The Limits of
Market
Organization

The Limits of Market Organization

RICHARD R. NELSON
EDITOR

Russell Sage Foundation | New York

The Russell Sage Foundation

The Russell Sage Foundation, one of the oldest of America's general purpose foundations, was established in 1907 by Mrs. Margaret Olivia Sage for "the improvement of social and living conditions in the United States." The Foundation seeks to fulfill this mandate by fostering the development and dissemination of knowledge about the country's political, social, and economic problems. While the Foundation endeavors to assure the accuracy and objectivity of each book it publishes, the conclusions and interpretations in Russell Sage Foundation publications are those of the authors and not of the Foundation, its Trustees, or its staff. Publication by Russell Sage, therefore, does not imply Foundation endorsement.

Library of Congress Cataloging-in-Publication Data

The limits of market organization / edited by Richard Nelson.
    p. cm.
  Includes bibliographical references and index.
  ISBN 0-87154-626-4
    1. Comparative economics. 2. Mixed economy. 3. Government ownership. 4. Capitalism.
5. Free enterprise. 6. Economic policy. I. Nelson, Richard R.

  HB90.L535 2005
  330.12′2—dc22

2004058806

Text design by Suzanne Nichols.

RUSSELL SAGE FOUNDATION
112 East 64th Street, New York, New York 10021
10 9 8 7 6 5 4 3 2 1

Contents

Contributors   vii

Chapter 1   Introduction   1
Richard R. Nelson

PART I   INFRASTRUCTURE, NATURAL MONOPOLY,   25
AND EQUITABLE ACCESS

Chapter 2   Electric Power   27
Kira Fabrizio

Chapter 3   Telecommunications Regulation: An Introduction   48
Nicholas Economides

Chapter 4   Passenger Rail   77
Elliott D. Sclar

Chapter 5   Financial Clearing Systems   114
John A. James and David F. Weiman

PART II   HUMAN SERVICES   157

Chapter 6   The Role of Markets in American K–12 Education   161
Richard J. Murnane

Chapter 7   Early Childhood Education and Care   185
Sheila B. Kamerman and Jane Waldfogel

Chapter 8   Market Versus State in Health Care and Health Insurance:
False Dichotomy   213
Dahlia K. Remler, Lawrence D. Brown, and Sherry A. Glied

PART III   SCIENCE AND TECHNOLOGY   231

Chapter 9   Basic Scientific Research   233
Richard R. Nelson

Chapter 10   The Internet   259
             David C. Mowery and Timothy Simcoe

Chapter 11   Satellite Data   294
             Roberta Balstad

PART IV   PROTECTING THE PUBLIC AND THE STATE   319

Chapter 12   Public Health   321
             Kristine M. Gebbie

Chapter 13   Campaign Finance   335
             Richard Briffault

Chapter 14   Conclusion   371
             Richard R. Nelson

             Index   377

Contributors

RICHARD R. NELSON is George Blumenthal Professor of International and Public Affairs, Business, and Law, Emeritus, at Columbia University.

ROBERTA BALSTAD is director of Columbia University's Center for International Earth Science Information Network (CIESIN).

RICHARD BRIFFAULT is vice-dean and Joseph P. Chamberlain Professor of Legislation at Columbia Law School.

LAWRENCE D. BROWN is professor in the Department of Health Policy and Management in the Mailman School of Public Health at Columbia University.

NICHOLAS ECONOMIDES is professor of economics at Stern School of Business at New York University.

KIRA FABRIZIO is a doctoral candidate at the Haas School of Business at the University of California, Berkeley, and is currently a visiting scholar at the Boston University School of Management.

KRISTINE M. GEBBIE is Elizabeth Standish Gill Associate Professor and Director of the Center for Health Policy at the Columbia University School of Nursing.

SHERRY A. GLIED is professor and chair of the Department of Health Policy and Management in the Mailman School of Public Health at Columbia University.

JOHN A. JAMES is professor of economics at the University of Virginia.

SHEILA B. KAMERMAN is Compton Foundation Centennial Professor for the Prevention of Children and Youth Problems at the Columbia University School of Social Work, director of the Columbia Institute on Child and Family Policy (ICFP), and codirector of the ICFP Clearinghouse on International Developments in Child and Family Policies.

DAVID C. MOWERY is the William A. and Betty H. Hasler Professor of New Enterprise Development in the Haas School of Business at the University of California, Berkeley.

RICHARD J. MURNANE is Thompson Professor of Education and Society at the Harvard University Graduate School of Education.

DAHLIA K. REMLER is associate professor in the School of Public Affairs at Baruch College, City University of New York.

ELLIOTT D. SCLAR is professor of urban planning and public affairs at Columbia University and holds appoints in the Graduate School of Architecture, Planning, and Preservation and the School of International Affairs.

TIMOTHY SIMCOE is assistant professor of management in the Rotman School of Management at the University of Toronto.

JANE WALDFOGEL is professor of social work and public affairs at Columbia University School of Social Work and research associate at the Centre for Analysis of Social Exclusion at the London School of Economics.

DAVID F. WEIMAN is Alena Wels Hirschorn '58 Professor and chair of the Department of Economics at Barnard College.

1

INTRODUCTION

Richard R. Nelson

T HE CLOSE of the twentieth century saw a virtual canonization of market organization as the best, indeed the only effective, way to structure an economic system.[1] This phenomenon, though strongest in the United States and, to a somewhat lesser extent, the United Kingdom, was widespread. The conception of market organization being canonized was simple and pure, along the lines of the standard textbook model in economics. For-profit firms are the vehicles of production. They decide what to produce and how, on the basis of their assessments about what is most profitable. Given what suppliers offer, free choice by customers, who decide on the basis of their own knowledge and preferences where they will spend their own money, determines how much of what is bought by whom. Competition among firms assures that production is efficient and tailored to what users want, and prices are kept in line with costs. The role of government is limited to establishing and maintaining a body of law to set the rules for the market game and assuring the availability of basic infrastructure needed for the economy to operate.

Economists of an empirical bent and political scientists and sociologists who have studied actual modern economies recognize the oversimplifications involved in this folk theory. If intended as a positive theory of how modern economies are actually structured, it misses the complexity of market organization in many spheres of economic activity and ignores the wide range of activities involving major investments of resources where markets play a limited role. The theory represses the extensive roles of government in modern economies. More generally, it misses the institutional complexity and variegation of modern economies.[2]

The folk theory clearly is intended more as a normative statement than as a positive one. In this role, it has been highly successful in recent years.

While the broad ideological argument is focused on the economy as a whole, it is at the sectoral or activity level that the details of economic organization are worked out. At this level, discussion today about the way a sector or activity should be structured almost always starts with the presumption that market organization, of a relatively simple kind, is the right solution. This is the "default" solution. In recent years, sectors and activities that were previously regulated have been subject to strong pressures for deregulation. Where there is a major public sector role, the pressures are toward privatization. Under this view, competition is always something to be fostered, and arguments for public support of any kind are viewed with suspicion. Propositions to the effect that perhaps market organization is not appropriate for the activity in question tend to be rejected out of hand. There is a strong preference to use the market as much as possible and to keep nonmarket elements to a minimum.

A case can be made that this apparent bias in favor of simple market organization at a sectoral level is, on net, a plus. It points policy discussion right from the start toward a mode of organization that, in fact, has served effectively as a central part of the governing structure over a wide range of activities and sectors. It is associated with bias against governing structures that rely heavily on central planning and top-down command and control, which often have proved problematic or worse in contexts in which they have been employed. However, the case for markets can be pushed too far. If the presumption in favor of market organization is accompanied by blindness to the complexity and variegation of modern economies, an ideological resistance to mixed forms of governance, and hostility to structures that make little use of markets, this can be a real problem.

Modern societies face a number of challenging and often contentious choices regarding how to organize and govern a variety of activities that together employ a large and growing share of their resources. For some of these, a satisfactory solution can quite likely be found through market organization that is not too far away from the folk theory. However, in other cases, to make market organization work tolerably well will almost surely require strong and fine-grained regulation and perhaps a number of other supplementary elements. For some activities, it will prove best to rely centrally on other basic organizational modes, with markets in an ancillary role.

Each of the chapters that follow is concerned with a sector or area of economic activity in which there have been strong pressures to use market organization more. However, in each sector there are important features that make market governance of the simple textbook kind problematic. In each, also, strong voices argue against what they consider overdue reliance on market forces. The project that resulted in these studies was organized to call attention to a fact that seems overlooked in many contemporary discussions: that modern economies involve a variety of different kinds of activities. For some of these, market organization can do a fine job of governance. But it is also important to recognize the complexities and limits of markets as economic governing structures.

Economic Governance as a Political Issue

I use the term "governing structure" to highlight what is at stake in choosing a mode of organization for an activity or an industry—who is to get what, who pays, who is responsible for provision, mechanisms of control—and to call attention to the fact that society can and does have a choice about the matter, a choice that is ultimately political. Economists tend to see the governing structure (my terminology) of an industry as involving both a demand side and a supply side. Political scientists recognize a similar distinction between the processes of policy making and administration for the areas of public sector activity they study. In the discussion that follows, I also use this rough distinction between demand- and supply-side governance.[3]

In its canonical form, market organization brings together potential users, on the demand side, who decide how to spend their own money, and suppliers, on the supply side, who seek profit. Canonical market organization in combination with limited regulation is one form of governance structure. However, it is far from ubiquitous.

First, there are many goods and services for which benefits are spread among the public rather than being private. For these goods and services, public, generally governmental, processes need to be used to determine how much is wanted, and public funds used to pay for what is procured. National security and public health measures are classical examples. Until recently, there was little argument against the proposition that basic scientific knowledge was a public good and its creation and terms of access should be supported publicly. There also are certain activities the supply of which is regarded as an innately governmental function. Providing and running the police system and the courts is an obvious example. Structuring elections and developing legislation are others.

Other cases of society's using collective demand determination machinery, or public provision, are more controversial. Thus debate continues about the extent to which medical care should be publicly, as contrasted with privately, funded. Countries differ in the extent to which they consider rail and airline service to provide public as well as private benefits and thus warrant public financial support, direct or indirect. In many countries, most of primary and secondary education is provided through public organizations, an arrangement challenged in the United States by proposals for vouchers. There is controversy regarding the appropriate role of public spending and public provision of supplemental family child care.

Of course, many activities and sectors that generally are thought of as market governed have in fact a mixed governing structure. Thus the production and sales of pharmaceuticals are regulated, and public moneys go into the basic research that pharmaceutical companies draw from in their development work. Most of the old "public utilities,"—for example, the telephone system and electric power—are still quite regulated, and some, like passenger rail service, are subsidized to some degree. Government programs provide the infrastructure—airports and the air traffic control system—that enables private for-profit airlines to operate. The Internet was brought into existence through a combination of private and public efforts. Today, society is struggling with the question of whether and how the Internet should be regulated.

That struggle is, in part, about the appropriate role of government. However, it is a mistake to see the governance issue as strictly about the balance between markets and government. Child care, an activity that absorbs an enormous amount of resources, is largely provided by family members, with market institutions and government both playing a subsidiary role. Not-for-profit organizations principally govern organized religion and Little League baseball.

Market organization is a widely used and useful governing structure, though in many cases it is complemented by various nonmarket elements. And just as one size shoe does not fit all feet, a single mode of sectoral governance cannot cope with the great variety of human activity. Modern economies are made up of many different sectors. There is no way that a single form of organization and governance is going to be appropriate for all of them.

The chapters in this volume deal with sectors or areas of activity in which the issue of the role of market organization is highly controversial. This introductory chapter sets the stage.

The Past as Prologue

The presumption and fact that markets play a pervasive role in the governance and organization of economic activity are relatively recent phenomena. A significant expansion in the role of markets occurred first in Great Britain around the beginning of the eighteenth century and later spread to continental Europe and the United States, still later to Japan, and recently to large portions of the world. Of course, certain kinds of markets have existed from virtually the dawn of history but until recently were central in only a small portion of human activity. It is the pervasiveness of markets, and the broader system legitimating and supporting market organization, which came to be called capitalism, that is relatively new on the historical timescale.

With the spread of markets, of production that was largely for sale on markets, and of an economy in which either net receipts from sales or wages garnered on labor markets largely determined the access of an individual or family to goods and services, a sphere of economic activity began to emerge in its own right as a system that was distinct from the broader society and polity. Thus Adam Smith's *The Wealth of Nations* (1776/1937) is about a market economy, influenced profoundly, to be sure, by the culture and government of the nation containing it but also an object in its own right, with its own basic rules of operation. Smith's book could not have been written a century earlier.

However, it is important to recognize that many activities continued to be outside the market system. Both government and families remained important institutions. Moreover, throughout the period of capitalism's ascendancy many sophisticated observers and analysts gave it mixed grades, arguing that there were minuses as well as pluses and activities in which the market should not be dominant.

Although the British "classical school" is often thought of as a strong proponent of markets, as unencumbered as possible and extended to as wide a range of human activity as possible, that is not quite accurate. Adam Smith's enthusiasm for markets was nuanced, and he clearly saw a downside. John Stuart Mill did not like many aspects of the capitalism he saw rising in mid-nineteenth-century England. The United States today is regarded as the locus of almost unwashed enthusiasm for unfettered markets. However, Alexander Hamilton, in his "Report on Manufactures" (1791/1965), argued that protection and subsidy were needed if American industry were to survive and prosper. Many of the founders of the American Economic Association, established in the late nineteenth century, believed that the capitalism emerging in the United States badly needed regulation.

For all the enthusiasm today for market capitalism of a relatively extensive and unrestricted sort, it is easy to forget that half a century ago some of the most distinguished scholars were predicting capitalism's demise. In the 1940s Joseph Schumpeter (1942) published his classic *Capitalism, Socialism, and Democracy,* and Karl Polanyi (1944) his *The Great Transformation.* Both saw raw capitalism as a system whose time had passed, the former with regret and the latter with relief. Both saw capitalism as it had developed during the first part of the twentieth century as politically unviable in a democracy.

The evidence indicates they were correct, at least at that time, although what happened was not quite as they predicted. In Western Europe and in the United States, the early postwar era saw major reforms in the system. It was widely recognized that the reformed capitalism was significantly different from what it had replaced. The roles of government had expanded greatly. Unemployment insurance became widespread and in many countries quite generous, and similarly Social Security. Public support of education became much more extensive, particularly at the university level, and governments became the principal supporters of scientific research. Many countries expanded the scope of national health insurance or instituted new programs. Several authors considering the reforms speculated as to whether the new economic system was capitalism or something new and different (see, for example, Dahl and Lindblom 1953; Crosland 1956; Bell 1960; Myrdal 1960; Schonfeld 1965).

In the United States and the United Kingdom, economists increasingly used the term "mixed economy" to describe the system as it was coming to be. The basic themes were well articulated in the 1962 report of the Kennedy administration's Council of Economic Advisors, which contained a number of the country's best-known and most-respected economists. Whereas market organization was assumed to be the standard way of governing and managing industry, the theory of market failure was very much part of the notion of a mixed economy. Monopoly was recognized as a condition that could negate many of the advantages of market organization, something to be guarded against by rigorous antitrust or, where inevitable, to be controlled through regulation in lieu of competition or through public sector management. The provision of public goods, like national security and scientific knowledge, under this view required public support and, in some cases, public undertaking. Externalities required regulation or a regime of taxes and subsidies. Government needed to proceed actively to ensure that the workings of the economic system did not generate unrelieved poverty.

Of course, these changes in economic policy and, more broadly, changes in the view of what capitalism was and what was needed to make it effective did not go unchallenged. By the middle or late 1970s, there was loud advocacy for rolling back many of the changes or, at least, blocking further moves in these directions. The administrations of Margaret Thatcher and Ronald Reagan clearly marked a watershed. Since that time the conventional wisdom has been that a simple lean capitalism is best and that the earlier chatter about a mixed economy was badly misguided. Daniel Yergen and Joseph Stanislaw (1998), in *The Commanding Heights,* have written about how the marketplace has won out over government in the battle for supremacy, and they see the outcome as victory for the right cause, expressing few qualms that the issues might be more complex than the ideological arguments of the victors. Francis Fukuyama (1992) proclaimed "the end of history and the last man" as a final victory for capitalism (along with liberal democracy), with hardly a mention of the earlier discussions that modern economies, while relying heavily on markets, needed to be "mixed."

Mark Blyth (2000) has proposed, in his *Great Transformations, Economic Ideas, and Political Change in the Twentieth Century,* that there may be a natural cycle regarding popular opinion on the appropriate level and kind of government regulation and involvement more generally, a cycle that involves both policies and ideologies, with a tendency to overshoot in one direction and then, with a lag, reverse directions. He ascribes the turning of the 1980s to an overshooting in a liberal direction during the earlier postwar era. My argument is that we have overshot again.

As I have emphasized, the principal concern of the authors of this volume is how a society governs different economic activities at the level of a sector. Our argument is not about macroeconomics or about whether or not broad reliance on market organization is a reasonable thing. Rather, we argue that in the current climate there is a strong tendency to rely on market organization of a relatively pure and simple kind, not only in contexts in which this can work reasonably well but also where simple market organization is at best problematic.

The Case for Market Organization: The Perspective from Economics

Since the days of Adam Smith, British and American economists have generally touted the virtues of the "invisible hand" of market organization. For the most part, Smith's was a qualitative argument, supported by a set of empirical cases drawn from his own experiences and those of others. It is important to remember that Smith was making his case for market organization partly as argument against a particular alternative: mercantilism.

Noneconomists seem to be under the impression that modern economists have built a theoretically rigorous and empirically well supported case for market organization, one that tightens up the logic of Smith's argument. However, I argue that in fact the most commonly cited theoretical argument in modern economics can support little weight, the empirical case for market organization is rough and ready, and the persuasive part is pragmatic and qualitative rather than rigorous and quantitative. In my view, at least, the arguments for market organization that are most compelling are quite different from that contained in the standard modern textbook formulation.[4]

That formulation is that given a particular set of assumptions, a theoretical model of a market economy yields results that are Pareto optimal. An important implication of this line of theoretical argument is that one need not look at other forms of economic organization because market organization "can't be beat." This perspective on the virtues of markets invites no comparative analysis except for the purpose of exposing the weaknesses of nonmarket forms. In any case, the argument is a nonstarter for considering the real advantages of market organization vis-à-vis other forms of governance.

It is a nonstarter, first of all, because no one really believes that the model is a close approximation of how a market economy actually works or that the real economy actually generates outcomes that, even in principle, "can't be beat." On the other hand, real market economies are much richer institutionally than the simple model, and thus theoretical arguments (for example, those contained in market failure theory) may not be an indictment against the actual market economies that we have. What clearly is needed is careful empirical evaluation of quite complex alternative governing structures. There has been little of this kind of hard research. Unfortunately, therefore, analysis of the pluses and minuses of governing structures that make significant use of markets has to rest on a mixture of the rather rough comparisons that history does allow in addition to efforts at sensible, if somewhat ad hoc, theorizing.

Thus though market organization as it actually is does not achieve Pareto optimality, most economists and many lay persons would argue that market organization and competition often does seem to generate results that are moderately efficient. There are strong incentives for firms to produce goods and services that customers want, or can be persuaded they want, and to produce them at the lowest possible financial cost. Under many circumstances, economic sectors organized around competitive markets seem to respond relatively quickly to changes in customer demands, supply conditions, and technological opportunities. Thus to the extent that producing what customers value is treated as a plus, and so long as factor prices roughly measure opportunity costs, there is a strong pragmatic case for market organization, broadly defined, on economic efficiency grounds, at least in certain domains of activity. It is not the case presented in textbook theory. But in my view it is far more persuasive.

Why Not Top-Down Planning?

The kind of economic governance needed would certainly seem to depend on the nature of the salient needs. Thus in wartime, virtually without protest, capitalist economies have abandoned market governance and adopted centrally coordinated mechanisms of resource allocation, procurement, and rationing. The rationale has been that such economic governance is essential if production is to be allocated to the highest priority needs and conducted effectively. By and large, there is agreement that remarkable feats of production have been achieved under these arrangements.

The experience with wartime planning has led some analysts to propose that a number of the mechanisms used then would vastly increase economic efficiency during peacetime. However, most knowledgeable analysts have argued strongly against that position. It is one thing to marshal an economy to concentrate on a central set of consensus high-priority demands over a short period of time, as in wartime production or in the early years of the communist economies, when the central objective was to build up a few basic industries. It is something else again to have an economy behave reasonably responsively and efficiently in a context of diverse and changing demands, supply conditions, and technological opportunities over a long time period. The experience with central planning in the former Communist countries after the era had passed, when building up standard infrastructure sufficed as a central goal, bears out this argument.[5]

However, I propose that the argument behind the scenes here for market organization is more complex than, and in fact different from, the standard textbook argument that profit-maximizing behavior of firms in competitive market contexts yields economically efficient results. It hinges on the multiplicity, diversity, and unpredictable changeability of wants, resources, and technologies in modern economies that experience shows defies the information-processing and resource-allocating capabilities of centrally planned and controlled systems. It also presumes that the chances of appropriate responses to changed conditions are enhanced when there are a number of competitive actors who can respond without acquiring approval for proposed action from some central authority, or gaining the approval of a large number of people, before acting. Friedrich Hayek and the modern "Austrian" economists (for example, Kirzner 1979) have stressed the ability of market economies to experiment, searching for unmet needs and unseized opportunities, and argue that centralized systems are poor at this. This argument is not what standard textbook theory is about. It hinges on the desirability of consumer sovereignty, expressed through market choices. It is mute regarding how to mind social or collective demands.

A Schumpeterian Perspective

Many observers have proposed that it is in dynamic long-run performance, rather than in short-run efficiency, that market capitalism reveals its greatest strength. As Karl Marx and Schumpeter have stressed, capitalism has been a remarkably powerful engine of economic progress. Here, too, one can make a rather explicit comparison. Indeed, a good case can be made that a central reason for the collapse of the old Communist economies was their inability to keep up with and take advantage of the rapid technological progress that was going on in market economics.

The characteristics and capabilities of market organization that contribute to technological progress, however, are very different than those that relate to static efficiency and the textbook normative model. Indeed, Schumpeter made a great deal of those differences. Some commentators on Schumpeter have proposed that he did not believe that, in modern capitalism, competition was important. That is not correct. Rather, his argument was that the kind of competition that mattered was not the sort stressed in the economics textbooks but competition through innovation. The capitalism of his *Capitalism, Socialism, and Democracy* was an effective engine of progress because competition spurred innovation. His theory places high value on pluralism and multiple rival sources of invention and innovation. However, under this view of what socially valuable competition is all about, the presence of large firms, with research and development laboratories as well as some market power, was welcomed, despite the fact that such a market structure diverged from the purely competitive one associated with the static theorem about Pareto optimality.

It is interesting that Schumpeter, in his late writings, argued that, as science became more powerful, the unruly and inefficient competition of capitalist systems would no longer be needed for industrial innovation, which increasingly could be planned. History has showed him to be very wrong on this point. Centrally planned systems often have achieved strong success in allocating research and development resources where the objectives are sharply defined and the likely best routes to success quite clear. The Manhattan Project and Project Apollo are good examples. However, for the most part, potential innovators are faced with the problem of guessing just how much users will value various innovations they might introduce and also of judging how easy or difficult it would be to develop various alternatives. The answers to these questions are seldom clear. Furthermore, well-informed experts are likely to disagree on the answers. Under these conditions, the competitive pluralism of market-organized research and development systems is a great advantage.

It can be argued that, at least in recent years, the strong performance of market capitalist economies on the industrial innovation front also has a lot to do with features of modern capitalist economies not highlighted in Schumpeter—for example, public support of university research and training. However, the pluralism, flexibility. and competition of modern capitalism surely are essential aspects of any effective innovation system.

The Positive Case for a Mixed Economy: Market Failure Theory

Although I and the other authors of this volume find the argument in favor of market organization of economic activity broadly compelling, it is too broad. Its breadth disguises the fact that economies include a large variety of sectors and activities, with different properties. As noted earlier, one size shoe does not fit all feet. It is important to consider the details of an activity before deciding whether it fits neatly into the simple market shoe.

It is clear that most high-level argument about where market organization works effectively and where it works poorly is conducted using the economists' market failure language. Market failure theory takes as its benchmark the theory that, under the set of assumptions about behavior built into neoclassical economic theory, and given a particular set of context assumptions, market governance of economic activity yields Pareto-optimal outcomes. Market failure theory is oriented toward context conditions that upset that result.

Because this body of theory is so well known, I can telescope here the standard account of the basic market failure categories. My emphasis, instead, is on the blurry edges of the standard categories and on some cases that seem to strain the underlying economic theory more generally. In my view, a large share of the current controversies about the role of markets fall into these areas.[6]

The Public Goods Bestiary

Economists use the concept of public good to flag a class of goods and services whose benefits are collective and communal rather than individual and private. Under this body of conceptualization, a pure public good has two attributes. The first is that, unlike a standard private good like a peanut butter sandwich, which can benefit only one consumer (although of course it can be split and shared), a public good provides atmospheric benefits that all can enjoy. In the language of economists, public goods are nonrivalrous in use. Your benefiting from a public good in no way diminishes my ability to benefit from it. The second is that if a public good or service is provided at all, there is no way to deny access to any person or to require direct payment for access. Clean air and national security are standard examples of pure public goods. Scientific knowledge often is used as another example. For a neighborhood, the quality of access roads has some public good attributes.

For the procurement of a pure public good, society is virtually compelled to put in place some kind of collective choice mechanism to decide how much to buy and some kind of collective revenue source to pay for it. Standard market governance simply will not work. For some local public goods, the mechanism can be informal. Thus a neighborhood association may collect voluntary dues for maintenance of access roads. But for public goods that benefit a wide range of people and groups, and to which, if provided, access cannot be blocked, there is no option but to use the machinery of government.

However, pure public goods are rare; and for a variety of goods and services with some public goods properties, using the market for provision is feasible. First, there is a class of goods and services for which, though they are marked by nonrivalry in use, potential beneficiaries can be made to pay if they are to have access. Thus access to scientific knowledge or data can be restricted by secrecy on the part of its creator. In recent years, legal changes have made certain kinds of scientific research results, and certain kinds of data, protectable under patent and copyright law.

Where access can be blocked, there is the option of using market organization for supply and making individuals and groups pay for what they want to get. The problem with this governance structure is that if the good or service is nonrivalrous in use, or largely so, use may be restricted when there is no social cost of extending use. The losses from restricting use here can be small or considerable. Argument about this is now prominent in the face of moves to make greater use of the market for the support of scientific research and the collection and distribution of scientific data.

Second, and somewhat related, many goods and services are partly private and partly public, in the sense that they provide identifiable benefit to particular individuals, who can be made to pay for access, and at the same time broad atmospheric benefits from the availability or provision of the good or service. Education is a prominent example. Vaccination for contagious diseases is another. It can be argued that mass transport, in addition to generating benefits to the users, also benefits society at large by reducing the congestion and other costs associated with greater use of private transport were public transport not available.

Society has a choice here to rely largely on market provision by making the individuals who directly benefit pay the full costs, thus minimizing needed public support. This is the proclivity of the American government these days regarding rail transportation. We seem to be moving in that direction regarding higher education. However, primary and secondary education continue to be largely publicly financed, even though the benefits to individual students are usually substantial; and vaccination may be required by law.

In many cases the perceived public benefits of a good or service are associated with beliefs about what is appropriate for a society or a polity. Many citizens in a democracy support funding for universal education not because they or their children will take advantage of public schools or because they believe it will reduce the incidence of crime that can affect them but because they believe that universal free education is a necessary condition for equality of opportunity in a society. Similar arguments have been put forth for public funding of universal preschool child care. Many people clearly believe it is wrong for people in need to be denied access to medical care because they cannot afford it. The values at stake here seem different in kind from the utility that an individual might get from a nice steak.

Whether a good or service has significant public good properties clearly depends on how the benefits it yields are viewed. In the cases mentioned here, the benefits that are seen as public are not easily analyzed in terms of the standard kinds of benefits that are the focus of standard economics. Rather, their "publicness" resides in values defined in terms of perceptions about what makes a society a decent and just one. For this reason, for many goods and services the argument is not about whether innate publicness requires public funding to ensure a decent level of provision but rather about whether the good or service should be made available to all, on reasonable or nominal terms, with public moneys footing the bill. That is, a considerable part of the debate is about what goods and services ought to be public.

Significant costs are involved in employing public choice machinery instead of or supplementary to market demand-side machinery. There is, first, the question of how to decide how much is to be provided, in contexts in which individuals and groups may value the public provision of the good or service differently. There is, second, the question of who is to pay. Because of the number of individuals and groups who may try to have a say in these matters, the process will be either time consuming and cumbersome or pruned back and simplified in a way that will certainly outrage certain parties. The outcomes of collective demand–generating processes are inevitably going to be considered by some to be unfair and inefficient. But if a good or service has strong innate public good properties or is deemed by some as something that ought to be public, this argument is inevitable.

The Externalities Problem: Bringing in Broader Interests to the Governing Structure

In economics, the concept of externalities refers to by-products of economic activity that have negative or positive consequences that are not reflected in the benefits and costs perceived by those who engage in the externalities-generating activity. Environmental contamination is an obvious example of a negative externality and a clear case in which there is a value at stake in the operations of an activity, with no one to represent and fight for it, at least in the simple model of market governance put forth in economics textbooks.

In a famous article written some time ago, Ronald Coase (1960) argues that, if property rights are clear and strong and the number of interested parties relatively small, markets can, in fact, deal with these kinds of problems. Those who value clean air or water can simply "buy" from the potential polluter behavior that respects those values. The problem arises when those who care about the values, which could be neglected, are dispersed. In this case some kind of collective action machinery is needed to bring them in. A good way to think about regulation or a tax on pollution is to see these measures as the result of governance machinery that has brought in a broader range of interests and values bearing on decision making in an activity or sector than would be there under simple market organization.

The general problem for society is to delineate the range of interests that should be represented, their relative influence, and the mechanisms through which they can operate to make their values felt. The latter can range from public interest advertising and boycotts, which can proceed without direct access to governmental machinery, to lawsuits, which involve general governmental apparatus, to particular pieces of special regulation and associated control machinery.

As suggested earlier, one of the major advantages of market governance of an activity or sector is that it tends to avoid the costs and inefficiencies of central planning. One of the reasons for its flexibility and responsiveness to certain kinds of needs is that simple market governance tends to count a rather narrow range of interests. Yet it is hard to identify an activity, or a sector, in which there are not some values at stake that go beyond the direct interests of the customers and the suppliers. Severe externalities from an activity clearly call for amending simple market organization to give those interests an effective voice. On the other hand, the greater the number of interests and values that have to come to some collective conclusion before action is taken, or have a veto power over change, the more cumbersome the governance system. The question, of course, is where to draw the line.

The Costs of Competition and the Problem of Private Monopoly

The benefits of competition are part of virtually all arguments extolling the advantages of market organization. Of course, one can have competition without having for-profit firms. Indeed, there are a number of proposals for reforming primary and secondary education by giving parents and students a wider range of school choice and providing stronger incentives to schools to attract and hold students, which do not necessarily involve introducing for-profit schools into the supply side of the picture. Some of those who oppose this kind of reform, or doubt its advantages, argue that parents and students do not, in general, have the knowledge or motivation to make good choices in such a setting and that stimulating competition among schools would invite catering to ill-informed tastes. There are similar arguments, for and against competition, regarding choice of medical plans and doctors.

In a number of activities or sectors there are significant economies of scale of provision relative to the size of the market, or strong advantages of having an internally coordinated system, or both. Activities with these characteristics are called by economists "natural monopolies." If a sector or an activity is a natural monopoly, competition is not a desirable or a viable element of a governing structure. This traditionally has been the assumption regarding the range of sectors that have been called "public utilities," including, prominently, the telephone system, electric power, and railroads. Until recently, public utilities tended to be operated as government corporations in much of Europe and as franchised private but regulated corporations in the United States.

Over the past quarter century, there have been strong pressures to denationalize, or deregulate, the old public utilities. This argument has often been associated with the proposition that these activities are, in fact, no longer natural monopolies, if they ever were. However, the generation of competition has in many cases proved difficult or costly. As a result, customers now tend to face a relatively unregulated private utilities monopoly, as contrasted with a regulated or public one.

American economists are inclined to rationalize the use of antitrust, to prevent undue market power from arising, and regulation, to deal with cases in which there is natural monopoly, on the grounds that monopolists tend to charge too high a price. It is clear, however, that much of the force behind the policies to break up or rein in monopolies, or regulate them closely, has to do with concerns that arise when private bodies gain considerable power over people's lives, a matter that may involve but also may transcend being forced to pay monopoly prices. Economists are inclined to rationalize that governments not only fund but directly control activities related to national security and the criminal justice system on the grounds that these activities yield "public goods." But the near consensus that it would be highly dangerous to place power over these activities in private hands is probably at least as relevant. Although clearly there is widespread concern about undue governmental powers, in the arena of public utilities there is concern about unregulated private power, as well.

I propose that concern about the lack of accountability to the public of private power over activities and services that many people believe are of vital importance to them lies at the heart of the current debate about how to govern activities like telephone service, electricity generation and distribution, urban water supply, the railroad system, and urban mass transport. To ignore this aspect of the debate about how to govern these sectors is to miss the point. However, as with the issue of regulation to deal with externalities, the key question of regulation of industries in which monopoly or a highly concentrated structure is inevitable is where to draw the line.

The Issue of Uneven Expertise and Agency

Economists have become more interested recently in how asymmetric information between buyer and seller, or, more generally, insufficient expertise to judge quality on the part of customers, complicates the workings of markets. I propose that a number of the current controversies about the efficacy of market organization, about regulation of market supply, and about alternatives to market supply reflect this issue.

The problem is clearly fundamental in medical care. The medical community long has professed that, though doctors do sell their services on the market, they most emphatically do not try to maximize their profits but rather prescribe in the patient's interests. Analysts have observed that to some extent that may be true, but still the capabilities of patients to choose among physicians or physician groups remains problematic. Thus the questions of what information needs to be provided to those choosing among doctors or plans and what controls there should be on advertising are important matters in considering the role that competition should play in the provision of medical care. There is also the question of whether, even under suitable regulatory constraints, competition among health plans and physicians for patients is a useful component of the governing structure, or even whether competition may be, on net, pernicious.

The same issues, of course, come up in arguments over the wisdom of adopting a voucher plan, and about school competition, in education. There is considerable resistance on the part of many citizens, not simply public school teachers, to the notion that for-profit schools should receive public support and can thereby act as useful competitors to public schools. Similar issues are involved in the debate about the rules and regulations that should be required of extrafamily child care and whether to encourage for-profit firms in that line of activity.

My point here is not that those who oppose simple market organization in areas in which there is considerable consumer ignorance have a fully persuasive argument for heavy regulation or nonmarket provision; these alternatives to market organization have their own liabilities. Rather, it is that where one cannot count on informed customers to make good choices, the argument in favor of lean market organization is problematic.

The Peculiar Bias of Market Failure Theory

I conclude this survey of market failure theory by pointing out a bias built into that theory. By the way it is formulated, market failure theory carries a heavy normative load to the effect that unless they are basically flawed in some sense, markets are preferred to other forms of governance. Thus the only reason why government should provide for national security and protect citizens from crime is that markets cannot do these jobs well. Similarly, parents need to take care of their children because of market failure. As one reflects on it, the argument that we need government because markets sometimes "fail" seems rather strange, or at least incomplete. Can't one make a positive case for government, or families, for that matter, as a form that is appropriate, even needed, in its own right?

The Functions of the State and the Community

An ancient body of theorizing puts forth a positive case for government. In much of its early incarnation, and some of its more recent, the state is viewed as the structure through which values are defined at the level of the community and decisions regarding the community as a whole are made. Reflect on Plato's discussion in *The Republic,* or Georg Hegel's definition of the good state in terms of the quality of its justice and the character of its citizens. This formulation of the role of the state, of course, does not resolve the issue of differences among individuals who make up the state. Indeed, disputes about values are likely to be even more heated than disputes involving choices that affect economic interests differently. The issue of how to decide may be even more contentious. Plato saw the answer in government by philosophers. For better or worse, modern societies are stuck with democratic process.

A liberal position on how to deal with value differences within the population would be to keep the state out of it and to try to avoid forcing the values of one group to be imposed on another. But in many cases there is no way to do that. Abortion either is legal or it is not.

This theory clearly captures a lot of the flavor of contemporary debates about matters like the right to life and the right to choose, the commitment of a society to ideals of equal opportunity and fairness, and whether there should be universal health insurance regardless of ability to pay. Arguments about these matters involve beliefs about appropriate collective values, or values of the collective, that transcend those of particular individuals. Under this theory, in these areas, at least, the state, which defines the collective, is the natural vehicle of governance in contexts in which a collective position on something has to be taken one way or another. In these areas the state may choose to use markets to further some collective values, but the purpose being served is a public purpose, and the responsibility for furthering it is ultimately a state responsibility.

Providing the Context for a Fruitful Civil Life and Economy

Another, but not mutually exclusive, body of theorizing about the state does not focus so much on collective values but rather sees the state as the necessary vehicle to set the context for fruitful private lives and actions. From at least the time of Thomas Hobbes and John Locke, theories about the need for a strong state have involved, centrally, the proposition that an effective state is needed for individuals to lead secure, decent, and productive lives. Originally, this body of theorizing had little to do with economics, much less the role of the state in market economies. Thus Hobbes's case for a strong state to establish and enforce a clear body of law is posed in terms of the need to avoid the "war of every man against every man" (Hobbes 1651/1994, 13.13). Although this case involved security of property, that is not Hobbes's central orientation. Locke's orientation is more toward security of property, but his greatest writings were before capitalism emerged as a recognizable economic system.

The argument here for a strong state is an argument for a single ultimate source of legal authority and police power. In the language of market failure theory, it is a natural monopoly argument as well as a public good argument. But the orientation to these issues in the political philosophy literature is that authority and power are natural basic functions of the state and do not simply fall to the state by default because of some kind of market failure.

A closely related proposition is that the state has principal responsibility for assuring the provision of needed basic infrastructure, physical as well as legal. Adam Smith's (1776/1937) emphasis in *The Wealth of Nations* was on the need for a reliable government and legal system if an economy were to work decently, but as economies grew more complicated provision of basic services soon became viewed as a responsibility of the state.

The question of what infrastructure needs to be provided for markets to work well, and what markets themselves can be expected to provide, often is not an easy one. But this issue is not generally argued out strictly under the concepts of market failure theory. Thus consider activities like providing a system of contract law, building and maintaining a road or railroad system, or supporting the development of basic scientific knowledge. These activities can be viewed as public goods, in the sense of market failure theory, the market failure stemming from the fact that their benefits are to a considerable extent collective rather than individual and hence for-profit firms would have great difficulty collecting for their provision on a conventional market. Alternatively, they can be considered as "needed infrastructure," provision of which falls to governments, by their very functions. Whereas the former theory sees the reason for government provision or overview and control in the inability of markets to do an adequate job, the latter sees provision of such goods and services as a central responsibility of government, even if they could be provided through market mechanisms. Where market mechanisms are used as part of the machinery for provision, the latter perspective sees government as still responsible for overseeing the operation, at least to some degree.

The State and the Community

Several of these theories of the state rest heavily on the concept of a natural community of individuals, families, and extended social structures, tied to one another by community bonds. Under this conception, the state is the vehicle through which the community makes collective decisions and takes coordinated collective action, when that is appropriate. From another point of view, however, it is clear that much of the decision making and action taking of the community does not involve state-mediated collective action. Indeed, ensuring that the state not interfere too much in the life of the civil community has been a central issue in Anglo-American political theory.

I believe it is fruitful, and illuminating, to view the economy as an aspect of community life rather than as a set of institutions that stand separate.[7] From this perspective, the economy is the term used to denote and focus attention on the activities of the community that use scarce resources to achieve human purposes. It is clear that much of economic activity in this broad sense does not involve markets, in the standard sense of that term.

Adam Smith is mostly known today, particularly among economists, for his *The Wealth of Nations,* in which he stresses the value of the "invisible hand" of market mechanisms. The orientation of Smith's (1853) *Theory of Moral Sentiments* is quite different in a number of ways. There he stresses the extended empathy that humans in a community have for one another, along with feelings of rivalry and sometimes of hostility. Extended empathy can be a powerful ingredient in a governing structure, in some cases an ingredient that can be deemed vital for effective governance. But extended empathy is not what markets are about. Thus, to pick up on an earlier theme, the family is the standard governance structure for child care, and for many other economic activities, not because of simple "market failure" but because the family can be counted on (mostly) to hold the extended empathy toward its own and related children that seems essential to good care. Similarly, in a wide variety of other activities involving members of the community, it is neighborhood groups, voluntary associations, clubs, and the like, not formal government and not markets, that play a central role in the governing structures.

Karl Polanyi (1944) is one in a long line of social analysts who see the extension of markets as an enemy of society, a destroyer of communal modes of governance. This is not a "market failure" argument. It is an argument that markets should be fenced off from certain kinds of activities.

The reality, but even more the myth, of the community structure that was undermined by market capitalism included, first, that the community took care of its own and, second, that each community member, depending on his or her status, had certain rights as well as certain obligations. With the rise of the modern state, formal government gradually took on responsibility for taking care of its citizens and for ensuring their basic rights. Over time, arguments about the appropriate domain of such rights have moved from political rights to economic rights.

Thus under traditional democratic theory, all citizens of a state ought to have the right to vote, to equal treatment under the law, and to a variety of freedoms of action regarding personal matters. Access to these basic rights of citizenship are seen as something that should not be rationed through markets and for which government has a fundamental responsibility. During the nineteenth century, government also came to be charged with protecting those who were regarded as too weak to protect themselves from market arrangements that would hurt them: thus child labor laws were passed, and laws limiting hours of work for certain classes of labor. The right of all citizens to a free public education, at least to a minimal level, gradually came to be recognized. The core arguments of modern welfare state theories add to these venerable political and protective rights a set of rights to access to certain kinds of goods and services. This decoupling of access to a considerable range of goods and services from normal market process is the hallmark of the modern welfare state.[8]

Note that the proposition here regarding the role of government has a family resemblance to that associated with the position that government is responsible for needed infrastructure. The difference is that the orientation is not so much to what is needed to make the economy work as to what is needed to make a society viable. Note also that in both theories there is a strong notion of collective values. Although the base values in this theory are associated with individual well-being, the notion that society is simply a collection of individuals and families with their own independent wants and purposes misunderstands this perception of what human societies are. Solidarity is a word often used by advocates of this position. From another (sometimes closely related) tradition, we all are our brothers' keepers.

Economic Governance as a Continuing Challenge

Arguments about appropriate governing structures are difficult for many reasons. In the first place, often there are significant conflicts of interest and differences in views regarding the salient values at stake. Because a central aspect of a governing structure involves the mechanism that determines what interests and values count, it is easy to see why this may be a contentious issue. Moreover, the question of who is responsible for supply, and under what set of rules, often involves contenders with strong interests in how that question is resolved. Reflect on the conflicts involved in proposals in the United States for a "patients' bill of rights" in dealing with managed care organizations or in proposals for a voucher scheme for publicly funded education. Deregulation of the electric power system and the telephone system was supported strongly by certain firms and interests, and a tightening of regulation will be strongly resisted by those interests.

The problem is difficult not just because of competing interests and values but also because of real uncertainties—the better term might be ignorance—regarding the consequences of adopting one governance scheme or another. Given the analytic limitations of the social sciences or the complexity of the subject matter, or both, it simply is impossible to foresee reliably the consequences of a patients' bill of rights or a voucher scheme for public education. The developing argument about whether, and if so how, to regulate spam and pornography on the Internet is additionally complicated by the fact that it is impossible to forecast how different regulatory regimes will, in fact, work.

Furthermore, for better or for worse, decisions that lead to the establishment of and changes in a governance structure almost always are made in a highly decentralized manner, and much of the action is taken by private parties doing things they think are in their best interest. The current modal structure and the range of variants of managed care in the United States is the result largely of decisions made by organizations seeing potential profit in managed care or striving to reorganize their managed care operation so as to make it profitable, on the one hand, and individuals and organizations with a responsibility to fund health care making their decisions regarding with whom to do business, on the other.

Of course, in this case and others the evolution of public programs and policies is an important part of the story. Indeed, the ratification of a governance structure or changes in it is ultimately a political decision, even if that decision does not involve new law. However, because of the way issues arise and are dealt with in a democracy, policies are made and remade piece by piece. Thus today the U.S. Congress is treating patients' rights and coverage of pharmaceutical costs as if they were separate issues. The issues of school reform and of the appropriate policy for support and organization of preschool child care are complicated by the fact that there are many government agencies that will have a say, some at the national level, some at the state level, and some, in education, at the local level.

Some analysts would blame the problems societies have had in developing coherent and effective governing structures for areas like medical care or the Internet on this fragmentation. However, from another point of view this decentralization and the serial nature of the policy-making process largely has protected us from grand coherent plans, the reach of which extends well beyond what can be well predicted.[9] Although ex ante analysis can serve to rule out certain proposals as obviously inadequate in certain areas, the development of governance structures for various activities has to rely to a considerable extent on evaluation of experience with attempts to reform.

It would be nice if experience with prevailing systems and their variants provided sharp, clear feedback of what is working and what is not so as to guide the next round of adjustments. However, even putting aside that the interests and values of different parties might lead them to evaluate the same thing differently, and even where there is agreement that the current regime is unsatisfactory in certain ways, it may be extremely difficult to identify just what aspect of the current regime is causing the problem or how to fix it. Ex post evaluation of a reform may be somewhat easier than ex ante prediction of the effects of that reform, but it still is very difficult (see Rivlin 1971).

Plan of the Book

The heart of this volume consists of chapters concerned with a number of sectors and activities in which society currently is struggling with the question of how best to organize and govern. The chapters are grouped into four clusters, with considerable commonality among the sectors treated in each cluster and significant differences between the clusters.

One cluster is concerned with sectors that for many years were broadly assumed to be "natural monopolies" and hence where competition was seen as impossible or, where it existed, counterproductive. The sectors treated here are electric power, telecommunications, passenger rail service, and bank clearance operations. Sectors of this sort have tended to be governed as regulated private monopolies in the United States, as state-owned enterprises in Europe. But beliefs and technologies have changed, and over the past quarter century more market elements and more competition have been introduced to the governing structure of each of these sectors. The consequences have been controversial, and in each sector there is continuing argument about how much reliance there should be on simple market governance and how much need there is for regulation.

The second cluster is concerned with human services and includes chapters on primary and secondary education, extrafamily child care, and medical care. There are no issues of natural monopoly regarding these activities; in each case, efficient service providers can be relatively small and are usually local in scope. Rather, the reluctance to employ simple market organization has to do with widespread beliefs that access is more or less a human right, together with concerns that public control is necessary to ensure the quality and appropriateness of what is provided. However, as is the case with the sectors in the first cluster, in recent years attitudes have changed. In each of these sectors there have been strong pressures to rely more on market governance and less on regulation and public provision, along with strong counterarguments.

The third cluster addresses activities associated with the advance of science and technology: basic research, the development of the Internet, and the acquisition and distribution of satellite data. Governments and public funding have traditionally been involved in the support of science and the development of many areas of technology, partly because of widespread beliefs that scientific and basic technological knowledge has strong public good properties and partly because of the importance of many technological fields to national security. However, the lines between the areas that are publicly and privately funded, and between what was deemed appropriately in the public domain and what was appropriately private property, have always been somewhat controversial in the domain of science and technology. These chapters discuss the recent pressures to move these lines, so that market governance covers more, and the reactions to these pressures.

The fourth cluster concerns itself with activities for which there is little argument about the central importance of government but limited agreement regarding the appropriate range and extent of regulation of market forces. One of the areas considered is public health. Here, the debate focuses on how much regulation of private activities there should be on the grounds of protecting public health. The other is elections and the making of legislation and the efforts to prevent these from being for sale.

Notes

1. For a statement in this spirit, see Francis Fukuyama (1992) and Daniel Yergen and Joseph Stanislaw (1998).

2. David Mowery and Richard Nelson (1999) describe in detail the involvement of government programs in sectors conventionally thought of as "market organized." See also Joseph Rogers Hollingsworth and Robert Boyer (1997), Douglas North (1990), and Geoffrey Hodgson (1999), stressing the institutional complexity of modern economies.
3. For a good discussion, see Richard Lipsey, Paul Courant, and Christopher Ragan (1999, chap. 3).
4. The discussion that follows develops some of the themes first introduced in my article, "Assessing Private Enterprise: An Exegesis of Tangled Doctrine" (Nelson 1981).
5. C. Edward Lindblom's (1977) discussion of these issues in *Politics and Markets* is particularly good.
6. Of the many expositions of the many facets of market failure theory, I find Joseph Stiglitz (1986) especially fine. See also Lipsey, Courant, and Ragan (1999, chap. 18).
7. This is very much the position taken by Lindblom (2001).
8. Gøsta Esping-Andersen (1990) provides a broad and incisive picture of the modern welfare state. See also Robert Goodin et al. (1999).
9. The dangers of detailed planning where understanding is limited have been stressed by Friedrich Hayek (1988) and Lindblom (1977; 2001).

References

Bell, David. 1960. *The End of Ideology.* Cambridge, Mass.: Harvard University Press.

Blyth, Mark. 2000. *Great Transformations, Economic Ideas, and Political Change in the Twentieth Century.* Baltimore: Johns Hopkins University Press.

Coase, Ronald. 1960. "The Problem of Social Cost." *Journal of Law and Economics* 3: 1–44.

Crosland, C. Anthony. 1956. *The Future of Socialism.* London: Jonathan Cape.

Dahl, Robert, and C. Edward Lindblom. 1953. *Politics, Economics, and Welfare.* New York: Harper and Brothers.

Esping-Andersen, Gøsta. 1990. *The Three Worlds of Welfare Capitalism.* London: Oxford University Press.

Fukuyama, Francis. 1992. *The End of History and the Last Man.* New York: Avon Books.

Goodin, Robert, Bruce Headey, Ruud Muffelss, and Henk-Jan Dirven. 1999. *The Real Worlds of Welfare Capitalism.* Cambridge: Cambridge University Press.

Hamilton, Alexander. 1791/1965. "A Report on Manufactures." Reprinted in *The Reports of Alexander Hamilton.* New York: Harper Torchbooks.

Hayek, Friedrich. 1988. *The Fatal Conceit: The Errors of Socialism.* Chicago: University of Chicago Press.

Hobbes, Thomas. 1651/1994. *Leviathan: The Matter, Form and Power of a Commonwealth Ecclesiastical and Civil,* edited by Edwin Curley. Indianapolis: Hackett.

Hodgson, Geoffrey. 1999. *Economics and Utopia.* London: Routledge.

Hollingsworth, Joseph Rogers, and Robert Boyer. 1997. *Contemporary Capitalism: The Embeddedness of Institutions.* Cambridge: Cambridge University Press.

Kirzner, Israel M. 1979. *Perception, Opportunity, and Profit: Studies in the Theory of Entrepreneurship.* Chicago: University of Chicago Press.

Lindblom, C. Edward. 1977. *Politics and Markets.* New York: Basic Books.

———. 2001. *The Market System: What It Is, How It Works, and What to Make of It.* Cambridge: Cambridge University Press.

Lipsey, Richard, Paul Courant, and Christopher Ragan. 1999. *Economics.* New York: Addison-Wesley.

Mowery, David, and Richard R. Nelson. 1999. *The Sources of Industrial Leadership.* New York: Cambridge University Press.

Myrdal, Gunnar. 1960. *Beyond the Welfare State.* London: Duckworth.

Nelson, Richard R. 1981. "Assessing Private Enterprise: An Exegesis of Tangled Doctrine." *Bell Journal of Economics* 12(1): 93–111.

North, Douglas. 1990. *Institutions, Institutional Change, and Economic Performance.* Cambridge: Cambridge University Press.

Polanyi, Karl. 1944. *The Great Transformation.* Boston: Beacon Press.

Rivlin, Alice. 1971. *Systematic Thinking for Social Action.* Washington, D.C.: Brookings Institution Press.

Schonfeld, Andrew. 1965. *Modern Capitalism.* London: Oxford University Press.

Schumpeter, Joseph. 1942. *Capitalism, Socialism, and Democracy.* New York: Harper and Row.

Smith, Adam. 1776/1937. *The Wealth of Nations.* New York: Modern Library.

———. 1853. *The Theory of Moral Sentiments.* London: Henry G. Bohn.

Stiglitz, Joseph. 1986. *The Economics of the Public Sector.* New York: W. W. Norton.

Yergen, Daniel, and Joseph Stanislaw. 1998. *The Commanding Heights.* New York: Simon & Schuster.

Part I

INFRASTRUCTURE, NATURAL MONOPOLY, AND EQUITABLE ACCESS

T HE CHAPTERS in part I are concerned with four "systems" activities: electric power, telephone service, passenger rail service, and bank funds clearing. Three different but overlapping attributes profoundly affect the ongoing arguments regarding the role that markets should play in their governance and needed regulation.

First of all, all these activities are widely regarded as "infrastructure," that is, as activities that need to be performed if the overall economy is to work well. The infrastructure category innately has blurry edges. However, most people would include these four systems as infrastructure. This means that, innately, there is going to be a public interest in their effective performance.

Second, up until recently at least, there was widespread belief that these systems were "natural monopolies" (at least locally) and that they could be operated more efficiently as unified, comprehensive systems serving all users in a particular region, or along a particular route, than under a pluralistic competitive regime of market governance. Unlike in other sectors of the economy, competition in service provision in these activities was regarded as inevitably leading to inefficiencies.

Third, there is broad philosophical support for the principle of universal, equitable access to these services, at least at a basic service level. This has led in several of the cases to the requirement that certain user groups or uses be served at prices that are below cost and, therefore, to cross-subsidy of certain users and services in the name of equity. While cross-subsidies are often viewed by economists as causing economic inefficiencies, they tend to have strong political support.

For all these reasons, electric power, telephone service, and railroads, though they started out as competitive regimes, became regulated in the United States, with regulation determining both prices and who was allowed to serve. In Europe, after World War II at least, all three of these systems generally became government enterprises. In both the United States and Europe, bank funds clearance mechanisms were largely under the auspices and supervision of the central bank.

Of course, the picture presented here is that of the past, not the present. At the present time, all four of these systems are marked by more market elements, more competition, less central control and administration, and less regulation (or, at least, different regulation) than in the past. Deregulation (denationalization in Europe) clearly is spurred by the growing strength of promarket sentiments and arguments as discussed in chapter 1. In the cases of telephone service and electric power, the deregulation movement was focused initially on opportunities for competition in parts of the system that had been opened up by new technologies and called into question the idea of natural monopoly. The same is true, if to a lesser extent, regarding bank funds clearance.

The U.S. passenger rail case is different, in that the initial conditions for movement toward deregulation were set by the financial troubles of passenger rail service after World War II, which led to government overview (in some cases, management) and significant subsidy. Here, deregulation and denationalization were seen as reforms to increase efficiency and reduce the need for subsidy. However, the argument that passenger rail was not a natural monopoly was involved here, too.

We think it fair to say that the deregulation experiences with electric power and passenger rail now are widely seen as mixed bags. The recent blackout in the eastern United States has called attention to the fact that if a system is divided up to facilitate competition, no one may be responsible for systems integrity. A similar issue arose when British rail was privatized and divided up. In parts of the telephone system, deregulation has indeed engendered a competitive market structure, but parts of the system continue to defy reform. In all four cases, there is continuing controversy regarding the role markets ought to play in the governance structure and whether the marketization that has taken place is a good start and ought to be pushed forward or whether, on the contrary, the whole issue of governance needs to be rethought, again.

2

ELECTRIC POWER

Kira Fabrizio

S INCE THE mid-1980s, there has been a movement to restructure or privatize industries that were traditionally regulated or nationalized monopolies. The natural gas, telecommunications, and electricity industries involve several horizontal sectors, one or more of which is an integrated network and thus a natural monopoly. Historical development, previous regulation, and coordination benefits from vertical integration led to vertically integrated monopolies in these industries, governed by regulation or nationalization. In each of these industries, it was determined that one sector of the vertically integrated monopoly was not a natural monopoly on its own but had been subjected to regulation (or nationalization) owing to the integrated nature of the market participants.

Restructuring efforts in the electricity industry have focused on the potentially competitive generation sector. The push to restructure has been motivated by technology changes, some (perceived) shortcomings of regulation, and a general ideological shift toward less government intervention in favor of the market mechanism. This movement in the United States follows other restructuring efforts in the telecommunications, airline, and natural gas industries, among others, indicating the impact of the prevailing ideology. From the perspective of electricity customers, regulation brought benefits such as reliability and decreased prices over time (Victor 2002). The challenge for restructuring is to maintain the benefits of regulated utilities while encouraging cost savings, innovation, and productive efficiency more strongly than under the regulated system. The importance of establishing institutions that allow for efficient market transactions, and the costs of relying on the market mechanism, may have been underappreciated at the start of the restructuring process.

Although these efforts have been labeled "deregulation," a perfectly competitive market would not develop simply by removing the price and entry regulations that were in place. New institutions and regulations must be established along the way. The electricity generation sector is linked (physically, financially, and operationally) with the transmission and distribution sectors of the industry, which remain natural monopolies. Effective restructuring policy must consider the history of the industry: not only did the industry develop as vertically integrated for good reason, but the vertical integration influences the institutional structures necessary in the move to a competitive market. An understanding of the complex problems faced in the restructuring process suggests the importance of postrestructuring governance structures that replace the regulatory rules being dismantled. Sally Hunt (2002) suggests five major areas of change that must be dealt with to successfully implement a competitive generation market. These include exposing the demand side of the market (customers) to the market, creating trading arrangements run by a central system operator separate from traders, establishing a feasible transmission model with control separate from traders, opening the supply side to entry, and eventually allowing retail choice for all customers.

Measuring the success of restructuring raises the question of defining the goals of restructuring, which may include greater efficiency, lower costs, less regulation, improved innovation incentives, or simply achieving a competitive market for its own sake. There is some evidence that the restructured system may provide benefits, but considerable new regulations and well-publicized difficulties with the transition have left many wondering if we would not have been better off leaving well enough alone.

Industry Overview

The electricity industry comprises three sectors. The generation sector encompasses the creation of electricity. Moving electricity at high voltage from the generation plant to substations that transform it to lower voltage is the most prominent role of the transmission sector. The transmission sector also includes the complicated system that keeps the entire grid of the transmission network stable, including the interconnection and integration of distributed generation facilities into a stable alternating current (AC) network, scheduling and dispatching of generation to balance demand and supply in real time, and management of equipment failures, network constraints, and interconnection with other electricity networks. Finally, carrying the lower-voltage electricity from the substation to the customer is the role of the distribution sector.

Several characteristics of the electricity industry complicate the market. Most important, the transmission grid is an integrated network that must be operated in coordination with the generation plants. The electricity transmission grid is a free-flowing AC network on which electricity follows the path of least resistance from the generator interconnections to the places where electricity is being drawn from the system. The location of each generator on the grid and how much electricity each generator is producing at any time affect all other connected generators and the operation of the transmission system. The demand for electricity varies widely across hours of the day and days of the year. Electricity is not economically storable, so supplies must be generated simultaneously with the demand being served, leading to significant coordination requirements. To maintain a stable transmission grid and serve all customers reliably, generation plants need to be ready to run when called upon, and transmission operators need to coordinate the generation plants on the grid, constraints of the transmission system, and demand (or "load") drawing electricity from the grid. Compounding these issues, the aggregate short-run demand elasticity is small because customers do not know the real-time price of electricity, and shifting the use of electricity across time may take considerable adjustment.

Other characteristics of the generation, transmission, and distribution assets also affect how the market functions. Generation assets are site specific: once located at a particular point on the transmission grid, they cannot be practically relocated to serve changing demand patterns or adjust to changes in the transmission grid. The transmission and distribution sectors of the electricity industry are natural monopolies. Once a distribution or transmission network has been established in an area, it would be inefficient for a second provider to duplicate the infrastructure. Although the generation sector is no longer characterized by natural monopoly attributes, vertical integration between the three sectors effectively turns the generation sector into a monopoly, as well (Joskow 1997; 1999).

All these aspects of the electricity industry mean that the generation sector cannot be meaningfully contemplated independently of the transmission and distribution sectors. The high level of coordination and extreme time specificity require interaction and cooperation between sectors of the industry that may not be available through the spot-market transactions associated with competitive markets. As Paul Joskow (1997, 122) states, "The primary economic rationale for vertical integration between generation and transmission is that it internalizes within an organization the operating and investment complementarities between these supply functions, with their associated public goods and externality problems." The characteristics of the market make complete contracting for the transaction between generation and transmission operators nearly impossible, and certainly costly. As described by Oliver Williamson (1985), when contracting is costly and transaction hazards are significant, the governance structure of last resort—vertical integration—is employed. In this light, it is understandable why a market structure of vertical integration has dominated the electricity industry.

History of Regulation

To understand the challenges facing the restructuring movement, it is useful to briefly review the history of regulation in the electricity industry in the United States and other parts of the world. From the 1870s through the 1920s, the U.S. electricity industry was highly fragmented. Utility companies served separate populated areas, and the lack of a comprehensive transmission network limited interconnection. Initially, there was competition between electricity suppliers in some densely populated areas and also competition with the existing energy sources, such as gas and kerosene. However, by 1900 electricity had won out, and scale economies had come to dominate the industry. Once a utility had been established to serve an area, it was uneconomical for another utility to build duplicative assets to compete. As more of the population was connected to electric service, the industry consolidated to take further advantage of the scale economies.[1]

During the period between the 1920s and World War II, governments in developed countries became more heavily involved in the electricity industry. Electricity came to be seen as more of a necessary product than a luxury item, giving the government reason to regulate prices and ensure provision of service. In the United States, states began to establish regulatory commissions to oversee the utility companies (Victor 2002).

In the United States, the industry became concentrated, and electric utilities became vertically integrated. Generation, transmission, and distribution services were provided by integrated monopolists serving exclusive service territories. By 1932, when about two-thirds of households in the United States were wired for electricity, the eight largest holding companies controlled 73 percent of the country's investor-owned utility companies, and almost half of the electricity generated in the United States was controlled by three holding companies (EIA 2000). This prompted the 1935 Public Utility Holding Company Act, limiting the holdings of these conglomerates and requiring the breakup of large electricity holding companies until each was a consolidated vertically integrated utility serving a particular geographic area (EIA 2000). The governmental intervention in the electricity market was justified as a means of controlling prices in a natural monopoly industry and preventing the exercise of market power, but it was also part of a pattern of government activity favoring state ownership and control of industries providing public goods (Victor 2002). During this time the "regulatory compact" developed, establishing a contract between the state government and electricity service providers that in exchange for the exclusive right to serve customers in an area, the utility company would serve all customers in that area at rates set by a state-level regulatory body to allow a fair rate of return on the generation, distribution, and transmission assets of the utility company.

Following World War II, the minimum efficient scale of generating plants increased dramatically owing to technological change and the fact that the transmission and distribution grids were much more complete. This technological and infrastructure development provided opportunities for consolidation and monopolistic behavior on the part of electric utility companies. Many European governments decided that the electricity sector was a natural monopoly and merged small companies into nationwide, government-owned monopolies.[2] In keeping with Public Utility Holding Company Act regulations and the granting of limited exclusive service territories to utility companies, the U.S. market remained horizontally fragmented and vertically integrated. Private investor–owned monopolies, regulated by state-level regulatory commissions, were the major owners of generation, transmission, and distribution assets. These asset owners constituted an interconnected nationwide system, with many owners each controlling small portions of the system and a low level of overall network control.[3]

Laying the Groundwork for Restructuring

In the 1970s doubts began to emerge regarding whether the regulated monopoly was the best market structure for the electricity industry. A movement toward privatization and restructuring was driving policy in many industries. Pressure built for reform of the generation sector of the electricity industry to increase reliance on market governance and introduce competition. Restructuring of the electricity industry was complicated in part by the divided jurisdiction between the federal government, responsible for oversight of wholesale trade, and state governments, responsible for the oversight of generation, distribution, and transmission for retail sales. This divide tied the hands of all policy makers with respect to which aspects of the highly interconnected industry each could influence. Federal policies on two fronts paved the way for later state-level restructuring policies. The first was the encouragement of power production from non-utility generators, which are a class of independent power producers. The second was the establishment of wholesale trading rules to facilitate competition at the wholesale level.

The Emergence of Independent Power Producers

Federal legislation, starting with the Public Utility Regulatory Policy Act of 1978, encouraged more competition in the wholesale generation sector by requiring utilities to buy power from small independent power producers and co-generator facilities at the utility's avoided cost.[4] The act had a significant impact on the industry because it demonstrated that generation by independent companies was possible and that independent producers could sell power into the grid without compromising the stability of the system. This opened the door for at least partial restructuring of the generation sector. Low gas prices and investment by independent power producers stimulated innovation in combined-cycle gas turbines, which shortened construction time and decreased the minimum efficient scale of generation plants from about 1,000 megawatts (MW) in the early 1980s to between 50 and 350 MW in the 1990s.

The avoided-cost-based prices agreed to in the Public Utility Regulatory Policy Act power contracts were soon much higher than the spot-market price of electricity as natural gas prices fell during the 1980s and 1990s and new technology improved generation efficiency, leaving utility companies purchasing power at out-of-market prices (Borenstein and Bushnell 2000). These high-fixed-price contracts were seen as a failure of regulation to mimic the benefits of the market and encouraged calls for true "deregulation" of the generation sector.[5]

The development of a market for power produced by independent generators also created an interest group of independent power producers with an interest in opening up the generation market to competition and gaining access to the transmission grid (Joskow 2000; Hogan 2001). Access to the transmission assets of the incumbent monopolies was critical to independent power generators, especially because the horizontally disaggregated nature of the U.S. market necessitated transmission across the transmission assets of several companies (Joskow 1999).

Federal Wholesale Trading Policies

The decentralized structure of generation and transmission asset ownership led to the development of wholesale power markets and "wheeling" services, or power transmission between and across different companies' transmission systems. Wholesale power trades grew during the 1970s owing to increased costs and varied demand and capacity conditions across utilities in regions connected by the transmission grid. However, the wholesale energy market was inhibited by the traditional regulatory structure for transmission. Under the Federal Power Act of 1935, the Federal Energy Regulatory Commission (FERC) could not order a utility to provide interstate transmission service or related network services. The system of bilateral contracting and wholesale wheeling that evolved during the late 1970s was reasonably good at dealing with short-term wholesale transactions between connected utilities where the utilities were not in competition and the operating rules were viewed as mutually beneficial (Joskow 1996). Large-scale wholesale and retail competition, however, require that significantly more wholesale trading and wheeling services be provided by utilities in competition with one another, stretching this model beyond its capacity to function efficiently. Independent power producers were faced with the prospect of negotiating for transmission services with many different operators in order to transmit power across the many interconnected control areas of the network. Transmission rates for this type of service were often "pancaked" on top of one another, so that the cost of transmission made otherwise economic trades inefficient (Joskow 2000). The existing institutional structures did not go far enough to promote market transactions.

In 1988 FERC issued several notices of proposed rule making encouraging independent power production and wholesale trading of energy. The agency never passed these rules, but it did put many of the policies into effect through case-by-case decisions (Joskow 2000). In 1992 the Energy Policy Act expanded FERC's authority to order that utilities provide access to transmission assets to support wholesale power transactions and created a new class of generating units that would produce electricity for wholesale sales, called exempt wholesale generators.[6] However, utilities were still not required to file generic tariffs for transmission wheeling services and instead underwent case-by-case negotiations. Requests for wheeling services often turned into lengthy, contentious negotiations (Joskow 2000). Contracting for wholesale transmission was too complicated and costly, and the transmission asset owners had the incentive to hold up the power producers. In 1996, in response to these difficulties and the initiation of retail restructuring proceedings in California, FERC established additional rules standardizing the wheeling rates and rules.[7] These rules did not go far enough to solve transmission access problems, and further FERC policy in 1999 encouraged investor-owned utilities to establish regional transmission organization, in an attempt to achieve some benefits of regional coordination of transmission activities and separate the control of transmission assets from other functions to avoid conflicts of interest between transmission and generation operation.[8] These activities at the federal level encouraged non-utility generation investment and facilitated wholesale trade. However, because FERC's jurisdiction is limited to wholesale transactions, it was prohibited from ordering open access for final (retail) customers, and so this was left to the states.

Thus the electricity industry in the early 1990s was undergoing significant changes at the wholesale level, with considerable growth in wholesale trading and new rules established to facilitate negotiations and trade. The improved technology associated with long-range transmission and the reduction in the minimum efficient scale of generation plants owing to the development of combined-cycle gas turbines provided the technological opportunity for a more competitive generation sector. Decreasing information technology costs and the increasing ability to monitor and coordinate the complex, interconnected system also facilitated the decentralization of generation supply. The growth of independent power producers demonstrated the feasibility of more decentralized generation. At the same time, there was an increase in the influence of market-oriented thinking and an emphasis on maximizing economic efficiency, especially through the market mechanism. In short, the electricity industry was ripe for reform. It would not be long before the pressure was on the state regulatory commissions to pursue competition in search of lower electricity prices.

Restructuring the Industry

Pressure for state-level reform of the electricity sector in the United States was building during the 1980s and 1990s. In 1988 Chile privatized its generation sector, followed shortly by the Nordic countries and New Zealand, and in 1990 by the United Kingdom, which formed the model for the U.S. restructuring (Victor 2002). In the United States, especially in states with the highest electricity prices, prices for electricity generation were perceived as higher than those that would result from a competitive market system, owing in part to regulation and misaligned incentives but perhaps mostly from mistakes of the past such as Public Utility Regulatory Policy Act contracts and nuclear power investments (Borenstein and Bushnell 2000). The states with higher generation costs were those that moved most quickly to restructure their retail generation markets (White 1996). Large industrial customers (looking for lower rates) and independent power producers (looking to profit by selling to customers at the current wholesale rates) led the charge.[9] Years of debate over how to restructure the electricity market ensued.

As interest in restructuring spread throughout the United States, state-level politics took over and largely determined the course that each state took. As David Victor (2002, 408) writes, "In all the countries that have led this wave, restructuring was the product of an idea—that government should intervene less in the economy—rather than a particular crisis or opportunity knocking on the door." In the pursuit of the idea of competition, the details and complexities of the necessary institutions and transition policies were sometimes overlooked. Proposals for restructuring quickly became subject to the pressures for compromise inherent in the political process.

Basic Model of Restructuring

The fundamental idea behind restructuring is to establish a competitive market for generation at the wholesale level and allow customers to purchase generation services from any one of the competing suppliers serving their market at the retail level, rather than receiving service only from the incumbent utility. As in other restructuring network industries, the competitive segment in the electricity industry is separated (functionally or structurally) from the natural monopoly segments. Price and entry regulations are removed in the generation sector, natural monopoly services are "unbundled" from the generation portion, and regulators establish mandated access to the network facilities with prices set by new regulatory mechanisms.[10] Customers contract with electricity suppliers, who supply customers with electricity through the transmission and distribution assets owned by other companies. Electricity suppliers may or may not own generation assets. Although prices in the wholesale market fluctuate in real time and are likely to be volatile at times, retail customers may choose to contract with electricity suppliers offering fixed-price contracts. Moving toward this ideal model, however, has been difficult in reality.[11]

Policy makers in all markets pursued restructuring with similar goals: greater efficiency and less regulatory overhead through reliance on competition. Academics and policy makers expected efficiency improvements to come through improvements in investment decisions and construction costs, decreased politicization of resource development decisions (that is, avoiding high-cost results such as Public Utility Regulatory Policy Act regulations), improved operating performance of plants, increasing productivity of labor and decreased wage costs, retirement of uneconomical plants, and provision of incentives for investment and innovation. Regulation of this potentially competitive sector came to be seen as unnecessarily extending the weakened incentives, overhead costs, and politicized processes associated with regulation. Regulation leaves customers to bear the risks associated with demand, prices, investment, maintenance, and management because the utilities receive rate payments to cover their incurred operating costs. In contrast, a competitive market places the risks with the asset owners and electricity suppliers and thereby provides incentives to operate efficiently (Joskow 1997; Hunt 2002). Just as the involvement of independent power producers following the Public Utility Regulatory Policy Act helped stimulate technological innovation in combined-cycle gas turbines, competition in the generation sector as a whole may stimulate innovation.

The value of these competitive market benefits must be considered in light of the potential costs of reliance on a market-based structure. Although restructuring offers potential benefits from competition, including lower regulatory costs, efficient investment incentives, and lower operating costs, it may also bring new costs owing to incentives to exercise market power, contracting costs, and costs incurred because of misaligned or lacking governance structures. As Joskow (2000, 124) notes, the realization of the potential benefits of competition "depends on designing a sound transmission network, competitive wholesale power market, and retail market institutions and on mitigating serious market power problems efficiently where they arise in power or transmission markets." Designing these institutions was more difficult than anticipated. The basic model of restructuring attempted to solve these problems. As experience has shown, the details of the market matter considerably, and some states have been more successful than others in achieving the desired benefits and avoiding potential costs.

Challenges of Restructuring and Institutional Solutions

Ideally, competition would alleviate the need for regulation. However, successful implementation of competition in the generation sector requires institutional structures and governance mechanisms to provide solutions and safeguards for the market transactions. How to create an efficient competitive market and encourage free entry of new competitors has proved to be a complicated question. Generally speaking, the competitive marketplace must be established in such a way as to avoid conflicts of interest between the competitive entities and the owners and operators of the assets to which all competitive players need access, such as transmission, while also facilitating coordination among portions of the system that function interactively and assuring that market prices are the result of a truly competitive market (Hunt 2002). The movement from a regulated monopoly to competitive market necessarily alters the incentives of the market players. Failure to anticipate the incentive structures results in unexpected market activity, some of which may undermine the competitive market. As Hunt (2002, 69) writes, "For virtually all dimensions of markets, the preexisting situation does not provide underpinning that would lead to competitive markets if the regulations simply went away and did nothing. This is especially true in the United States, where every aspect of the competitive market requires some sort of institutional, structural, or regulatory change." Four broad areas—a functioning wholesale market, potential self-dealing between sectors, coordination of generation and transmission, and the exercise of market power—require considerable attention in the design of new institutions for the competitive market, though this is by no means a complete list.

Functioning Wholesale Markets

Establishing a well-functioning wholesale market is critical to restructuring the electricity market. Competition in the wholesale market controls the prices of electricity and protects customers from high prices. The wholesale spot-market price also provides incentives for efficient investment, plant operation, and transmission, allows settlement of real-time discrepancies between sellers and buyers in the market, and provides a benchmark against which customers can compare competitive generators' offers.

The competitive wholesale market depends on establishing a supply side without too much market power and making the rules of the market flexible enough to allow efficient behavior. Encouraging entry of generators depends on guaranteeing access to vital assets, such as transmission and distribution, in a way that does not disadvantage new entrants. The supply side of the market can also be expanded and made more competitive by removing transmission constraints to enable more geographically dispersed suppliers to sell into the market.

Clear, understandable, known, and stable rules of the marketplace are also critical to efficient trades. As described by Severin Borenstein and his colleagues (2003), the complexity and lack of stability of the wholesale market rules in California led to inefficiencies in the markets for power and limited the ability of the market actors to compete efficiently. This was part of the reason that Enron was able to manipulate the market unchecked. The initial chaos and confusion in the California market allowed Enron to profit from arbitrage trading in a way that it would not have been able to had the market been conducted with more transparency (Hunt 2002).

Preventing Self-Dealing Between Transmission and Generation Sectors

A competitive market in generation requires that new entrant competitors be protected from unfair dealings by the incumbents. Owing to the vertically integrated nature of the market in the United States before restructuring, some separation of control or ownership between the generation and transmission sectors was necessary to prevent strategic self-dealing by the operators of the transmission assets. If the owners and operators of the incumbent generation facilities were allowed also to be the operators of the transmission networks in a competitive market, these companies would have the incentive and ability to favor their own generation assets at the expense of competitors. The general solution has been functional or structural separation of the generation and transmission assets.

Most of the restructuring states in the United States followed an approach in which vertically integrated utilities may still own transmission assets but must turn over the operation of these assets to an independent system operator (ISO). The ISO is responsible for network functions. This avoids the problem of forced divestiture of privately held generation assets but also prevents self-dealing on the part of owners of transmission and generation assets. However, the separation of operation of transmission and generation assets raises the problems of coordination: the generation and transmission assets were integrated for a reason. As Hunt (2002, 6) writes, "If transmission expansion is in the hands of competing generators, there are issues of discrimination. If it is in too many hands, there are issues of coordination."

Coordination of the Transmission and Generation Sectors

Operation of the transmission grid requires coordination among many parties, including operators of generation facilities, power marketers and other energy suppliers, and companies selling power to end-use customers. Primarily, there is a need for coordination between transmission and generation operators in the dispatch of plants, investment in new assets, and maintenance of existing assets. As mentioned earlier, the electricity industry in the United States was characterized by a low degree of horizontal integration in any of the three sectors but was highly vertically integrated (Joskow 1997). The prerestructuring vertical integration helped solve coordination and technical problems, and also aligned incentives between the segments of the industry, without reliance on a pricing mechanism for transmission. Under that model, transmission constraints were solved by the monopolist dispatcher's adjusting its own plants to balance the system with the transmission constraints. When an optimization is based on bids of generation plants at different locations on the grid, rather than the vertically integrated system of generation and transmission, prices for transmission across congested areas are required. It is critical to integrate the operation of the generation and transmission assets so that the efficient dispatch and pricing signals are sent to asset owners.

Policy makers in restructuring states have generally recognized the need for a central system coordinator to maintain and coordinate the grid system, determine the economic dispatch of generating plants, coordinate demand and supply, and maintain system stability in a way that accounts for all transmission constraints. Reliance on the ISO as a replacement for the vertical integration of generation and transmission functions raises some complicated issues regarding how to allocate transmission rights, price transmission, deal with network constraints, coordinate investment decisions between generation and transmission, and provide incentives for transmission asset maintenance and investment. Many of these difficulties have not been completely solved. However, as mentioned earlier, getting the wholesale spot-market price right provides the correct incentives for these other decisions. Setting the transmission prices correctly matters, as well. Without prices reflecting the actual differences in cost between locations on the grid, the incentives for efficient investment in generation and transmission do not exist. Nodal pricing reflects the true prices that result from the plant dispatch process while the locational pricing model provides an approximation of the correct prices, resulting in difficulties and requiring additional fixes to make up the differences. Integration of the nodal pricing method for transmission with plant dispatch, spot-market prices, and congestion management operations allows the elements of the system to work together coherently and efficiently.

The roles of the ISO and the generation assets owner in decisions regarding the operation of and investment in transmission assets are unclear. Who decides when and where to invest in maintenance and upgrades of the system and who pays for these improvements are problematic issues. There are considerable negative externalities and free rider problems associated with investment in generation and transmission assets. The placement of generation (or transmission) assets on the grid relative to other generation assets and to customer load affects the operation of the transmission grid and may also impact the dispatch of generators on the grid in a way that creates negative and positive externalities for generation asset owners. In addition, investments in transmission assets are lumpy, long-lived sunk costs characterized by economies of scale.[12] There is still no clear answer to these difficult questions (Hunt 2002).

Market Power

Realizing the benefits of competition in the generation sector depends on ensuring sufficient wholesale competition. Several states required or strongly encouraged divestiture of incumbent utilities' generation assets to bring multiple generation owners into the market and promote competition. However, simply having many generation owners in the market does not ensure efficiency and low prices. Once the generation market is restructured, companies have incentives to exercise market power that they did not have when they were integrated companies.

Even with a low concentration of ownership of generation assets, owners of some plants may be able to exercise considerable market power. In the wholesale spot market, generation asset owners bid into the market, and all plants selected to run are paid the bid of the marginal plant dispatched. Because the marginal plant sets the market price, the plants not dispatched at that time provide the relevant competition. When demand is high, all of the base load plants and most of the peaking units may already have been dispatched, leaving little competition on the margin. As a result, firms may be able to exercise market power even in markets that, by typical measures of concentration, would be considered only modestly concentrated (Borenstein and Bushnell 2000; Joskow 2000). "The combination of (completely) inelastic demand and tight supplies created opportunities for individual suppliers to exercise market power without engaging in collusion, driving prices up still higher" (Joskow 2001, 35). Real-time pricing, which would allow customers to know the price for electricity when they make their consumption decisions, would make the demand curve less inelastic and provide the opportunity for demand response to high market prices. This would help limit the exercise of market power and would decrease the high peaks owing to capacity constraints.[13]

With all of these difficulties and complexities, restructuring policy makers faced plenty of challenges. In addition, many other factors were unknown at the time the policy was crafted. Despite these issues, several markets have experienced some success with restructuring, though the negative experience with restructuring in California has been influential in other markets considering restructuring.

Restructuring in Action

These challenges to restructuring, among others, influenced the transition process in all states attempting to promote competition in the electricity generation sector. Policy makers in several states, including Pennsylvania, Rhode Island, and New York, responded to the difficulties encountered and adjusted restructuring policy accordingly. Most of the restructuring states have been moderately successful in creating a functioning wholesale market, coordinating generation and transmission, and preventing the exercise of market power and self-dealing. The competitive retail market has been slow to develop in many places, owing in part to mandated low prices offered by the incumbent suppliers that new competitive suppliers have difficulty competing with.[14] There is a considerable amount to be learned from the policy-making, implementation, and transition experiences in restructuring states. Most important, these experiences offer the lesson that successful restructuring requires carefully crafted institutions to govern transactions in the market and mitigate transaction costs to promote a competitive market.

The wholesale market in California offers an example of a failure of policy making to anticipate market incentives or establish the necessary institutions in the market. The design of the wholesale market in California constituted a compromise between many interests rather than a coherent body of policy. "Getting it done fast and in a way that pandered to the many interests involved became more important than getting it right. The end result was the most complicated set of wholesale electricity market institutions ever created on earth and with which there was no real-world experience" (Joskow 2001, 14). The California policy attempted to separate the forward energy market (run by the power exchange, or the PX) from the transmission markets (run by the ISO), relying on the market system to provide the coordination required between these functions. This policy took decisions that required coordination and moved them from a vertically integrated system to a completely separated system. As John Chandley, Scott Harvey, and William Hogan (2000, 3) state, "The flawed premise of the California market design was that this inescapable reality could be ignored or minimized in an effort to honor a faith in the ability of markets to solve the problems of coordination." Hogan (2002) has dubbed this premise the "separation fallacy" and has described in detail the need for these functions to be integrated in the same decision-making body. No other state or country that has pursued restructuring has established a dual market like the California PX and ISO system. Since its inception, the system has experienced difficulties. "As we now know from painful and expensive experience, the decision to separate system operations from short-term markets in California was a failure" (Hogan 2002, 2).

In addition, California policy makers opted for a zonal approach to determining transmission prices, as opposed to a more rigorous nodal pricing approach. As described by Chandley, Harvey, and Hogan (2000, 21), "The California zonal system is fundamentally flawed because it cannot get the prices right. The zonal experiment has failed and it must be replaced. It is the source of persistent gaming, infeasible schedules, and poor locational signals. It encourages over-scheduling of constrained transmission, fosters market power, and muffles the price signals that loads need to respond to high prices."

The failure of restructuring in California owes to more than badly formed wholesale markets and inefficient transmission pricing. The strain on the wholesale markets was increased by supply shortages, increased demand, high natural gas prices, inefficient dispatch of plants, tightening markets for emission allowances, and the possible exercise of market power. The scarcity conditions in the California market drove up the market price. Because of the lack of real-time pricing and the inelasticity of customer demand, there was little demand reduction in response to the high prices. Hunt (2002, 279) claims that "if demand response had been built into the trading arrangements there would never have been a crisis—the market prices could never have risen so high." During June and July 2000, utilities were purchasing power from the wholesale market at prices up to $300 per megawatt hour (MWh) to serve customers from whom they were only allowed to collect $60 per MWh owing to the frozen retail rates (Hirst 2001). The mounting debt of the utilities led potential electricity suppliers to restrict sales to these companies out of fear of nonpayment, which further exacerbated the demand-supply strain in California and forced even higher wholesale rates (Hirst 2001; Joskow 2001). In December 2000, FERC issued an order that eliminated the requirement that utilities sell their power into the PX, as a result of which the PX ceased to operate in January of 2001.

On March 27, 2001, the California Public Utilities Commission finally raised the fixed retail rates by an average of 30 percent to help pay for the debts incurred by the utility companies, but it was too late. Pacific Gas and Electric declared bankruptcy. In an attempt to control the wholesale cost of power to California utilities, the state entered into long-term contracts with power suppliers in mid-2001.[15] Between January and May of 2001, California spent more than $7 billion on purchases of power for the state (Hirst 2001). It signed long-term contracts for up to twenty years into the future amounting to more than $43 billion (Hunt 2002). By the end of August 2001, the wholesale price had dropped to 90 percent of the December 2000 price, a function of reduced natural gas prices, reduction in electricity demand, increased capacity owing to generators coming back on line and some new generation, the exemption of generators from the emissions program, and FERC's price mitigation programs to end strategic withholding by generators. The prices dictated by the contracts for power signed by the state now appear much higher than expected future market prices (Joskow 2001), reminiscent of the Public Utility Regulatory Policy Act contracts. On September 20, 2001, the California Public Utilities Commission issued an interim order suspending retail choice in California. Although the ISO continues to operate a real-time market for energy, it relies increasingly on power procurement through the Department of Water Resources (Joskow 2001).

This brief example demonstrates the potential problems that can occur when the market governance structure created by policy is not well suited to managing the challenges of the particular market structure. The dual PX-ISO system exists only in California; other states and countries have been much more successful at implementing workable restructuring policies, but many required adjustment along the way as the true difficulties of the market became clearer. Both the New York and the Pennsylvania–New Jersey–Maryland (PJM) markets integrated dispatch decisions, reliability functions, and market operations within one system operator (Hogan 2002). The pricing systems in those markets, which rely on the nodal pricing method for transmission, provide incentives for generators to bid into the market efficiently (Chandley, Harvey, and Hogan 2000).[16]

The market for generation services in Pennsylvania was built upon the existing PJM power pool that managed central economic dispatch based on marginal cost pricing for wholesale trades in the region (Joskow 2000). The power pool comprised the transmission assets of utilities in Pennsylvania, New Jersey, and Maryland. The system relied heavily on the nodal pricing method for pricing transmission, and the transmission and energy markets were integrated and consistent. Parties were free to use the forward market and the spot market in whatever way most efficiently served their needs, with few restrictions on contracting (Chandley, Harvey, and Hogan 2000). The PJM ISO determines locational prices at more than two thousand locations in the system every five minutes, demonstrating the feasibility of a full locational pricing model. This system provides efficient incentives for generation and investment (Hogan 2001).

Policy makers in some states, such as Pennsylvania, implemented retail rates based on the realized market price, avoiding the gap between market prices and fixed retail rates that bankrupted the utilities in California. In addition, other states allowed adjustments to the fixed rates employed during the transitional period of restructuring for significant changes in costs incurred by utilities. As natural gas prices rose across the country, many states increased the rates that utilities were allowed to charge customers, often through fuel adjustment clauses. This prevented utilities in other states from experiencing the wholesale-retail price imbalance faced by California utilities.

Is Restructuring Worth It?

Consumers in California are now left with a compromised electricity market, lacking a comprehensive plan going forward, and high electricity rates. In restructuring states in which competitive markets have been more successful, consumers have a choice of electricity suppliers and a competitive market that promises lower prices through greater investment and operating efficiency.

The failure of competition in California has prompted many other states to conclude that restructuring is not worth the trouble or is perhaps too difficult a transition for policy to implement successfully. As stated by Borenstein and James Bushnell (2000, 46), "In general, the nonstorability of electricity, combined with very little demand elasticity and the need for real-time supply/demand balancing to keep the grid stable, has made restructuring of electricity markets a much greater challenge than was inferred from experience with natural gas, airlines, trucking, telecommunications, and a host of other industries." Is the challenge presented by restructuring worth the potential benefits? Although the recent nature of the policy changes in the electricity industry precludes analysis of long-term gains, some evidence regarding the success of restructuring programs can be identified.

Goals of the restructuring efforts in the United States included improved efficiency, lower retail electricity rates, improved incentives for innovation, less regulation, and development of a competitive market. Following privatization and reforms, the electricity industry in the United Kingdom displayed significant cost savings, increased labor productivity, and labor reductions (Newbery and Pollitt 1997). The average price of electricity has fallen, and the retail market has become fairly competitive (Littlechild 2001). In New Zealand, costs savings in the generation and transmission sectors were approximately 10 to 15 percent, and there was significant new entry of generation capacity. In Norway, most prices have also fallen (IEA 1999). In an analysis comparing day-ahead prices in the Western Systems Coordinating Council (WSCC) before and after the advent of operation of the California ISO (CAISO) and California PX (CALPX), Joskow (2000) finds no evidence that the deregulated market structure has led to a significant change in wholesale prices. However, there is some evidence suggesting that investor-owned utilities in the United States have decreased labor, operation, maintenance expenses in order to become more competitive (EIA 2000; Fabrizio, Rose, and Wolfram 2004).

In general, the restructuring transition process has not decreased the amount of regulation or the involvement of regulators in the electricity market in the United States. Perhaps achieving the goal of less regulation will be realized in the longer term. Several states are on their way to having established competitive generation markets, but the California experience serves as an example of why careful policy making is critical. "California shows that poor market design, coupled with inappropriate regulatory and political intervention, can rapidly produce extremely unsatisfactory outcomes when capacity is tight, particularly if the shortages are unexpected" (Newbery 2002, 5). Restructuring clearly does not mean complete reliance on the market; it is more accurately described as a replacement of the old regulation with a new regulatory framework. The institutional structures, market rules, and resulting incentive structures put in place make a tremendous difference to the realized benefits of competition in the generation sector.

Are we better off with restructured electric generation markets than under the old regulatory regime? As Hunt (2002, 12) writes, "We do not have the option of going back a decade—the appropriate comparison is what is happening now, which in many cases is not as good as it was pre-1992. We have taken the industry apart and have put nothing comprehensive in its place." The challenge for policy makers now is to take what we have learned and create a workable system of cohesive institutions to support an efficiently functioning electricity industry. The fractured nature of the U.S. electricity industry has become a barrier to cohesive policy and workable institutions. The split jurisdiction between state and federal governments has created a situation in which neither part can implement policy affecting all parts of the integrated system. The electricity transmission system connects areas larger than states, which necessitates a set of policies applicable to regions larger than states. Hunt (2002) suggests that to establish a workable competitive generation market, the United States must take a national approach, with nationally established trading arrangements and coherent policy across broad geographical regions, in place of the highly fragmented system that currently exists.

This chapter has benefited from the comments of Richard Nelson, David Mowery, and participants in the conference on the Complexities and Limits of Market Organization at Columbia University, School of International and Public Affairs, February 24, 2003.

Notes

1. From 1914 to 1929, the average capacity of a generating unit grew from 12.5 megawatts (MW) to 24 MW, while at the same time the capital costs per MW decreased by 70 percent (Victor 2002).
2. For example, France established EdF in 1946. Italy was the last country in the European trend, creating the state-owned ENEL in 1962. Australia and New Zealand adopted similar models. These nationalized systems typically established legislatively mandated entry barriers or at least protected incumbents from competition.
3. There were approximately 150 separate control areas over three large synchronized AC networks (Eastern Interconnection, Western Interconnection, and Texas Interconnection). Within these control areas, individual utilities were responsible for generation dispatch, network operations, and maintaining reliability on specific portions of the network.
4. "Avoided cost" is the hypothetical marginal cost avoided or not incurred by the utility by producing one less unit of electricity.
5. The growing dissatisfaction with the traditional model of regulated vertically integrated monopolies was punctuated by the Three Mile Island nuclear disaster and the $2.25 billion bond default by the Washington Power Supply System

(appropriately referred to as "Whoops") following its failure to complete five nuclear reactors (Hogan 2001).

6. The Energy Policy Act and state programs that followed further increased contracting for power by requiring or encouraging utilities to meet generation needs through competitive bidding rather than by building additional generation assets. In the mid-1990s, independent producers accounted for more than half of the new generation capacity (Joskow 1997).

7. These rules were issued in Order 888, which required transmission owners to file open-access tariffs with FERC that would be available to all wholesale customers, and accompanying Order 889.

8. This was in Order 2000. It is still unclear whether FERC has the jurisdiction to order participation of investor-owned utilities in regional transmission organizations.

9. Many states did not move toward restructuring their electricity markets. In fact, some states explicitly voted against the move. In Idaho, Iowa, and Florida, for example, utilities, consumer groups, legislators, and regulators believed that restructuring would increase their relatively low retail rates and potentially compromise reliability. In addition, many states had strong interest groups opposed to restructuring. Rural cooperative and municipal power suppliers were concerned that large investor-owned utilities would skim off the most lucrative customers, leaving them with geographically dispersed rural users and rising costs. See *Electrical World* (1997).

10. The same basic model forms the backbone of the electricity restructuring policies in many markets, including the United Kingdom, Chile, Argentina, New Zealand, Norway, California, New England, New York, Pennsylvania, and Illinois (Joskow 1997).

11. It should be noted that restructuring of the industry clearly invalidated the regulation compact, under which generation companies were required to serve all customers in their protected service territory at the regulated rates in exchange for the monopoly right to serve the customers in that service territory. This raises the question of whether or not the generation companies still have the obligation to serve customers living in what was previously their service territory. States have dealt with this question in various ways, using various names (such as "default service" or "provider of last resort"). Often, the responsibility to serve customers who have not chosen another provider is assigned to the incumbent generating company. In states that have required or encouraged divestiture of all generation assets by the incumbent utilities, this default service is sometimes assigned to the incumbent distribution company and is sometimes bid off to competitive service providers. Most restructuring policies envision phasing out this service as customers switch (or are switched) to competitive generation supply companies. The potential for leaving those in need without access to electricity has been the subject of considerable debate in formulating restructuring policy.

12. Paul Joskow (1997, 132) states, "Transmission investment decisions do not immediately strike me as being ideally suited to relying on the invisible hand," but he goes on to note that private parties may play an important role in identifying transmission investment opportunities if a "reasonably good" allocation of capacity rights has been created. The network operator would still need to be involved in the investment process to determine the externalities on network users

or to identify situations in which the private market is providing inadequate incentives for investment owing to scale economies or free riding.

13. Promoters of restructuring policy often referred to the potential for real-time pricing and increased demand elasticity as potential benefits of competition. However, with the exception of a few large industrial users, real-time pricing and metering has not materialized in markets that have implemented restructuring policy.

14. Restructuring policy in California mandated that retail rates be frozen at a discounted level throughout the transition to a competitive market. The policy mandated a 10 percent reduction from June 1996 rates for residential and small commercial customers and a rate freeze for industrial and large commercial customers until March 2002 or the utilities recovered their stranded costs, whichever occurred first (California Bill AB 1890). Massachusetts law mandated a 10 percent rate reduction in 1998 and another 5 percent reduction in 1999. The price for default service was set at an increasing rate over the eight years following restructuring and was expected to exceed the market price, so that retail customers could save money by switching to a competitive supplier offering the market price. As it turned out, market prices in both of these states were higher than anticipated, and competitive suppliers could not often beat the default service price. In Pennsylvania, utilities agreed to mandated price reductions much smaller than those in other states. Default service prices were set above the expected wholesale price, with a premium known as the "shopping credit" added to the realized market price. By switching to a competitive supplier for generation services, retail customers could avoid paying the "shopping credit" premium on the market price (Joskow 2000, 180).

15. Authorized in California Bill AB 1X in February 2001.

16. See John D. Chandley, Scott M. Harvey, and William W. Hogan (2000) for a detailed discussion of the problematic policies of the California market and some discussion of how policies in Pennsylvania and New York created more efficient markets with better incentive systems.

References

Borenstein, Severin, and James Bushnell. 2000. "Electricity Restructuring: Deregulation of Reregulation?" *Regulation* 23(2): 46–52.

Borenstein, Severin, James Bushnell, Christopher R. Knittel, and Catherine Wolfram. 2003. "Trading Inefficiencies in California's Electricity Markets." Working Paper PWP-086. Berkeley, Calif.: Program on Workable Energy Regulation.

Chandley, John D., Scott M. Harvey, and William W. Hogan. 2000. "Electricity Market Reform in California." Working paper. Cambridge, Mass.: Center for Business and Government, John F. Kennedy School of Government, Harvard University.

Electrical World. 1997. "Deregulation: It's Not a Done Deal." *Electrical World* 211(5, May): 21.

Energy Information Administration (EIA). 2000. *The Restructuring of the Electric Power Industry, A Capsule of Issues and Events.* DOE/EIA-X037. Washington, D.C.: National Energy Information Center.

Fabrizio, Kira, Nancy L. Rose, and Catherine Wolfram. 2004. "Does Competition Reduce Costs? Assessing the Impact of Regulatory Restructuring on U.S. Electric Generation Efficiency." NBER Working paper w11001.

Hirst, Eric. 2001. "The California Electricity Crisis: Lessons for Other States." Washington, D.C.: Edison Electric Institute.

Hogan, William W. 2001. "Electricity Market Restructuring: Reforms of Reforms." Paper presented to the Twentieth Annual Conference of the Center for Research in Regulated Industries. Rutgers University (May 23–25).

———. 2002. "Electricity Market Design and Structure: Avoiding the Separation Fallacy: Comments." Report submitted to the Federal Energy Regulatory Commission. Docket RM01-12-000, Washington, D.C.

Hunt, Sally. 2002. *Making Competition Work in Electricity.* New York: John Wiley and Sons.

International Energy Agency (IEA). 1999. *Electricity Market Reform: An IEA Handbook.* Paris: Organization for Economic Cooperation and Development.

Joskow, Paul. 1996. "Introducing Competition into Regulated Network Industries: From Hierarchies to Markets in Electricity." *Industrial and Corporate Change* 5(2): 341–82.

———. 1997. "Restructuring, Competition, and Regulatory Reform in the U.S. Electricity Sector." *Journal of Economic Perspectives* 11(3): 119–38.

———. 1999. "Introducing Competition into Regulated Network Industries: From Hierarchy to Markets in Electricity." In *Firms, Markets, and Hierarchies,* edited by Glenn Carroll and David Teece. New York: Oxford University Press.

———. 2000. "Deregulation and Regulatory Reform in the U.S. Electric Power Sector." In *Deregulation of Network Industries: The Next Steps,* edited by Sam Peltzman and Clifford Winston. Washington, D.C.: Brookings Institution Press.

———. 2001. "California's Electricity Crisis." Working paper. Cambridge, Mass.: Massachusetts Institute of Technology.

Littlechild, Stephen. 2001. "Electricity: Regulatory Developments Around the World." Beesley Lectures on Regulation, Series 11. London: IEA/LBS.

Newbery, David M. 2002. "Mitigating Market Power in Electricity Markets." Working paper. Cambridge: Department of Applied Economics, University of Cambridge.

Newbery, David M., and Michael Pollitt. 1997. "The Restructuring and Privatization of Britain's CEGB: Was It Worth It?" *Journal of Industrial Economics* 45(3): 269–303.

Victor, David G. 2002. "Electric Power." In *Technological Innovation and Economic Performance,* edited by Benn Steil, David Victor, and Richard Nelson. Princeton, N.J.: Princeton University Press.

White, Matthew. 1996. "Power Struggles: Explaining Deregulatory Reforms in Electricity Markets." *Brookings Papers on Economic Activity: Microeconomics* 1996: 201–67.

Williamson, Oliver. 1985. *The Economic Institutions of Capitalism.* New York: Free Press.

3

TELECOMMUNICATIONS REGULATION: AN INTRODUCTION

Nicholas Economides

T HE U.S. TELECOMMUNICATIONS sector is going through a significant change. A number of factors contribute and define this change. The first is the rapid technological change in key inputs of telecommunications and computer-based services and in complementary goods, which have dramatically reduced the costs of traditional telecommunications services and have made many new services available at reasonable prices. For example, telecommunications cost reductions have made access to the Internet affordable to the general public.

The second reason for the revolutionary change has been the sweeping digitization of the telecommunications and the related sectors. Not only has the underlying telecommunications technology become digital, but the consumer and business telecommunications interfaces have become more versatile and closer to multifunction computers than to traditional telephones. Digitization and integration of telecommunications services with computers create significant business opportunities, impose significant pressure on traditional pricing structures, especially in voice telephony, and threaten the fundamental features of the traditional regulatory regime.

The third reason for the current upheaval in the telecommunications sector was the passage of an important new law to govern telecommunications in the United States, the Telecommunications Act of 1996. Telecommunications has traditionally been subject to a complex federal and state regulatory structure. The 1996 act attempted to adapt the regulatory structure to technological reality, but various legal challenges by the incumbents have so far delayed, if not nullified, its impact.

In general, regulation should be used only when it is clear that deregulated markets are likely to fail even in the presence of reasonably strict antitrust enforcement. Clearly, the success or failure of a market in the absence of regulation depends crucially on the demand and cost conditions under the present technology. Progress and innovation in telecommunications technologies have been rapid for the past forty years and are expected to continue at a fast pace. As a result of technological change, cost conditions shift considerably over time and can transform a market that requires regulation into one that does not. This is crucial for telecommunications and has lead to progressive deregulation. For example, the market for long-distance telecommunications services, starting as a near monopoly in the mid-1970s, was formally completely deregulated in 1995, after strong competition in the 1980s and early 1990s emerged following the breakup of American Telegraph and Telephone (AT&T) in 1984 and the opening of the long-distance market to competition. However, the process of deregulating some services while other services (often produced by the same firms) remain regulated is a complicated task with many pitfalls. Given the complex incentives of firms that participate in many markets and often face competitors who participate in just a few, it would be foolish to proceed with complete deregulation of the telecom sector without a careful analysis.

Telecommunications services are based on an increasingly sophisticated and complex network able to produce a rich variety of services that differ in distance traveled, quality, amount and nature of data or voice transmitted per unit of time, requirement of immediate (real-time) delivery, and so on. Making effective use of elements of market organization in many telecommunications contexts often requires considerable and detailed regulation. Many times, these regulations, even if they work well for existing markets, have pretty poor results when applied to markets for new products. This lack of flexibility of regulation is particularly important in modern telecommunications because new telecommunications services are continually produced, helped by the availability of complementary goods and services. For example, the demand for low-level data transmission as required by the World Wide Web and the Internet would not be possible without the wide availability and low prices of computers. But it would be foolish to start applying the traditional regulatory framework to the Internet, and the Federal Communications Commission (FCC) has correctly understood this.

Finally, telecommunications regulation is hampered by the various exigencies of regulation in general, such as political intervention and lobbying. Political intervention is complicated because some telecommunications services (such as access to emergency services) are essential for all and others, such as basic service, are considered necessities.

A number of factors drive the U.S. telecommunications industry today:

- dramatic and continuing reductions in the costs of transmission and switching
- digitization
- the 1984 breakup of AT&T's monopoly, resulting in a competitive long-distance service sector and a monopolized local telecommunications sector

- restructuring of the regulatory environment through the implementation of the 1996 Telecommunications Act, twelve years after the breakup of AT&T
- the move of value from underlying services (such as transmission and switching) to interfaces and content
- the move toward multifunction programmable devices with programmable interfaces, such as computers, and away from single-function, nonprogrammable consumer devices, such as traditional telephone appliances
- reallocation of electromagnetic spectrum, allowing for expanded wireless services interconnection and interoperability of interconnected networks
- standardization of communications protocols
- the existence of network effects whereby connection to a large network is more valuable for each customer, and the fact that small networks unable to reach critical mass are unlikely to survive

These, in turn, have a number of consequences:

- increasing pressure for cost-based pricing of telecommunications services
- price arbitrage between services of the same time immediacy requirement
- increasing competition in long-distance services
- the possibility of competition in local services
- the emergence of Internet telephony (voice-over Internet protocol [VOIP]) as a major new telecommunications technology

Why Have Telecommunications Regulation?

To answer the question, "Why have telecommunications regulation?" one must first answer the question, "Why have regulation in general?" The logic of competition law in the United States is that efficiency (allocative, productive, and dynamic) is the desired outcome of antitrust policy, and competition is the means of achieving it. Thus antitrust laws are used to guard against restrictions on competition. Economic regulation has been established as a last resort for those markets where it is clear that competitive outcomes cannot be achieved by market forces;[1] where deviation from economic efficiency is deemed socially desirable; where the social and private benefits are clearly different, including cases in which minimum safety standards increase social welfare; and to allow for coordination in technical standards or market equilibriums.[2] Telecommunications can qualify under all four of these criteria as an industry in which some form of regulation is appropriate.

The main reason proposed for regulating telecommunications has been that a desirable competitive outcome could not be achieved by market forces.

In the last decade of the nineteenth century and the first three decades of the twentieth century, AT&T, after many of its patents had expired, faced significant competition in local telecommunications by independent telephone companies. The independents typically started at the local level and wired many businesses and households in small and midsize towns, sometimes also creating regional long-distance networks. There were periods in the first decade of the twentieth century when independents had in total more local lines than AT&T, although the near monopoly of AT&T in long distance was never seriously challenged until the 1970s. AT&T refused to interconnect with the independents, forcing many businesses to subscribe to two telephone companies with disconnected and incompatible networks, an independent to reach local customers (mainly households) and AT&T to reach suppliers.[3]

AT&T stated that it was concerned with the quality standards of independents and offered to incorporate most of them in the Bell System, but clearly there were also business and strategic reasons behind AT&T's refusal to interconnect. The benefit to an independent telephone company of access to the AT&T long-distance network was much larger than the benefit to AT&T of adding to its network the mostly residential customers of an independent. Although not clearly articulated in network economics terms, the issue facing the independents and AT&T was clearly a fundamental issue in network economics. Modern network economics teaches us that the incentives of firms of different sizes to interconnect differ depending on the value and size of the new demand that is created by interconnection (Economides 1991; 1996). Typically, a large and high-value network has a significantly smaller incentive to interconnect with a smaller, low-value network than the smaller one has to interconnect with the larger one. This can easily lead to a refusal by the larger, high-value network to interconnect.

In summary, market incentives led AT&T to refuse to interconnect with smaller (local and long-distance) networks, though such interconnection was considered socially desirable. This was the first reason for which regulation at the federal and state levels was imposed with a requirement to interconnect public switched telecommunications networks.[4] There were clearly some service markets in the time period leading to the 1930s in which only one firm could survive. Monopoly prices in general are predicted to be high, and AT&T's long-distance prices during this period were high. This gave a further justification to regulation, since free entry was unlikely to increase the number of competitors in many service markets.

The second and third reasons for regulation (deviation from social efficiency being desirable and a difference between the social and private value of telecommunications) were generally articulated after regulation was already in place. In the 1960s regulators did not let prices of basic local service rise in their attempt to achieve "universal service," that is, to include as many households as possible in the telecommunications network, on the basis that this was desirable even if it were allocatively inefficient. The ability of customers to receive calls and make emergency calls also played a role in setting the goal of universal service. Basic telecommunications service is now considered a necessity, and its inexpensive and ubiquitous provision is guaranteed by regulation.[5]

The fourth reason for regulation, that the regulator can help the industry achieve technical compatibility and avoid fragmentation, has had only limited application to telecommunications. Clearly, technical compatibility in a network industry is important since it allows all users to get the full benefits of the combined networks rather than the benefits of only the one they subscribe to. In practice, the present de facto compatibility standards in voice transmission and in higher data protocols are largely the legacy of the pre-1984 AT&T monopoly and the adoption of Internet protocols that were created with government subsidization, with the requirement that they be made public. The regulatory requirements are typically on interconnection and at the level of voice transmission. There is no regulatory requirement of compatibility in many areas, including wireless equipment, wireless text messaging, higher data protocols, and interfaces.[6]

In understanding telecommunications regulation in the United States, it is useful to keep in mind the particular factors that made regulation the appropriate policy answer at some point in time. As technology and population densities change, some markets that may have been natural monopolies in the past may not be natural monopolies any more, and it may be better to allow competition in those markets while keeping regulation in the rest. The question of the desirability of regulation in various markets has been asked repeatedly over time, resulting in the present regime of progressive deregulation.

The public interest objective of telecommunications regulation is vague. Most economists agree that a valid objective is to increase total surplus, that is, consumers' surplus plus profits of active firms. Most economists also agree that the public interest should promote innovation and growth. Although it is difficult to quantify the exact effect of innovation and growth on income, there is wide consensus that these should be promoted and are part of the public interest. Finally, the public interest may include subsidization of telecommunications services that are considered necessities, such as basic local service, or those that are deemed to increase productivity and growth, such as Internet access. Given the vagueness of the concept of the public interest, various groups lobby politicians and regulators to include their objectives as part of the public interest. This rent-seeking behavior sometimes leads to telecommunications regulators to impose policies that have little to do with telecommunications markets.

Having outlined the potential benefits of regulation, I should also note that there are significant drawbacks and costs created by regulation. First, regulators generally do not have the latest technological information. In an industry with fast technological change, such as telecommunications, this can lead to significant divergence between costs and prices as costs fall much faster than prices. This has happened consistently both in the old regulated AT&T and in regulated local-exchange carriers. Second, regulated firms may be able to use the regulatory setup to create barriers to entry and thereby perpetuate their profitable existence. For example, the first application of MCI to provide switched long-distance service was rejected by the FCC; MCI had to sue and was allowed in long-distance service only after a court decision. Third, the regulatory setup is slow, cumbersome, bureaucratic, and, in many cases, politically influenced. In practice, the regulatory system is much easier to influence by politicians than the judicial system. Fourth, because of the public interest provision, there can be significant rent-seeking activity by various groups, especially in issues relating to mergers that have strict, externally imposed deadlines. Fifth, in an industry with fast technical change, it is hard to define the appropriate array of regulated products; and new and evolving products are difficult to regulate correctly. Thus regulation should be used sparingly, and only when there are no good alternatives.

A new problem in regulatory supervision has been added with the recent aggressive intervention of the Competition Committee of the European Union in telecommunications matters. The European Union intervened in the mergers of MCI and WorldCom and of WorldCom with Sprint. This has created a situation in which large telecommunications companies contemplating a merger have to argue their case in front of the United States Department of Justice, the European Union Competition Committee, the public utilities commissions in fifty states, and other foreign regulatory bodies. This not only adds to the complexity and the cost of the merger but also creates the possibility that the requirements imposed by different regulatory bodies will contradict one another, and it would not be feasible to meet all of them. It also creates the possibility that conditions in financial markets may change considerably between the time a merger is announced and the time it is consummated, so that one of the merging parties may not find the merger desirable at the later date and may use a regulatory objection to abandon the merger without penalties. This increases the incentives of private parties opposing a merger to intervene, attempting to lengthen the approval process in hope that financial conditions may change during the approval process.

U.S. Telecommunications Regulation

Telecommunications has traditionally been a regulated sector of the U.S. economy. The market for telecommunication services and equipment went through various stages of competition after the invention of the telephone by Alexander Graham Bell. Regulation was imposed in the early part of this century and remains today in various parts of the sector.[7]

The Period of AT&T's Near Monopoly

Following a period of expansion and consolidation, by the 1920s AT&T had an overwhelming majority of telephony exchanges and submitted to state regulation. Federal regulation was instituted by the 1934 Telecommunications Act, which established the Federal Communications Commission. In its heyday, from the 1930s to 1981, AT&T dominated all aspects of telecommunications in the United States. It had approximately 90 percent market share of local access lines and more than 90 percent of the long-distance revenue. It used almost exclusively equipment of Western Electric, its equipment division. It owned a top research laboratory, Bell Laboratories, which conducted both applied and theoretical research. Crucial scientific inventions of the twentieth century, such as the transistor and the integrated circuit, occurred at Bell Laboratories. By the 1970s, AT&T had achieved universal service—more than 90 percent of U.S. households had a telephone—and it kept improving the quality of its services.

Regulation of the U.S. telecommunications market was marked by two important antitrust lawsuits that the U.S. Department of Justice brought against AT&T and the Bell System. In the first one, United States v. Western Electric, filed in 1949, the U.S. Department of Justice claimed that the Bell operating companies practiced illegal exclusion by buying both production equipment and customer premises equipment (telephone appliances and switchboards) only from Western Electric, a part of the Bell System. The government sought a divestiture of Western Electric, but the case was settled in 1956, with AT&T agreeing not to enter the computer market but retaining ownership of Western Electric. The second major antitrust suit, United States v. AT&T, was started in 1974. The government alleged the following:

- that AT&T's exclusive relationship with Western Electric was illegal
- that AT&T monopolized the long-distance service market
- that AT&T refused to interconnect telecommunications competitors as well as customers' premises equipment, thus being liable for a "refusal to deal"
- that AT&T used various discriminatory practices that raised the costs of competitors
- that AT&T abused the regulatory process and did not provide complete information to regulators
- that AT&T set prices to exclude competitors, including practicing predatory pricing

The Department of Justice sought divestiture of both manufacturing and long-distance service from local service.[8] Late in the Carter administration, the department offered to accept only the divestiture of manufacturing. AT&T refused and later had to accept a much more onerous breakup. The case was settled by the modified final judgment in 1984. AT&T retained its long-distance network, but seven regional Bell operating companies (RBOCs) were broken away from it.[9] Each RBOC comprised a collection of local telephone companies that were part of the original AT&T. Regional Bell operating companies remained regulated monopolies, each with an exclusive franchise in its region, and were not allowed to provide long-distance service.

Microwave transmission was a major breakthrough in long-distance transmission that created the possibility of competition in long distance. Microwave transmission was followed by technological breakthroughs in transmission through satellite and fiber-optic wire. By the time competition took root in long distance, fiber-optic technology had become the dominant technology of transmission.

The Postbreakup Years

The breakup of AT&T crystallized the recognition that competition was possible in long distance while the local market remained a natural monopoly (see, for example, Crandall 1991). The biggest benefits to consumers during the past eighteen years have come from the long-distance market, which was transformed during this period from a monopoly to an effectively competitive market. However, consumers often do not reap the full benefits of cost reductions and competition because of an antiquated regulatory framework that, ironically, was supposed to protect consumers from monopolistic abuses and instead sometimes protects the monopolistic market structure.

Competition in long distance has been a great success. The market share (in minutes of use) of AT&T fell from almost 85 percent in 1984 to barely 50 percent in 1998, as shown in figure 3.1, and presently below 45 percent. The revenue market share of AT&T, shown in figure 3.2, also fell dramatically. Since the 1984 modified final judgment, the number of competitors in the long-distance market has increased dramatically. Soon after the judgment, two nationwide facilities-based competitors, MCI and Sprint, emerged as strong competitors of AT&T. Facilities-based competitors deployed their own fiber-optic switched network. Over the past decade, a number of new strong facilities-based competitors entered with nationwide (or significant-coverage) networks, including Qwest, Level 3, Williams, and Global Crossing.[10] There are also a number of smaller regional facilities-based carriers as well as a large number of "resellers" that buy wholesale service from the facilities-based long-distance carriers and sell to consumers. For example, there are currently about five hundred resellers competing in the California interexchange market, providing strong evidence for the ease of entry into this market. At least twenty new firms have entered the California market in each year since 1984.

FIGURE 3.1   *AT&T's Market Share of Interstate Minutes, 1984 to 1998, at Three-Month Intervals*

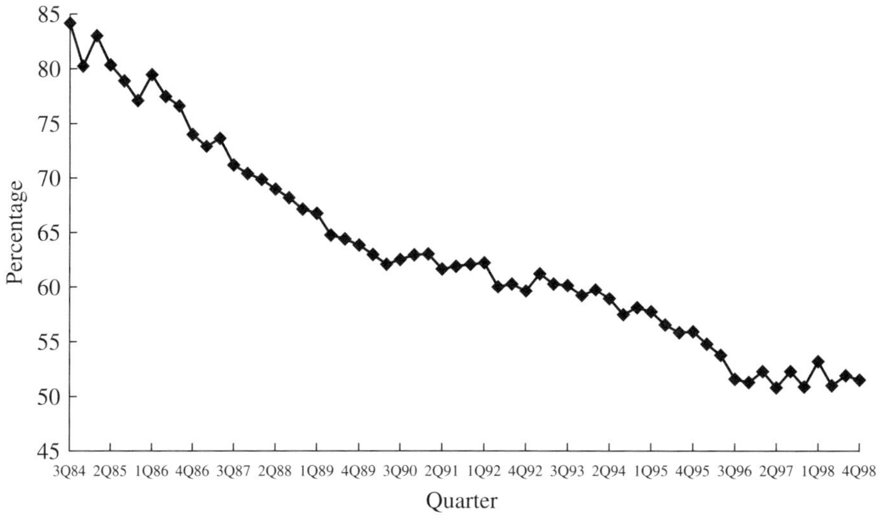

Source: Data from FCC (2003a; 2003c).

Prices of long-distance phone calls have decreased dramatically. The average revenue per minute of AT&T's switched services was reduced by 62 percent between 1984 and 1996. Figure 3.3 shows the average revenue per minute for AT&T relative to 1984 (upper line) as well as the average revenue per minute for AT&T net of access charges relative to 1984 (lower line).[11] The FCC declared AT&T "nondominant" in the long-distance market in 1995 (FCC 1995). Most economists agree that presently the long-distance market is effectively competitive.

The modified final judgment did not allow the RBOCs to provide "in-region" long-distance phone service: that is, each RBOC was prohibited from offering long-distance service that originated in its local area. The main reasons for that restriction were to avoid three types of anticompetitive actions by a local service monopolist that would also own a long-distance service subsidiary: vertical price squeeze, price discrimination against the opponents of the local monopolist's long-distance subsidiary, and nonprice discrimination against the opponents of the local monopolist's long-distance subsidiary.

A long-distance phone call is carried by the local telephone companies of the place it originates and the place it terminates, and only in its long-distance part by a long-distance company. Originating access and terminating access

FIGURE 3.2   *AT&T's Share of All Long-Distance Revenues, 1984 to 2001*

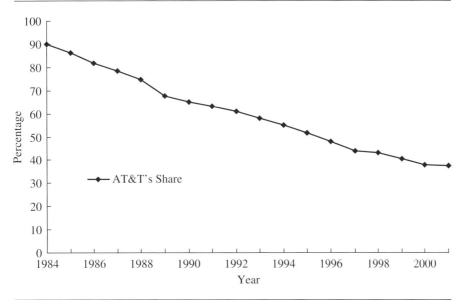

Source: Data from FCC (2003a; 2003c).

are provided by local-exchange carriers to long-distance companies and are es-sential bottleneck inputs for long-distance service. A local-exchange monop-olist sets a per minute originating fee (a) paid by all long-distance companies for calls originating from its region. Origination and termination fees are ap-proved by the state public utility commission.[12] If the local-exchange monop-olist also provides long-distance service, it can influence the maximum price per minute (p) that an independent long-distance company can charge. Thus a local-exchange monopolist that has vertically integrated in long-distance ser-vice can control the gross revenue per minute (p − a) of its long-distance rivals. By setting its long-distance price and influencing the access charge, the verti-cally integrated local-exchange monopolist can squeeze or even make nega-tive the gross per minute revenue (p − a) of the long-distance rivals so that they are marginalized or even driven out of business. This is called a "vertical price squeeze." A local-exchange monopolist with a long-distance subsidiary can also use price and nonprice discrimination against long-distance competitors to disadvantage them (see Economides 2003; Economides, Lopomo, and Woroch 1996; Economides and White 1995; Faulhaber 2004). Thus to insu-late long-distance competition from leveraging in the long-distance market of the RBOC monopoly power in the local exchange and to protect the public

FIGURE 3.3   *Average Revenue per Minute (ARPM) of AT&T's Switched Services and ARPM Net of Access Charges, 1984 to 1998*

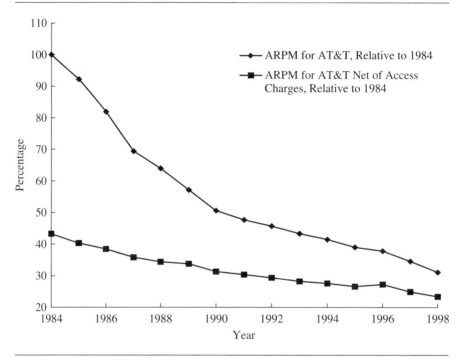

Source: Data from Hubbard and Lehr (1998).

interest, the 1984 modified final judgment restricted the RBOCs from providing in-region long-distance service.[13]

Local telephone companies that came out of the Bell System (RBOCs) actively petitioned the U.S. Congress to be allowed to enter the long-distance market. To a large extent in response to this pressure, Congress passed the Telecommunications Act of 1996. The great success of competition in long distance allowed Congress to appear balanced in the Telecommunications Act of 1996 by establishing competition in local telephony while allowing RBOCs into long distance after they had met certain conditions. However, the transition of local markets to effective competition will not be as easy or as quick as it was in the long-distance markets. This is because of the nature of the product and the associated economics.

Many telecommunications companies are presently trying to be in as many markets as possible so that they can bundle the various products. Companies believe that consumers are willing to pay more for bundled services for which the consumer receives a single bill. Bundling also discourages consumers from migrating to competitors, who may not offer the complete collection of services, so that consumer "churn" is reduced.

The 1996 Telecommunications Act and Its Impact

The Telecommunications Act of 1996 attempted a major restructuring of the U.S. telecommunications sector. The act will be judged favorably to the extent that it allows and facilitates the acquisition by consumers of the benefits of technological advances. Such a function requires the promotion of competition in all markets. This does not mean immediate and complete deregulation. Consumers must be protected from monopolistic abuses in some markets as long as such abuses are feasible under the current market structure, which was in many ways determined by the legacy of regulation. Moreover, the regulatory framework must safeguard against firms exporting their monopoly power in other markets.

In passing the Telecommunications Act of 1996, Congress took radical steps to restructure U.S. telecommunications markets. These steps had the potential to result in significant benefits to consumers of telecommunications services, telecommunications carriers, and telecommunications equipment manufacturers. But the degree of success of the act depends crucially on its implementation through decisions of the FCC and state public utility commissions and the outcome of the various court challenges that these decisions face.

The 1996 act envisioned a network of interconnected networks that are composed of complementary components and generally provide both competing and complementary services. The act used both structural and behavioral instruments to accomplish its goals. It attempted to reduce regulatory barriers to entry and competition. It outlawed artificial barriers to entry in local-exchange markets in an effort to accomplish the maximum possible competition. Moreover, it mandated interconnection of telecommunications networks, unbundling, nondiscrimination, and cost-based pricing of leased parts of the network, so that competitors can enter easily and compete component by component and service by service.

The act imposed conditions to ensure that de facto monopoly power would not be exported to vertically related markets. Thus it required that competition be established in local markets before the incumbent local-exchange carriers would be allowed in long distance. It preserved subsidized local service to achieve universal service but imposed the requirement that subsidization be transparent and that subsidies be raised in a competitively neutral manner. Thus it led the way to the elimination of subsidization of universal service through the traditional method of high access charges.

It crystallized changes that had become necessary because of technological progress. Rapid technological change has always been the original cause of regulatory change. The radical transformation of the regulatory environment and market conditions that is presently taking place as a result of the 1996 act is no exception.

Logic of the Act

The logic behind the 1996 act was essentially to break the network into components and let everyone compete in every part, as well as in end-to-end services. To achieve this, the act mandates interconnection, unbundling, and nondiscrimination. Moreover, it takes away some of the incumbent's advantages that arise purely from historical reasons by mandating the lease of unbundled network elements at cost, mandating wholesale provision of any service presently provided by the incumbent local exchange carriers, and imposing phone number portability. To preserve the competition in long distance, the act attempted to ensure that monopoly power arising from historical or other reasons in the local exchange is not exported in other markets. Finally, it attempted to impose nationwide standards for competition and take some regulatory power away from the states.

The 1996 Act allows entry of RBOCs in long distance after they open their local-exchange networks to competition. Thus from the point of view of an RBOC, entry into long-distance service provision was supposed to be the reward for allowing competition in the local exchange and losing its local-exchange monopoly. The act was based on the belief that the individual private incentives of the RBOCs would be sufficient to drive the process. Thus it did not impose penalties for delay or noncompliance. This has proved to be a serious deficiency. Congress thought that the "carrot" of entry in long distance would be sufficient reward for RBOCs to open their local networks. Events have shown that Congress erred in this; RBOCs' behavior showed that they were willing to pay the price of staying out of long distance for a while rather than open their local networks.

Entry in Local Services as Envisioned by the Act

At the time of this writing, the "last mile" of the telecommunications network that is closest to the consumer (the "local loop") still remains a bottleneck controlled by a local-exchange carrier. The Telecommunications Act of 1996 boldly attempted to introduce competition into this last bottleneck, and, before competition took hold, to imitate competition in the local exchange.

To facilitate entry in the local exchange, the act introduced two novel ways of entry other than through the installation of owned facilities. The first allowed entry in the retailing part of the telecommunications business by requiring incumbent local-exchange carriers to sell to entrants at wholesale prices any retail service that they offer. Such entry is essentially limited to the retailing part of the market.

The second and most significant novel way was through the leasing of unbundled network elements from incumbents. In particular, the 1996 Act required that incumbent local-exchange carriers unbundle their networks and offer for lease to entrants network components (unbundled network elements) at prices "based on cost" (sect. 252[d][1][a][i]) that "may include a reasonable profit" (sect. 252[d][2]) and be "nondiscriminatory" (sect. 252[d][1][a][ii]).[14] Thus it envisioned the telecommunications network as a decentralized network of interconnected networks.[15]

Many firms, including the large interexchange carriers AT&T and MCI-WorldCom, attempted to enter the market through "arbitration" agreements with incumbent local-exchange carriers under the supervision of state regulatory commissions, according to the procedure outlined by the act. The arbitration process proved to be extremely long and difficult, with continuous legal obstacles and appeals raised by the incumbent local-exchange carriers. To date, more than eight years after the signing of the act by President Bill Clinton, entry in the local exchange has been limited in most residential markets.

As of June 2003, entrant competitive local-exchange carriers provided service to 14.7 percent of the approximately 183 million local telephone lines nationwide (FCC 2003c, sec. 8, table 6), but only 3.4 percent of end users were served over facilities owned by competitive local-exchange carriers.[16] Forty-two percent of all competitive local-exchange carriers' lines served medium and large business, institutional customers, and government customers.[17] For services provided over leased facilities, the percentage of service by competitive local-exchange carriers, which is total service resale of services by incumbent local-exchange carriers, declined to 19 percent at the end of December 2002, while the percentage provisioned over acquired unbundled-network-element loops grew to 55 percent.

Entry of RBOCs in Long-Distance Service

In 1996 RBOCs had 89 percent of telephone access lines nationwide. Most of the remainder belonged to GTE and independent franchise holders. Competitive access providers (who did not hold a franchise monopoly) had less than 1 percent of all residential access lines nationwide. Besides providing access to long-distance companies, local-exchange carriers also provide lucrative custom local-exchange services such as call waiting, conference calling, and automatic number identification. Basic local service provided by local-exchange carriers is considered not to be particularly profitable.

The act allowed for entry of RBOCs in long distance once a list of re-quirements had been met and the petitioner had proved that its proposal is in the public interest. These requirements are supposed to be met only when the market for local telecommunications services becomes sufficiently competi-tive. If the local market is not competitive when a monopolist incumbent local-exchange carrier enters into long distance, the local-exchange carrier can leverage its monopoly power to disadvantage its long-distance rivals by in-creasing their costs in various ways and by discriminating against them in its pricing. If the local market is not competitive when a monopolist incumbent local-exchange carrier enters into long distance, an incumbent local-exchange carrier (ILEC) controls the price of a required input (switched access) to long-distance service while competing for customers in long distance. Under these circumstances, an ILEC can implement a vertical price squeeze on its long-distance competitors whereby the price-to-cost ratio of long-distance com-petitors becomes so low that they are driven out of business.[18]

In allowing entry of local-exchange carriers into the long-distance market, the 1996 Telecommunications Act tried not to endanger competition that has developed in long distance by premature entry of RBOCs in the long-distance market. However, on this issue, the act's provisions guarding against premature entry may have been insufficient. Hence, to guard against anticompetitive con-sequences of premature entry of RBOCs in long distance there is need for a deeper analysis of the consequences of such entry on competition and on con-sumers' and social welfare. The FCC has not demanded significant competition before allowing RBOCs to enter long distance, and RBOCs are currently ap-proved for long-distance service in all states. The history of the approval pro-cess is summarized in table 3.1 (see also FCC 2003b).

Universal Service

Traditionally, the United States has adopted a policy to maximize the sub-scribership of the public switched telecommunications network, commonly called universal service. Because universal service requires that some con-sumers be provided with basic telephone services below cost, from an effi-ciency standpoint there is overconsumption of those services. Most studies report very small price elasticities of demand for access, so the overconsump-tion effect may be small, and most of the distortion caused by universal ser-vice may be a wealth transfer effect. However, depending on how universal service is structured and provided, a host of other inefficiencies may also be created.

Historically, attaining the goal of universal service has focused on keeping basic rates for local-exchange telephone service low. To achieve this goal, the funds required to subsidize service were extracted from inter- and intra-LATA (local access transport area) long-distance service. Thus rates for carrier access

TABLE 3.1   *FCC Approval of Local-Exchange Carriers into the Long-Distance Market, 1997 to 2003*

State	Filed by	Status	Date Filed	Date Resolved
Arizona	Qwest	Approved	September 4, 2003	December 3, 2003
Illinois, Indiana, Ohio, Wisconsin	SBC	Approved	July 17, 2003	October 15, 2003
Michigan	SBC	Approved	June 19, 2003	Due by September 17, 2003
Minnesota	Qwest	Approved	February 28, 2003	June 26, 2003
Michigan	SBC	Withdrawn	January 15, 2003	April 16, 2003
New Mexico, Oregon, South Dakota	Qwest	Approved	January 15, 2003	April 15, 2003
Nevada	SBC	Approved	January 14, 2003	April 14, 2003
District of Columbia, Maryland, West Virginia	Verizon	Approved	December 18, 2002	March 19, 2003
Colorado, Idaho, Iowa, Montana, Nebraska, North Dakota, Utah, Washington, Wyoming	Qwest	Approved	September 30, 2002	December 23, 2002
California	SBC	Approved	September 20, 2002	December 19, 2002
Florida, Tennessee	BellSouth	Approved	September 20, 2002	December 19, 2002
Virginia	Verizon	Approved	August 1, 2002	October 30, 2002
Montana, Utah, Washington, Wyoming	Qwest	Withdrawn	July 12, 2002	September 10, 2002
New Hampshire, Delaware	Verizon	Approved	June 27, 2002	September 25, 2002
Alabama, Kentucky, Mississippi, North Carolina, South Carolina	BellSouth	Approved	June 20, 2002	September 18, 2002
Colorado, Idaho, Iowa, Nebraska, North Dakota	Qwest	Withdrawn	June 13, 2002	September 10, 2002
New Jersey	Verizon	Approved	March 26, 2002	June 24, 2002
Maine	Verizon	Approved	March 21, 2002	June 19, 2002
Georgia, Louisiana	BellSouth	Approved	February 14, 2002	May 15, 2002
Vermont	Verizon	Approved	January 17, 2002	April 17, 2002
New Jersey	Verizon	Withdrawn	December 20, 2001	March 20, 2002
Rhode Island	Verizon	Approved	November 26, 2001	February 24, 2002
Georgia, Louisiana	BellSouth	Withdrawn	October 2, 2001	December 20, 2001
Arkansas, Missouri	SBC	Approved	August 20, 2001	November 16, 2001
Pennsylvania	Verizon	Approved	June 21, 2001	September 19, 2001
Connecticut	Verizon	Approved	April 23, 2001	July 20, 2001

(Table continues on p. 64.)

TABLE 3.1   *Continued*

State	Filed by	Status	Date Filed	Date Resolved
Missouri	SBC	Withdrawn	April 4, 2001	June 7, 2001
Massachusetts	Verizon	Approved	January 16, 2001	April 16, 2001
Kansas, Oklahoma	SBC	Approved	October 26, 2000	January 22, 2001
Massachusetts	Verizon	Withdrawn	September 22, 2000	December 18, 2000
Texas	SBC	Approved	April 5, 2000	June 30, 2000
Texas	SBC	Withdrawn	January 10, 2000	April 5, 2000
New York	Verizon	Approved	September 29, 1999	December 22, 1999
Louisiana	BellSouth	Denied	July 9, 1998	October 13, 1998
Louisiana	BellSouth	Denied	November 6, 1997	February 4, 1998
South Carolina	BellSouth	Denied	September 30, 1997	December 24, 1997
Michigan	Ameritech	Denied	May 21, 1997	August 19, 1997
Oklahoma	SBC	Denied	April 11, 1997	June 26, 1997
Michigan	Ameritech	Withdrawn	January 2, 1997	February 11, 1997

Source: FCC (2003c).

and certain other services were set at artificially high levels to provide implicit subsidies to support the objective of universal service.

The historical method of promoting subscribership raised subsidies through taxing of traffic-sensitive services through the imposition of the federal, and in some cases state, common carrier line charges and was based on implicit and hidden subsidies. The historical method of raising subsidies for universal service compares poorly with the economically efficient method for a number of reasons. First, the historical subsidy is not explicit. Therefore, it is unclear who is subsidizing whom. For example, in the traditional regime, a rural customer who makes a significant number of toll calls in a high-cost area may not be subsidized in net terms. Second, the traditional mechanism is not targeted to those subscribers who require the subsidy. Instead, the local-exchange carrier receives the subsidy for serving all consumers regardless of their ability to pay the full cost, even if they live in an area where costs do not exceed revenues. Third, the burden of universal service is borne by inter- and intra-LATA toll users, rather than being funded broadly, thereby introducing inefficiencies in the provision of those services. Fourth, the traditional system is not competitively neutral because the benefits of the current system inure only to the incumbent local-exchange carrier and not to any of their potential competitors. This system not only inhibits the introduction of competition in the local exchange (because the subsidies flow to the incumbent local-exchange carrier instead of to the carrier chosen by the consumer) but also may bestow unwarranted benefits on the incumbent local-exchange carrier to the extent the subsidies are inflated above amounts necessary to provide basic universal service at cost.

The 1996 act introduced fundamental changes in the structure of telecommunications markets in the United States. The most important thrust of the Telecommunications Act is its goal of establishing competition in all telecommunications markets. Competition generally drives prices closer to cost and imposes a strict discipline. As a result, and once competition takes hold, the prior implicit method of subsidization would no longer be viable. The act explicitly rejects such a process by requiring universal service support to be explicit (Telecommunications Act of 1996, sec. 254[e]) and by forbidding the continued use of universal service subsidies to cross-subsidize competitively provided services (sec. 254[k]).

The 1996 act aims to "preserve and advance universal service" (sec. 254[b]). This translates to the following:

- high quality at low rates
- access to advanced services in all states
- access in rural and high cost areas at prices comparable to those in other areas
- service supported by "equitable and nondiscriminatory contributions" by "all providers of telecommunications services"
- specific and predictable mechanisms to raise the required funds
- access to advanced telecommunications services for schools, health care facilities, and libraries

Regulatory policy that explicitly deviates from the market outcome in the market for subscription creates a number of complex questions. Among them are who will be subsidized, by how much, by whom, and how the money will actually flow from the subsidizers to the subsidized. If these issues are not resolved in an efficient manner, economic distortions ("secondary distortions") may result that may be more significant than their original cause. For example, if the subsidy is extracted from subscribers of a single service, demand for that service will necessarily be impacted in ways that would not be consistent with the goals of the 1996 act. On the other hand, an efficient solution to these questions can guarantee that no further distortions are created by universal service, that is, no distortions over and above the original distortion created by the decision to maximize subscribership.

Funding for universal service should be achieved in a manner that is both efficient and competitively neutral. An economically efficient universal service fund should conform to the following criteria:

- All subsidies to promote universal service should be made explicit.
- Universal service should be funded broadly.
- Universal service subsidies should be targeted narrowly.
- Universal service should be achieved in a competitively neutral fashion.

- The existence and operation of any universal service fund should minimize distortions to other telecommunications services.
- Subsidized consumers should be served in the most efficient way possible.

These characteristics are embodied in the 1996 Telecommunications Act. The act specifies that universal service subsidies should be made explicit (Telecommunications Act of 1996, sec. 254[e]), funded broadly (sec. 254[d]), and achieved in a competitively neutral fashion (sec. 254[b]). This framework minimizes to the maximum extent possible the problem of secondary distortions identified earlier in this chapter.

The Failure of the 1996 Act and the Current Wave of Mergers

Congress made a crucial miscalculation of the incentive of RBOCs to open their local networks to competition so that they would be rewarded with entry in long distance. In the summer of 1996, the RBOCs decided to delay entry of their local networks to competition as long as possible, even if that would lead to delay of their entry into the long-distance service market.

The various legal challenges have derailed the implementation process of the act and have increased uncertainty in the telecommunications sector. In the absence of reasonable final prices, given the uncertainty of the various legal proceedings, and without final resolution on the issues of nonrecurring costs and the electronic interface for switching local-service customers across carriers, entry in the local exchange through leasing of unbundled network elements has been slow. Moreover, entry in the retailing part of the business through total service resale has been minimal, since the wholesale discounts have been small.

In the absence of entry in the local exchange market as envisioned by the act, the major long-distance companies are buying other companies that give them some access to the local market. For example, MCI has merged with WorldCom, which had just merged with Brooks Fiber and MFS, which, in turn, also own some infrastructure in local-exchange markets. MCI-WorldCom has focused on the Internet, having acquired Internet backbone provider UUNET as part of MFS, and the business long-distance market.[19] WorldCom proposed a merger with Sprint. The merger was stopped by both the U.S. Department of Justice and the Competition Committee of the European Union. The Department of Justice had reservations about potential dominance of the merged company in the market for global telecommunications services. The European Union had objections about potential dominance of the Internet backbone by the merged company.[20] In June 2002 WorldCom filed for Chapter 11 bankruptcy protection after a series of revelations about accounting irregularities; as of this writing, the full effects of these events on the future of WorldCom and the entire industry are still open. MCI (WorldCom having reverted to its old name) has emerged from bankruptcy, and competitors are concerned that MCI will be a formidable competitor with no debts.

AT&T acquired TCG, which owned local-exchange infrastructure that reached business customers. AT&T unveiled an ambitious strategy of reaching consumers' homes by using cable television wires for the "last mile." With this end in mind, AT&T bought TCI with the intent of converting the TCI cable access to an interactive broadband, voice, and data telephone link to residences. AT&T had also entered in an agreement with Time Warner to use its cable connection in a way similar to TCI's, and in April 1999 AT&T outbid Comcast and acquired MediaOne, the cable spin-off of U.S. West.

TCI cable at the time reached 35 percent of U.S. households. Together with Time Warner and MediaOne, AT&T could reach a bit more than 50 percent of U.S. households. Without access to unbundled network elements to reach all residential customers, AT&T had to find another way to reach the remaining U.S. households. The provision of telephony, Internet access, broadband, data, and two-way video services exclusively over cable lines in the "last mile" requires significant technical advances, significant conversion of the present cable networks, and an investment of at least $5 billion (some say $30 billion) just for the conversion of the cable network to two-way switched services. Moreover, there is some inherent uncertainty in such a conversion, which has not always been successful in the past. Thus it was an expensive and uncertain proposition for AT&T, but, at the same time, it was one of the few remaining options of entry in the local exchange.

Facing tremendous pressure from financial markets, slow cable conversion, and a steep reduction in long-distance revenues, AT&T decided on a voluntary breakup into a wireless unit, a cable TV unit, and a long-distance and local service company that retained the name AT&T and the symbol "T" on the New York Stock Exchange. Before the breakup, financial markets tended to underestimate the value of AT&T by looking at it only as a long-distance company. After the breakup, the cable part of AT&T was bought with by Comcast, and since then Comcast has generally not tried to attract new cable telephony customers using the AT&T technology.

Attempts by the RBOCs to maximize their foothold, looking forward to the time when they would be allowed to provide long-distance service in all states, include Southwestern Bell's acquisition of Pacific Bell and Ameritech and Bell Atlantic's merger with NYNEX, despite some antitrust objections. Southwestern Bell also bought Southern New England Telephone, one of the few companies that, as an independent (not part of AT&T at divestiture), was not bound by restrictions imposed under the modified final judgment and had already entered into long distance. Bell Atlantic has merged with GTE, creating Verizon. Thus the eight large local exchange carriers of 1984 (seven RBOCs and GTE) have been reduced to only four: Verizon, BellSouth, Southwestern

Bell, and U.S. West. U.S. West recently merged with Qwest. The smallest one left, BellSouth, is widely reported to be a takeover or merger target.

A crucial crossmedia merger occurred with the acquisition of Time Warner by AOL at the height of AOL's stock price. The merger was achieved with the requirement that AOL/Time Warner allow independent Internet service providers access to its cable monopoly for broadband services. Synergies and new joint products failed to materialize at AOL/Time Warner. AOL has already been dropped from the trading symbol of the merged company, and there is wide speculation that AOL will be divested.

The Telecom Meltdown of 2000 to 2003

The present crisis in telecommunications arose out of an incorrect prediction of the speed of expansion of the Internet and therefore of the demand for all the new markets "living" on the Internet. It was widely believed that the Internet would grow at 400 percent in terms of transmitted bits per year. In retrospect, it is clear that for the years 2000 and 2001 growth of only 100 percent was realized. Of course, it is always difficult to pin down the growth rate in early stages of an exponential network expansion, and the Internet was growing at 400 percent a year when the original predictions were made. The rate of growth slowed down in the number of new hosts connected, however, and since no new "killer application" that required a lot of bandwidth was unveiled, the rate of growth in bits transferred also slowed down. This is despite the fast growth of transfers of bits in peer-to-peer (P2P) transfers of files among computers, mainly songs in MP3 format, popularized by Napster and still going strong even after Napster has been practically closed down.[21]

Based on the optimistic prediction of Internet growth, there was tremendous investment in Internet transport and routing capacity. Moreover, because capital markets were liberal in providing funds, a number of companies invested in and deployed more telecommunications equipment than would be prudent, given their present market share. This was done for strategic reasons, essentially in an attempt to gain market share in the process of the rapid expansion of the Internet.

Once the growth prediction was revised downward, the immediate effect was a significant reduction in orders and in investment in fiber-optic, switching, and router equipment. Before making significant new investments, telecommunications service companies are waiting for higher utilization rates of their existing capacity as the Internet expands. There is presently a temporary but significant overcapacity of Internet transmission capacity in the United States. As mentioned earlier, since it is easy to run the Internet backbone as a long-distance network, the significant overcapacity of the Internet backbone, combined with new investment and overcapacity of traditional long-distance networks, has led to significant pressure and reductions of long-distance prices. Thus the incorrect prediction of the Internet expansion has had negative repercussions not only in Internet-based business but also in the long-distance business and in the market for telecommunications equipment.

Internet Telephony and Regulatory Breakdown

The Telecommunications Act of 1996 did not legislate any framework for the most revolutionary of all current innovations in telecommunications, Internet telephony, or more precisely Internet protocol–based telephony, more generally known as "voice-over IP." This is despite the emergence of IP (internet protocol) telephony as the favorite mode of operation of new telecommunications networks, such as those built by Qwest and Level 3, as well as the required conversion of traditional telecommunications networks, such as AT&T's.

Digitization of telecommunication services imposes price arbitrage on the bits of information that are carried by the telecommunications network, leading to the elimination of price discrimination between voice and data services. Elimination of such price discrimination can, in turn, lead to dramatic reductions in the price of voice calls, precipitating significant changes in market structure. These changes were first evident on the Internet, a ubiquitous network of applications based on the transmission control and Internet protocols (TCP/IP). Internet-based telecommunications are based on packet switching. There are two modes of operation: a time-delay mode, in which there is a guarantee that the system will do whatever it can to deliver all packets, and a real-time mode, in which packets can be lost without possibility of recovery.

Many telecommunications services do not have a real-time requirement, so applications that "live" on the Internet can easily accommodate them. For example, a number of companies currently provide facsimile services on the Internet, all or part of the transport of the fax taking place over the Internet. Although the Internet was not intended to be used in real-time telecommunications, despite the loss of packets telecommunications companies presently use the Internet to complete ordinary voice telephone calls. Voice telecommunications service started on the Internet as computer-to-computer calls. In 1995 Internet telecommunications companies started offering termination of calls on the public switched network. In 1996 firms started offering Internet calling that originated and terminated on the public switched telecommunications network ("PSTN"), that is, from and to the regular customers' phone appliances. The last two transitions became possible with the introduction of PSTN-Internet interfaces and switches by Lucent and others.

Traditional telephony keeps a channel of fixed bandwidth open for the duration of a call. Internet calls are packet based. Because transmission is based on packet transport, IP telephony can utilize bandwidth more efficiently by varying in real time the amount of it used by a call. But because IP telephony utilizes Internet real-time mode, there is no guarantee that all the packets of a voice transmission will arrive at the destination.

Internet telephony providers use sophisticated voice sampling methods to decompose and reconstitute voice so that packet losses do not make a significant audible difference. Since such methods are by their nature imperfect, the quality and fidelity of an Internet call depends crucially on the percentage of packets that are lost in transmission and transport.

This, in turn, depends on other factors, including the allocation of Internet bandwidth (pipeline) to the phone call, the number of times the message is transmitted, and the number ("hops") of routers over which the phone call passes. Internet-based telecommunications services pose a serious threat to traditional telecommunications service providers, including long-distance service, international service, and local service providers. In the present U.S. regulatory structure, a call to an Internet service provider that originates from a computer (or terminates to a computer) is not charged an access charge by the local-exchange carrier. This can lead to substantial savings owing to the inflated access fees charged by local-exchange carriers.

Computer-to-computer Internet telephony has been available since 1998 but has not been widely used except for international calls, especially in countries where international rates are astronomical (see Garcia-Murillo 2003). However, a number of competitors, including AT&T, have recently entered the voice-over IP telephony market, attempting to substitute traditional local telephone service with IP telephony over a cable television or digital subscriber line (DSL) Internet connection. These companies provide appliances that look and feel like traditional phones and, because they deliver all calls over the Internet, have low prices.

In summary, although the Internet was not created for real-time interaction, its user datagram protocol (UDP) mode has been used for voice telecommunications (Internet telephony). Internet telephony will mature as the quality of routers and the meshing of the IP database with the U.S. phone-numbering system improve. As Internet telephony improves in quality and Internet phone calls become widely available, artificially high prices of voice calls will not be sustainable because of arbitrage in the bits. This will cause a major problem of regulatory breakdown in which it is likely that major telecommunications companies will ask for regulation of the Internet so that voice-call prices do not collapse.

The Coming World

The intent of the Telecommunications Act of 1996 was to promote competition and the public interest. It will be a significant failure of the U.S. political, legal, and regulatory systems if the interests of entrenched monopolists, rather than the public interest as expressed by Congress, dictate the future of the U.S. telecommunications sector. The market structure in the telecommunications sector two years from now will depend crucially on the resolution of the local-exchange carriers' legal challenges to the 1996 Telecommunications Act and its final implementation.[22] At the time of this writing (June 2004), the prospects for competition in the local exchange in the manner anticipated by the 1996 act are bleak. The Appeals Court in Washington, D.C., has thrown out substantial parts of the triennial review order of the FCC (United States Telecom Association v. FCC, no. 00-1012, decided March 2, 2004), which defined a framework for continuing leasing of unbundled network elements by RBOCs. The solicitor general and the FCC decided not to appeal this decision to the Supreme Court. The Supreme Court did not intervene, and now cost-based leasing of unbundled network elements is likely to be quickly phased out, and the RBOCs will be allowed to charge monopoly prices for unbundled network elements, resulting in a classic vertical price squeeze of entrants in the local exchange who lease unbundled network elements. Facing an imminent vertical price squeeze by the RBOCs and the increasing sale of "buckets" of combined local and long-distance minutes, which it would not be able to match in the vertical price squeeze situation, on July 22, 2004, AT&T decided to stop marketing both local and long-distance services to residential customers. Thus the 1996 act's vision of competition in the local exchange through leasing of unbundled network elements essentially is dead. As wireless service is still not of the same quality as traditional fixed service, the only significant challenge to the RBOCs' dominant (and, in many states, near monopoly) position in the residential and small-business market is voice-over IP, and there is much uncertainty over the viability of competition based on voice-over IP.

AT&T's decision to stop marketing long distance to residential customers because of the leveraging of the RBOCs' dominance of the local market is exactly the type of undesirable event that was not supposed to happen as a consequence of allowing RBOCs to compete in the long-distance market. Thus the Telecommunications Act of 1996 has failed in its fundamental goals. First, competition in local markets through leasing of incumbents' networks did not materialize to a sufficient extent before it was abruptly killed by regulatory action. Second, the premature entry of RBOCs in long distance allowed them to implement a vertical price squeeze on local entrants, driving the largest one, AT&T, out of the local market. Third, the liberalization of regulatory pricing rules on RBOCs allowed them to sell buckets of combined minutes of local and long-distance service, thereby implementing a vertical price squeeze with such force that even marketing stand-alone long distance to residential customers became unprofitable for the largest provider of residential long-distance services, AT&T. The failure of the goals of the 1996 act is immense. Residential and small-business customers are likely to be significantly harmed by this enormous regulatory failure to protect them from monopoly.

Already, we have seen a series of mergers leading to the remonopoliza-tion of local telecommunications. As the combinations of former RBOCs have been approved for long distance in all states, we see a reconstitution of the old AT&T monopoly (without the present AT&T). We have also seen significant integration in the cable industry as a result of the acquisitions and eventual di-vestitures of cable companies by AT&T.

The local telephone companies have already entered the long-distance market without earlier significant decreases of their market shares in local markets. Local telephone companies have merged to expand their customer base and become stronger competitors in the next battle among carriers that sell both local and long-distance services. Twenty years after the government broke up the longstanding Ma Bell monopoly, the remonopolization of telecommunications is almost here.

Computers are likely to play a bigger role as telephone appliances and in running intermediate-size networks that will compete with local-exchange carriers and intensify the arbitrage among interexchange carriers. Computer-based telephone interfaces will become the norm. Firms that have significant market share in computer interfaces and computer operating systems, such as Microsoft, may play a significant role in telephony.[23] Hardware manufactur-ers, especially firms like Cisco, Intel, and 3Com, that make switches and local networks will play a much more central role in telephony. Internet telephony (voice, data, and broadband) is expected to grow fast.

Finally, I expect that, slowly but steadily, telecommunications will drift away from the technical standards of the signaling-system seven established by AT&T before its breakup. As different methods of transmission and switch-ing gain a foothold, and as new interfaces become available, wars over techni-cal standards are likely.[24] This will further transform telecommunications from the traditional quiet landscape of regulated utilities to the mad-dash world of software and computer manufacturing. This change will create significant busi-ness opportunities for entrants and impose significant challenges on traditional telecommunications carriers.

Notes

1. For example, if the production technology has such high fixed costs that it is clear that only one firm will survive in the marketplace, resulting in a natural monopoly, regulation can be used to stop the monopolist from charging the high monopoly price.
2. Often, market interactions that can be modeled as economic games have multi-ple equilibriums, where each equilibrium is defined by a number of firms or in-dividuals taking the same or similar actions. Then intervention by a regulatory body can coordinate the actions of firms or individuals, resulting in a more ben-

eficial outcome. For example, cars can be driven on the left or the right side of the street, and, in principle, there is no particular advantage to an equilibrium in which all cars are on the left or all cars are on the right; but there are considerable disadvantages if some cars go on the right and some go on the left. Thus a regulatory body can create substantial benefits by imposing a rule whereby one of the two equilibriums is chosen.

3. See David Gabel and David F. Weiman (1998) and Weiman and Richard C. Levin (1994). Occasionally, AT&T allowed interconnection to some independent local monopolists under the guarantee that these would not interconnect with any non-AT&T exchange.

4. However, it should be noted that the requirement to interconnect could also have been imposed by antitrust authorities since the no-interconnection policy of AT&T was equivalent to a "refusal to deal" and thereby broke antitrust law.

5. Still, there is no convincing evidence that the price for basic service is below cost, except possibly for some rural households. Moreover, adding households to the telecommunications network, even at a subsidized rate, may be desirable because of the network effects they produce to the rest of the consumers. Thus it is unclear that the provision of universal service has produced a considerable allocative efficiency distortion—if any.

6. Even when the FCC was auctioning spectrum and approving licenses for personal communication services (PCS) wireless services, it did not impose the same technical standard for wireless transmission; the result is three incompatible networks in the United States, in contrast to the single-standard global system for mobile communication (GSM) network in Europe.

7. The telecommunications sector is regulated both by the federal government, through the FCC, and by all states, typically through a public utilities commission or a public service commission. Usually a public utility commission also regulates electricity.

8. For a detailed exposition of the issues in this case, see Roger G. Noll and Bruce Owen (1989).

9. These were Ameritech, Bell Atlantic, BellSouth, NYNEX, Pacific Bell, Southwestern Bell, and U.S. West.

10. MCI merged with WorldCom, which had earlier expanded its original LDDS network and had acquired the Internet backbone of UUNET.

11. This is on a relative scale over time, since the carriers do not disclose actual price-to-cost margins.

12. Origination and termination of calls are extremely lucrative services. Access has an average cost (in most locations) of $0.002 per minute. Its regulated prices vary. The national average in 2001 was $0.0169 per minute. Such pricing implies a profit rate of 745 percent. Access charges reform is one of the key demands of the procompetitive forces in the current deregulation process.

13. However, non-RBOC local-exchange monopolists, such as GTE, had been traditionally allowed to provide long-distance service and were not restricted by the modified final judgment.

14. In FCC (1996), the FCC and state regulatory commissions have interpreted these words to mean total element long-run incremental cost, which is the forward-looking, long-run (minimized) economic cost of an unbundled element and in-

cludes the competitive return on capital (see Gregg 2001 for a recent survey of UNE prices).

15. The implementation of the 1996 act started with the FCC's "First Report and Order" (see FCC 1996).

16. The nationwide percentage of end-user lines served over facilities owned by competitive local-exchange carriers (3.4 percent) is derived by dividing the number of lines owned by competitive local-exchange carriers nationwide (FCC 2003a, table 10) by the total number of lines nationwide (FCC 2003a, table 6).

17. In contrast, 22 percent of reported incumbent local-exchange carriers' switched access lines served such customers.

18. Avoiding a vertical price squeeze of long-distance competitors, such as MCI, was a key rationale for the 1981 breakup of AT&T in the long-distance division that kept the AT&T name and the seven RBOCs that remained local monopolists in local service, as discussed earlier in this chapter. Also see Nicholas Economides (1998; 1999).

19. The MCI-WorldCom merger was challenged by the European Union Competition Committee, the Department of Justice, and GTE on the grounds that the merged company would have a large market share of the Internet backbone and could sequentially target, degrade interconnection, and kill its backbone rivals. Despite a lack of an economically meaningful definition of the Internet "backbone," the unlikelihood that MCI would have such an incentive because any degradation would also hurt its customers, and the unlikelihood that such degradation would be feasible, the Competition Committee of the European Union ordered MCI to divest itself of all its Internet business, including its retail business, where it was never alleged that the merging companies had any monopoly power. MCI's Internet business was sold to Cable and Wireless, the MCI-WorldCom merger was finalized, and MCI-WorldCom is using its UUNET subsidiary to spearhead its way in the Internet.

20. The merged company proposed to divest Sprint's backbone. The European Union's objections were based on WorldCom's market share of about 35 percent in the Internet backbone market. The European Union used a peculiar theory predicting that "tipping" and dominance to monopoly would occur starting from this market share because WorldCom would introduce incompatibilities into Internet transmission and drive all competitors out of the market. Time proved that none of these concerns were credible.

21. Clearly, the Internet provides a superior way of distribution of music in digitized form. However, because of concerns that the music will be freely downloaded, the recording industry has avoided using this distribution process and is currently suing hundreds of individuals for allowing digitized music to be downloaded from their computers. Distribution of music and video in digitized form could significantly increase the amount of bits traveling on the Internet, but the present copyright dispute makes it unlikely that this will happen any time soon.

22. In one of the major challenges, GTE and a number of RBOCs appealed the 1996 FCC rules (among others) on pricing guidelines to the Eighth Circuit. The plaintiffs won the appeal; the FCC appealed to the Supreme Court, which ruled on January 25, 1999. The plaintiffs claimed (among other things) that the FCC's rules on the definition of unbundled network elements were flawed; that the FCC

"default prices" for leasing of unbundled network elements were so low that they amounted to confiscation of incumbent local-exchange carriers' property; and that the FCC's "pick and choose" rule, allowing a carrier to demand access to any individual interconnection, service, or network element arrangement on the same terms and conditions the local-exchange carrier has given anyone else in an approved local competition entry agreement without having to accept the agreement's other provisions, would deter the "voluntarily negotiated agreements." The Supreme Court ruled for the FCC in all these points, thereby eliminating a major challenge to the implementation of the act.

23. Microsoft owns a share of WebTV, has invested in Qwest and AT&T, and has broadband agreements with a number of domestic and foreign local-exchange carriers but does not seem to plan to control a telecommunications company.

24. A significant failure of the FCC has been its silence in defining technical standards and promoting compatibility. Even when the FCC had a unique opportunity to define such standards in PCS telephony (since it could define the terms while it auctioned electromagnetic spectrum), it allowed a number of incompatible standards to coexist for PCS service. This led directly to a weakening of competition and higher prices, as wireless PCS consumers have to buy a new appliance to migrate across providers and are unable to set up service with more than one provider using the same appliance.

References

Crandall, Robert W. 1991. *After the Breakup: U.S. Telecommunications in a More Competitive Era.* Washington, D.C.: Brookings Institution.

Economides, Nicholas. 1991. "Compatibility and the Creation of Shared Networks." In *Electronic Services Networks: A Business and Public Policy Challenge,* edited by Margaret Guerin-Calvert and Steven Wildman. New York: Praeger.

———. 1996. "The Economics of Networks." *International Journal of Industrial Organization* 14(2): 675–99. Also available at: http://www.stern.nyu.edu/networks/94-24.pdf (accessed November 19, 2004).

———. 1998. "The Incentive for Non-Price Discrimination by an Input Monopolist." *International Journal of Industrial Organization* 16(3): 271–84. Also available at: www.stern.nyu.edu/networks/1136.pdf (accessed November 19, 2004).

———. 1999. "The Telecommunications Act of 1996 and Its Impact." *Japan and the World Economy* 11(3): 455–83.

———. 2003. "The Tragic Inefficiency of M-ECPR." In *Down to the Wire: Studies in the Diffusion and Regulation of Telecommunications Technologies,* edited by A. Shampine. New York: Nova Science Publishers, Inc. Also available at: http://www.stern.nyu.edu/networks/tragic.pdf (accessed November 19, 2004).

Economides, Nicholas, Giuseppe Lopomo and Glenn Woroch. 1996. "Regulatory Pricing Policies to Neutralize Network Dominance." *Industrial and Corporate Change* 5(4): 1013–28. Also available at: http://www.stern.nyu.edu/networks/96-14.pdf (accessed November 19, 2004).

Economides, Nicholas, and Lawrence J. White. 1995. "Access and Interconnection Pricing: How Efficient is the Efficient Component Pricing Rule?" *The Antitrust*

Bulletin XL(3): 557–79. Also available at http://www.stern.nyu.edu/networks/95-04.pdf (accessed November 19, 2004).

Faulhaber, Gerald. 2004. "Bottlenecks and Bandwagons: Access Policy in the New Telecommunications." In *Handbook of Telecommunications,* edited by Martin E. Cave, Sumit K. Majumdar, and Ingo Vogelsang. Amsterdam: Elsevier Publishers.

Federal Communications Commission. 1995. "In the Matter of Motion of AT&T Corp. to be Reclassified as a Non-Dominant Carrier." CC Docket 95-427. Order (adopted October 12). Washington: FCC. Available at: www.fcc.gov/Bureaus/Common_Carrier/Orders/1996/fcc96454.wp (accessed November 19, 2004).

———. 1996. "First Report and Order." CC Docket N. 96-98, CC Docket No. 95-185. Report (adopted August 8, 1996). Washington: FCC.

———. 2003a. "Local Telephone Competition: Status as of June 30, 2003." Report (December 22). Washington: FCC Wireline Competition Bureau.

———. 2003b. "Report and Order On Remand And Further Notice Of Proposed Rulemaking." CC Docket 01-338, 96-98, 98-147. Report (adopted February 20; released August 21). Washington: FCC.

———. 2003c. "Trends in Telephone Service." Report (August 7). Washington: FCC Wireline Competition Bureau. Available at: http://www.fcc.gov/Bureaus/Common_Carrier/Reports/FCC-State_Link/IAD/trend803.pdf (accessed November 19, 2004).

Gabel, David, and David F. Weiman. 1998. "Historical Perspectives on Interconnection Between Competing Local Operating Companies: The United States, 1894-1914." In *Opening Networks to Competition: The Regulation and Pricing of Access,* edited by David Gabel and David F. Weiman. Norwell, Mass.: Kluwer Academic Press.

Garcia-Murillo, Martha. 2003. "Assessing the Impact of Internet Telephony on the Deployment of Telecommunications Infrastructure." Working Paper 03-04. New York: Networks, Electronic Commerce, and Telecommunications (NET) Institute. Also available at: www.netinst.org/Garcia.pdf (accessed November 19, 2004).

Gregg, Billy Jack. 2001. "A Survey Of Unbundled Network Element Prices In The United States." Columbus: Ohio State University. Available at: http://www.nrri.ohio-state.edu/documents/intro0703_000.pdf (accessed November 19, 2004).

Hubbard, R. Glenn, and William H. Lehr. 1998. "Improving Local Exchange Competition: Regulatory Crossroads." Mimeo (February). New York: Columbia University.

Noll, Roger G., and Bruce Owen. 1989. "The Anti-competitive Uses of Regulation: *United States v. AT&T.*" In *The Antitrust Revolution,* edited by John E. Kwoka and Lawrence J. White. New York: HarperCollins.

Weiman, David F., and Richard C. Levin. 1994. "Preying for Monopoly? The Case of Southern Bell Telephone Company, 1894-1912." *Journal of Political Economy* 102(1): 103–26.

4

PASSENGER RAIL

Elliott D. Sclar

THE STRENGTHS and limits of market governance in the production of intercity passenger railroad service is a topic worth considering, both for its relevance to an exploration of the limits of market governance, the focus of the present volume, and because the public policy precepts that presently govern this service are now up for review and revision. Passenger rail service is a quasi-public good, as are transportation services in general. It can be simultaneously a private market product, exhibiting the classic characteristics of excludability and rivalry in consumption while also creating larger positive and negative externalities.

Because of its "boundary" status between the public and private realms, passenger rail service has been subject to a long political-economic history of alternations between tight public control and unregulated markets. This back and forth is as old as the industry itself. We are fortunate to have this rich historical experiential base to draw upon in analyzing this "gray" policy area. Throughout its history, U.S. passenger rail service has been provided under several alternative public-private regimes. These have gone from the purely private (with public subsidy, of course) in the early years of railroad development (the early nineteenth century) to the purely public during World War I. Since that war, several other variations of public-private balance have existed.

Although the history of American rail and its passenger component is by definition a single case, the underlying economic principles that shape it and the political economics that drive policy responses are universal. Internationally, the policy dynamic with regard to passenger rail policy has run parallel to the American experience. Although the unique history and social institutions of individual countries drives this dynamic, each country has typically moved toward solutions in which public regulation and public subsidy become central to service delivery. Although the material presented here is primarily based on the American case, I supplement it by drawing upon recent British experience to underscore the larger points about the role and limits of market governance in the provision of passenger rail service.[1]

It is also an opportune moment for a reconsideration of public policy related to passenger rail service because in the summer of 2003 the Bush administration proposed a reorganization of the National Passenger Rail Corporation (Amtrak). The intent of the Bush proposal is to shift the policy balance away from an emphasis on public regulation and public subsidy and toward a level of service determined by market forces. The proposal is predicated on the assumption that intercity passenger rail service is or should be a market-provided service. Presently, it is provided under an organizational model that privileges its externality characteristics and hence its public service functions. As a purely abstract proposition, a transformation such as the one the Bush administration suggests is conceptually possible. However, if the public service functions have significant value, such market-oriented policies may prove to be neither practically sustainable nor socially desirable.

Although the dominant thesis of this chapter is a case for a public goods approach to rail service provision, it is not in and of itself an argument against the use of market-based incentives to deliver the service. In terms of the contemporary policy debate about "privatization," however, the issue that frames the present debate—the determination of who the direct service provider should be (government or a private contractor)—is the least consequential portion of the current problem. This particular way of framing the debate has a real cost. If the decision is made to privatize the provider, deregulate the service, and cut the subsidy, it will waste valuable resources and time and ultimately fail as long as we continue to believe that the service provides valuable external public benefits. The privatization question—that is, the identification of the direct service provider—can be meaningfully resolved only in a broader context that clearly recognizes the limits of market governance in the face of such externalities.

Recent technological changes that make safe high-speed (over one hundred miles per hour) and very-high-speed (over two hundred miles per hour) train travel possible transform the question into one about the configuration of twenty-first-century travel on the North American continent. The extent to which the benefits of this technologic innovation will be captured depend crucially upon our ability to draw a wise and balanced approach to the use of market governance in the area of transportation.

A Stylized Introduction to the Contemporary Policy Debate

The contemporary debate over the future of Amtrak, the United States not-for-profit public passenger rail operation, is complex in its details and simple in its overarching political approach. To appreciate the way the present policy options have been framed it is necessary to understand the political-historic architecture of the Bush administration's market liberalization argument. It is this context that defines the "policy culture" in which the members of Congress, who make the ultimate determination, act.

The political case for more extensive market governance is rooted in a selective interpretation of railroad experience in the United States. This interpretation is characterized by two themes: the historic centrality of the private sector to the creation and operation of railroads and the contemporary policy conventional wisdom that public regulation almost invariably fails. The historic role of the private sector is privileged by an interpretive history that views the nineteenth-century establishment of a national rail network as a triumph of entrepreneurial ingenuity and the soundness of competitive market signals. The nineteenth-century infrastructure investments that define the twenty-first-century U.S. railroad system are seen as the result of the actions taken by risk-tolerant and bold entrepreneurial visionaries financed by similarly inclined venture capitalists. The concept of "competitive market signals" refers to the multiplicity of services along the competing trunk-line, or mainline, routes connecting the nation's two coasts and burgeoning urban centers to one another. Competition was rarely the case along the branch lines that served America's small towns and farming communities. Monopoly would be a more accurate characterization.

It was in reaction to the abusive monopolistic behavior of the rail entrepreneurs along these branch lines that federal public regulation was created. The rail lines began to engage in egregious forms of price discrimination along these monopolized branch lines. This economic discrimination engendered a strong political reaction from the farmers in the Midwest and the South, who bore the brunt of this discrimination. They led a populist political revolt in the late nineteenth century that eventually forced the federal government to begin to regulate the entire industry through the creation of a new Progressive Era bureaucracy, the Interstate Commerce Commission.

Viewed retrospectively through contemporary policy lens tinted by a public choice critique that views government failure as endemic and pervasive, the best that can be said of early regulation is that though it may have been politically inevitable, it was not necessarily wise. Regulation in this market liberalization orientation is almost always wrong. Accordingly, the problems that plagued the industry throughout the twentieth century are viewed as the result of such government intrusion in the late nineteenth century. President Woodrow Wilson, at the tail end of the Progressive Era and in the heat of World War I, nationalized the entire railroad system to ensure that it would serve the war effort. Although the system was restored to private operation in the 1920s, the railroad companies never fully recovered from this "inappropriate" overregulation and war-based "deprivatization." The private industry did recover sufficiently that nationalization was never seriously considered during World War II, when it performed admirably in meeting the challenge of a bicoastal transcontinental nation fighting a world war across two oceans. However, in the decade after the war, fate, in the guise of highway and air travel, dealt both passenger and freight services a cruel blow. These two "newer" travel modes, heavily subsidized by the federal government, effectively destroyed the market for rail service. At the same time, the industry regulated by the heavy hand of the Interstate Commerce Commission was in no position to reorganize itself in response to new market realities.

By the early 1960s, as a result of the market share lost to these newer subsidized travel modes, the conditions of the entire rail industry were so precarious that the federal government once again intervened, intending to stabilize the newly shrunken industry and permit it to continue to function in the private market. This third intervention was successful with freight operations, which were restored to a self-sustaining and deregulated private market niche, but passenger rail became an apparent white elephant carried by the U.S. taxpayer all the way into the twenty-first century.

According to this stylized and compressed regulatory history, intercity passenger rail service never made it back to viable private operation because, as a result of public takeover in the guise of Amtrak, it never gained the proper market-based efficiency incentives. Instead, Amtrak became an inefficient and unaccountable "public monopoly." The theory supporting this conclusion derives from one or another variant of public choice theory. Bureaucrats and public employee unions, shielded as they are from the competitive marketplace, are free to engage in rent-seeking behavior that results in higher subsidy costs to taxpayers and higher fares and worse service for rail travelers. The policy implication is obvious. The only way that passenger rail service can be effectively revitalized is to relinquish government "ownership" by devising a privatization scheme to restore the service to the realm of market-based competition with other intercity travel modes. If that transformation is permitted to occur, either a profitable and self-sufficient industry will emerge or the service will disappear. But if it were to disappear in the context of a competitive travel market, that would not necessarily be a bad thing. The disappearance would be a result of the judgment of consumers in the competitive marketplace for intercity travel literally "voting with their feet." They would have cast a judgment that rail service is inferior to the air and auto alternatives.

Although some would disagree with particular aspects of this stylized promarket and antigovernment interpretation of rail policy history, it is in essence the dominant conventional wisdom behind the contemporary advocacy for market-based reform. Two themes implicitly run through it: government regulation is almost impossible to "get right," and markets make better decisions. However, while there are elements of truth in these stylized facts, they are scarcely universal. They are at best only partial truths. Partial truths are a good basis for more in-depth inquiry, but they are a poor basis for sound public policy. It is important that we develop a more sophisticated and comprehensive understanding of the subject matter if we are to draw a better, if not necessarily "correct," policy line between market governance and regulation in this important area of transportation.

Passenger Rail Service and Market Preference

Arguments of market governance aside, of all transportation modes, passenger rail is arguably the least subsidized by the federal government. One of the largest obstacles to the creation of a more generous public policy is the widespread belief that intercity passenger rail service is in trouble not because it is underfunded or because it is publicly supplied but because people do not want to use it. According to this view, passenger rail service is outmoded. It has failed the crucial market test that air travel and auto travel have passed. At the dawning of the twenty-first century, passenger rail service is a nineteenth-century mode of travel for which there is insufficient demand. The entire policy debate about a public need is deemed to be politically manufactured by environmentalists, trade unionists, and sentimentalists. The traveling public has voted with its feet. Their overwhelming choice is to travel by more flexible private automobiles or faster commercial jet planes.

The aggregate national transportation statistics certainly lend credence to this argument. According to the 1995 National Household Travel Survey, approximately 96 percent of trips of more than one hundred miles are completed either by personal motor vehicle (77 percent) or commercial airline (19 percent). Passenger rail accounts for a mere 1 percent of all such trips (U.S. Department of Transportation 1997). Clearly, if these aggregate statistics are taken as an indicator of consumer preferences, an extremely small proportion of the traveling public prefers to make intercity trips by train. However, the situation is not that simple. For starters, it is important to remember that these travel statistics reflect the direct personal costs and benefits of the alternative travel modes consumer face. Accordingly, for the vast majority, air and auto provided the best "deal" in terms of cost, convenience, flexibility, and safety. But the direct personal costs and benefits are not the total costs and benefits of these choices. Since all modes are subsidized by federal, state, and local governments to a greater or lesser extent, the direct personal costs are merely those costs that, as a matter of public policy, consumers are asked to consider in their decision calculus. A de facto public policy heavily subsidizes auto and air travel, while it only lightly subsidizes rail. Thus when statistics are used, the outcomes analyzed do not reflect purely inherent consumer preferences. Rather, they reflect choices that are a conflation of individual preferences and public policy decisions. I argue that it is policy decisions, far more than consumer bias, that shape these statistics.

There is much evidence to bear this out. Despite Amtrak's precarious funding structure, which has led to diminished train capacity and to fare increases that surpass the rate of inflation, its trains travel at high levels of capacity utilization. Systemwide, ridership on Amtrak grew almost 20 percent between 1996 and 2001 (Mead 2002, 8). In addition, evidence from several other sources indicates that there is no inherent consumer bias against rail-based travel. "A *Washington Post* poll taken July 26 to 30, 2002 (and reported August 5, 2002) found 71 percent support for continued or increased federal funding of Amtrak" (NARP 2003). In November 2000 Floridians voted by a margin of 53 to 47 percent for a ballot initiative instructing the state to begin constructing a high-speed rail system (NARP 2002). These citations are indicative of the larger point that there is no inherent antirail bias in the intercity travel market. Travelers are merely choosing the best option given the available alternatives.

In places where intercity passenger rail service has adequate infrastructure and high service frequency, it is highly competitive with air and highway travel. In the Northeast Rail Corridor, between Boston and Washington, D.C., and the New York–Albany corridor, where this infrastructure sufficiency and train density exist, Amtrak dominates the airlines and offers a significant alternative to automobile travel. Amtrak handles about half of all New York–Washington airline and railroad traffic. If offered a good rail-based alternative, many travelers will most likely choose rail.

For our purposes, consideration of consumer preferences, though important as a general principal, is not central to the present analysis. The working assumption here is that unless all modes are equally subsidized or unsubsidized, existing usage figures reflect policy decisions. Given the present state of national public policy, with its significant differentials in subsidy by transportation mode, attempt to infer preferences by looking only at travel statistics is a bit like adding apples and oranges.

Passenger Rail Service and Technological Possibilities

The twenty-first-century technological possibilities for passenger rail are truly revolutionary. Magnetic levitation trains, or "mag levs," are capable of reaching speeds of three hundred miles per hour or better. These are speeds that can effectively compete with air travel at distances of between one thousand and fifteen hundred miles. Using magnetic repulsion, the technology essentially lifts the train from the rail bed and floats it just above the tracks. This permits both high speeds and a smooth ride. Isolated mag levs are operational in Japan and Germany. The German and Chinese governments recently announced that the two countries will cooperate in the installation of a mag lev system in metropolitan Shanghai (Xinhuanet News Agency 2003). The U.S. government is considering spending upward of $600 million to install a demonstration system in a major American city (CBICC 2001).

Mag-lev technology is futuristic technology. Although it is possible that it will impact travel later in the century, it is not by itself a basis for present policy. In terms of present possibilities, it is important to be aware of contemporary working high-speed technologies using conventional power sources. High-speed rail is used extensively in developed nations all over the world, and it could be put in place in the United States if the public commitment to invest in it was also in place. About two years ago, one of France's older high-speed TGV (train à grande vitesse) trains broke a speed record when it traversed the 662 miles between Calais and Marseilles in 3.5 hours—an average speed of about 190 miles per hour. At that speed, Boston is only three hours from Washington by train, and Atlanta to Chicago is a four-hour trip (NARP 2002). High speeds do not require new and exotic technology. They can be achieved on present trains by significantly upgrading existing rail beds to support such speeds. The Acela Express, which travels along the Northeast Rail Corridor, is designed to travel at far higher speeds than its tracks now permit. While the needed investments are not inexpensive, they are well within the range of what we could afford if we had the political desire to create them. Indeed, with only comparatively modest upgrading of existing rail beds it would be possible to achieve average sustained operating speeds of approximately 110 miles per hour. On trips of less than five hundred miles, that speed would make an enormous difference in shifting travelers from the less fuel efficient highways and allow for more efficient use of crowded airport runway capacity for longer hauls.

This last point is not trivial. According to the transportation survey cited previously, 60 percent of all intercity passenger travel in the United States is in distances of less than five hundred miles, and 80 percent is for distances of less than a thousand miles (U.S. Department of Transportation 1997). At these distances, a higher-performance passenger rail system would be able to take pressure off both our highways and air lanes.

Over the past half century, Japan's "bullet trains," France's TGV, America's Metroliner and Acela, and the international Eurostar have all demonstrated that, with public sector leadership and new public investment, the demand for rail travel is alive and well. Each of these trains has been able to attract new riders and succeed in competition with automobiles and air travel. As of 2004, 66 percent of travelers from London to Paris and 52 percent of travelers from London to Brussels take Eurostar trains (Paul Charles, letter to the editor, *New York Times,* May 19, 2004, p. A23). According to a Eurostar spokesman, "In 2007 (when the entire British portion of the trackage is at high speed standards) we can see the airlines withdrawing from the London-to-Paris route because they can't beat us from city center to city center" (Alan Cowell, "Eurostar Picks Up Speed To Stem Ticket Decline," Travel section,

New York Times, September 14, 2003, p. 3). Each of these high-speed systems is a result not of private market forces but of a strong and active public policy commitment backed up with significant public investment. It was the Japanese government that funded the first bullet train in 1958. It was the U.S. government, through the High Speed Ground Transportation Act of 1965, that launched the upgraded service in the Boston–New York–Washington corridor. It was the French government that decided in 1973 to finance the first TGV between Paris and Lyons. Eurostar, which links London, Brussels, and Paris by high-speed trains traveling under the English Channel, is a joint public-private venture, but the leadership and the investment guarantees are all public. Clearly, market preferences cannot be considered in isolation from public transportation investment decisions.

Public investment and public leadership must play a prominent role in the process of developing modern transportation infrastructure. Private markets never sustain these types of investments for two reasons. First, private investors are not able to absorb the hugely expensive long-term risks in creating products for markets that do not yet exist. Second, private investors are reluctant to enter markets in which the likelihood of an unsubsidized positive market return is small in the best of circumstances. Indeed, it was not private investments that were the primary drivers of the original rail system in the United States; it was massive public investment.

Passenger Rail Economics: An Introduction

The fundamental economic issue critical to establishing an effective and sustainable national passenger rail policy is recognition of the need for ongoing public subsidy. Passenger transportation systems rarely, if ever, cover their total costs through user charges. As a general proposition, this is often hard to accept because there is no intuitive theoretical explanation for this situation. Yet this observation holds true with remarkable and universal consistency. It does not matter whether it is aviation, highways, mass transit, commuter rail, intercity rail, or fixed-route buses being considered. As high-volume systems, they all require more funding than can be obtained from revenue generated by travelers. The reason for this lies in part on the demand side of the market but, even more important, on the supply side. On the demand side of the market, public subsidy is provided as an incentive for individuals to engage in more travel than they would otherwise willingly undertake. The policy rationale is that transportation is not an end product but literally a means to an end. As individuals, we value transportation because it permits us to engage in other activities: work, family visits, vacations, and so on. These activities, in turn, benefit a larger segment of society than the traveler alone. Public subsidy, by inducing larger passenger volumes than an unsubsidized market would create on its own, thus creates large positive benefits beyond those gained by individual travelers. Inexpensive transport access (regardless of mode) enlarges the market area for both products and inputs, with all the attendant productivity gains of specialization and higher productivity that come with these larger markets. Subsidized transport makes cities, in particular, valuable centers of production and consumption. In an era when pollution and congestion from automobile travel are becoming ever more costly negative externalities, subsidies to public transport systems create positive benefits by lessening these negatives.

On the supply side, the use of tax revenues and public expenditures is necessitated by the inability of transportation systems easily to employ private market pricing systems to collect the full cost of producing transportation directly from travelers. Passenger rail is quite typical in both these respects.

Transportation systems are infrastructure intensive: they require spatially extensive and generally expensive investments in roads, streets, rail beds, signaling equipment, rail and air terminals, air traffic control systems, and the like. These fixed investments are apart from and additional to the direct and variable operating costs associated with the vehicles (trains, planes, and cars) and personnel needed to provide service at the time of use. If these capital and operating costs are not covered by user charges, then subsidy becomes necessary.

To understand the challenge in transportation it may be helpful to consider it in relation to two other infrastructure-intensive industries: telecommunications and electric power. Despite the similarities in infrastructure requirements, transportation systems stand in sharp contrast to both because of a more limited ability to recoup infrastructure and operating costs. The principal difference is that telecommunication and electric power services can more easily use market pricing schemes. This is especially the case in high-income countries where telephones and electric power use are virtually universal. In these places, providers have the ability to spread the costs of fixed infrastructure effectively over the entire population. In these situations, direct user charges, because of their universal impact, are tantamount to a privatized system of public finance.[2] This "taxation" is possible because the electric power and telecommunications infrastructures are physically tied to site-specific locations or, in the case of cell phones, to specific users. This permits the imposition of comparatively inexpensive long-term contractual billing that is easy to enforce at a low cost. The pricing structure of these contracts contains both a fixed charge, related to infrastructure access and maintenance, and a use charge, related to intensity of individual use. More important, because of the universality of market penetration, the high aggregate costs of infrastructure are effectively spread over the entire population. This leads to significantly lower average unit costs for these expensive items of fixed capital. This, in turn, negates the need for public subsidy to ensure the positive externalities created by these infrastructure-based services. Service providers in effect "tax" virtually the entire population. As a result of these characteristics, telecommunications and electric power providers typically cover the full costs of their operation through user-generated revenues. As a result, the salient public policy debate in these areas of natural monopoly relates solely to regulation.

The situation in transportation is different. Because there is a multiplicity of modally separate transportation systems that simultaneously compete with and complement one another, the universality of use that would permit a private pricing system to cover full systems costs by modality does not exist. Moreover, the specific elements of needed transportation infrastructure are so diverse and so extensive that an economically viable unitary pricing system is impossible to create. The dependency of bus companies, for example, on the multiple units of government that supply highways, through streets and access streets over which their vehicles must travel, are more complex than can be handled by an interorganizational billing scheme that approaches the simplicity and low transactions costs of an electric bill or a telephone bill. Even if travelers paid a cost per ride sufficient to cover the myriad of charges for the infrastructure needed to convey them from point A to point B, the transactions costs of sorting out the revenue distribution through a private market framework would be impossible. Thus formal public finance schemes are used to provide the needed transportation infrastructure for the individual transportation service providers.

While it is possible to conceive of locational taxes, such as property taxes that reflect the value of area access created by transport, and user taxes, such as gasoline taxes to approximate use intensity by travelers, these are at best imperfect public financing and subsidy approximations to a market. A market is typically made by a two-party exchange relationship. Transportation financing, because it must follow the nature of the service, always becomes a situation in which government must become a third party to the transaction between supplier and traveler, and hence it is reflective of the limitations of markets in the transportation sector. Exacerbating the situation is the fact that only a comparatively small percentage of the population in even the highest-income countries uses any particular transport service mode at any time and then only for a short use period. As a result of this smaller population base, the average unit (per ride) costs for the amortization of the fixed infrastructure costs tend to be high on a per user fully allocated cost basis. Thus the need for subsidy also results from the fact that the amount that users are willing to pay is usually insufficient to generate the necessary ridership numbers to capture the social benefits of a modern high-volume transportation system.

Because users have only an intermittent relationship with transportation, the transactions costs of prepayment systems comparable to those used for electricity and telecommunications are usually too high to be practicable for highways, streets, and roads. The only possible exceptions are monthly rail and bus commuters who continually use the service at the same time of day all year long. Rail commuters can be sold monthly tickets, and bridge users can be given a differential rate. But in these cases, the peak period users represent only a portion of total users and if charged more than a small peak period differential would find the service prohibitively expensive.[3] Charging intermittent users on anything remotely resembling a fully allocated cost basis would seriously reduce the revenue stream from those users with the lowest marginal cost to the system and discourage users who contribute the most to offsetting total system costs.

Thus in practice, fares and tolls are set to capture as much of costs as possible with the expectation that to maintain the service, public subsidy is a necessary ongoing element. The proportion of total costs absorbed by the users is called "the farebox recovery ratio."[4] The gap between revenues and costs is typically financed through general systems of public expenditures sustained by various forms of taxation. The rationale for providing the service at a subsidized price is that low-cost transportation is necessary to create sufficient use volumes to generate broader social and economic benefits that are external to the market for the service (Schaeffer and Sclar 1980).

From the perspective of transportation policy, the debate is further complicated by the fact that while all modes are publicly subsidized, they are not equally subsidized. Since 1971, Amtrak has received approximately $21 billion in federal operating and capital funding. To put that in proportion, over approximately three decades, Amtrak received less federal funding than highways alone received in the single year of 1999 ($23.6 billion). Passenger rail receives slightly more than 1 percent of all federal transportation moneys and approximately one-third of 1 percent of combined federal, state, and local funding. Highways receive forty-three times the amount of federal funding that rail receives; aviation receives twenty times as much. Even transit—the other stepchild in the federal budget—receives eight times as much funding (U.S. Department of Transportation 2003b). It could, of course, be argued that the comparative level of subsidy is nothing more than a reflection of the comparative level of service use. However, the reverse is equally true, if not more plausible; the level of subsidy drives the level of use. Because of the complexity of the simultaneity of the relationship between use levels and subsidy, it is more important to focus the policy debate on the larger goal of efficient and effective intercity movement than on individual mode.

Furthermore, given the comparatively small amount of subsidy now given to passenger rail, much of the rhetoric in the present policy debate used to justify cutting subsidy to Amtrak because of its alleged inefficiency and its potential drain on the taxpayer is, in the broader context of federal transportation funding, a tempest in a teapot. The charge that Amtrak wastes its resources is insignificant compared with the issue of Amtrak's inadequate funding. Although Amtrak has made intermittent progress in increasing revenues and reducing losses, it has never achieved self-sufficiency. From 1997 to 2001, Amtrak lost between $762 million and $1.072 billion each year

(Mead 2002). From 1997 to 2002, Amtrak received a total of $5.7 billion in federal assistance. Given the political pressure on Amtrak to close the deficit, the operating losses have left little or no moneys for the capital improvements Amtrak must make to be a twenty-first-century transportation system. In the larger scheme of things, the five-year Amtrak subsidy is only slightly more than the approximately $5 billion cash subsidy that the Department of Transportation hurriedly paid to the airline industry under the Air Transportation Safety and System Stabilization Act of 2001, passed in wake of the attacks of September 11 (U.S. Department of Transportation 2003a).

In the policy debate over intercity passenger service, one frequently heard argument is that while an economic case could be made for rail service along certain high-density corridors, that does not make a case for subsidizing a national system. Discussions about Amtrak take the form of making a distinction between corridor trains and long-distance trains. Amtrak currently oversees a service network spanning roughly twenty-three thousand miles of rail over which approximately 270 trains operate on a typical day.[5] It serves more than five hundred communities in forty-seven states, services 23 million passengers annually, and generates more than $1 billion in annual ticket sales (AASHTO 2002). These services are divided between corridor routes, defined as markets in which trip distances typically run from one hundred to five hundred miles, and long-distance routes, defined as trip distances exceeding five hundred miles.

The economic distinction between corridor trains and long-distance trains is far more complex than a simple distinction based on distance alone would imply. Consider the densest routes such as Boston-Washington, Seattle-Portland, Los Angeles–San Diego, and Chicago–St. Louis: where population density is high, there is a combination of long-distance business and personal travel along with a small amount of longer-distance daily commuting. On these routes, the farebox recovery ratio ranges from 90 to 100 percent. This provides the basis for the argument that the most efficient and effective public policy would be one that focuses on using scarce resources to develop high-speed capacity in dense corridors with a demonstrated market demand and not a national system through places with lower population density and sparse use of long-distance trains. From a static perspective, this is a powerful argument. However, when viewed through a dynamic lens that stresses the future needs of the nation and the potentials of new technology, the future of long-distance trains has both new possibilities and new risks. In deciding how to answer this longer-term question it is critical that decision makers balance the potentials and risks against the short-term financial implications of closing down services.

In the short term, the issue should be framed as the classic textbook problem of deciding when to shut down a business. In this case, we must compare the cost savings from eliminating services (called avoidable costs) and the revenue loss of these actions. The Los Angeles–Seattle route, of which the Portland-

Seattle corridor is just one part, can serve as an illustration of the substantive complexities that a decision to shut down entails. The route is 1,389 miles long. When viewed as an end-to-end product, the question arises: Why would someone choose a long, slow train ride from Los Angeles to Seattle at a relatively high price over a quick flight on a low-cost commercial air carrier? The answer to the question as posed is that most people do not choose to make this trip by train.

The decision to shut down the route in favor of smaller corridor segments becomes compelling when the issue is defined as the effectiveness of an end-to-end long-distance train. Indeed, an analysis of travel patterns on this route reveals that two-thirds of all the passengers use it for distances of less than five hundred miles. But how do we separate the long-distance features from the corridor features? In a sense, the long-distance features are really an aggregate of a series of smaller overlapping "corridor" services. Moreover, because the decision to shut down has financial implications, it is also important to analyze the revenue generation patterns of its passengers. The one-third of passengers who use this train to travel distances greater than five hundred miles generate two-thirds of the revenue needed to support the service (NARP 2002, 13). Consequently, even in a static analysis focused solely on present service issues, the economics of passenger use make a determination to write off this long-distance train on a corridor versus long-distance criterion far less compelling. An analysis that focuses only on end-to-end travel is misleading.

Amtrak cannot avoid the overhead and other fixed costs of its operations by eliminating these long-distance trains. In 2002 revenue from the long-distance trips totaled approximately $380 million (Richard Slattery, Amtrak senior director of planning and business development, personal communication, April 23, 2003), yet Amtrak president David L. Gunn (2003) estimates the avoidable cost reductions resulting from eliminating these trips at $70 million a year. Shutting down these long-distance trains would result in a short-term net revenue loss of $310 million on an annual budget of about $1.8 billion. That is a sizable impact. As the textbooks suggest, as long as the added revenue from operation exceeds the added costs of operation, shutdown is more costly than continued operation.

Evaluating the potential shifts in market structure that will come with the introduction of even presently available high-speed technology further complicates the decision in a long-term and dynamic context. With investments that significantly shorten travel times, passenger trains will become even more competitive with air travel and thus increase the demand for rail and restructure air travel to focus more on the longer-distance markets, where its comparative advantage is greatest. As long as these long-distance routes are contributing more to revenues than to costs, it would seem wise to continue them until the larger federal technology and investment policy is definitively clarified. Although high-speed rail may never make the Los Angeles–Seattle trip cost effective, it will begin to change the spatial relationships among smaller regional markets along the way. In short, it is important that as we think about the future system we avoid using analytic constructs based upon what will become outmoded distinctions derived from the older technology. Any decision on the future of the rail system should be based on consideration of a national high-speed rail system as it can be, not as it presently is.

Long-distance routes serve areas that would otherwise lack any rail or air connection to major urban centers (Charles Sheehan, "Small towns may be off the track," *Philadelphia Inquirer,* April 6, 2003). The only trains linking twenty-four states are Amtrak long-distance trains. Passenger rail reaches 42 percent of the nation's rural population and is the sole transportation mode for more than three hundred thousand people (U.S. Department of Transportation 2003b). As much as we subsidize roads, postal services, and telephone lines to remote locations, surely we can justify subsidized rail connections.

The Case for Public Intervention

Why have governments in advanced industrial nations seen fit to invest in passenger rail services, and why should the United States follow suit? Modern high-speed national passenger railroad systems are crucial drivers of economic prosperity, and the role of high-speed passenger rail systems will be of growing importance in the rapidly evolving and competitive global economy. Four factors are of particular relevance here: passenger rail strengthens the competitive advantages of metropolitan centers, it improves the overall energy efficiency of intercity travel, it contributes to environmental improvement, and it is a necessary element in the creation of improved homeland security.

The highest value-added segment of the world economy is the service sector. Services are labor intensive. Productivity in services depends on both the education and skills of individual workers and the efficiency of their working environment. This is especially true for urban-centered professional services that make up the bulk of value added in globally traded services. Put simply, a national infrastructure that facilitates ease of travel among metropolitan areas for business and other purposes (leisure travelers, foreign visitors, students, and so on) is crucial to contemporary economic life. Better rail access will make America's metropolitan centers more attractive locations for global business. Railroads can move travelers from center city to center city more efficiently than any other travel mode. A network of high-speed rail connections among the centers of America's great metropolitan areas can only strengthen these places as locational nodes in an increasingly competitive global economy.

Intercity rail travel is the most energy-efficient mode of travel among rail, highway, and air. In terms of Btus per passenger mile, Amtrak is 125 percent more efficient than air travel, 278 percent more efficient than private automobile travel, 94 percent more efficient than a transit bus, and even 6 percent more efficient than a motorcycle. Improving the rail alternatives for intercity travelers can only mean less highway congestion, which means improved fuel economy. Environmentally, it means less wasteful burning of nonrenewable fuels by drivers stuck in slow or stalled traffic. Although air travel was down as a result of the September 11, 2001, attacks and the stagnating American economy, the reality is that air travel has resumed its long-term growth trend (Travel Industry Association of America 2004).

It is now virtually impossible to build new airports in suitable proximity to our large metropolitan areas. Rail systems, especially those that connect to airports and provide trips of less than five hundred miles, could complement and strengthen aviation as well as play a major role in alleviating the impending airline capacity crisis. By helping the airline industry fly with fuller planes on longer flights, an integrated intercity passenger rail system could also boost the fuel efficiency of aviation and strengthen it in its most competitive area—long-distance travel.

Increasingly, concerns surround U.S. dependence upon imported oil. By enhancing the overall fuel efficiency of various travel modes, improved intercity passenger rail will allow us to travel farther and more often on less petroleum. In addition, security and hazards experts agree that redundancy in transportation infrastructure better enables us to respond to and recover from terrorist attacks and natural calamities (AASHTO 2002). The U.S. air travel system has been shown to be vulnerable to terrorism. The entire system was shut down by the 2001 attacks. Passenger rail has added value, in this light, if it provides a viable transportation alternative.

Should Congress treat intercity passenger rail as a relic of a bygone era or a private sector business fallen on hard times, it will either defund Amtrak entirely or continue to fund it at a starvation level. The result will be either no system or a skeletal one with extremely low return on taxpayer investment. In either case, it will confine the U.S. service sector to a higher-cost business context. There will be no progress on the environmental front nor any relief from our dependence on foreign oil. Nor will the nation be more secure from terrorism.

From a competitive standpoint, moribund urban centers cannot be helpful to the U.S. economy. At the margin, mediocre rail service will induce high value-added urban-based sectors of the service economy to seek locations elsewhere in the world for some if not all of their activities. The multiplier effects of such location decisions will lead to a proportionate drop in domestic employment and a worsening balance of payments. From an environmental standpoint, favoring highway over rail subsidies can only mean dirtier air, with all its attendant health and social problems—problems that will show up as taxpayer costs, bereft of offsets from higher productivity. In effect, we will be paying for the damage of a flawed policy decision rather than using tax dollars to increase productivity.

America's First Railroads

The history of rail service in the United States illustrates two important issues. The first is the abiding role of federal subsidy to and regulation of railroads in general—that is, in both freight and passenger service. The second pertains to passenger service as a separate and distinct entity.

Contrary to popular belief, from its start rail development was a publicly financed undertaking (Fogel 1964; Fishlow 1965; Stover 1997). The initial grants from government to entrepreneurs were made by state and local governments in the years between 1826 and approximately 1850. The impetus for these investments was the realization that improved overland transportation generated strong localized economic externalities. This was especially true after New York State opened the Erie Canal in 1826. By 1830, thanks to the strong connections this created between the Port of New York and the westward expanding nation, New York grew from just one of five major East Coast ports (the others being Boston, Philadelphia, Baltimore, and Charleston) to the preeminent center of the new nation's economy. The city fathers of Baltimore in 1828, seeing any hope for their economic future beginning to slip away, followed New York's lead with public investment in transport infrastructure for both a canal and a railroad. The history of rail investing for the rest of this period is largely a story of cities and states understanding that good access is a comparative economic advantage.

After 1850 the public investment scene shifted from the cities and states to the federal government. The technological potential for railroads to unite the continent had became obvious, and the political need imperative. The first federal involvement came in 1853, when Congress appropriated $150,000 to survey four possible transcontinental routes (Stover 1997, 49–50). Full-fledged subsidy began in 1862, when President Abraham Lincoln signed the Pacific Railway Act authorizing the Central Pacific and Union Pacific to build rail routes to the Pacific Coast. The Union Pacific Railway Company built westward from the Missouri River, and the Central Pacific built eastward from Sacramento. In 1869, with the driving of a golden spike at Ogden, Utah, the nation had two transcontinental railroad links. By 1885 the number had grown to four, and by 1895 to five. The federal government granted these companies public land in exchange for completed track. Long-term low-interest government loans were also made to the companies, the size of the loan varying with the difficulty of terrain.[6] The land grants created secure collateral against which the companies could obtain private funding. Most of this funding came from Great Britain. Between 1865 and 1914, the United States was a debtor nation, with most of the capital repatriation going back to the British Isles. Most of the foreign debt was tied to the building of the several transcontinental railroads.

It is estimated that the federal government granted title to more than 131 million acres of land to all of the interstate railroads constructed between the late 1850s, when some initial modest grants were made, and 1943, the year the last of the railroads received full title to its lands. To put this in perspective, this acreage amounts to an area about 80 percent the size of the five states in the old Northwest and larger than all the land granted to settlers under the 1862 Homestead Act (Stover 1997). The total subsidy value of these enormous land grants in 1941 prices has been estimated at more than $500 million (Stover 1997, 82–83). It is impossible to fully estimate the size of the public subsidy in today's terms. However, if the 1941 estimate is adjusted to current prices, the present dollar amount would be at least $15 billion. This is clearly an underestimate of the actual total value of public investment, but it does put an approximate floor under it.

Passenger Rail Becomes a Separate Service

In response to the Penn-Central collapse in 1970, Congress established two separate corporations: Conrail, to take over freight service in the Northeast, and Amtrak, to provide national intercity passenger service, as railroads all over the country were losing money on passenger service. Amtrak was, in effect, a corporate bailout for all U.S. railroads.[7] It was at that point that freight and passenger service were divorced from each other and the need to fund a separate passenger system became a federal policy imperative. It was also at that point that intercity passenger rail service moved from being a privately supplied but publicly subsidized service to a directly supplied public service.

From the founding of the first American railroads until the creation of Amtrak in 1970, passenger rail was not a separate "product." Railroad companies supplied both freight and passenger service. Freight service was almost always profitable (indeed, as the history of the founding of the Interstate Commerce Commission suggests, it was perhaps too profitable), but passenger rail service was a hit-or-miss proposition. There was intense passenger competition on the well-traveled trunk routes, such as New York to Chicago, but little on the branch lines (Schaeffer and Sclar 1980). Passenger fares were competitive on the trunk routes, and services were frequent. On the branch lines, the opposite was the case: fares were excessive, and the service was infrequent and inadequate. As with air travel today, passenger rail service was always a highly cyclical and only marginally profitable business for the railroads.

In reaction to the local monopolies that the railroads were able to achieve in individual agricultural markets, pressure to redress the balance through public regulation began to grow after the Civil War. By the 1880s, public regulation of passenger fares and freight rates was a reality. This regulation continued until the closing decades of the twentieth century. Although the conventional wisdom views the series of regulatory acts promulgated during the Progressive Era as gestures to protect the public interest from the special interest of the railroad trusts and others, the regulatory framework also helped to save the industry from itself. (Kolko 1963; 1970). One of the drawbacks of the system of land grants and public subsidies used to construct the first lines was that because capital was cheap and plentiful, routes were overbuilt. The new era of regulation provided a way for the industry to reduce the overcapacity it had built itself into along its trunk lines. Just before the turn of the twentieth century, five separate transcontinental rail routes spanned the nation (Stover 1997, 77). By 1906, as a result of consolidations fostered in part by the new regulated environment, nearly two-thirds of the 225,000 miles of rail lines in the nation were controlled by just seven ownership groups. After the wave of industry consolidations there followed a period of abandonment as the lines sought to cut capacity to stabilize costs and prices. In 1916 total rail mileage in the United States peaked at 254,000 miles. By 1940, the eve of World War II, total mileage was down almost 10 percent, to 233,000 (Stover 1997, 219, table 8.6).

World War II boosted both the passenger and freight businesses of the railroads. At the beginning of the war, railroads were carrying 72 percent of all commercial freight traffic and 74 percent of all intercity passenger traffic. From 1941 to 1944 the railroads handled 77 percent of the new intercity passenger traffic and 83 percent of the new commercial freight business (Stover 1997, 187). These gains were short-lived. With the end of the war, the federal government shifted the historical emphasis of its transport subsidies away from rail and toward highways and aviation. The Interstate Highway Act of 1956 was the largest public works project in human history: in 1955 the official estimate in mid-1954 dollars was $27 billion (U.S. Department of Transportation 2003c). This was just the down payment, as it covered only the years through 1964. In contemporary terms the comparable estimate would be about $100 billion. That highway system is the backbone of the entire contemporary infrastructure for truck and auto travel in the United States.

For the railroads the result of the massive shift of federal subsidy was devastating. By 1965, as increasing highway mileage came on line, the railroads controlled less than 18 percent of the total intercity commercial passenger business and 44 percent of the intercity freight traffic (Stover 1997, 192–93). As a result of the enormous drop in passenger volume and the squeeze on freight volumes, the railroads sought to get out of the passenger end of the business as quickly as possible. In 1957, for the first time, air passenger volume surpassed rail passenger volume. The 1958 Transportation Act allowed the Interstate Commerce Commission to act quickly on railroad company petitions to abandon passenger service. In 1958 passenger trains serviced 107,000 miles of line. By the time Amtrak was created in 1970, there were only 49,000 miles of passenger rail service (Stover 1997, 228).

The justification was obvious from a business perspective. Passenger rail had no future as a "business," and the railroads were running businesses, not public services. But while passenger rail was shorn of a business rationale, its vital public service externalities did not disappear. The public nature of rail travel came sharply into focus, and the federal government was forced to enter the picture.

The problems of market shrinkage for railroads in the 1960s were manifest in both freight hauling and passenger service. By then, the cumulative impact of the changed federal investment priorities had became manifest in a series of corporate financial crises that began to convulse the industry and prompt a second large wave of rail mergers and consolidations. In 1966 the Pennsylvania Railroad and the New York Central merged to form the Penn-Central. Four years later, in 1970, this vast northeastern carrier declared bankruptcy—at that time, the largest corporate failure in history. Penn-Central's bottom-line problems were a direct result of the loss of top-line freight and passenger revenue to air and highway modes. These, in turn, were a direct result of federal public investment decisions.

The Birth of Amtrak

Because of its roots in private railroading, the working policy assumption when Amtrak was created was that, as with freight, public control would be temporary. Intercity passenger service was viewed by policy makers at the time either as a vital business that had fallen on hard times or as a perhaps technologically obsolete mode that was being gently guided to its final demise. As a result, from its inception in 1970 onward, Amtrak had two structural problems built into its existence. The first was that it was now a freestanding service running over rail lines mainly owned by freight operators with different corporate missions and profit-making options from the passenger carrier. The second was that, as a result of the "policy culture" that defined it, funding bills always moved grudgingly through Congress. The policy culture was defined by an implicit assumption that the National Rail Passenger Corporation (NRPC), Amtrak's corporate parent, was at best only a temporary agency. The ongoing external benefits of passenger rail either were never properly or fully valued by policy makers or were dismissed as being superseded by highways and aviation. While it is easy to understand this state of affairs historically, these operative policy assumptions were wrong. Certainly, experts understood even then what has since emerged as a worldwide consensus: passenger rail service is important as a public service and not viable as a freestanding business. The evidence was abundant in the experiences in other modes, the history of American railroading, and the railroading experiences of every other developed nation: nowhere in the world is there a wholly private, profitable, and unsubsidized passenger rail system. The information was there, but it was not properly taken into account.

Because of its unique pathway into public receivership, as a bailout for the rail freight industry, and the belief that it had at best a short future, intercity passenger rail service entered public service without the public agency protection typically afforded to other transportation systems in the United States. Airlines originally had the Civil Aviation Board and the Federal Aviation Administration. With the advent of airline deregulation, the Civil Aviation Board, the industry's market regulator, was dissolved. But because the government retains responsibility for the national air space and flight safety, the new Transportation Security Administration, which is ultimately intended to secure our entire transportation infrastructure, is presently primarily an airport security operation. The federal government has been subsidizing the construction and maintenance of highways in the United States since the Federal Aid Road Act of 1916. The Federal Highway Administration (FHWA) sees its mission as advocating for, funding, and maintaining the national highway system. With the Urban Mass Transit Act of 1964, a federal agency to oversee and channel aid to urban transit aid was created, originally the Urban Mass Transit Administration and presently the Federal Transit Administration.

There is no comparable agency with a mandate to nurture intercity rail. In a technical sense the Federal Rail Administration should play the role, but its agency mission, especially in the Bush administration, has been defined as transforming Amtrak into a competitive business, not advocating for its current needs. Congress, in creating Amtrak, established an arms-length relationship with it. The NRPC is a semiprivate orphan in the disguise of an independent nonprofit corporation. It was given a mandate to provide national passenger rail transportation with as little public help as possible and was asked to restore passenger service to profitable private operation as quickly as possible. In short, Congress never fully embraced its responsibility for this public service in the same way in which it embraces its obligation for all other transport modes.

When Amtrak officially opened for business on May 1, 1971, the passenger rail system had shrunk from the forty-nine-thousand-mile network that existed in 1970 to the twenty-one-thousand-mile network that became the basis of Amtrak's service. It inherited a fleet of old and poorly functioning equipment from the financially strapped freight railroads. Because of the way it was established as a secondhand and temporary agency with no rail infrastructure of its own, it had virtually no chance to become excellent. The federal government struck a bargain with freight operators, who would be relieved of providing passenger service but had to allow Amtrak access to their tracks at a very low marginal cost.

Amtrak did acquire the 456-mile-long Northeast Rail Corridor between Boston and Washington, D.C., as a result of the Penn-Central bankruptcy. While the corridor is expensive to maintain, it is important to the competitiveness of passenger rail in this part of the country. Because Amtrak controls this critical asset, it was able to upgrade its rail beds to create Metroliner service in the 1970s and the potentially high-speed Acela services in the late

1990s. Both of these are successful services. A major problem facing Amtrak almost everywhere else is that it does not similarly control the rights-of-way on which most of its trains travel. Because of the original agreement between the lines seeking to drop passenger service and the NRPC, giving Amtrak access to these rights-of-way, this access does not generate meaningful revenue for the freight lines. Consequently, the freight lines give a lower priority to Amtrak's trains when there is congestion along the lines. One result of this is poor on-time performance by Amtrak. The proportion of total hours of delay to Amtrak caused by freight rose from 41 percent in 1994 to more than 55 percent in 1999 (NRPC 2000). If intercity passenger rail is to play an important role in the future of the U.S. economy, it must be punctual and well capitalized, and it must have more rights vis-à-vis its critical infrastructure.

The Amtrak Policy Debate

From the inception of Amtrak, the core belief underlying the creation of the NRPC was that intercity passenger rail service was essentially a private good. Thus in designing the new public corporation it was assumed that Amtrak would come close to breakeven, if not eventually make a profit and perhaps be returned to complete and unsubsidized private operation. Remarkably, the popular belief in the private market viability of Amtrak has stood for more than three decades as a core policy principle, despite the contrary evidence of actual experience. The truth is that over the past thirty-plus years Amtrak has run a deficit every year.

The Amtrak deficit has been a highly charged political issue. Although transportation experts and academic specialists always understood the structural nature of this deficit, that knowledge never translated politically into the congressional policy dialogue. Instead, the chronic deficit was rationalized as a result of either excessive labor costs caused by unionization or managerial incompetence bred by lack of market discipline or some combination of the two. Whatever truth there might be in these observations is marginal to the larger structural problem: Even the most efficiently run passenger rail system cannot cover its full costs through passenger revenue.

Regardless of the reasons, the underlying policy debate in Congress took a distinct turn toward more market governance with the accession to power of the Republicans in 1994. In 1997 Congress passed the Amtrak Reform and Accountability Act, which mandated the creation of the Amtrak Reform Council (ARC), an oversight body to monitor Amtrak's performance and propose changes in the structure of the NRPC if Amtrak continued to run a deficit. The ARC had a five-year life span and issued its final report in February 2002. The membership of the ARC was shaped to reflect the prevailing ideological view that privatization was the answer to Amtrak's problems (as to virtually all governmental problems). According to a press release from the ARC, "In 1997, Congress debated de-funding Amtrak, and instead Congress gave it one more chance. The Amtrak Reform and Accountability Act of 1997 stated that Amtrak had to be operational[ly] self-sufficient by December 2002" (Amtrak Reform Council 2002b, 1). Amtrak was essentially set up for failure, and needless to say, fail it did.

Consistent with the longstanding conventional wisdom that Amtrak is an inefficient bureaucracy, the ARC asserted that "the roots of Amtrak's flaws lie in its institutional structure" (Amtrak Reform Council 2002a, 2). The solution they proposed was a new "business model." The implicit assumption, never proved but continually stated, was that the cost problems Amtrak faced were the result of bureaucratic inefficiency bred of its multiple responsibilities for train service operation and infrastructure maintenance and improvement—particularly in the Northeast Corridor, where it is responsible for maintaining and upgrading rail rights-of-way. According to the ARC, all of this is too complex a mission for one agency. It keeps them from focusing adequately on service provision.[8] One particularly bad result of this organizational overreach is that it has deterred innovation.

Under the ARC's new business model, the NRPC would be recharted as a small administrative agency that is largely responsible for administering contracts. Instead of providing service, it would oversee services provided by other entities. Initially two entities, or, as the ARC prefers to call them, "companies," would be created; one would provide train operating services and the other would manage maintenance operations. The newly shrunken NRPC's mandate would be similar to that of a federal bureau charged with dispensing public funds. It would be empowered to review the business plans of the operating companies, monitor their progress in reaching their goals, disperse as well as withhold federal funds for intercity rail, and have strategic planning oversight for capital improvements leading to high-speed rail corridors.

The rationale behind the proposal for the two smaller operating units is that it is a basis for breaking down the natural monopoly inherent in rail operation. The initial breakout into two companies is intended to evolve into an expanding market of multiple outside providers who will eventually "compete" for the train and maintenance operations. Although the ARC identifies this latter step as something to be considered eventually, in many ways it is the ideological heart and soul of what it views as reform. There is a tendency among privatization advocates to conflate "contracting" with "competitive contracting" and "competitive contracting" with "efficient market governance." Therefore, in this mental construct, privatization equals efficiency. In fact, however, this causal chain exists mainly in the minds of a small group of free market ideologues, and only rarely does it make an appearance under the most highly constrained conditions—conditions that are difficult to achieve in public contracting in general and especially when the services are as expensive and complex and involve a single system of tracks, as is the case with passenger rail. More important, even when these conditions can be achieved, the equilibrium is precarious and is almost never sustainable.[9] The experience of the privatization of British Rail, examined later in this chapter, is a good illustration of this point.

Although the deficits cited by the ARC could be evidence of incompetence and inefficiency, by themselves they are evidence of neither. They are as plausibly, if not more so, evidence of the fact that passenger rail is a public service and not viable in the private market. In that regard it is important to remember that Amtrak exists because passenger rail was not viable as a private service in the past and is unlikely to be viable as such in the future. It is not clear that Amtrak is any more inefficient than most public or private organizations. According to a 1996 study by the Bureau of Transportation Statistics, labor productivity in rail transportation has been steadily improving. Between 1959 and 1992, rail transportation productivity grew an average of 5.9 percent. By way of comparison, this metric outperformed both aviation (4.6 percent) and trucking (2.8 percent) (U.S. Department of Transportation 1996). That finding is not necessarily evidence that Amtrak is a paradigm of efficiency, but it is consistent with the notion that it might not be all that inefficient. The ARC study never looked at productivity; it is certainly plausible that the organizational form is fatally flawed by inefficiency, but before it is so judged, its actual operations should at least be studied. This was not done by the ARC.

From all available evidence it would appear that the fiscal challenges Amtrak faces are better explained by inadequate funding than by performance efficiency. Amtrak's chronic fiscal crisis, in light of its 1997 mandate requiring operational self-sufficiency, has forced it into ever more questionable financial transactions in an attempt to improve its cash position. In 2000 Amtrak engaged in a leaseback of substantially unencumbered Amtrak equipment to raise $124 million that had not been projected as a cash source in its strategic business plan for that year. More notably, in 2001 Amtrak mortgaged a portion of Penn Station to obtain a $300 million loan to fund cash shortfalls. These transactions and other borrowings have increased Amtrak's debt threefold since 1995 and saddled it with $200 million of debt service annually (Mead 2002). The insistence on an unrealistic breakeven for a public service does not save taxpayer money; it forces increased spending to fund the debt service that was a de facto result of a foolish policy goal.

The assertion by the ARC that Amtrak was institutionally flawed by its range of responsibilities is similar. The provision of any service is always accomplished through the completion of a multiplicity of tasks. There is no reason in either experience or organizational theory to conclude that any particular "make-buy" organizational arrangement is better or worse than another. At best, theory would suggest that the bureaucratic costs of the present arrangement should be compared with the transactions costs of interorganizational operations that the advocated breakup would impose (Williamson 1996). That, too, was not done.

The ARC proposal seriously underestimates the important abiding role of public investment in rail innovation. Passenger rail travel was created only through active, sustained, and sufficient public investment in new technology. The newly constituted NRPC is envisioned to have a planning function, but it is given direct control of neither adequate investment funds with which to implement a plan or any direct operating control of the critical national railbed assets needed to make change. In such situations a planning function is a toothless gesture.

The ARC cited the return of Conrail to private operation as evidence that privatization can work. Overlooked in this were the vast differences between the nature of freight and passenger services and the crucial role of ownership of the rail infrastructure that the freight lines maintained and that passenger rail lost in the reorganizations of the late 1960s. These differences play an important role in explaining the apparent success of one and the difficulties of the other. Historically, rail freight has largely been a profitable enterprise, and once the losses of the 1960s and 1970s caused by shifting national transportation priorities were absorbed through reorganization, Conrail was able to sell a profit-making venture to private owners. The ARC proposal called for Amtrak to yield one of its most valuable assets, ownership of the Northeast Corridor, to some unspecified amalgam of the states that border the line.[10]

In June 2002 the Bush administration's Federal Rail Administration adopted the ARC approach as the policy basis for its five principles of intercity passenger rail. In July 2003 the dismantling of Amtrak became official administration policy. The central principle of the Bush administration's approach identifies Amtrak's organizational structure as the problem. More specifically, it asserts that because Amtrak is a public service with a "monopoly" on rail travel and not a market-driven company, it is an inefficient operation. Because it is inefficient it is losing money. The approach takes as an article of faith the belief that it is possible to restructure what is now run as a public service because of its natural monopoly features into competitive passenger rail "industry."

In economic terms, the Bush proposal seeks to overcome the natural monopoly features of passenger rail by breaking the internal operation into component parts that can be more easily contracted out to different bidders. In essence, the proposal calls for a large increase in the transactions costs of operating intercity passenger rail with absolutely no evidence that the time and money costs of fostering an external interorganizational relationship will be less than the costs of internal reorganization. That is precisely the approach that Great Britain took in the 1990s. Everyone who has examined that disastrous experience with rail privatization has uniformly come to the conclusion that the cause of the implosion was precisely the high transaction costs engendered by the organizational disaggregation that the Conservatives then in power mistook for a market (see, for example, Murray 2001 and Wolmar 2001). The disaster was so bad that the current Conservative shadow secretary of transportation has recently pledged that if the voters of Great Britain return the Tories to power, they will not try to reprivatize the rail system (National Corridors Initiative 2003).

Been There, Done That: The United Kingdom Experience

In the early 1990s British prime minister John Major's government, imbued with an expansive zeal for the transformative powers of competitive markets, attempted a larger version of the present Bush administration proposal. It was the last large privatization initiative of the Conservative governments that ruled the United Kingdom from the late 1970s through 1997. The British Rail privatization spawned twenty-four of the top one hundred corporations on the London Stock Exchange (Shaoul 2001). The British model was more extreme than the present Bush proposal because American railroads had been separated into freight and passenger service in 1971. Moreover, the U.S. freight lines are entirely private. In Great Britain, the challenge involved the devolution of a completely integrated system. In both cases, the underlying idea is the same: A natural monopoly somehow becomes more "competitive," and hence more efficient, when it is broken into smaller, self-interested units operating in negotiated arrangements with one another and governed by marketlike mechanisms. Although the scale is different, an analysis of the British experience can give us insight into the likely change dynamic that will occur if the Bush proposal is implemented.

In a period of about eighteen months, beginning in 1994 and ending in 1996, the United Kingdom's entirely publicly run national freight and passenger rail service, British Rail, was completely transformed into what its designers imagined a "competitive" railroad would look like. The Railways Act of 1993 stipulated that a single public agency, British Rail, was to be transformed into a collection of approximately one hundred independent companies. The newly created companies engage in various aspects of rail service: operation, maintenance, capital investments, and infrastructure improvements. Passenger service was divorced from freight and carved into twenty-five separate passenger train operating companies. These companies staff the trains, sell tickets, and service the train stations, where they are the principal service providers and perform routine maintenance on their rolling stock. But they own no physical assets. They do not own the rolling stock, the stations, the tracks, or the signals. The trains are owned by "rolling-stock leasing companies," which are responsible for heavy maintenance on the rolling stock.

The physical infrastructure of rail beds, signals, and stations are owned by a different entity. Originally, it was a publicly traded corporation known as Railtrack. However, in 2001 the British government placed a bankrupt Railtrack into receivership and turned its assets over to a new not-for-profit entity called Network Rail, established in 2002. The rolling-stock leasing companies, which were the major customers of Railtrack, now Network Rail, negotiate and compensate that entity for use of the infrastructure. These companies, in turn, are expected to recoup their costs through the leasing charges they collect from the train operating companies, which, in turn, recoup their expenses through the fares collected and, because the fare revenue does not cover the full cost of operation, from negotiated subsidies from the government.

Overseeing the entire operation are two direct governmental regulators. Because Railtrack (originally, and now Network Rail) controls the essential strategic core of the entire system and cannot be subdivided into competitive alternatives, it is deemed to be a natural monopoly. To offset this unequal power relationship, the 1993 legislation made provision for the office rail regulator (ORR), "an independent statutory officer appointed by government" (Office of the Rail Regulator 2003, n.p.). The ORR does just what the title describes: he or she adjudicates between the infrastructure monopolist and the rolling-stock leasing companies to ensure that the infrastructure owner is maintaining the system in good order and selling access at fair prices. The regulator expressly does not deal with the consumer protection functions of the system.

That falls to a second overseer, added in 2001, the Strategic Rail Authority, one of whose important functions is to ensure that the various train operating companies fulfill the terms of their franchise agreements and enforce safety and on-time performance requirements. They are empowered to levy fines for noncompliance and can cancel contracts if necessary. The Strategic Rail Authority was not part of the original legislation; it was established when it became clear that important strategic decision making had disappeared from the system. Its mission is to impose important overall strategic public interest direction on this business-oriented agglomeration of companies. The added regulator was established when it became clear that one by-product of the fragmented contracting was that no one was in charge of long-term strategic planning and organizing the subsequent financing for future investment in the entire British railroad system. Such strategic planning was initially thought to be unnecessary because market prices would provide all the needed signals and information for long-term investing. The theory was that Railtrack, as a profit-maximizing entity, would see the benefits of future investments and be motivated to use private capital markets to undertake capital improvements. Moreover, it was assumed that Railtrack, as the profit-seeking owner of the infrastructure, would fully appreciate the real costs of any new investments and hence undertake them efficiently. The train operating and the rolling-stock leasing companies would similarly understand both the broader market-building benefits and the direct future revenue enhancements and hence would support the innovations. Thus market signals, not direct regulation, were supposed to be sufficient to achieve the goal of continual planning and innovation.

This fragmented scheme guided by market signals turned out to be less a textbook exemplar of efficient market allocation than a classic example of moral hazard. Because of the nature of the revenue relationship between the monopolist (originally Railtrack and now Network Rail) and the operating entities, the monopolist has every incentive to overstate the costs and value of improvement to justify higher fees. The operating entities, for their part, have every incentive to understate the benefits to justify lower fees. The net effect is that long-range planning in such a context is an adversarial proceeding adjudicated by a third party with no stake in long-term planning or innovation per se. All that the office of rail regulator can do is determine a structure of fair charges for any new capital investments (Nash 2000). The regulator has not been charged with contemplating the values, uncertainties, and scenarios that a planning agency is supposed to think about. The operational regulator, whose prime responsibility is day-to-day operation in the context of fair present returns to the parties, is perhaps the least able to be in charge of such an important long-term mission, with all its implications for reshaping the structure of transportation options. Markets are never good planning devices because of their need to discount the future heavily in the service of the present.

The repair solution to this in the British situation was the introduction of the Strategic Rail Authority as both a consumer service regulator and a long-term planning agency. How well it will work in practice remains to be seen. Much depends upon the willingness of the government to give it meaningful control over capital investment decisions and defend it against the onslaught of reaction to any decision it makes.

In addition to the problem of long-term planning, the system rapidly revealed a series of major flaws in day-to-day operation. In response to these flaws, the current government has undertaken a series of alterations to the original arrangement that have the net effect of moving it away from the originally envisioned market system and toward a more publicly regulated alternative. It should be emphasized that this turnabout is based on real system failings and not ideology or politics. The New Labor government (the Blair government) is quite comfortable with the privatization schemes originated by their Conservative predecessors. In fact, its 1997 election manifesto was noteworthy for lacking any commitment to renationalize the rail system. Despite widespread criticism, the Blair government is proceeding with its own plan to partially privatize the London underground (Wolmar 2002). The turnaround is rooted in the series of events that quickly followed the implementation of privatization.

In October 1999 two passenger trains traveling through Ladbroke Grove collided, resulting in thirty-one deaths and five hundred injuries. This was the worst rail disaster in the United Kingdom in a decade. A three-hundred-page report indicted Railtrack for its "lamentable failure" to respond to several warnings of problems on the route. Drivers had previously reported that the misread signal that was a central cause of the accident was badly positioned and easy to miss because of overhanging cable and sunlight reflection. The problem had been the subject of a series of meetings between representatives of the train operating companies, Railtrack, and its maintenance contractors. Meetings were followed by letters, and letters were followed by memos, and memos by more meetings in a caricature of the worst kind of bureaucratic buck passing that is supposed to be the exclusive province of public administrators.

The delay in this case was, quite literally, fatal. The report found that the newly recruited thirty-one-year-old driver of Thames Trains had insufficient training and when he set out had only a set of "hand-written notes" describing the train's route. This tragedy forced senior company officials of Thames Trains to admit to "flaws" in their driver recruitment policies. Moreover, had the train been fitted with an automatic braking system, as used elsewhere in Europe, at least the speed at impact might have been reduced, but investment in that safety technology by the rolling-stock leasing companies was an early victim of the cost-cutting pressures demanded by privatization. The Ladbroke Grove crash was not an isolated incident, just the worst. A previous accident earlier in 1999 killed seven people, and it was followed in October 2000 by another derailment, at Hatfield. In this incident, an intercity train traveling at nearly 100 miles per hour derailed and shattered into three hundred pieces, killing four passengers. These tragic events dramatically illustrated the disorganization of service and severe undermaintenance that were direct results of dismantling a unified operating system and then attempting to motivate all the component parts to engage in cost cutting in the name of good business practice. Although these accidents were the most publicly dramatic feature of the failure of the rail privatization, they were in some regards the tip of the iceberg in terms of the ongoing problems of deteriorated day-to-day service.

Railtrack was placed in receivership by the British government in the fall of 2001 after this series of fatal mishaps and a major cash hemorrhage that would have required a massive government bailout to keep it afloat. In July 2002 Railtrack was replaced by Network Rail. Unlike Railtrack, Network Rail is not a publicly traded for-profit corporation. Instead, it is a governmentally chartered not-for-profit similar to the present NRPC in the United States.[11] The alternative for the government would have been to renationalize the infrastructure. However, for a variety of political reasons that was not an appealing alternative for the Blair Government. Instead, they chose a transfer of ownership, as such an arrangement kept the costs of the takeover off the government's books.

The structural cause of Railtrack's bankruptcy was that it was squeezed between the clashing demands of two separate masters: its public service mission as conservator of important public infrastructure and its private corporate mission to earn a competitive profit. As a result, Railtrack became ground zero in the collapse of the entire system. All it took was one train wreck too many. Following the Hatfield crash in October 2000, things began to go from bad to worse for Railtrack. On the one hand, it continued to make dividend payments to shareholders, even though its cash flow position was deteriorating because of its efforts to mollify the capital markets upon which it depended for future investment capital. Thus even as it made its quarterly dividends it was simultaneously seeking £600 million ($1.1 billion) in government subsidies to address the immediate safety requirements exposed by this string of accidents. In October 2001 Railtrack was in a desperate situation. It was in need of a massive infusion of money to meet its obligations, but given its shaky financial condition, it had no access to private markets. The government, seeking to avoid any new debt on its books yet in need of a functioning rail system, forced Railtrack into receivership and created the new quasi-public corporation— Network Rail—to take over the operation.

Network Rail, with a guarantee of government backing in the event of default, secured a £9 billion ($16.65 billion) bridge loan from a syndicate of investment and commercial banks, financed by floating bonds backed by leasing revenues. However, the loan does not include sufficient funding to meet planned increases in both passenger and freight use of the system, an amount estimated at £10 billion ($18.5 billion). In addition, the *Economist* ("Anybody got £15 billion?" January 13, 2002) has estimated that Network Rail needs approximately £1 billion ($1.85 billion) of new working capital. It is not at all clear that leasing revenue and private lenders will meet this need.

With the establishment of Network Rail, the British government has repudiated a core belief of the original privatization. Network Rail takes as its core mission "operating, maintaining and renewing Britain's rail network" (Network Rail 2003b), not earning a profit. The not-for-profit status of the new organization relieves a major mission conflict that dogged Railtrack. Unlike its predecessor, Network Rail is not trapped in a conflict between the profit-seeking interests of shareholders and an important public service mission. Consistent with this newly defined core mission, Network Rail specifically rejects one of the central tenets of the original privatization, namely, that only profit incentives can motivate managers and employees to behave efficiently. Instead, they correctly point out that nonprofit organizations and public agencies have many ways to provide incentives for efficient and effective management and workplace operation (*Railtrack* 2003).

There is some indication that Network Rail, in pursuit of efficiency, is going to begin to maintain its infrastructure directly. Under the original Tory scheme, maintenance companies were supposed to contract competitively with the rail owner to perform infrastructure maintenance. The transactional complexities of managing these relationships are now considered more expensive than the bureaucratic costs of internal provision. According to Network Rail's chief executive officer, John Armitt, taking maintenance back in-house "is a significant step in enabling us to improve the efficiency of maintenance of the rail infrastructure in the future" (Network Rail 2003a, n.p.).

The rationale for the Tory privatization was similar to the Bush rationale, namely, that the system of public ownership is always inherently flawed. However, in 1994, the year that the Tories moved forward with their radical privatization scheme, British Rail was not in bad shape by many objective measures. Its labor productivity, perennially the highest in Europe, increased between 1976 and 1994 as the system's labor force shrunk by about one-third. It was also the least subsidized system in Europe. In 1976, 26 percent of its revenues came from government grants; by 1994, that figure had fallen to 15 percent (Shaoul 2001).

Fares on British Rail, always the highest in Europe, began to rise rapidly as the new private owners sought to extract more revenue from the system. Between June 1995 and March 1999, average fare increases exceeded the 12 percent rate of inflation in that time period. On some lines the increase was as much as 30 percent (Keith Harper, "Rail fares speed ahead of inflation," *Guardian,* March 13, 1999, p. 9). There were serious problems with on-time performance and system reliability. In August 1999 passenger complaints had increased 27 percent in one year and more than 154 percent in the previous two years (Barrie Clement, "Rail complaints rise by nearly 30%," *Guardian,* August 19, 1999, p. 11). As a result of the fragmentation of the system into many lines with different business models and goals, the private rail operators were unable to coordinate schedules among themselves for the benefit of travelers needing to make connections.

The cost cutting had a direct impact on maintenance, and the problem was noticeable even to casual riders.[12] The cause of this change was a decrease in the size of the workforce. Between 1992 and 1997 the total number of employees on the British system fell from 159,000 to 92,000. Infrastructure maintenance staff fell from 31,000 to between 15,000 and 19,000 (Jack Ian, "Breaking point," *Guardian,* April 3, 2001, p. 4). As a result, the incidence of breakdowns increased and maintenance of even crucial systems became lax, and it was just a matter of time before that translated into the series of fatalities previously described.

The system at present gives the public sector the worst of two worlds. On the one hand, the government has to make up any shortfalls because railroads provide vital public service. On the other hand, given the complex set of interorganizational arrangements government must now work through to achieve any policy goal, it has little control over system costs. The best present estimates are that subsidy demands from the train operating companies will rise significantly over the next several years in response to the pressures to upgrade performance and safety and the need to keep fares reasonable.

When looked at in the aggregate, it is clear that government is moving inexorably, if somewhat reluctantly, away from privatization and toward the imposition of a mixed system guided by strong and active public regulation. At the end of the day, what Great Britain will have is a better-funded version of the present Amtrak system. Its exact contours will be shaped by the unique history of that system. The move away from privatization that is now taking place will not result in a return to the older nationalized railroad, but it will create one with extensive public control, public investment, and public subsidy.

At this time the organizational form of passenger rail service in Great Britain is a work in progress. However, the underlying structural issues are sufficiently known that the more regulated system that is emerging will clearly be better than the disjointed privatized system it is replacing. In a larger sense, however, it is not clear that it will necessarily be better than the older nationalized system. The new system will most likely be different from the old in terms of relative strengths and weaknesses. Most striking among the differences is that its higher degree of transactional complexity will require a far higher level of expenditure on external regulation. Moreover, as the government moves toward establishing systemwide stability and reliability, any hope for the use of competitive contracting as an efficiency check will most likely also fade, as the costs of "churning" providers—if there are truly any at all— are likely to be offset by sufficient gains in system efficiency. Instead, what will occur is that the contracted operations created by the Tories in hopes of evoking "competition" will be transformed by Labor into a de facto, if not de jure, ongoing series of cost-plus franchise arrangements. What is also clear is that the new mixed system is certainly not less expensive for government. According to one estimate, over the next four years alone the British rail system will need as much as £15 billion ($27.75 billion) (*Economist,* "Anybody got £15 billion?" January 13, 2002). However, given the confusing state of affairs, no one knows for sure whether this is the outside limit.[13]

One of the major outcomes of this change was the devaluation of the larger public mission of public service from a primary to a secondary goal. Each of the new profit-seeking companies that now manages a piece of the process has a primary fiduciary concern with cost minimization in the face of its contractually derived income. This is, of course, consistent with a larger goal of maximizing shareholder value. The public service mission that is central to a national railroad system became of necessity secondary to the individual suppliers.

The entire British Rail privatization arrangement is similar to a symphony orchestra in which the various musicians enter into contracts with one another in deciding how to perform a musical work. The principal problem is that the need for contracting among actors with far different stakes in the system causes everything to work poorly. The principal problem in both the British situation and the proposed American one is a misidentification of the challenge. In both instances, key policy makers, viewing the problem through ideological lenses, defined it as a matter of organizational inefficiency brought on by lack of competitive pressure. They viewed the symptoms as the cause. The primary problem is structural. Passenger rail service requires public subsidy. If we are not prepared to do without it, then we need to fully embrace this reality. To the extent that we desire quality improvements, the problem is one of adequate investment in relation to the desired goal. While there is always room for more efficiency in every operation, and contracting has a part to play, these are secondary problems. Where competition is an inappropriate market structure, attaining efficiency by forcing competition is the wrong approach. Furthermore, where future investments and economic development are key public concerns, actors responding to day-to-day price signals will not necessarily make the type of long-range decisions in the face of uncertainty that a public agency with a longer time horizon might more reasonably make.

Some Concluding Observations

The present debate about privatization of the railroad industry is framed in terms of the relative merits of market governance versus those of public supply. In the context of a service that because of its infrastructure is inherently a natural monopoly, that debate makes little sense without a clearer discussion of its context. In the end, the success or failure of the policy will depend heavily on the quality of the regulation and the degree of investment in the system. The danger in debates over operation cut loose from these larger substantive contextual considerations is that they lead the policy discussion down a path that will potentially waste resources in the short run and time in the long run. It is a debate in which the subject that is the focus of concern, the interstate passenger rail system, takes a back seat to an ideological need to "prove" that markets do a better job of serving the public interest than public oversight. In reality, each has a place, but context must be the determining factor.

Based on experience from all over the world, it is clear that it really does not matter whether the passenger trains themselves are run directly by a quasi-public entity such as Amtrak, a private monopoly, or some combination of several private providers. The critical factor in terms of the viability and quality of the service is the quality and effectiveness of the public regulatory structure that is imposed on the chosen delivery configuration. There can be no "free" entry and exit of suppliers into and out of this system. Consequently, if we want a well-used system of intercity passenger rail service, we must recognize that the rail lines themselves are a natural monopoly similar to the electric power grid. There can be many generators of power, but there is only one grid, and the key to transmitting that power efficiently is an effective public regulator. In a similar vein, whether there are one or many providers of actual train trips, there is only one rail grid over which they can traverse. Thus while many trains run by many different suppliers over the same set of tracks is conceptually possible, it is economically dubious. In choosing among the alternatives, then, the critical question for policy makers concerns the comparative transactions costs of the various alternatives. To date, that analysis has not been done in the promulgation of the present proposal.

Based on recent British experience, which is heading in the direction of something akin to the present Amtrak, the wisest course forward is not the abandonment of Amtrak in its current organizational form but rather working with it in highly specific ways to improve aspects of its organization. History matters, and institutional experience is an important form of public capital. These assets should be leveraged and not discarded unless the organization is egregiously and hopelessly incompetent. No one has made that case in the present debate. Indeed, the only charge against Amtrak is that it needs subsidy. But what major rail system anywhere in the world does not need subsidy?

The crucial issue facing Amtrak is not its competence but the lack of an effective plan for upgrading, maintaining, and managing the entire system of rail "roads" and investing in modern rolling stock. To call for such a plan and such investment is to call for no more than the approach we take to maintaining a system of highways to which many different suppliers of freight and passenger services have access.

The experience of Great Britain is instructive in this regard. The Strategic Rail Authority now closely monitors the on-time performance of all the individual service providers. While there is variance in how well they do vis-à-vis one another, these differences are slight. For example, in a recent audit, Midland Mainline's on-time performance deteriorated from 76.3 percent to 74.5 percent, while Virgin West Coast's rose from 77.4 percent to 78.2 percent (Robert Wright, "Long-distance train time-keeping worsens," *London Financial Times,* September 20–21, 2003, p. 4). However, these are variations around the basic level of infrastructure quality that is completely determined by the actions or inactions of Network Rail. Stewart Francis, the chairman of the Rail Passengers' Council, echoes the concerns of Richard Bowker, the Strategic Rail Authority chairman, when he notes, "We welcome the good efforts by many train companies to boost their performance, but further analysis of these figures shows that *Network Rail's performance is deteriorating and it is the ongoing problems with tracks and signals which are holding back progress*" (quoted in Robert Wright, "Long-distance train time-keeping worsens," *London Financial Times,* September 20–21, 2003, p. 4, emphasis added).

Finally, the issue must be reframed at a macroscopic level as well. The present debate makes an implicit assumption that passenger rail service can be viewed in isolation from alternative modes of transportation. That is to say, passenger trains as a mode of travel should "compete" with automobiles and planes for intercity passenger business. Thus not only should passenger train companies compete with one another, but the aggregate railroad industry itself should compete with other industries for the same intercity customer base.

This view is entirely consistent with an approach that makes competition the central goal of public policy. But if our central goal is not competition per se but rather overall transportation efficiency and equity in moving people between cities, then a focus on competition stands a high probability of being destructive rather than constructive.

An alternative framing, and one that I advocate, views modes of intercity travel not as competitors but as complements to one another. That reframing places an emphasis on ensuring a great deal of intermodal connectivity among the alternatives. High-speed trains should connect not only between cities but between outlying airports and city centers. This is increasingly the case in other developed countries. High-speed rail now takes travelers from Heathrow Airport to Paddington Station in fifteen minutes. From Paddington Station, travelers can connect to the rest of Great Britain by rail or reach any part of metropolitan London by the underground or by taxi. The Metro Park station in New Jersey, along Amtrak's Northeast Corridor, permits motorists to park and board an intercity train that can take them south to Philadelphia, Wilmington, Baltimore, or Washington or north to New York, New Haven, Providence, or Boston. It can also give them access to a commuter rail network heading either to New York or to Philadelphia. The larger the burden that rail can take from highways and aviation, the better these modes can do in fulfilling their functions without congestion. In the case of aviation this is particularly important, as it removes pressure to build new runways and airports for which the environmental costs and political opposition can be formidable if not totally prohibitive. But if we are to capture these advantages, we must reorient our own thinking. Markets do many things well, but they do many things poorly. Any debate that totalizes issues of service delivery into an either-or context at best promises delay and avoidable costs and at worst can hasten environmental disasters and cripple the economy.

I would like to acknowledge the help of my research assistants, Christine Grimando, Ana Puszkin-Chevlin, Robert Chevlin, and Elizabeth Currid.

Notes

1. Although the substantive case material in this chapter is drawn from experience with intercity passenger rail service, the lessons, by analogy, apply more generally to other services with similar private and social characteristics.
2. I am grateful to Jean Shaoul for this insightful point.
3. Moreover, it should be noted that regular peak users, for whom system capacity is built and who therefore should pay the highest user charges, are given a price that discounts or "commutes" the charges they pay.

4. The farebox recovery ratio is the proportion of total costs recovered through direct user charges.
5. This excludes commuter trains, which Amtrak also operates on contract in certain corridors.
6. "Both companies were to receive ten alternate sections of public lands (increased to twenty sections in 1864) for each mile of track. In addition, each of the two lines received a thirty-year government loan in United States bonds. The amount of the loan per mile of track varied with the terrain, $16,000 per mile being granted across the plains, $48,000 per mile for the high mountain area, and $32,000 per mile for the plateau region between the Rockies and the Sierras. Both the Union Pacific and the Central Pacific were permitted to issue first-mortgage bonds up to the amount of the government loan or subsidy" (Stover 1997, 64).
7. Part of the agreement between the federal government and the freight lines was that Amtrak's trains would be permitted to use the lines at marginal cost, which was close to zero. If some version of the Bush proposal is ever put into effect, there is no guarantee that the monopoly owners of the existing rail lines will cut the new entity as favorable an arrangement.
8. Of course, one could plausibly argue that this breakout of tasks is arbitrary. After all, it is the combination of rail beds and rolling stock that generates rail service. Why slice it at the point where the wheels meet the tracks?
9. For a more complete discussion of the reasons for this, see Elliott Sclar (2000).
10. A key recommendation of the ARC is that Amtrak yield control of the Northeast Corridor to the several states it runs through. Once more, there is no apparent explanation for why this fragmentation would be better than unitary management in the context of creating a high-speed system. However, if one believes that fragmentation is analogous to competition, it makes some sense as an explanation, though it is still wrong as a theory.
11. In British terminology it is a "company limited by guarantee." Although its mission is to earn a surplus of revenues over costs, the intention is not to distribute them as profits but to reinvest them "in improvements in the infrastructure" (*Railtrack* 2003, n.p.).
12. "I began to notice weeds . . . that grew . . . to the size of small shrubs" (Jack Ian, "Breaking Point," *Guardian,* April 3, 2001, p. 4).
13. Four months later, the *Economist* ("Make me an offer," May 25, 2002, p. 34) pushed the estimate up to £20 billion ($37 billion).

References

American Association of State Highway and Transportation Officials (AASHTO). 2002. *Intercity Passenger Rail Transportation.* Washington, D.C: AASHTO.

Amtrak Reform Council. 2002a. "An Action Plan for the Restructuring and Rationalization of the National Intercity Rail Passenger System." Report to U.S. Congress. Washington, D.C.: Amtrak Reform Council.

———. 2002b. "Today, the Amtrak Reform Council releases its action plan for the restructuring and rationalization of the national railroad passenger system."

Press release, February 7. Available at: www.amtrakreformcouncil.gov/report/pressrel.html (accessed November 17, 2004).

Chamber of Business and Industry of Center County (CBICC). 2001. "Hopes float again for mag-lev connection: high speed trains across commonwealth?" *Chambernet* 901(September–October). Available at: www.cbicc.org/newsletters/sepoct01.pdf and www.cbicc.org/newsletter.asp?ID=329 (accessed January 5, 2003).

Fishlow, Albert. 1965. *American Railroads and the Transformation of the Ante-Bellum Economy.* Cambridge, Mass.: Harvard University Press.

Fogel, Robert W. 1964. *Railroads and American Economic Growth: Essays in Econometric History.* Baltimore: Johns Hopkins University Press.

Gunn, David L. 2003. Testimony Before the House Committee on Appropriations, Subcommittee on Transportation, Treasury, and Independent Agencies. April 10, 2003. 108th Congress.

Kolko, Gabriel. 1963. *The Triumph of Conservatism: A Reinterpretation of American History, 1900–1916.* New York: Free Press of Glencoe.

———. 1970. *Railroads and Regulation, 1877–1916.* New York: W. W. Norton.

Mead, Kenneth. 2002. Statement before the U.S. Senate Committee on Commerce, Science, and Transportation. March 14, 2002.

Murray, Andrew. 2001. *Off the Rails: The Crisis of Britain's Railways.* London: Verso.

Nash, C. A. 2000. "Privatisation and Deregulation in Railways: An Assessment of the British Approach." In *Privatisation and Deregulation of Transport,* edited by William Bradshaw and Helen Lawton Smith. London: Macmillan.

National Association of Railroad Passengers (NARP). 2002. "Modern Passenger Trains: A National Necessity." Report. Washington, D.C.: NARP.

———. 2003. "Debunking Common Myths About Amtrak." Washington, D.C.: NARP. Available at: http://www.narprail.org/default.asp?p=home%2Ehtm (accessed November 17, 2004).

National Corridors Initiative. 2003. "Tories won't reprivatize rail." *Destination Freedom Newsletter,* January 7. Available at: nationalcorridors.org/df/df01062003.shtml#Tories (accessed November 17, 2004)

National Railroad Passenger Corporation (NRPC). 2000. "On-time Performance." In *Amtrak Annual Report,* statistical appendix. Washington, D.C.: NRPC.

Network Rail. 2003a. "Network Rail to take direct responsibility for maintenance in the reading area." Available at: www.networkrail.co.uk/pressoffice/pressreleases.asp?newsId=17B5AA77-04E5-4A75-897A-CA129EC9CE93 (accessed February 7, 2003).

———. 2003b. "Welcome to Network Rail." Available at: www.railtrack.co.uk and www.railtrack.co.uk/our_business/qa.cfm (accessed February 7, 2003).

Office of the Rail Regulator. 2003. "About the ORR." Available at: www.rail-reg.gov.uk/server/show/nav.001008 (accessed November 17, 2004).

Railtrack. 2003. "Many companies successfully incentivise staff without share option schemes." *Railtrack.* February 3. Available at: www.railtrack.co.uk/our_business/qa.cfm (accessed February 7, 2003).

Schaeffer, K. H., and Elliott Sclar. 1980. *Access for All: Transportation and Urban Growth.* New York: Columbia University Press.

Sclar, Elliott. 2000. *You Don't Always Get What You Pay For: The Economics of Privatization.* Ithaca, N.Y.: Cornell University Press.

Shaoul, Jean. 2001. "Britain: Railtrack collapse sparks political crisis." Available at: www.wsws.org/articles/2001/oct2001/rail-o22.shtml (accessed February 7, 2003).

Stover, John. 1997. *American Railroads.* Chicago: University of Chicago Press.

Travel Industry Association of America. 2004. "TIA Research: Travel Forecasts." Available at: http://www.tia.org/travel/travelforecast.asp (accessed November 3, 2004).

U.S. Department of Transportation. 1996. Bureau of Transportation Statistics. *Annual Report.* Washington: U.S. Department of Transportation.

———. 1997. Bureau of Transportation Statistics. "1995 American Travel Survey Profile." BTS/ATS95-US. Washington: U.S Department of Transportation (October).

———. 2003a. Bureau of Transportation Statistics. "Carrier payments." Available at: www.dot.gov/affairs/carrierpayments.htm (accessed December 7, 2003).

———. 2003b. Bureau of Transportation Statistics. "Scheduled Intercity Transportation: Rural Service Areas in the United States." Available at: www.bts.gov/products/scheduled_intercity_transportation_and_the_us_rural_population/ (accessed August 7, 2003).

———. 2003c. Federal Highway Administration. "Target: $27 Billion: The 1955 Estimate." Available at: www.fhwa.dot.gov/infrastructure/target.htm (accessed August 7, 2003).

Williamson, Oliver. 1996. *The Mechanisms of Governance.* New York: Oxford University Press.

Wolmar, Christian. 2001. *Broken Rails: How Privatisation Wrecked Britain's Railways.* London: Aurum Press.

———. 2002. *Down the Tube: The Battle for London's Underground.* London: Aurum Press.

Xinhuanet News Agency. 2003. "Le train 'Mag lev' " de Shanghai: exemple d'une étroite coopération germano-chinoise, selon M. Schroeder." Available at: http://202.84.17.11/French/htm/12311544421.htm (accessed November 3, 2004).

5

FINANCIAL CLEARING SYSTEMS

John A. James and David F. Weiman

OLLOWING its establishment in 1913, the Federal Reserve Bank (the Fed) assumed dual roles. In addition to the traditional central-bank functions of bank regulator and lender of last resort, it entered the market for the clearing and settlement of check transactions with the goal of forging a more efficient, integrated national payments system (Spahr 1926; Stevens 1996). Since this initial foray into the payments system, the Fed has extended its reach in both the clearing and settlement markets. Alongside its regional check clearinghouses, the Fed operates a national automated clearinghouse (ACH), providing an electronic alternative to retail check payments. Additionally, it furnishes net settlement services to private clearinghouses and a book-entry system for storing and transferring U.S. government and related securities.

Paralleling debates in other network industries, economists and policy makers have increasingly questioned the extent of the Fed's direct intervention in payments markets. Their focus has been on the greater involvement of the central bank in check-clearing and ACH markets, as compared with the more private systems in other Group of Ten countries. Advocates of deregulation or privatization point to comparative and historical evidence to demonstrate the viability of a more private system (Weinberg 1997; Lacker, Walker, and Weinberg 1999; Kroszner 2000). Moreover, they argue, recent economic, political, and technological changes have opened up potential markets for the private provision of payments services and so diminished the Fed's share.[1] Some have even taken aim at the Fed's discount window, which competes directly with the private federal funds market in the allocation of liquidity among banks (Goodfriend and King 1988; Kaufman 1991; Schwartz 1992).

In 1980 Congress partially resolved the matter by passing the Monetary Control Act (MCA), which both recognized and sought to decouple the Fed's dual roles. The MCA finally mandated universal access to the Fed's clearing and settlement networks and subjected all depository institutions to uniform standards like reserve requirements.[2] At the same time, the act treated the Fed like a regulated monopoly in the provision of payment services. The Fed could no longer subsidize its products with surpluses earned in markets protected by its central-bank authority. Instead, its prices had to cover all "direct and indirect costs" as well as imputed charges for "the taxes that would have been paid and the return on capital that would have been provided had the services been furnished by a private business firm."[3]

The Federal Reserve Board, in turn, translated this legislative mandate into a market survivor test to determine the scope of the Fed's direct intervention in the payments system.[4] According to the test, the Fed should exit existing markets, where it lacked competitive advantage as evidenced by declining market share or chronic losses. Similarly, the test would justify Fed entry into emerging markets only if it could expect to operate as efficiently as private suppliers and so satisfy the criterion of full cost recovery, including the private sector markup. The board did, however, admit to a public interest exception, justifying Fed intervention if it would yield significant social benefits, such as universal access to critical payment services, or bolster the integrity of the payments system.

In principle, the new policy regime drew a stark line between the private and public sectors in the payments system, with a clear nod in favor of the former. In the absence of any compelling social benefits or large political-economic barriers to entry, it regards the private sector as the default option in existing and emerging markets. So, for example, the Fed can supply payment services, but only when it enjoys economies of scale and scope or it is necessary to supply "an adequate level of services nationwide" (Federal Reserve Board of Governors 1990, n.p.).[5]

The critical question, of course, is whether in practice the Fed's more market oriented policies can achieve a sharp separation between the public and private sectors in the payments system. Our answer is firmly no, because Fed (or, more generally, public) intervention is a necessary condition to constitute essential payments systems.[6] To put our point another way, we argue that for essential payments services, the public interest exception trumps the market logic and so warrants the Fed's continued direct intervention in two areas. The first corresponds to a core central-bank function as a lender of last resort. The second is more novel and conceives the Fed as a standards coordinator and clearinghouse of last resort in essential payments networks.

Making Payments

The payments system is a complex of financial instruments and relationships that quite literally grease the wheels of commerce, that is, transfer value (or good funds) between buyers and sellers to complete their transactions. Cash is considered the simplest means of payment. Cash transactions directly transfer good funds from buyer to seller and so constitute final settlement without

FIGURE 5.1   *Check Transactions and the Circulation of Deposits*

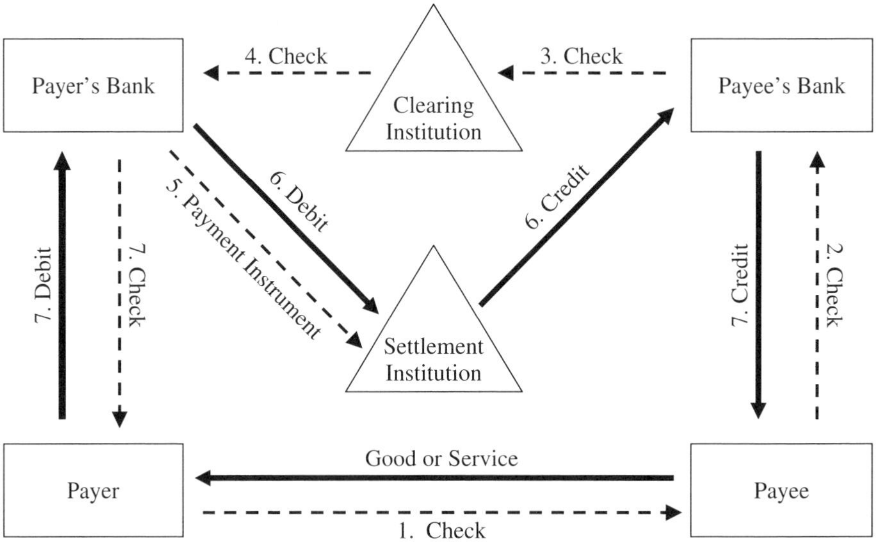

Source: Authors' compilation.

mediation by third parties.[7] Most transactions, especially in developed economies, involve noncash payments instruments like checks or credit card receipts. Unlike cash, they represent payment orders directing intermediaries to transfer good funds to each party's transactions account.[8]

The use of noncash instruments in the payments process typically involves several steps referred to as clearing and settlement. The former corresponds to the transmission of the payment order to the buyer's intermediary, its verification and approval, and the calculation of interbank payment obligations. Settlement involves the reverse delivery of funds to the seller's intermediary and the crediting and debiting of the party's account.[9] Each step, in turn, corresponds to distinct services supplied by payments intermediaries (Juncker, Summers, and Young 1991; CBO 1996, 3–4; Bank of Canada 1997, 12–21).

Consider the familiar case of a check transaction that transfers deposits through the banking system (see figure 5.1). Banks furnish individual and business customers with access to this payments system through deposits lodged in transactions accounts. Bank customers make and receive payments by writing and depositing checks (steps 1 and 2).[10] Another layer of intermediaries supply banks with the remaining services, which effectively knit them into a system. The payee's bank forwards the check to a clearing institution (step 3)—a correspondent or clearinghouse—which transmits the item physically or electronically to the paying bank (step 4). The paying bank verifies and approves the check and then authorizes payment by issuing an order to the settlement institution (step 5).[11] The settlement institution completes the transaction by debiting and crediting the accounts of the two banks (step 6), which in turn debit and credit their customers' accounts (step 7).

As the figure illustrates, the payments system operates at two levels. We focus on interbank transactions and markets because they are the primary domain of central-bank intervention in the United States and other developed countries. The Fed, in particular, provides the full range of interbank payments services. It operates clearinghouses for check and retail electronic payments. It also operates an electronic large-value funds transfer system known as the Fedwire, which processes interbank payments by debiting and crediting banks' reserve accounts at the Fed.[12] The Fedwire also supplies funds transfer or settlement services for other interbank intermediaries like private clearinghouses and correspondents and depository and transfer services for U.S. government and related securities.[13]

In each of these markets the Fed faces competition from the private sector and so forms but one facet in a more complex public-private system. The extent and nature of competition in each segment and hence its market structure vary greatly. At one extreme the markets for settlement services are virtual duopolies, in which the Fed competes against joint ventures of financial institutions—CHIPS (Clearing House Interbank Payment System) in the large-value funds transfer market and DTC (Depository Trust Company) in the securities depository and transfer markets. CHIPS, for example, both complements and competes with the Fedwire. It mediates the domestic leg of international transactions, which are outside the Fed's domain, but also clears and settles domestic transactions between its members—either on their own account or for their customer banks. The extent of competition or degree of substitution between CHIPS and Fedwire services is limited, at least in the short-run, because of significant differences in their organizational structures and operating procedures.[14] It is greater, however, for the largest domestic and international banks, located mainly in the Second (New York) Federal Reserve district. Because of their greater size and geographical scope, they can take advantage of and afford the fixed costs of CHIPS membership (Biehl, McAndrews, and Stefanadis 2002, 25–27).[15]

The check-clearing market lies at the other end of the spectrum. It embraces myriad arrangements, from direct bilateral transactions between banks to correspondent relationships and joint ventures of local banks. Table 5.1 presents evidence from a 1998 Federal Reserve System report by the Committee on the Federal Reserve in the Payments Mechanisms, informally known as the Rivlin Committee and a more recent study by the Federal Reserve Retail Payments Research Project (FRS 1998; 2002) illustrating the relative importance of each type. Excluding transactions between customers of the same bank,

TABLE 5.1   The Fed in the Check-Clearing Market, 1996 and 2000

Clearing System	1996		2000			
	Volume (Billions of Checks)	Share of Volume (Percentage)	Volume (Billions of Checks)	Share of Volume (Percentage)	Value (Trillions of U.S. Dollars)	Share of Value (Percentage)
Federal Reserve	16	35 to 37%	17.223	50.1%	$14.625	49.4%
Private clearinghouse	10 to 11	23 to 24	10.002	29.1	8.318	28.1
Direct presentment	6	14				
Correspondent	10 to 11	23 to 24				
Bankers' bank	Less than 1	1				
Third-party provider	Less than 1	1				
Same-day settlement			4.779	13.9	3.881	13.1
Other			2.402	7.0	2.785	9.4

Source: Data from FRS (1998, 14; 2002, 31–32).
Note: Same-day settlement refers to checks presented directly to banks for collection before 8:00 a.m. and so eligible for collection or settlement on the same day.

estimated to be 30 percent of all payments, the Fed clearinghouses handled 35 to 37 percent of the volume of check transactions in 1996 and one-half of both the volume and the value of check transactions in 2000.[16] Thus approximately one-half to two-thirds of the clearing business was mediated by the private sector. Private clearinghouses accounted for approximately one-quarter of all check clearings, and a significant fraction were cleared through correspondents and direct presentment.[17]

The ACH market combines elements of the other two. Like the check-clearing market, it includes twenty-three regional payment associations, joint ventures of local banks, and large corporate users.[18] Few, however, operate their own networks; most instead rely on the Fed and other private national vendors to process ACH transactions. The Fed was the first mover in this market, but in the mid-1990s it faced entry by three private organizations, two based on regional clearinghouses and one on the Visa credit card association. Intense "competitive pressure" over the past year has winnowed the number down to one, the Electronic Payments Network, which, like CHIPS, is a subsidiary of the New York Clearing House (EPN 2003, 14).[19]

Missing from our discussion is any mention of the systems for clearing the growing nexus of "plastic" credit and debit card payments.[20] By conscious decision, the Fed had delegated these markets to the private sector, as joint ventures of mainly depository institutions. The most familiar are the dominant Visa and MasterCard credit card associations. Together, they process more than three-quarters of all credit card transactions through vast electronic networks connecting terminals in retail outlets to depository institutions (Evans and Schmalensee 1999, 173–75; Thomson Media 2002).

Reflecting their origins in and joint use by regional ATM (automated teller machine) networks, the clearing systems for debit card transactions are more decentralized. In 2001 there were twenty-five point-of-sale regional networks for transferring funds electronically. Still, the evidence indicates a tendency toward increasing concentration in this sector, as well. Despite the rapid diffusion of merchant terminals in the 1990s, the number of networks declined by almost 50 percent, and the largest five regional networks accounted for more than 90 percent of all transactions in 2001 (Evans and Schmalensee 1999, 311; BIS 2002; Thomson Media 2002, 32–36).[21] Moreover, we are currently witnessing the convergence of credit and debit card systems into a more integrated, national electronic retail payments system (BIS 1999; Evans and Schmalensee 1999).

Network Perspectives on the Payments System

Like the other vital infrastructure analyzed in this section, payments systems are economic networks, consisting of links that transmit information and funds between the nodes (Economides 1993, 1996; McAndrews 1997). Debit and credit card systems, for example, are organized into familiar hub-and-spoke networks in which the nodes—a merchant card reader and the acquiring bank—are connected to a central switch through telecommunications lines. The switch, operated by the joint-venture ATM or credit card association, mediates all interbank transactions. The clearing and settlement of check transactions through a private clearinghouse has a similar centralized structure.[22] In this case, however, the links consist of physical transport and communications lines but also less tangible contractual relationships that constitute the joint venture.

Regardless of its structure, the critical or defining feature of an economic network is the strong complementary relationships among the various components. The synergies between nodes and their corresponding links are the most obvious. An automated teller machine and the communications line connecting it to the central switch must operate in tandem to deliver payment services—a cash withdrawal from a bank account or funds transfers between accounts. As important, complementarities between distinct and even competing nodes can bolster the transmission of information and funds throughout the network and so yield pervasive externalities as well as market failures. In a shared ATM network like NYCE or PULSE, for example, a bank's investments in new ATM locations will benefit other members, whose customers will have more convenient access to their deposit accounts.

The example of the shared ATM network illustrates what is termed a demand externality. Put simply, it implies that a vaster network with more ATMs in convenient locations will enhance the value of deposit accounts and hence the willingness of customers to pay for member banks' deposit services.[23] The externality depends on all members adopting compatible ATM technologies to ensure the smooth, rapid flow of information through the network, regardless of origination and destination points—the ATM and the cardholder's bank, respectively. Under this condition, a customer can send a payment message to his or her bank from any ATM in the network and receive immediate authorization for the transaction. The extent of the benefit also depends on banks' operating policies. For example, high surcharges on "foreign" ATM transactions can discourage customers from using the ATMs of other member banks and so diminish the value of the demand externality.

A second, liquidity externality derives from the complementary flows of funds through vaster, more centralized networks for settling banks' mutual claims.[24] By liquidity we mean the capacity of banks to meet depositors' withdrawal demands at minimum cost and risk.[25] Banks generally fund these outflows from three sources: excess reserves, current inflows of payments, and short-term (overnight) loans from other banks and, if necessary, the Fed. With the recent diffusion of ATMs, for example, banks now hold larger excess reserves of vault cash to satisfy customers' more frequent cash withdrawals.

The largest liquidity demands in value terms are banks' payments to other banks in final settlement of their customers' check and other noncash transactions. Depending on the size and scope of the settlement network, these interbank payments can be more or less self-financing. In other words, they can make lesser or greater demands on banks' reserve balances and, if necessary, their holdings of other, more liquid assets. A bank could fully fund its interbank payments from this source if, over the settlement period, it could accumulate an equal value of claims on other member banks. At the end of the period it would simply offset its due-to items with those due from other banks.

Banks can enjoy the liquidity benefits of mutually offsetting payments and receipts even when their own are not sufficiently synchronized over each settlement period so that their total settlement credits just match their total debits. Facing transitory deficits, they can liquidate secondary reserve holdings or, what amounts to the same thing, borrow excess reserves from other member banks in the overnight federal funds market, for example.[26] Under normal conditions, larger, more economically diverse settlement networks will support a more robust funds market, one in which banks can rely on adequate supplies of excess reserves and so collectively minimize their costly reserve holdings.[27] The greater network size and scope imply that interbank payments will be more complementary, that is, less correlated in time. By effectively pooling the reserves of all member banks, the funds market smooths out idiosyncratic fluctuations in banks' net positions and so ensures a more stable aggregate supply of reserves (Economides and Siow 1988, 10; Weinberg 1997, 38–39; Kashyap, Rajan, and Stein 2002).

In addition to enhancing banks' payments services, demand and liquidity externalities foster the concentration of clearing and settlement markets among a small number of networks. In late-nineteenth-century America, for example, their combined impacts centralized the holding of correspondent balances in New York and, to a lesser extent, in regional metropolises (Myers 1931, 229–31; Conzen 1977; Odell and Weiman 1998; James and Weiman 2003).[28] A New York correspondent greatly facilitated the clearing and settlement of check transactions, especially between distant banks with limited direct interactions. Instead of more costly and risky forms of direct presentment through express agents, banks could remit checks to their New York correspondent for collection and then settle the resulting claims through ledger entries to their correspondent accounts. The spatial concentration of correspondent balances in New York banks also enhanced their liquidity as reserves and so reinforced their dominant position in the payments system.[29]

Although Fed clearinghouses have largely displaced New York banks in mediating interregional transactions, private correspondent banks and the same agglomeration economies continue to operate at the regional level (see Gilbert 1983).[30] The extent of concentration is even greater in electronic payments networks, where demand and liquidity externalities reinforce large economies of scale. The evidence on scale effects comes mainly from econometric studies of the Fed's payments services (Bauer and Ferrier 1996; Adams, Bauer, and Sickles 2002). Still, the recent rapid consolidation in ATM and ACH markets attests to their force in the private sector.

The development and smooth, stable functioning of payments systems depends on some form of conscious coordination and regulation to harness network effects. The value of coordination—that is, the impact of demand and liquidity externalities—can be best shown by its absence. The fragmentation of retail intermediaries because of incompatible standards would limit the convenience value of the payments instrument and hence its adoption as a general means of payment. This fate applies even to legal tender, such as the Susan B. Anthony dollar, which did not fit in most vending machines and so could be used only in over-the-counter transactions, where it competed directly with the lighter and more familiar paper dollar (Caskey and St. Laurent 1994).

Even (and perhaps especially) within an integrated payments system, the lack of synchronization of funds transfers can result in a maldistribution of liquidity and payments system gridlock. This condition, as James McAndrews and Samira Rajan (2000) show, regularly occurs in the Fedwire, as banks delay payments until the end of the day to economize on intraday liquidity costs (Angelini 1998; Kahn and Roberds 2001a). More severe disruptions occur when a large bank with large due-to obligations (or correspondent balances) defaults or when vital communications networks are jammed (Garber and Weisbrod 1992, 540–41; McAndrews and Potter 2002). These instances of operational and systemic risk can propagate liquidity shortages throughout the payments system, resulting in a self-reinforcing spiral of contraction.

Our analysis also implies a significant role for regulatory intervention to ensure equal, competitive access to payments networks. The problem of market power typically afflicts network industries like payments systems because they are prone to higher levels of market concentration.[31] It is particularly acute when the vertically related segments of the industry converge on a bottleneck facility, defined as one that supplies an essential input for successful entry into adjacent markets. Under these conditions, dominant firms can lever their control over the critical input to gain market power in related competitive markets.

The most notable recent antitrust cases involving vertical foreclosure have come from the telecommunications and computer industries. Still, the payments system has had its share of high-profile cases, notably, in private credit card market. The dominant MasterCard and Visa associations have faced frequent charges of tying arrangements to limit competitive entry into existing markets and to extend their dominance into new electronic payments markets. A more relevant case, however, involved the fledgling ACH network and implicated the Fed itself. In 1977 the Department of Justice successfully applied the "essential facilities" doctrine against two regional ACH associations that sought to wield network access as a means to thwart the competitive entry of thrift institutions into the check payments market (Kuprianov 1985, 28–30). This case figured significantly in subsequent congressional deliberations over access to and the pricing of Fed payment services, leading to the passage of the Monetary Control Act.

The last issue relates to but transcends the problems of market failure and market power. As a cumulative process, the diffusion of payments systems is often slow and uneven and in its wake can strand communities and individuals for extended periods of time. More conscious coordination and rigorous antitrust enforcement mitigate these "divides" by fully realizing the potential externalities from robust access competition.[32] These interventions cannot, however, overcome entry barriers owing to critical mass effects that tend to limit access in more sparsely settled, lower-income communities.

The solution to the problem depends, of course, on the nature of the service and suggests an alternative, broader conception of essential facility. The limited diffusion of ATMs, for example, may inconvenience individuals, who must rely more on bank offices and perhaps banking hours for cash withdrawals. By contrast, costly or unreliable access to payments networks that mediate more vital transactions such as regional check clearinghouses and national ACHs may reinforce the spatial-economic isolation of individuals and their communities. For these more essential services, a "universal" access mandate defies any narrow economic logic and instead must refer to broader notions than efficiency and fair competition. In addition to serving state interests such as efficient tax collection and social security disbursements, this form of public intervention would both signify and solidify a common political identity by integrating all communities into a unified national market with a common means of payment.

The Fed in the Market for Payments Services

Following Bruce Summers and Alton Gilbert (1996), we apply a simple survivor test to the Fed's payment services. We estimate their market shares at five-year intervals since the passage of the MCA in 1980 and interpret the resulting trends as a sign of their economic viability. A steady decline, for example, would imply that the Fed secured its initial market position through subsidies and so could not effectively compete with private suppliers in the post-MCA environment. To assess the impact of competition in what are deemed core central-bank and ancillary services, we compare the trends in the large-value funds transfer and clearing markets.[33]

Despite the claim of the Rivlin Committee (FRS 1998), the Fedwire has faced increasing private sector competition since the 1980s. From their vantage point in the mid-1990s, Summers and Gilbert saw a steady erosion of the Fed's share of the funds transfer market, although recent evidence, presented in table 5.2, paints a rather different picture.[34] Between 1980 and 1995 the

TABLE 5.2   Federal Reserve Bank's Share of the Clearing and Settlement Markets, Various Years

	1980		1985		1990		1995		2000	
	Transactions (Millions)	Value (Billions)	Transactions (Millions)	Value (Billions)	Transactions (Millions)	Value (Billions)	Transactions (Millions)	Value (Billions)	Transactions (Millions)	Value (Billions)
Settlement Services										
Large-value funds transfers										
CHIPS	13.2	$35,300.0	24.9	$78,400.0	37.3	$222,100.0	51.0	$310,021.2	59.8	$292,147.1
Fedwire	25.8	$49,700.0	45.0	$109,100.0	62.6	$199,100.0	75.9	$222,954.1	108.3	$379,756.4
Fed's share (percentage)	66.2	58.5	64.4	58.2	62.7	47.3	59.8	41.8	64.4	56.5
Government and related securities										
DTC	n.a.	n.a.	n.a.	$300.0	72.6	$13,900.0	119.0	$41,000.0	230.3	$116,400.0
Fedwire	n.a.	n.a.	7.7	$74,200.0	10.9	$99,900.0	12.8	$149,800.0	13.6	$188,100.0
Fed's share (percentage)				99.6	13.1	87.8	9.7	78.5	5.6	61.8
Clearing Services										
Check transactions										
Miscellaneous private	9,992.5	$10,000.0	16,802.8	$21,800.0	19,944.0	n.a.	28,145.0	n.a.	17,413.0	n.a.
Federal Reserve	15,599.7	$9,400.0	16,687.0	$10,100.0	19,307.0	$13,154.0	16,128.0	$12,083.0	17,486.0	$14,161.9
Fed's share (percentage)	61.0	48.5	49.8	31.7	49.2		36.4		50.1	
ACH transactions										
Private	n.a.	n.a.	n.a.	n.a.	n.a.	n.a.	249.7	$1,095.2	532.4	$2,417.3
Federal Reserve	227.0	$300.0	585.0	$2,100.0	1,427.0	$4,661.0	2,645.0	$8,934.8	5,152.2	$14,024.4
Fed's share (percentage)							91.4	89.1	90.6	85.3

Sources: Data for 1980 and 1985 from Summers and Gilbert (1996, 12–13); for the remaining years, BIS (2002).
Notes: Checks exclude "on-us" transactions and so record only interbank transactions through clearinghouses, correspondents, and direct presentment.

Fed's share fell sharply from 66.2 to 59.8 percent of the volume and from 58.5 to 41.8 percent of the value of all transactions. The MCA and increasing global trade, Summers and Gilbert reason, decisively shifted competitive advantage to the private sector. In the late 1990s, however, the Fed's share rebounded to approximately its 1980 levels—64.4 percent of the volume and 56.5 percent of the value of transactions. This dramatic turn of events derives in part from the Fed's adoption of technological innovations and more aggressive pricing policies that reinforced its prior "dominant" position. Still, a recent Fed study (Biehl, McAndrews, and Stefanadis 2002) cautions against complacency because of potential competition from CHIPS as well as new entrants such as the CLS (Continuous Linked Settlement) bank.[35]

Since 1980 the Fed has not fared as well in the clearing markets for retail check and electronic payments. In 1980 the Fed's regional clearinghouses handled 61.0 percent of all check transactions, amounting to approximately one-half of the total value of check payments. Over the next two decades, the Fed's share of the total volume declined to between one-third and one-half. The figures on the total value are more speculative but point to an even sharper drop by almost one-half.[36]

Over the 1990s, the Fed's share in the ACH market has declined slowly but surely. In 1992 the Fed occupied a virtual monopoly position, accounting for 94 percent of the volume and value of ACH transactions. Nearly a decade later, the market share of its private sector competitors had doubled to 12 percent of the total volume and 13 percent of the total value of transactions. Private operators benefited from innovations in information and communications technology and from the rapid adoption of electronic payments technologies in the private sector. For example, government transactions fell to only 15 percent of the volume and 17 percent of the value of Fed ACH payments, while the private sector share of interbank commercial transactions grew from 3.5 to 13.7 percent over the past decade.[37]

Our evidence indicates the increasing privatization of ancillary but not necessarily core central-bank functions since 1980. This simple test cannot, however, discern the exact impact of the MCA and related Federal Reserve Board policies. By leveling the playing field in clearing markets, these initiatives may have directly spurred competition from existing and new entrants.[38] Alternatively, they may have simply accommodated the profound structural economic changes over the period—for example, new spatial-economic patterns of payments and payments technologies—that, in turn, created new economic opportunities for private suppliers.

Setting aside the question of cause, we turn to the equally important one about consequences. What do these trends imply about the role of the Fed (and, more generally, the public sector) in the payments market? Summers and Gilbert's (1996) response is illuminating, especially as they were writing during a period when the Fed was losing market share across the board. Interpreted in light of the market survivor logic, their evidence clearly implies a more marginal Fed role. Interestingly, they resist the stark conclusion not only for the Fed's core settlement services but for its ACH and check-clearing services as well.

Their argument in support of a significant, enduring role for Fedwire funds and securities services echoes in part the position of the Rivlin Committee. They create the critical channels for the Fed to inject reserves into the banking system through its discount window and open market operations. Moreover, through its direct support of the federal funds market in which banks purchase and sell excess reserves, these Fedwire services reinforce the private sources liquidity in the banking system.

Summers and Gilbert are more ambivalent when it comes to the Fed's ACH and check-clearing services. They foresee a persistent if not accelerating decline in the Fed's share of these markets, as changes in technology and the increasing consolidation of the banking system expand opportunities for payments intermediaries to bypass Fed facilities.[39] Comparative evidence lends support to their prediction. With the spread of nationwide branched banks and electronic payments technologies, the U.S. payments system will more closely resemble those in other Group of Ten countries, where central banks have little if any operational presence in clearing systems.

At the same time Summers and Gilbert (1996, 17–19) identify several contravening factors—"public interest" exceptions—that may qualify the Fed's strict market criterion. From its inception, they observe, the Fed has served as "rule maker" or "de facto . . . coordinator" in orchestrating a national payments system, whether based on paper or electronic technologies. It has also functioned as a clearinghouse of last resort, supplying essential clearing services to all depository institutions under all economic conditions (see also Kane 1982, 114). While acknowledging possible private alternatives to the Fed's continuing operational presence in these markets, they also recognize their potential social costs in the form of concentration and market power, on the one hand, and greater systemic risk, on the other.

These examples of direct public intervention, while consistent with our earlier analysis, represent only one solution to the problems of market failures and market power that can plague economic networks. To explain the anomaly of greater public intervention in the U.S. case, Summers and Gilbert emphasize the combined impacts of technology and market structure. A study by the Bank for International Settlements (BIS 2000, 8) puts the point more sharply. It sees the Fed's role as a historical legacy of an older, paper-based transactions technology that mediated interbank transactions within a highly decentralized banking system (see also Mester 2000, 18).

We find this explanation to be too facile. After all, it cannot account for the unusual and dominant position of the Fed in the ACH market, a more recent innovation based on electronic transfers of information and funds. The case of the credit card market reinforces the point. During its formative years in the 1960s, the clearing of credit card receipts also involved massive flows of paper receipts through a highly fragmented banking system (Evans and Schmalensee 1999, 62–68). Yet in 1960s the Federal Reserve Board of Governors ignored bankers' lobbying efforts and consciously decided to relegate this retail payments system to the private sector (Summers and Gilbert 1996, 9).

Both examples imply a weak, if any, causal connection between the nature of the transactions media and technology and Fed intervention. Banking market structure and the indispensability of the payments system, we hypothesize, are more pertinent factors in explaining the location of Fed intervention. A highly decentralized banking system with many small community banks magnifies the incidence and costs of market failures and market power. For example, the greater number and heterogeneity of banks increases the inherent complexity of coordinating technological standards, including the transactions cost of cooperation. Given their size and spatial-economic location, moreover, community banks tend to have narrower access to essential payments networks and so face greater risks of vertical foreclosure and even isolation through the termination of service.

Essential payments systems supply the equivalent of money in myriad local and long-distance transactions and so knit banks, regardless of their size and location, into a national market. Check payments certainly qualify, at least over the next decade (FRS 1997, 19). At the same time, recent evidence from the Fed's retail payments survey shows a striking shift from check to newer electronic payments systems, notably ACH transactions (Gerdes and Walton 2002, 361). With the increasing universality of ACH payments in such critical domains as social security and direct deposit payments and the integration of ACH and electronic point-of-sale networks, smaller banks certainly perceive access to the ACH network as vital to their long-term economic viability and to the well-being of their customers.

Put another way, we see direct intervention by a neutral public payments intermediary such as the Fed as a necessary support for the complex transactions within a highly decentralized banking system.[40] Quantitative evidence in the Rivlin Committee report and accompanying documents make abundantly clear the Fed's critical niche in mediating payments between larger and smaller banks, as well as the latter's strong endorsement of continued Fed intervention. In the ACH market the Fed disproportionately transmits payment orders from large to small depository institutions (see table 5.3). The largest one hundred depository institutions originate 75 percent of all ACH payment orders but receive less than one-third.

In the check-clearing market the net flows are in the same direction but are less pronounced. The largest one hundred institutions account for 46 percent of the checks sent to the Fed for clearing and collection but only 31 percent of the checks presented for payment. Not surprisingly, then, the Fed's share of the check collection market exceeds 60 percent in regions with

TABLE 5.3   *Federal Reserve Bank's Share of Funds Transfers, 1996 (Percentage)*

Bank Size	Check Payments		ACH Payments	
	Collecting	Paying	Origination	Receipt
Ten largest bank holding companies	16	11	30.4	11.5
Next ninety largest bank holding companies	30	20	45.0	20.1
All other depository institutions	54	69	24.6	68.4

Source: Data from FRS (1998, 14, 27).
Notes: Collecting banks are the banks presenting checks to the Fed clearinghouse for collection. Origination and receipt banks are those that originate and receive the ACH payment.

smaller, more rural banks (such as the New Orleans and Helena clearinghouse districts) but is less than 30 percent in metropolitan districts around Chicago, New York, and Los Angeles.

The Fed as Standards Coordinator and Clearinghouse of Last Resort

In reviewing the role of the Fed in the payments system, Paul Connolly and Robert Eisenmenger (2000) focus on the development and diffusion of vital innovations that have greatly reduced the time and cost in clearing noncash retail payments. In the case of checks, the list ranges from magnetic-ink character recognition to digital imaging technologies. It has also fostered the development and diffusion of check substitutes like ACH transactions.

All of these examples fall under the general rubric of standards setting, in which a central authority coordinates the operational and technical standards of payments intermediaries to ensure their mutual compatibility (see Kindleberger 1983; Farrell and Saloner 1985; Katz and Shapiro 1985; David and Greenstein 1990). The Fed's intervention in the check-clearing and ACH markets nicely illustrates both types of standards coordination. In both cases, the Fed filled in the gaps left by private banks and so forged a truly national bank–based payments system.

The Fed entered the check-clearing market to displace the myriad private correspondent relations that orchestrated the clearing and collection of non-local checks under the post–Civil War national banking system. According to contemporary reformers, the latter patchwork arrangement was plagued by erratic if not inefficient practices. They frequently cited the circuitous routing of checks and nonpar settlement, which literally diminished the value of checks as means of payment, at least to sellers or their banks.[41] Additionally, under this more decentralized system, country banks maintained multiple correspondent relations and so held excess clearing balances.

Private clearinghouses pursued two reforms, neither of which could fully remedy these more systemic problems. Extending its scope to include a "foreign" department, the Boston clearinghouse forged a regional clearing system covering virtually all New England banks. Like its predecessor the Suffolk system, it ensured rapid clearing and par settlement of check transactions within but not outside of the territory (Cannon 1910, 259–74). The New York Clearing House, by contrast, tried to regulate prices—the interest paid on correspondent balances and the collection (or presentment fees) on nonlocal check payments. It could not, however, effectively enforce these dubious regulations, which even its former president James Cannon (1910, 12–22, 185–87) saw as collusive and thereby in likely violation of antitrust legislation (U.S. House of Representatives 1913, 137–45, 224–25).

Based on its statutory authority to organize a clearinghouse among reserve banks, the Fed began providing retail check-clearing services in 1915. Its purported goal was to enhance the efficiency of this vital payments system by standardizing banks' procedures for clearing and settling check transactions and by centralizing their reserve holdings. As a closed voluntary system, the Fed clearinghouse enlisted only about one-quarter of its members and so could not effectively compete with the more extensive networks of New York correspondent banks. In response, the Fed altered its policies in April 1916. For member banks, it mandated the par clearing of checks sent to the Fed for collection and also charged collection fees ranging from 0.9 to 2.0 cents per check. In 1918 the Fed launched a more efficient electronic system to transfer funds among reserve banks and eliminated collection fees.

These policy changes significantly enhanced the size and scope of the Fed's par clearing network and the value of its collection services for member banks. In turn, the value of Fed check clearings, relative to private clearinghouses, multiplied from a mere 2.9 percent in 1915 to more than 35 percent in 1919 and to nearly half by the late 1920s (Gilbert 2000, 131). While most local check transactions were still cleared privately, the Fed tended to mediate longer-distance, interregional payments (Gilbert 1998, 137).

Whether Fed intervention improved the allocative efficiency of the payments system is an open question.[42] The Fed did, however, wield its increasing leverage in the clearing market to promote par settlement as a standard and so rendered checks a more perfect substitute for currency in nonlocal transactions. The Federal Reserve Act mandated par settlement only of member bank checks cleared through the Fed's clearinghouse, even those remitted through the mail. Using the carrot and eventually the stick, the Fed attempted to extend the policy to nonmember banks as well.[43] After a protracted political struggle, it was ultimately rebuffed by the Supreme Court, which in 1923 ruled that the Fed had exceeded its legal mandate in insisting on universal par settlement (Farmers and Merchants Bank of North Carolina, et al. v. Federal Reserve Bank of Richmond, Virginia, 262 U.S. 649 [1923]).[44]

Despite this political setback, the Fed would nearly achieve its goal through another means—the exclusion of nonpar banks from its clearing system. In requiring all member banks to join the Fed clearinghouse and thereby to adopt par settlement, the Fed created a critical mass of par clearing institutions. In turn, access to the Fed clearinghouse became an increasingly vital asset at least in competitive markets and induced nonmember banks to accept par settlement voluntarily. After the Fed adopted its policy in 1916, more than seven thousand nonmember banks joined the ranks of the Fed's par list, which nearly doubled in size (Spahr 1926, 247). Moreover, even after the 1923 Supreme Court decision, nonpar banking did not revive significantly. To be sure, in the subsequent year the number of nonpar banks rose by about 50 percent to 3,240, but the latter figure still represented only 16 percent of nonmember banks and an even smaller share of deposits or assets. More revealing, virtually all of these banks were located in isolated rural towns and quite likely possessed some degree of local monopoly power, insulating them from competitive pressures.[45]

In the case of the ACH, the Fed solved the "chicken and egg" problem that plagues all new complex network technologies (Evans and Schmalensee 1999, 137). Like all major innovations, the early adoption of network technologies is limited by relatively high costs and low uncertain returns. The latter, however, are magnified by the availability of multiple, incompatible formats. Consequently, the user base may be too small and narrow—that is, below a critical mass—to generate demand externalities that would enhance its value to potential adopters and so spur its more rapid diffusion. While the resulting delays in diffusion may represent a rational response to high adoption (and switching) costs, it may also reflect a collective action problem. The adoption of the new technology may be in the interest of a sufficient number of users if they act collectively but not if they act individually.

The idea of an electronic system for recurrent small payments originated in the private sector, among banks in Los Angeles and San Francisco.[46] In their original formulation, the Fed would take a purely operational or "back-office" role, adapting its critical technical know-how and Fedwire network to mediate retail electronic payments. With the spread of ACH technology to other urban centers, the American Bankers Association formed the National Automated Clearinghouse Association as an alternative to Fed control and hence to the dependence of the private on the public sector (Frisbee 1986, 5). The National Automated Clearinghouse Association would assist local bankers' associations in developing and coordinating a uniform standard to integrate their local clearinghouses into a national system.

Urban bankers' associations continued to form local ACHs, but the Fed ultimately spurred the development and diffusion of this new payments technology and forged local networks into a national system. The Fed assumed this catalytic role because private associations, including the National Auto-mated Clearinghouse Association, lacked the organizational capacity and fi-nancial resources to do so (Stone 1986, 25–26). Their inertia reflects, in part, internal divisions among member banks. As Bernell Stone (1986, 22–24) ob-serves and the Fed data in table 5.3 clearly corroborate, a relatively small frac-tion of banks originate a disproportionate share of all ACH transactions and so fully realize the economic benefits of the new technology. The rest are "pas-sive" receivers, which have less incentive to commit the resources to devel-oping and updating the technology.

The Fed, by contrast, had strong, direct interests in promoting the ACH payment system because of its functions as a national check clearinghouse and depository agent of the federal government. Fed officials regarded the ACH as a "natural extension" of its check clearinghouse business, which would reduce mounting congestion and other operational costs in handling paper-based trans-actions (Frisbee 1986, 5). Additionally, several large government agencies—the Social Security Administration and the Treasury and Defense Departments—embraced the new technology and worked with the Fed to automate their widely dispersed but recurrent payments. To this end, for example, the Fed developed low-cost microelectronic technology that enabled smaller banks to receive (but not originate) ACH payments.

While more circumstantial, the evidence also supports Summers and Gilbert's notion of the Fed as an open, fair, neutral, and stable intermediary or clearinghouse of last resort. Under the MCA, the Fed must supply its critical clearing services to all depository institutions at competitive prices. Its man-date therefore guarantees all banks universal access to essential payments sys-tems and so helps to prevent disruptions in the flow of funds owing to systemic and operational risks as well as the equivalent of digital divides in the Internet.

The early history of the ACH certainly justifies concerns of smaller, more marginal banks over equal access to emerging electronic payments technolo-gies (Kuprianov 1985, 24–30). The establishment of fair access rules, how-ever, was only a necessary condition for their integration into a national ACH network. It also depended on the Fed's strategic investments to develop and diffuse affordable gateway technologies. Consequently, small banks favor continued direct Fed investments in new electronic payments technologies and in an efficient public electronic payments networks (FRS 1997, 25–26). Even some larger banks acknowledge the value of these Fed investments, which will accelerate the diffusion of new payments technologies to smaller banks and so enhance the scale, scope, and value of emerging electronic pay-ments networks. In turn, these banks advocate the relaxation of the MCA pric-ing rule to afford the Fed a longer time horizon to recoup the substantial development costs of more "public" goods.[47]

Even in existing clearing markets the Fed has provided these universal service guarantees. During banking crises the Fed has strategically intervened by supplying backup facilities to stem potential systemic risks to the payments system. In the wake of financial troubles at Continental Illinois, for example, the Fed took a more active role and (along with the Federal Deposit Insurance Company and the comptroller of the currency) bailed out uninsured depositors, including nearly 2,300 commercial banks of which 179 were deemed at risk of failure (Garber and Weisbrod 1992, 540–41; Clair, Kolson, and Robinson 1995, 15).[48] About four years later, in the wake of the Texas banking crisis, the Fed's role was more passive but no less vital in containing the impacts of default risk by large correspondent banks. In this case, respondents took more preventive measures to avoid losses and possible disruptions to clearing services from the impending bankruptcy of their correspondents and shifted their business to the Fed clearinghouse during the peak of the crisis.[49] The critical condition for Fed intervention was sufficient backup clearing capacity, which could handle the 57 percent annual increase in "payment-processing arrangements" (Clair, Kolson, and Robinson 1995, 16–19).

Finally, the Fed's credible commitment to supply payments services at a competitive price has served as an alternative to the threat of antitrust prosecution in curbing the market power of alternative private vendors.[50] Banks can access ACH and check-clearing networks through regional clearinghouses and correspondents, but potential competition in these arenas is limited. Most territories, whether large urban centers or multistate regions, tend to be served by a single joint-venture clearinghouse, which in some cases supplies both ACH and check-clearing services.

Regional correspondent markets are also highly concentrated. In the St. Louis Federal Reserve district, for example, the largest four correspondents in each subregion accounted for 80 to 90 percent of correspondent balances in 1979 (Gilbert 1983, 484). Increasing consolidation in the banking industry has reduced the number of existing correspondents in regional markets, although this trend is offset by more liberal branching restrictions that allow new entry by correspondent banks from other money centers. Overall, however, the consolidation effects have been greater and have led to a steady rise in the concentration of correspondent balances at the national and state levels between 1984 and 1996 (Osterberg and Thomson 1999, 14–15; McAndrews and Strahan 2002).

With increasing vertical integration comes the real risk of vertical foreclosure. Correspondents can use access fees like the price of clearing services to raise rivals' costs and so leverage their wholesale market power to reap greater returns from their retail branches (Economides 1996; McAndrews and Strahan 2002, 324–27). From their pivotal vantage point, private correspondents can also glean and strategically exploit valuable confidential payments information about their competitors' customers. McAndrews and Philip Strahan (2002, 334–38) find evidence that following the deregulation of statewide branching restrictions, small banks in more concentrated correspondent markets tend to shift their clearing balances to the Fed.

The Fed as Lender of Last Resort

Closing the Fed's discount window may suffice during normal times, when private lenders can assess one another's financial condition in a timely and reasonably accurate fashion (Flannery 1996, 816). Not all times are normal, however, as evidenced by the recent hemorrhaging of the payments system in the aftermath of the September 11, 2001, disaster. By "recoordinat[ing]" interbank payments, Fed discount lending supported the vital flows of information and liquidity until normal Fedwire and federal funds transactions could be restored (McAndrews and Potter 2002, 72–73; see also Bernanke 1990, 148–49; Fleming and Garbade 2002). The social benefits from direct Fed intervention, in turn, justify its charging a discount rate below the market rate on federal funds transactions.

Kevin Dowd (1994) proposes an alternative private arrangement that falls between the competitive federal funds market and direct Fed intervention. To realize information and liquidity externalities, banks can form private "clubs." A prime example is the urban clearinghouse of the pre-Fed period. Originally established to orchestrate the clearing and settlement of check transactions, this voluntary organization quickly assumed core central-bank functions as lender of last resort and bank regulator (Timberlake 1984; Gorton 1985). Clearinghouses supplied emergency liquidity through the issue of loan certificates. First used in New York during the financial crisis of 1860, loan certificates substituted for legal tender in settling adverse clearinghouse balances and allowed banks to devote their cash reserves to satisfying customers' withdrawal demands. Like the Fed discount window, the clearinghouse loaned reserves on the basis of collateral approved by its loan committee and charged interest below prevailing rates (7 percent in 1860 and 6 percent in and after 1873) (see Moen and Tallman 2000, 148).[51]

The loan certificates were joint liabilities of clearinghouse members. If a member bank failed and did not post sufficient collateral, the others covered the loss through assessments in proportion to their capital. Such a coinsurance plan obviously created potential moral hazard problems. Clearinghouses therefore regulated member banks to limit excessive risk taking. They imposed minimum capital requirements and in some cases set maximum deposit rates. They also conducted periodic audits to assess the quality of bank assets. Violators were punished by fines and, if necessary, expulsion (Dowd 1994, 293–94). Although an extreme measure sending a negative if not fatal signal about a bank's solvency, expulsion required only a simple majority vote in New York.

TABLE 5.4   *National Bank Panics, 1873 to 1914*

	1873	1884	1890	1893	1907	1914
Panic onset	September 18	May 6	November 10	May 1	October 21	July 31
Issue of clearinghouse loan certificates in New York City	September 22	May 15	November 12	June 21	October 26	August 3
Aggregate loan certificate issue, New York Clearing House (millions)	$26.6	$24.9	$16.6	$41.5	$101.1	
Maximum amount outstanding (millions)	$22.4	$21.9	$15.2	$38.3	$88.4	
Bank reserves of New York Clearing House members (millions)	$57.1[a]	n.a.	$95.6[b]	$121.0[c]	$261.4[d]	
Ratio of maximum certificates issued to reserves (percentage)	39.2%	n.a.	15.9%	31.7%	33.8%	
Loan certificate issue nationwide (millions)	n.a.	n.a.	n.a.	$69.1	$238.1	$212
Restriction of cash payments in New York City	September 24			August 3	October 26	
Resumption of cash payments in New York City	November 1			September 2	January 1	

Sources: Data from Andrew (1908, 507); Sprague (1910, 34, 145, 163, 261–62, 432–33); Roberds (1995); Wicker (2000, 9, 121).
[a]On September 15, 1873.
[b]On November 8, 1890.
[c]On May 6, 1893.
[d]On October 19, 1907.

Table 5.4 documents the timing and extent of the New York Clearing House (NYCH) intervention in five of the six major financial crises or panics between the Civil War and the establishment in 1914 of the Federal Reserve System.[52] The NYCH authorized loan certificates in each instance, but with varying degrees of effectiveness in curbing systemic disruptions to the payments system.[53] Significantly, its successes came earlier in the period, and its failures, later.

Clearinghouse intervention in 1873 qualifies as only a partial success because member banks were ultimately forced to restrict local cash payments (Sprague 1910; Wicker 2000). In this case, the NYCH both issued loan certificates and pooled members' reserves. By drawing on the reserves of banks with more local business, the largest correspondent banks were able to satisfy the withdrawal demands of their out-of-town respondents.[54] Restrictions on cash payments were, therefore, "confined chiefly, if not entirely, to dealings with local individual depositors" (Sprague 1910, 90). Thus by alleviating liquidity pressures on the largest correspondent banks, the NYCH stemmed systemic disruptions to the payments system nationwide. As O. M. W. Sprague (1910, 70, 76, 90) notes with approval, this arrangement converted the private clearinghouse "to all intents and purposes into a central bank" by internalizing the liquidity externality among members.

The 1907 panic, by contrast, is a clear case of institutional failure (Wicker 2000, 15, 140). Sprague (1910, 114, 140, 257), for example, largely fixes the blame on the New York Clearing House for delays in responding to runs on the Knickerbocker and other trust companies (see also Wicker 2000, 14). Expressing genuine concerns about the trusts' "risky" assets, J. P. Morgan and other NYCH member banks initially refused to provide liquidity assistance. As important, because most trusts, including the largest, like Knickerbocker, were not members of the clearinghouse, the loan committee did not have detailed information about their asset portfolios nor sufficient time to gather it.

In the wake of the indiscriminate runs against trusts, Morgan organized a syndicate that supplied emergency liquidity but at a substantial cost, averaging in the extreme 50 percent per annum.[55] Only after a delay of five days, when the resources of the syndicate proved to be inadequate and the panic threatened to engulf the wider financial system, did the NYCH begin to issue loan certificates. This injection of liquidity eased pressures in stock and bond markets and as a result lowered interest rates (Donaldson 1993, 71–72, 76). It did not, however, completely halt bank runs, which lasted as long as three weeks for the Trust Company of America and the Lincoln Trust, and the resulting disruptions to the payments system (Sprague 1910, 257; Wicker 2000, 112–13).

A comparison with Chicago illustrates the negative impacts of NYCH policies. The larger trust companies in Chicago were full members of the clearinghouse and did not experience runs during the panic. According to Jon Moen and Ellis Tallman (2000), differences in the extent of clearinghouse membership, rather than in the quality of loan assets and reserve ratios, explain the differential experience of the two cities. Chicago trusts were spared runs by panicky depositors because their clearinghouse membership signaled soundness as well as access to an emergency liquidity facility.

The pattern of earlier success and later failure calls into question Gary Gorton's (1985, 283) rather sanguine observation that "by the early twentieth century clearinghouses looked much like central banks." We are more in-clined to concur with William Roberds (1995, 26) that private clearinghouses tottered "on the margin of success and failure." The timing, in fact, suggests that the NYCH was becoming less skillful, not more so, in dealing with the later and increasingly severe financial crises.[56]

The source of the problem lies in the conflicts of interest intrinsic to such private voluntary organizations (Goodhart 1988, 38–39). Mounting tensions within the larger, more differentiated New York financial sector eroded the consensus necessary for the clearinghouse to execute effectively its function as lender of last resort. Reserve pooling was one of the first casualties. The policy of paying interest on bankers' balances divided the mainly local banks from correspondent banks. In 1873 only twelve of sixty members paid inter-est on correspondent balances, and not surprisingly they held almost all of the correspondent accounts in New York. The other banks criticized the practice because it encouraged excessive risk taking. Correspondent banks held less rather than more excess reserves despite the higher turnover of bankers' bal-ances compared with other deposits. They also engaged in more call lending to stockbrokers.

After the panic of 1857 a plan to stop the practice failed to achieve unan-imous consent. In 1873 the "local" banks agreed to reserve pooling, but only because they expected the clearinghouse to impose a rule prohibiting the pay-ing of interest on deposits. When it failed to materialize, the pooling of re-serves in subsequent crises was never again a real option. During the next crisis in 1884, for example, opposition to reserve pooling was intense and quite general among NYCH members (Sprague 1910, 120).[57]

Internecine conflicts also delayed supplies of emergency liquidity to vul-nerable banks, another critical instrument in stemming panics.[58] On the eve of the 1907 panic, as the data in table 5.4 indicates, member banks certainly had sufficient clearinghouse reserves to fund subsequent issues of loan certificates. They did not deploy them because the troubled depository institutions were outside of their increasingly exclusive network.[59] Over time and across all cities, membership rates were declining as new financial institutions either did not satisfy clearinghouse rules or rejected their relatively high entry costs. The New York Clearing House encompassed all city banks at its founding in 1853 but less than a majority by 1909. Similarly, the Chicago clearinghouse expe-rienced a steady decline in membership from a maximum of thirty to twenty in 1909 (Cannon 1910, 164, 276, 288, 298).

The example of the New York trust companies shifts some of the blame to the fragmented or dual system of U.S. bank regulation, but in doing so it strengthens the case against Dowd's private solution. Trust companies defected en masse from the NYCH, when in 1903 and 1904 it imposed stiffer reserve requirements on them. The NYCH policy was a defensive response to lax state bank regulation that allowed trusts to skirt legal reserve requirements on deposit accounts and so gain a decisive cost advantage in deposit markets (Moen and Tallman 1992, 612–14; see also White 1983, 29–42). Ironically, the very same scenario was reenacted in the 1970s, as thrifts and other nonbank depository institutions exploited loopholes in the Federal Reserve Board's Regulation Q to enter the deposit market. The MCA finally resolved the problem by forcing all depository institutions to join the Fed's settlement network and to abide by its reserve requirements (Kuprianov 1985; Timberlake 1985).

The ability of private clearinghouses to supply emergency liquidity is "only half, and perhaps the less difficult half, of the exercise" (Goodhart 1988, 54; see also McAndrews and Roberds 1995). The power to print money during crises calls for greater restraint in noncrisis times. As Sprague (1910, 213) clearly perceived, "Unless associated with more conservative management it is highly probable that enlarged power to issue notes would be used in such a fashion in the years before crises as to place the banks in an extremely hazardous position through more unrestrained extension of credit than would otherwise have been granted." More generally, the prospect of meeting panics with emergency issues may well make it irresistible to profit-maximizing banks to hold fewer reserves in normal times. It seems unlikely that a private club would agree to and be able to enforce such restraint as compared with an outside party. In other words, a neutral central bank would more effectively combine expansionary policies during crises with restrictive policies during expansions (Goodhart 1988, 54).[60]

Conclusion

The Monetary Control Act of 1980 clearly envisioned a more private payments system like that in the pre-Fed period but with one important difference, namely, comprehensive regulatory oversight of depository institutions by the Fed and other agencies. Through an examination of the available evidence, we detect a decisive shift from the public to the private sector in the U.S. payments system since 1980, especially in clearing markets for check and ACH transactions. The result is especially striking in the case of the ACH market, where the Fed has realized large cost reductions through scale economies and innovation.[61] In turn, it raises a critical question of whether the Fed's early virtual monopoly was transitory, reflecting an initial lack of capacity in the private sector.[62] Put another way, if the market share of the Fed ACH should fall to levels comparable to those of, say, its regional check clearinghouses, would its early dominance reflect more than simply historical legacy or accident?

In forums organized by the Rivlin Committee, the "overwhelming majority" of participants rejected this conclusion, which implies that the Fed should liquidate or privatize its clearing facilities.[63] Not surprisingly, smaller (that is, more rural and urban "community") banks were the strongest advocates for the

Fed's role as clearinghouse of last resort. They questioned whether the private sector could supply adequate reliable access to critical check-clearing and ACH services. Private suppliers, they argued, would probably not devote sufficient resources to "legacy" check-processing facilities and would, in turn, leave significant gaps in the check market, notably in more rural regions and among smaller urban banks. In the ACH market, by contrast, most participants did not foresee problems of insufficient capacity, at least in the longer run. Still, they expressed concerns about whether the private sector would follow in the Fed's footsteps and supply all banks with advanced technologies to ensure the same level of access to electronic payments networks.

There was a more general consensus on the Fed's vital contribution to the development and diffusion of new payments technologies, although banks disagreed about the precise scope of its intervention. They saw electronic check payments on the horizon but also significant impediments to its widespread adoption, such as "the sheer size and fragmented nature of the check collection system" and inertia on the part of bank customers (FRS 1997, 19–20). The Fed was regarded as the appropriate "standards-setting" or "rule-making" body to foster the transition because of its regulatory authority, more open "structure and procedures" for deliberation, and legitimacy in the eyes of the public. Instead of mandates, however, participants stressed the value of collaboration between the Fed and industry participants in development of technological and operational standards, especially around the thorny legal issues of "privacy and security . . . [and] . . . liability and risk" (FRS 1997, 19–23).

Some participants, mainly larger banks, worried about potential conflicts of interest between the Fed's dual roles as aggressive innovator and regulatory authority. The more generally held view (FRS 1997, 23–24) asserts a complementary relationship. As payments intermediary, the Fed would acquire the critical know-how to work effectively with other industry participants in the development of new technological standards and regulations. Direct Fed intervention, it was thought, would also allay public concerns about "safety . . . and . . . equal access" (FRS 1997, 12) and so result in less onerous regulations that could curtail collaboration and innovation.

The bottom line is that the Fed's role as standards coordinator may be transitory in any particular market (like ACH payments) but not in the payments market as a whole. The nature of Fed intervention should change over the life cycle of individual payments systems and, in turn, evolve with the evolution of the payments system as a whole. In answer to our question about the ACH market, we do not believe that the Fed must continue as a dominant supplier of network services. At the same time, it must retain a sufficient presence in the ACH market to ensure access and stability to this vital payments network. In turn, it can redeploy its considerable research and development capacity to solve bottlenecks in other payments markets like check transactions.

While justifying a continued presence of the Fed in clearing markets, our analysis also questions the rhetoric and policies of privatization as applied to the payments system. We note, for example, a tension in the MCA between the Fed's competitive pricing and public interest mandates. As clearinghouse of last resort, the Fed must maintain sufficient excess capacity so that it can readily absorb banks' demand shifts in their flight to safety during periods of financial stress. The critical question, then, is how Fed clearinghouses can finance this investment and still satisfy the MCA pricing mandate. Prohibited from subsidizing their clearing operations with profits earned elsewhere, they would have to bear the burden in the form of higher fixed costs relative to private competitors. In the absence of offsetting operational economies, the Fed would most likely lose market share, at least during periods of relative tranquility, and so face mounting cost pressures from the additional but unintended excess capacity.

In strict accordance with its market survivor test, the Fed could respond to these demand shifts by scaling back its clearing operations. Of course, it could not then guarantee reliable timely clearing services during periods of financial stress. Under these conditions, banks would face greater risks from using private intermediaries and so would quite likely require some form of insurance. Private insurance would suffice only in cases of idiosyncratic failures (Bernanke 1990, 143–45). For systemic risks, the historical experience recounted in this chapter specifies two de facto public alternatives: unlimited deposit insurance and excess capacity in the Fed clearinghouse. The latter, we believe, is preferable. It not only avoids the obvious problems of moral hazard and closer regulation but also induces respondent banks to monitor closely their correspondents.

Drawing on the experience of other network industries, we could envision a partial solution in the form of an access fee like the fixed connectivity charge paid by all long-distance telephone customers. Revenues from the tax could subsidize private or nonprofit intermediaries to ensure the stability and dynamism of the payments system. Still, it could not address the other potential problems of privatization, such as increasing concentration and market power among payments intermediaries. Under current conditions, a likely model of private organization would be the joint venture, such as in the credit card market or the pre-Fed check-clearing market. Both cases have raised serious public policy concerns about the exercise of market power, ranging from fixing access fees (such as the merchants' discount or exchange costs) to restricting access.

Calls for the privatization of Fedwire services raise similar questions. As Summers and Gilbert (1996) observe, the relative growth of private settlement services like CHIPS and the Continuous Linked Settlement (CLS) bank would require an extension of the Fed's core central-bank functions to ensure the stability of the payments system. Their reasoning is a consequence of the "too big to fail" principle applied to interbank payments intermediaries. With the increasing size and importance of private networks, systemic and operational risks would propagate financial stress through the entire payments system and so require Fed intervention in the form of backup liquidity supplies and even processing facilities.

The expectation of a Fed bailout would, in turn, create potential moral hazard problems, the standard remedy to which is stiffer regulatory oversight. The problem, as Summers and Gilbert observe, is that the Fed currently has no direct regulatory authority over private clearing and settlement associations. Like its urban clearinghouse predecessors, it can wield only a "very blunt supervisory instrument," namely, closing the Fedwire to networks with lax security standards (Summers and Gilbert 1996, 21). Thus if the Fed's share in the funds transfer market should decline once again, it might be necessary to expand its supervisory and regulatory authority over private clearing organizations to maintain the integrity of the system overall.

In the end, both the abstract arguments in favor of privatization and the more concrete provisions of the MCA err in conceiving the public and private spheres as substitutes. Greater privatization, they imply, comes at the expense of public intervention. This notion of a simple trade-off ignores the unintended negative consequences of increasing privatization that would require further public intervention. As an alternative, we suggest conceiving recent trends in terms of an evolutionary process, leading toward new forms of public intervention involving different mixes of and relationships between the private and public sectors.

We are grateful to Barnard College for financial support and to Erica Wintermuth for research assistance. For their critical comments, we would like to thank R. Alton Gilbert, John Caskey, Michael Edelstein, Victor Goldberg, Jamie McAndrews, Rick Mishkin, Richard Nelson, Sidney Winter, and the participants of the Columbia University Macro Lunch Seminar and the research seminar at the New York Federal Reserve Bank.

Notes

1. Green and Todd (2001, 21), for example, see such changes as making the provision of payments services by the Fed superfluous to its core central-bank functions of conducting "monetary policy, banking regulation, and financial stabilization."
2. With the passage of the Expedited Funds Availability Act in 1987, the Fed acquired additional regulatory powers over the collection and clearing of check payments.

3. Federal Reserve Board of Governors (2002) reproduces the relevant section (IIA) of the Monetary Control Act.
4. The Federal Reserve Board of Governors (1981) enunciated its pricing principles and market test for payments services in 1980 and 1981; see also Federal Reserve Board of Governors (1990). In focusing on trends in market share, we adopt the Stigler (1958) version of the survivor test.
5. In this regard, the Fed functions like the post office and faces the same problems in competing against private suppliers, which do not operate under a universal service mandate.
6. Our notion of an essential facility is broader than that used in the antitrust literature, which emphasizes bottlenecks in access to critical vertical services (McAndrews 1995). Our notion also encompasses concerns about equity.
7. Cash is, in other words, "self-clearing" (Kuttner and McAndrews 2001, 40). By good funds, we mean a generally accepted means of exchange, one that agents can use to discharge other obligations. Finality connotes a payment in good funds that is irreversible (except in cases of fraud). In a cash transaction the transfer of value is not automatic but depends only on the seller's verification and acceptance of the notes. See Goodfriend (1990) and Kahn and Roberds (2001b; 2002).
8. In 1997, for example, cash payments accounted for only 40.8 percent of the volume and 17.4 percent of the value of consumer transactions (Mester 2000, 8–9). In the remainder of this chapter we use the terms demand, transactions, and bank deposits interchangeably.
9. Needless to say, noncash payments can take time and so rest on flows of credit in the money market. This dualism between flows of payments and short-term credit helps to explain the synergies realized by banks and other money market institutions in providing both payments and credit services (Goodfriend 1990; Garber and Weisbrod 1990; and McAndrews and Roberds 1999). Based on an examination of the practices of medieval money lenders, McAndrews and Roberds (1999) argue that mediating payments was central to the original function of banks of deposit.
10. The dashed lines correspond to the flows of information such as checks or other payment instructions. The continuous lines correspond to flows of funds or their equivalent in debits or credits to bank and reserve accounts.
11. Verification determines the authenticity of the check, approval indicates that the payer has sufficient funds (or line of credit). The sequence described here corresponds to a system of real-time gross settlement, in which banks "immediately" discharge their obligations upon receipt, verification, and approval of their customers' checks. Under the alternative of net deferred settlement, the clearing institution cumulates banks' credit and debit items and tallies their net surplus or deficit positions at the close of the settlement period, usually a day. Deficit banks then discharge their obligations with a single payment through the settlement institution.
12. Figure 5.1 depicts the organizational structure of the Fed's interbank payment services. The Fed divides the clearing and settlement functions between distinct

operating divisions, and the Fedwire is a real-time gross settlement system. In the pre-Fed period, by contrast, urban clearinghouses combined clearing and settlement services in a more tightly vertically integrated organization. Today, private clearinghouses and correspondents tend to specialize in clearing services and use the Fedwire for settlement services.

13. A description of each service, including data on annual flows, is available at: www.federalreserve.gov/paymentsystems/fedwire/default.htm. In Canada, by contrast, the central bank is but one member of a national clearing and settlement association (Anvari 1990; Redish 1991; Bank of Canada 1997). Along with large depository institutions, it constitutes a node in the distribution and clearing system but exclusively provides settlement services.

14. The comparative tables in the Bank for International Settlements (BIS 2002, 184–88) report on payments systems in Group of Ten countries succinctly depict the main features of the CHIPS and Fedwire funds transfer systems.

15. With an eye toward competing more directly with the Fedwire, CHIPS in 1999 adopted new policies of more continuous settlement and stiffer "prefunding" or collateral requirements for intraday credits, which closely approximate the Fed's policy of real-time gross settlement (see also TCHC 2003, 20).

16. The two studies may not be strictly comparable and so yield different results, notably on the Fed's share of the clearing market. For example, the Retail Payments Research Project (FRS 2002) surveyed paying banks at step 4 in the collections process (see figure 5.1). If a correspondent bank received checks for collection but routed them through a regional Fed clearinghouse for presentment to the paying bank, the survey would record this transaction as a paid check cleared through the Fed. The contribution of the correspondent would be overlooked. The Rivlin Committee report does not describe its survey design and question.

17. Correspondents are typically money center banks that hold interbank deposits of smaller regional banks and offer clearing and local settlement services.

18. For a map identifying each regional association and delineating its geographic boundaries, see www.nacha.org/map/nacha_map.html.

19. McAndrews (1994) discusses the early evolution of a private national ACH, which began in 1994 as a joint venture of the Arizona, Visa, and New York Clearing Houses and used the Visa electronic network.

20. We use the more familiar term debit card payment to refer to the electronic-funds-transfer–point-of-sale (EFT-POS) transaction. The Federal Reserve Board consciously decided not to enter either the credit card or ATM markets. Summers and Gilbert (1996, 9) regard the FRB's decision in the credit card case as early evidence of its more market-oriented position. We propose an alternative hypothesis, which implies that Fed intervention would be limited to an essential, national payments system. Credit cards, at least in the late 1960s, would not have qualified based on the former criterion, and ATM cards in the 1970s, on the latter. We are grateful to James McAndrews for informing us about the Fed's decision in the ATM market.

21. The share of regional ATM-POS networks is about the same whether we calculate total transactions or only point-of-sale transactions. Consolidation in this

sector has occurred through the formation of larger regional and transregional networks (McAndrews 1991; CBO 1998).

22. Compare figure 5.1 with the network diagrams in BIS (2000, 24–25) and Evans and Schmalensee (1999, 155–56). Check transactions involving local and large, metropolitan banks and cash payments are mediated by more decentralized, "geodesic" networks, corresponding to direct bilateral exchanges between the parties or their intermediaries (Huber 1987).

23. In one of the few empirical studies of network externalities, Saloner and Shepard (1995) apply this logic to explain the early diffusion of ATM systems. For a similar analysis of the diffusion of local ACH networks, see Gowrisankaran and Stavins (1999).

24. From this perspective, banks' special role as market makers in liquidity is systemic, a feature of settlement networks and not simply of the individual bank per se (Garber and Weisbrod 1990, 3; Economides 1993). Individual bank characteristics, such as its prudential management of assets and liabilities, are obviously important and have been the focus of much theorizing about the other special feature of banks, namely, information-intensive lending (see, for example, Calomiris and Kahn 1991). We do not dismiss the importance of information asymmetries in structuring financial arrangements but simply suggest that this literature has overlooked the reciprocal causal connections between the dual role of banks as payments and financial intermediaries (Garber and Weisbrod 1990; Goodfriend 1990; and McAndrews and Roberds 1999).

25. More formally, a liquid asset like a deposit account must have a "well-known and stable value relative to the unit of account" and not simply official sanction as legal tender (Garber and Weisbrod 1992, 3, 130; see also Keynes 1964, 229–36). The liquidity of bank deposits derives from the liquidity of the interbank payment or settlement market, including the formation of a well-functioning interbank loan market (Garbade and Silber 1979; Economides and Siow 1988).

26. The short term of the transaction is critical to ensuring the liquidity of the system and bears on the dual issue of information asymmetries. A priori it may not be possible to ascertain whether the borrowing bank is experiencing a transitory deficit or more serious structural problem. Thus even if deficit banks roll over these short-term loans for several periods and so effectively extend the borrowing terms, they are subject to periodic assessments to ensure that they can make good on their liquid liabilities; that is, they will have sufficient offsetting credits in the future (Garber and Weisbrod 1990, 33–34).

27. Redenius (2002) and Gilbert (2000) illustrate this liquidity externality in the private correspondent banking system of the late nineteenth century and in the early years of the Federal Reserve System. The liquidity economies (or externalities) of a net deferred settlement system explain its prevalence among private clearinghouses (BIS 2002, 184–85).

28. Under the National Banking System, New York, along with Chicago and St. Louis, were designated central reserve cities and so held the legal reserves of federally chartered banks. Still, New York banks accounted for 70 percent of the correspondent balances held in the three central reserve cities, including excess reserves above legal levels (Watkins 1929, 18–21).

29. Correspondent banks would routinely supply their customer banks with the equivalent of intraday credit to finance their transitory clearing deficits rather than require them to remit cash (Lockhart 1921). Given the size and scope of the New York correspondent market, New York banks could finance these loans directly through the transitory surpluses of other customer banks or by the sale of reserves on the call loan market and hence from the excess reserves of other New York banks (Watkins 1929, 210–28; Myers 1931, 275–78; Goodhart 1969; Miron 1986; Champ, Smith, and Williamson 1996).

30. McAndrews and Rajan (2000, 24–26) provide evidence of these agglomeration effects in the Fedwire.

31. The Federal Reserve Bank of St. Louis, for example, convened a symposium in 1995 on antitrust issues in the payments system; see, for example, Carlton and Frankel (1995) and McAndrews (1995, 1997). The credit card market has been the most contested terrain (Evans and Schmalensee 1999, chap. 11). On the most recent case involving the tying of credit and debit card payments, see Jennifer Bayot, "Master Card Settles Case with Retailers Ahead of Trial," *New York Times,* April 29, 2003, p. C1; and Jennifer Bayot, "Visa Reaches Settlement in Debit Card Case," *New York Times,* May 1, 2003, p. C1.

32. Mueller (1996, 22) coined the term "access competition" to characterize the intense competitive struggles between Bell and independent telephone operating companies before 1907 (see also Gabel 1994; Weiman and Levin 1994). Penetration pricing is an alternative, related notion (Farrell and Saloner 1986, 950–51; Katz and Shapiro 1986, 834). Downes and Greenstein (2002) nicely illustrate the problem of uneven spatial diffusion in the case of the Internet.

33. For completeness, table 5.2 includes the Fed's share in the securities depository and settlement services market. The calculation, however, is somewhat misleading, as the Fed specializes in U.S. government securities, while Depository Trust Company (DTC) tends to handle other government and private securities.

34. Trends in the market for securities transfers may corroborate their prediction. Since the entry of the DTC—a joint venture of banks and securities dealers—in the late 1980s, the Fedwire share has declined from virtually 100 percent in 1985 to only 5.6 percent of the volume and 61.8 percent of the value of all transactions in 2000.

35. According to Biehl, McAndrews, and Stefanadis (2002, 23–24, 29–33), these factors explain the almost 50 percent decline in average Fedwire prices since 1996 and a significant share of the growth in Fedwire transactions (given the elasticity of demand especially of larger banks). The CLS bank, a joint venture of large domestic and foreign banks, mediates international transactions in conjunction (not in competition) with central banks. Its entry favors the Fed in the short run but not necessarily in the long run. One unintended consequence, for example, has been a clear shift in CHIPS policies aimed at competing directly with the Fed in the domestic market. Additionally, the CLS Bank could eventually enter this market as well.

36. These estimates of the Fed's share of the clearing market are consistent with data on the institutional location of banks' holdings of "settlement media," that is, reserves used for settling interbank claims. In 1995 banks lodged 43.4 percent

of their reserve deposits in the central bank and the rest in "transferable" accounts in other banks such as correspondent accounts. The Fed's share declined sharply over the late 1990s to only 29 percent, as banks greatly reduced their central bank deposits. Because of changes in banks' reserve management, the figure for 1999 largely represents banks' clearing balances and excess reserves and so more closely gauges the role of the Fed in the clearing and settlement of checks and other noncash instruments (Clouse and Elmendorf 1997; Bennett and Peristiani 2002).

37. The Electronic Payments Network claims a larger market share of nearly 20 percent in 2001 (GAO 2002, table 1, n. g).

38. As an example, Summers and Gilbert (1996, 11–12) report a 12 percent decline in Fed check clearings after a change in its policy on presentment rules that diminished its competitive advantage in the check collection market relative to correspondent banks.

39. Preliminary results from the Fed's recent survey of the retail payments sector also points in the same direction (Gerdes and Walton 2002). It shows a decline in the use of checks and a corresponding increase in electronic payments services.

40. While it is not our intention to engage the thorny debate over the benefits and costs of U.S. bank branching restrictions, we do note that the evidence clearly shows a critical role of smaller, independent banks in fostering local development and innovation (Berger et al. 2003).

41. Circuitous routing increases the delays between the first deposit and final settlement of the check transactions and hence floats costs. According to the U.S. commercial code, banks were required to redeem checks at par value—that is, dollar for dollar—only when they were directly presented for collection at their offices. If checks, and hence payments, were remitted by mail, banks could charge a discount, known as a collection or presentment fee, and the payment would thus be a nonpar settlement.

42. See, for example, the current debate between researchers at the Richmond Fed (Weinberg 1997; Lacker, Walker, Weinberg 1999) and those at the New York and St. Louis Feds (McAndrews and Roberds 1995; McAndrews 1998; Gilbert 1998, 2000).

43. To induce compliance, the Fed in 1918 offered to pay for the additional transactions cost of remitting payments through the mail. When many nonpar banks resisted, the Fed resorted to the more aggressive tactic of direct presentment at their offices. This measure was also used by the Fed's predecessors, such as the Second Bank of the United States and the Suffolk System (see, for example, Bodenhorn 2002). Holdouts were mainly located in small rural communities in the South and in the Plains states, which restricted branch banking. Because of its policy of mandatory par settlement, 50 percent of the banks in the Richmond district and 75 percent in the Atlanta district did not join the Federal Reserve System (Watkins 1929, 115–22).

44. Spahr (1926, 232–90) and Jessup (1967, 9–13) recount the history of the par clearing controversy.

45. The figure of a 50 percent increase in the nonpar list may exaggerate the impact of the 1923 decision because the Fed tended to overstate the size of its par list

(R. Alton Gilbert, pers. comm., July 9, 2003). The rents earned from present-ment or remittance charges were probably an important source of revenue, but when par banks opened in town such charges were usually eliminated. Accord-ing to Stevens (1998, 19–20), 87 percent of nonpar banks in North Carolina in 1957 and 95 percent of those in the country as a whole in 1964, for example, faced no local competition from par banking rivals.

46. There is no comprehensive study of the early history of the ACH. Our analysis is based on Frisbee (1986), Stone (1986, 1990), Stone and White (1986), McAndrews (1994), and Connolly and Eisenmenger (2000).

47. As the Fed's potential and actual competitors, larger banks were more skeptical and worried that relaxation of the cost-recovery rules would allow the Fed to subsidize unfairly its emerging electronic payments services.

48. For related examples of the Fed's strategic use of the discount window in case of financial and operating crises, see Bernanke (1990, 148–49) and Garber and Weisbrod (1992, 286–88).

49. Private ACH networks explicitly designate the Fed as supplier of default set-tlement services for transactions between regional operators but also in case of systemic risk that threatens to disrupt their operations (see McAndrews 1993, 15–18).

50. By way of contrast, McAndrews (1998) points to the credit card (and, more re-cently, ATM) markets, where private clearinghouses can wield settlement fees as an instrument of "tacit collusion" to restrict entry.

51. The committee could also direct resources toward troubled banks, but it rarely exercised this power. It extended special assistance to the Metropolitan National Bank in 1884 and the Heinze-Morse banks in 1907 (Sprague 1910, 246–51, 352). Member banks generally were not allowed to fail during periods of sus-pension but were later expelled for failure to repay the loan certificates after re-sumption had occurred (Gorton 1985, 281–82).

52. Each panic was precipitated by a notable commercial failure (most famously, that of Jay Cooke in 1873) or an accompanying stock market crash (Calomiris and Gorton 1991). For detailed narratives of each panic, see Sprague (1910), Roberds (1995), and Wicker (2000). Sprague eschews the term "panic" for 1890, referring to it as a "financial stringency" instead, but for our purposes "panic" is a descriptive enough term.

53. Loan certificates were authorized but not issued in December 1895 and August 1896. In addition to New York, loan certificates were issued by the clearinghouses of Boston, Philadelphia, Cincinnati, St. Louis, and New Orleans in 1873 and in 1890 in Boston and Philadelphia. In 1893 clearinghouses in at least 12 cities is-sued certificates; in 1907 clearinghouse loan certificates or checks were issued in 71 of the 145 cities with populations greater than twenty-five thousand (Sprague 1910, 438–39; Dwyer and Gilbert 1989, p. 51).

54. In early 1873 nearly three-quarters of New York bankers' balances were con-centrated in seven banks. In contrast to the other New York banks with a pri-marily local business, these seven kept low levels of surplus reserves and so were particularly vulnerable to increased demands for cash by interior banks, seasonally but especially during financial crisis.

55. Even without a formal central bank, the federal government also assisted in the crisis. Beginning on October 24, the Treasury deposited $36 million in New York national banks, about half the amount paid out to interior banks and local depositors, including trust companies. The Treasury also made deposits in banks in several other cities until by mid-November it had used up all its available non-operating funds (Sprague 1910, 263–64; Wicker 2000, 98–99).

56. A. Piatt Andrew (1908, 497), the director of the United States Mint and a staff member of the National Monetary Commission, observes that the 1907 panic was "probably the most extensive and prolonged breakdown of the country's credit mechanism which has occurred since the establishment of the national banking system." One index, deposits in failed banks, was much larger in 1907 than ever before (Wicker 2000, 112).

57. Sprague (1910, 121–23) also notes that other divisions and opportunistic behavior almost prevented the pooling of reserves in 1873. Under the agreement, banks pooled their official reserves of legal tender and greenbacks. Banks with larger legal reserves, such as Chemical, initially refused to participate, agreeing only after being threatened with expulsion. To minimize their obligations, several other banks exchanged greenbacks for bank notes, which did not count as official reserves but could be used to satisfy customers' withdrawal demands.

58. According to Roberds (1995, 26), "The delay of a day or two was critical," as it could fatally weaken depositors' confidence in the liquidity of their institutions. These same problems plagued the Federal Reserve in the early 1930s. The Fed neglected the plight of nonmembers, which were failing in increasing numbers, but also was paralyzed by internal conflicts among members (Friedman and Schwartz 1963; Epstein and Ferguson 1984).

59. The loan committee's explanation for the delay suggests divisions among member banks as well: "It had been hoped that the crisis imminent for a week previous might be successfully met without the necessity for the issuance of Clearinghouse Loan Certificates, in spite of the urgent application for assistance from several bank members of the Association" (quoted in Wicker 2000, 97).

60. A staunch advocate of privatization, Richard Timberlake (1978, 223) describes the dilemma facing a quasi-private central bank: "[It] had to restrain itself during prosperous periods from lending on all good paper, which would have maximized its earning assets, so that it would have some metallic reserves to parlay among commercial banks if they were threatened by liquidity drains. When a panic occurred, the now-central bank had to lean into the wind, and, as Bagehot prescribed, lend on what might be call subjunctive paper—paper that would be good when general business conditions were again normal. Thus the commercial-public-central bank had to be more conservative than its fellows during a boom, and radical to the point of foolhardy in a crisis! . . . Central banking policies could never be rationalized by recourse to commercial banking principles." The NYCH would have faced a similar dilemma between private profit maximization and public responsibility, if it had envisioned any public role for itself.

61. Stone (1990, 25) depicts a nearly 96 percent drop in unit costs of the Fed's ACH operations over the 1980s. Econometric analysis by Bauer and Ferrier (1996, 1025) yields higher estimates of average unit costs (1.7 cents) but nonetheless shows strong increasing returns in ACH processing.

62. Langlois and Robertson (1989) make a similar argument to explain the vertical integration of large industrial corporations at the turn of the twentieth century—that is, for conscious control and coordination by private managerial bureaucracies.
63. The committee convened ten national and fifty-two regional forums, to which they invited various "payments system participants," including representatives of depository institutions and other private retail and wholesale intermediaries (FRS 1997, 3). To foster an open discussion, the committee ensured the anonymity of each participant and only issued a report summarizing the input from distinct groups.

References

Adams, Robert M., Paul W. Bauer, and Robin C. Sickles. 2002. "Scale Economies, Scope Economies, and Technical Change in Federal Reserve Payment Processing." Finance and Economics Discussion Paper 2002-57. Washington: Board of Governors of the Federal Reserve System.

Andrew, A. Piatt. 1908. "Substitutes for Cash in the Panic of 1907." *Quarterly Journal of Economics* 22(4): 497–516.

Angelini, Paolo. 1998. "An Analysis of Competitive Externalities in Gross Settlement Systems." *Journal of Banking and Finance* 22(1): 1–18.

Anvari, Mohsen. 1990. "The Canadian Payment System: An Evolving Structure." In *The U.S. Payment System: Efficiency, Risk and the Role of the Federal Reserve,* edited by David B. Humphrey. Boston: Kluwer Academic.

Bank for International Settlements, Committee on Payment and Settlement Systems (BIS). 1999. *Retail Payments in Selected Countries: A Comparative Study.* Basel: Bank for International Settlements.

———. 2000. *Clearing and Settlement Arrangements for Retail Payments in Selected Countries.* Basel: Bank for International Settlements.

———. 2002. *Statistics on Payment and Settlement Systems in Selected Countries.* Basel: Bank for International Settlements.

Bank of Canada. 1997. Department of Finance. *The Payments System in Canada: An Overview of Concepts and Structures.* Report 60. Ottawa: Bank of Canada.

Bauer, Paul W., and Gary D. Ferrier. 1996. "The Efficiency of Payment System Intermediaries: Scale Economies, Cost Efficiencies, and Technological Change in Federal Reserve Payments Processing." *Journal of Money, Credit and Banking* 28(4, part 2 "Payment Systems Research and Public Policy Risk, Efficiency, and Innovation"): 1004–39.

Bennett, Paul, and Stavros Peristiani. 2002. "Are U.S. Reserve Requirements Still Binding?" *Federal Reserve Bank of New York Economic Policy Review* 8(1): 1–16.

Berger, Allen N., Nathan H. Miller, Mitchell A. Peterson, Raghuram G. Rajan, and Jeremy C. Stein. 2003. "Does Function Follow Organizational Form? Evidence from the Lending Practices of Large and Small Banks." Unpublished manuscript. Washington: Board of Governors of the Federal Reserve System.

Bernanke, Ben S. 1990. "Clearing and Settlement During the Crash." *Review of Financial Studies* (3)1: 122–51.

Biehl, Andrew, James McAndrews, and Chris Stefanadis. 2002. "A Review of Retail and Wholesale Markets for Funds Transfers." Unpublished report. New York: New York Federal Reserve Bank.

Bodenhorn, Howard. 2002. "Making the Little Guy Pay: Payments-System Networks, Cross-Subsidization, and the Collapse of the Suffolk System." *Journal of Economic History* 62(1): 147–69.

Calomiris, Charles W., and Gary Gorton. 1991. "The Origins of Bank Panics: Models, Facts, and Bank Regulation." In *Financial Markets and Financial Crises,* edited by R. Glenn Hubbard. Chicago: University of Chicago Press.

Calomiris, Charles W., and Charles M. Kahn. 1991. "The Role of Demandable Debt in Structuring Optimal Banking Arrangements." *American Economic Review* 81(3): 497–513.

Cannon, James G. 1910. *Clearing Houses.* National Monetary Commission. Washington: U.S. Government Printing Office.

Carlton, Dennis W., and Alan S. Frankel. 1995. "Antitrust and Payment Technologies." *Federal Reserve Bank of St. Louis Review* 77(6): 41–54.

Caskey, John P., and Simon St. Laurent. 1994. "The Susan B. Anthony Dollar and the Theory of Coin/Note Substitutions." *Journal of Money, Credit, and Banking* 26(3, part 1): 495–510.

Champ, Bruce, Bruce D. Smith, and Stephen D. Williamson. 1996. "Currency Elasticity and Banking Panics: Theory and Evidence." *Canadian Journal of Economics* 29(4): 828–64.

Clair, Robert T., Joanna O. Kolson, and Kenneth J. Robinson. 1995. "The Texas Banking Crisis and the Payments System." *Federal Reserve Bank of Dallas Economic Review:* 13–21.

Clouse, James A., and Douglas W. Elmendorf. 1997. "Declining Required Reserves and the Volatility of the Federal Funds Rate." Finance and Economics Discussion Paper 1997-30. Washington: Board of Governors of the Federal Reserve System.

Congressional Budget Office (CBO). 1996. "Emerging Electronic Methods for Making Retail Payments." Washington: CBO.

———. 1998. "Competition in ATM Markets: Are ATMs Money Machines?" Washington: CBO (July).

Connolly, Paul M., and Robert W. Eisenmenger. 2000. "The Role of the Federal Reserve in the Payments System." In *The Evolution of Monetary Policy and the Federal Reserve System over the Past Thirty Years: A Conference in Honor of Frank E. Morris,* edited by Richard W. Kopcke and Lynn Elaine Browne. Boston: Federal Reserve Bank of Boston.

Conzen, Michael. 1977. "The Maturing Urban System in the United States, 1840–1910." *Annals of the Association of American Geographers* 67(1): 88–108.

David, Paul A., and Shane Greenstein. 1990. "The Economics of Compatibility Standards: An Introduction to Recent Research." *Economics of Innovation and New Technology* 1(1): 3–41.

Donaldson, R. Glen. 1993. "Financing Banking Crises." *Journal of Monetary Economics* 31(1): 69–95.

Dowd, Kevin. 1994. "Competitive Banking, Bankers' Clubs, and Bank Regulation." *Journal of Money, Credit, and Banking* 26(2): 289–308.

Downes, Tom, and Shane Greenstein. 2002. "Universal Access and Local Internet Markets in the US." *Research Policy* 31(7): 1035–52.

Dwyer, Gerald P., and R. Alton Gilbert. 1989. "Bank Runs and Private Remedies." *Federal Reserve Bank of St. Louis Review* 71(3): 43–61.

Economides, Nicholas. 1993. "Network Economics with Application to Finance." *Financial Markets, Institutions and Instruments* 2(5): 89–97.

———. 1996. "The Economics of Networks." *International Journal of Industrial Organization* 14(6): 673–99.

Economides, Nicholas, and Aloysius Siow. 1988. "The Division of Markets Is Limited by the Extent of Liquidity (Spatial Competition with Externalities)." *American Economic Review* 78(1): 108–21.

Electronic Payments Network (EPN). 2003. "The Electronic Payments Network and the Automated Clearing House—A History." Available at: www.epaynetwork.com/infofiles/EPN_History.pdf (accessed November 18, 2004).

Epstein, Gerald, and Thomas Ferguson. 1984. "Monetary Policy, Loan Liquidation and Industrial Conflict: The Federal Reserve and the Open Market Operations of 1932." *Journal of Economic History* 44(4): 957–84.

Evans, David S., and Richard Schmalensee. 1999. *Paying with Plastic: The Digital Revolution in Buying and Borrowing.* Cambridge, Mass.: MIT Press.

Farrell, Joseph, and Garth Saloner. 1985. "Standardization, Compatibility, and Innovation." *Rand Journal of Economics* 16(1): 70–83.

———. 1986. "Installed Base and Compatibility: Innovation, Product Preannouncements, and Predation." *American Economic Review* 76(3): 940–55.

Federal Reserve Board of Governors. 1981. "Federal Reserve Guidelines for the Provision of Financial Services." Available at: www.federalreserve.gov/paymentsystems/pricing/guidelines.htm (accessed November 19, 2004).

———. 1990. "The Federal Reserve in the Payments System." Available at: www.federalreserve.gov/paymentsystems/pricing/frpaysys.htm (accessed November 19, 2004).

———. 2002. "Statutory Authority for Services Pricing Policy." Available at: www.federalreserve.gov/paymentsystems/pricing/pricingpol.htm (accessed November 18, 2004).

Federal Reserve System, Committee on the Federal Reserve in the Payments Mechanism (FRS). 1997. "Summary of Input from Payments System Forums." Washington: Federal Reserve System.

———. 1998. "The Federal Reserve in the Payments Mechanism." Report 39. Washington: Federal Reserve System.

Federal Reserve System, Committee on the Federal Reserve in the Payments Mechanism (FRS). Retail Payments System Project. 2002. "A Snapshot of the U.S. Payments Landscape." Available at: http://www.frbservices.org:80/Retail/pdf/RetailPaymentsResearchProject.pdf (accessed November 18, 2004).

Flannery, Mark. 1996. "Financial Crises, Payments System Problems, and Discount Window Lending," *Journal of Money, Credit, and Banking* 28(4, part 2): 804–24.

Fleming, Michael J., and Kenneth D. Garbade. 2002. "When the Back Office Moved to the Front Burner: Settlement Fails in the Treasury Market after 9/11." *Federal Reserve Bank of New York Economic Policy Review* 8(2): 35–57.

Friedman, Milton, and Anna Schwartz. 1963. *A Monetary History of the United States.* Princeton, N.J.: Princeton University Press.

Frisbee, Paula. 1986. "The ACH: An Elusive Dream." *Federal Reserve Bank of Atlanta Economic Review* 72(3): 4–8.

Gabel, David. 1994. "Competition in a Network Industry: The Telephone Industry, 1894–1910." *Journal of Economic History* 94(3): 543–72.

Garbade, Kenneth D., and William L. Silber. 1979. "The Payments System and Domestic Exchange Rates: Technological versus Institutional Change." *Journal of Monetary Economics* 5(1): 1–22.

Garber, Peter, and Steven R. Weisbrod. 1990. "Banks in the Market for Liquidity." Working Paper 3381. Cambridge, Mass.: National Bureau of Economic Research.

———. 1992. *The Economics of Banking, Liquidity, and Money.* Lexington, Mass.: D.C. Heath.

Gerdes, Geoffrey R., and Jack K. Walton. 2002. "The Use of Checks and Other Noncash Payments Instruments in the United States." *Federal Reserve Bulletin* 88(8): 360–74.

Gilbert, R. Alton. 1983. "Economies of Scale in Correspondent Banking: Note." *Journal of Money, Credit, and Banking* 15(4): 483–88.

———. 1998. "Did the Fed's Founding Improve the Efficiency of the U.S. Payments System?" *Federal Reserve Bank of St. Louis Review* 80(3): 121–42.

———. 2000. "The Advent of the Federal Reserve and the Efficiency of the Payments System: The Collection of Checks, 1915–1930." *Explorations in Economic History* 37(2): 121–48.

Goodfriend, Marvin S. 1990. "Money, Credit, Banking, and Payment System Policy." In *The U.S. Payment System: Efficiency, Risk and the Role of the Federal Reserve,* edited by David B. Humphrey. Boston: Kluwer Academic.

Goodfriend, Marvin, and Robert King. 1988. "Financial Deregulation, Monetary Policy, and Central Banking." In *Restructuring Banking and Financial Services in America,* edited by William Haraf and Rose Marie Kushmeider. Washington: American Enterprise Institute.

Goodhart, Charles A. E. 1969. *The New York Money Market and the Finance of Trade, 1900–1913.* Cambridge, Mass.: Harvard University Press.

———. 1988. *The Evolution of Central Banks.* Cambridge, Mass.: MIT Press.

Gorton, Gary. 1985. "Clearinghouses and the Origins of Central Banking in the United States." *Journal of Economic History* 45(2): 277–84.

Gowrisankaran, Gautam, and Joanna Stavins. 1999. "Network Externalities and Technology Adoption: Lessons from Electronic Payments." Working Paper 40. Boston: Federal Reserve Bank of Boston.

Green, Edward J., and Richard M. Todd. 2001. "Thoughts on the Fed's Role in the Payments System." *Federal Reserve Bank of Minneapolis Quarterly Review* 25(1): 12–27.

Huber, Peter W. 1987. "The Geodesic Network: 1987 Report on Competition in the Telephone Industry." U.S. Department of Justice, Antitrust Division. Washington: U.S. Government Printing Office.

James, John A., and David F. Weiman. 2003. "Correspondent Banking Networks and the Formation of an Integrated National Payments System, 1880–1914." Unpublished manuscript.

Jessup, Paul. 1967. *The Theory and Practice of Nonpar Banking.* Evanston, Ill.: Northwestern University Press.

Juncker, George R., Bruce J. Summers, and Florence M. Young. 1991. "A Primer on the Settlement of Payments in the United States." *Federal Reserve Bulletin* 77(1): 847–58.

Kahn, Charles M., and William Roberds. 2001a. "The CLS Bank: A Solution to the Risks of International Payments Settlement?" *Carnegie-Rochester Conference Series on Public Policy* 54(0): 191–226.

———. 2001b. "Real-Time Gross Settlement and the Costs of Immediacy." *Journal of Monetary Economics* 47(2): 299–319.

———. 2002. "The Economics of Payment Finality." *Federal Reserve Bank of Atlanta Economic Review* 87(2): 1–12.

Kane, Edward J. 1982. "Changes in the Provision of Correspondent-Banking Services and the Role of the Federal Reserve under the DIDMC Act." *Carnegie-Rochester Conference Series on Public Policy* 16(0): 93–126.

Kashyap, Anil K., Raghuram Rajan, and Jerome C. Stein. 2002. "Banks as Liquidity Providers: An Explanation for the Coexistence of Lending and Deposit-Taking." *Journal of Finance* 57(1): 33–73.

Katz, Michael L., and Carl Shapiro. 1985. "Network Externalities, Competition, and Compatibility." *American Economic Review* 75(3): 424–40.

———. 1986. "Technology Adoption in the Presence of Network Externalities." *Journal of Political Economy* 94(4): 822–41.

Kaufman, George. 1991. "The Lender of Last Resort: A Contemporary Perspective." *Journal of Financial Services Research* 5(2): 95–110.

Keynes, John M. 1964. *The General Theory of Employment, Interest, and Money.* New York: Harcourt, Brace and World.

Kindleberger, Charles P. 1983. "Standards as Public, Collective, and Private Goods." *Kyklos* 36(3): 377–96.

Kroszner, Randall S. 2000. "Lessons from Financial Crises: The Role of Clearinghouses." *Journal of Financial Services Research* 18(2–3): 157–71.

Kuprianov, Anatoli. 1985. "The Monetary Control Act and the Role of the Federal Reserve in the Interbank Clearing Market." *Federal Reserve Bank of Richmond Economic Quarterly* 71(4): 23–35.

Kuttner, Kenneth N., and James J. McAndrews. 2001. "Personal On-Line Payments." *Federal Reserve Bank of New York Economic Policy Review* 7(3): 35–50.

Lacker, Jeffrey M., Jeffrey D. Walker, and John A. Weinberg. 1999. "The Fed's Entry into Check Clearing Reconsidered." *Federal Reserve Bank of Richmond Economic Quarterly* 85(2): 1–31.

Langlois, Richard N., and Paul L. Robertson. 1989. "Explaining Vertical Integration: Lessons for the American Automobile Industry." *Journal of Economic History* 49(2): 361–75.

Lockhart, Oliver C. 1921. "The Development of Interbank Borrowing in the National Banking System, 1869–1914." Pts. 1 and 2. *Journal of Political Economy* 29(2,3): 138–60, 222–40.

McAndrews, James. 1991. "The Evolution of Shared ATM Networks." *Federal Reserve Bank of Philadelphia Business Review*: 3–16.

————. 1993. "The Automated Clearinghouse System: Moving toward Electronic Payment." Unpublished manuscript. Philadelphia: Federal Reserve Bank of Philadelphia.

————. 1994. "The Automated Clearinghouse System: Moving toward Electronic Payment." *Federal Reserve Bank of Philadelphia Business Review:* 15–23.

————. 1995. "Antitrust Issues in Payment Systems: Bottlenecks, Access, and Essential Facilities." *Federal Reserve Bank of Philadelphia Business Review:* 3–12.

————. 1997. "Network Issues and Payment Systems." *Federal Reserve Bank of Philadelphia Business Review:* 15–25.

————. 1998. "Direct Presentment Regulation in Payments." *Research in Economics* 52(3): 311–26.

McAndrews, James, and Simon M. Potter. 2002. "Liquidity Effects of the Events of September 11, 2001." *Federal Reserve Bank of New York Economic Policy Review* 8(2): 59–80.

McAndrews, James, and Samira Rajan. 2000. "The Timing and Funding of Fedwire Funds Transfer." *Federal Reserve Bank of New York Economic Policy Review* 6(2): 17–31.

McAndrews, James, and William Roberds. 1995. "Banks, Payments, and Coordination." *Journal of Financial Intermediation* 4(4): 305–27.

————. 1999. "Payment Intermediation and the Origins of Banking." Staff Report 40. New York: New York Federal Reserve Bank.

McAndrews, James J., and Philip E. Strahan. 2002. "Deregulation, Correspondent Banking, and the Role of the Federal Reserve." *Journal of Financial Intermediation* 11(3): 320–43.

Mester, Loretta J. 2000. "The Changing Nature of the Payments System: Should New Players Mean New Rules?" *Federal Reserve Bank of Philadelphia Business Review:* 3–27.

Miron, Jeffrey A. 1986. "Financial Panics, the Seasonality of the Nominal Interest Rate, and the Founding of the Fed." *American Economic Review* 76(1): 125–40.

Moen, Jon, and Ellis Tallman. 1992. "The Bank Panic of 1907: The Role of Trust Companies." *Journal of Economic History* 52(3): 611–30.

————. 2000. "Clearinghouse Membership and Deposit Contraction during the Panic of 1907." *Journal of Economic History* 60(1): 145–63.

Mueller, Milton. 1996. *Universal Service: Competition, Interconnection, and Monopoly in the Making of the American Telephone System.* Cambridge, Mass.: MIT Press.

Myers, Margaret G. 1931. *The New York Money Market.* Vol. 1, *Origins and Development.* New York: Columbia University Press.

Odell, Kerry A., and David F. Weiman. 1998. "Metropolitan Development, Regional Financial Centers, and the Founding of the Fed in the Lower South." *Journal of Economic History* 58(1): 103–25.

Osterberg, William P., and James B. Thomson. 1999. "Banking Consolidation and Correspondent Banking." *Federal Reserve Bank of Cleveland Economic Review* 35(1): 9–20.

Redenius, Scott A. 2002. *Between Reforms: The U.S. Banking System in the Postbellum Period.* Ph.D. dissertation, Yale University.

Redish, Angela. 1991. "The Government's Role in the Payment Systems: Lessons from the Canadian Experience." In *Governing Banking's Future: Markets vs. Regulation,* edited by Catherine England. Boston: Kluwer Academic.

Roberds, William. 1995. "Financial Crises and the Payments System: Lessons from the National Banking Era." *Federal Reserve Bank of Atlanta Economic Review* 80(5): 15–31.

Saloner, Garth, and Andrea Shepard. 1995. "Adoption of Technologies with Network Effects: An Empirical Examination of the Adoption of Automated Teller Machines." *Rand Journal of Economics* 26(3): 479–501.

Schwartz, Anna. 1992. "The Misuse of the Fed's Discount Window." *Federal Reserve Bank of St. Louis Review* 74(5): 58–69.

Spahr, Walter E. 1926. *The Clearing and Collection of Checks.* New York: Bankers Publishing.

Sprague, O. M. W. 1910. *History of Crises under the National Banking System.* National Monetary Commission. Washington: U.S. Government Printing Office.

Stevens, Ed. 1996. "The Founders' Intentions: Sources of the Payment Services Franchise of the Federal Reserve Banks." Working Paper 0396. Cleveland: Federal Reserve Bank of Cleveland.

———. 1998. "Non-Par Banking: Competition and Monopoly in Markets for Payments Services." Working Paper 9817. Cleveland: Federal Reserve Bank of Cleveland.

Stigler, George. 1958. "The Economies of Scale." *Journal of Law and Economics* 1(1): 54–71.

Stone, Bernell K. 1986. "Electronic Payments at the Crossroads." *Federal Reserve Bank of Atlanta Economic Review* 72(3): 20–33.

———. 1990. "The Electronic Payments Industry: Change Barriers and Success Requirements from a Market Segments Perspective." In *The U.S. Payment System: Efficiency, Risk and the Role of the Federal Reserve,* edited by David B. Humphrey. Boston: Kluwer Academic.

Stone, Bernell K., and George C. White. 1986. "Scenarios for the Future of the ACH." *Federal Reserve Bank of Atlanta Economic Review* 72(4): 29–49.

Summers, Bruce J., and R. Alton Gilbert. 1996. "Clearing and Settlement of U.S. Dollar Payments: Back to the Future?" *Federal Reserve Bank of St. Louis Review* 78(5): 3–27.

The Clearing House Service Company (TCHC). 2003. "CHIPS Rules and Administrative Procedures." New York: The Clearing House Service Company.

Thomson Media. 2002. *Card Industry Directory.* New York: Thomson Media.

Timberlake, Richard. 1978. *The Origins of Central Banking in the United States.* Cambridge, Mass.: Harvard University Press.

———. 1984. "The Central Banking Role of Clearinghouse Associations." *Journal of Money, Credit, and Banking* 16(1): 1–15.

———. 1985. "Legislative Construction of the Monetary Control Act of 1980." *American Economic Review* 75(2): 97–102.

U.S. General Accounting Office (GAO). 2002. *Payment Systems: Central Bank Roles Vary, but Goals Are the Same.* Washington: U.S. General Accounting Office.

U.S. House of Representatives. 1913. "Investigation of the Financial and Monetary conditions in the United States under House Resolutions Nos. 429 and 504 before the Subcommittee of Banking and Currency." Washington: U.S. Government Printing Office.

Watkins, Leonard L. 1929. *Bankers' Balances.* New York: John Wiley and Sons.

Weiman, David F., and Richard C. Levin. 1994. "Preying for Monopoly? The Case of Southern Bell Telephone Company, 1894–1912." *Journal of Political Economy* 102(1): 103–26.

Weinberg, John A. 1997. "The Organization of Private Payment Networks." *Federal Reserve Bank of Richmond Economic Quarterly* 83(2): 25–43.

White, Eugene N. 1983. *The Regulation and Reform of the American Banking System, 1900–1929.* Princeton, N.J.: Princeton University Press.

Wicker, Elmus. 2000. *Banking Panics of the Gilded Age.* New York: Cambridge University Press.

Part II

HUMAN SERVICES

THE THREE studies in part II examine markets in basic human services. One of them—primary and secondary education—has for a long time been regarded as a responsibility of the state. The other two—preschool child care and medical care—have been accepted as state responsibilities in many countries, but that issue is contested in the United States. Even for these, however, in recent years no high-income country has left the governing structures simply to unregulated market operation.

Unlike the sectors considered in part I, none of the sectors considered here has ever been regarded as a natural monopoly. The suppliers of the service in question tend to be small and local. The issue of health insurance is something of an exception in that there is some argument that a "single-payer" system would be more efficient than one involving competitive private insurance companies. For the sectors and activities considered here, however, the debate about the efficacy of market governance and the need for government action centers mainly on two issues. One is the importance to the public of the services provided, beyond their value to the individuals receiving them, and, in light of that public interest, the adequacy of private decentralized decision making to ensure those benefits. The second is concern about the adequacy of the services that would be provided to the poor in the absence of public funding.

Primary and second education and preschool child care are canonical examples of services from which the benefits are at once private (the recipient child and family clearly benefit and may be willing to pay for services rendered) and public (it is widely agreed that society as a whole benefits when its children are brought up well educated and cared for). In addition, in many people's eyes, every child has a right to a decent upbringing and education, and provision of these is, in one way or another, a social obligation. This means that the government has at least a residual responsibility.

As with the chapters in part I, the chapters here focus on the United States, with comparative reference to other countries, particularly in Europe. In the United States, as in Europe, there is little argument against public finance of primary and secondary education. That is, the quasi-public nature of the benefits is not an issue. The debate is, rather, about who should provide the education and who should control the details of what goes on in schools. Private schools play a role in primary and secondary education in other countries as well as in the United States. But the arguments for private provision of public education in the United States seem much more couched in terms of the theoretical advantages of market organization and competition than in other countries. The debate is continuing and intense.

The debate about how to govern preschool child care has taken new form in the United States as, over the past forty years, the proportion of women with children who have jobs away from home has increased dramatically. While other nations have seen similar developments, and many have responded with significant increases in state financing of child care, in the United States the question of who should pay is still under debate; and the question of who should provide, while sometimes institutionally connected, is argued out on different terms. The argument for private provision, with or without public funding, like the argument over who should pay, is much more tied in the United States to propositions about the advantages of market organization and competition than is the case in other countries.

The argument that provision of quality services provides broad social benefits as well as private ones seems much more accepted with respect to primary and secondary education and child care than to private health care. It is widely accepted, of course, that governments have a responsibility for public health measures, and in some cases there is overlap between what is needed to ensure private health and public health, as, for example, in the case of vaccination. Public health is addressed later in this volume. Regarding private medical care, the main thrust behind the growing involvement of public funding and regulation, in the United States as in other countries, is the argument that all humans, or at least all citizens, should have access to adequate care when they need it, even if they cannot afford to pay for it.

Unlike a number of other high-income countries, the political process in the United States has not led to the adoption of a position that access to good health care is a citizen's right, at least not explicitly and broadly, although we may be moving in that direction. Public funding of health care is focused on particular segments of the population, the elderly and the poor. However, there is growing concern about people who, while not generally poor, would be hard pressed to pay for expensive medical treatment, should the need arise.

For a variety of reasons, over the past half century expenditures on medical care as a fraction of national income have risen significantly, as have average medical costs per person. Private insurance, usually associated with an employment contract, also has expanded; third-party payments, including Medicare, Medicaid, and Medicaid-related programs as well as private insurance, now cover the lion's share of medical expenses. On the other hand, there remains a significant block of people who are covered neither by private insurance nor by present government programs, and there is great political pressure to provide coverage for those who cannot afford to pay on their own and at the same time to contain costs.

Meanwhile in the United States, as in many other high-income countries, the supply of medical care remains principally in the hands of for-profit providers. There is continuing debate about whether and how, in the present demand environment, market competition among providers can play a useful role in making medical care responsive to needs while keeping costs under control. There are many strong advocates for the positive here. There is also a growing number of skeptics, who argue that, in the absence of government provision, regulation is needed to ensure quality and keep costs under control.

6

THE ROLE OF MARKETS IN AMERICAN K–12 EDUCATION

Richard J. Murnane

S INCE the publication in 1983 of "A Nation at Risk," a government-sponsored commission report noting "a rising tide of mediocrity" (National Commission on Excellence in Education 1983, 5), American kindergarten through twelfth-grade (K–12) education has come under intense scrutiny. One concern is that weaknesses in American education undermine the country's position in the world. Another is that inequality in access to good education contributes to the growing earnings inequality that may threaten the nation's democratic institutions. Some analysts and policy makers see greater use of markets in allocating educational services as the solution to these social problems. Others fear that greater reliance on markets will destroy a public education system that has served the country well. In this chapter, I argue that neither polar position is defensible. Moreover, the polar positions divert attention from the significant roles that markets currently play in the delivery of K–12 education in the United States and from the critical details of regulatory designs for proposals that would alter the role of markets in U.S. education.

Context: The Early Years of American Public Education

The nation's founding fathers saw popular education as a critical vehicle for building the new nation. Education would teach the citizenry to vote intelligently and behave virtuously. It would remedy the ignorance and passions that had plagued other countries' experiments with the republican form of government. Contrary to the situation in England, there was little opposition to the position that an educated citizenry was in the best interests of the nation.[1]

There was much less agreement in the early years of the nation on who should pay for schools and who should govern them. Although Thomas

Jefferson argued in 1779 for free public schools funded by taxes, his proposal was defeated. In the first fifty years of the republic, most children who attended school were either in private schools or in town-sponsored schools funded by a mix of taxes on property, fees charged to parents, and in-kind donations from parents. These schools were local institutions typically controlled by parents.

Only toward the middle of the nineteenth century did school reformers such as Horace Mann and Henry Barnard convince legislatures to embrace what became known as the common school. While the philosophies of the common-school reformers differed in details, they held common beliefs in "republicanism, Protestantism, and capitalism" (Kaestle 1983, 76). They shared with the founding fathers the belief that the republican form of government required an educated citizenry. Their Calvinist heritage emphasized the importance of inculcating in the young the importance of obedience, hard work, and upright behavior. They felt strongly that the common public school was the critical institution for "Americanizing" the rapidly growing number of immigrants, most of whom did not share the founding fathers' English Protestant heritage. In other words, Mann and Barnard saw the common school as providing critical public benefits to the emerging nation. They also believed that a greater role for state governments in regulating education was essential to achieving their reform agenda.

Not everyone supported the school reformers' agenda. Some felt that taxation to pay for the education of other people's children violated the freedom their forebears had fought for. Others resisted state infringement on local communities' decisions about the content and governance of their children's schooling. Still others, including many among the growing number of American Catholics, resented the use of the Protestant Bible in the public schools and the way their children were treated in these schools.

Although the school reformers' agenda evoked considerable controversy, the reformers carried the day. Elements of their reform program included a longer school year, better-educated teachers, higher teacher wages, and uniform textbooks. Eventually, reforms came to include complete public funding. Over the middle third of the nineteenth century, the percentage of children attending private schools dropped markedly. The percentage of New York City children in private schools, for example, dropped from 62 percent in 1829 to 18 percent in 1850 (Kaestle 1983, 116).

The historian Carl Kaestle summarizes this early history of the American common school as follows:

> Two enduring legacies of the common-school reform movement are the American faith in education and the cosmopolitan ideal of inclusive public schools. School reformers believed that common schools could solve the problems of diversity, instability, and equal opportunity. That faith has been resilient in

American history. Despite the periodic rediscovery that schools have not in fact solved our problems, and despite occasional periods of disillusionment with the education profession, the American common-school system has always revived, buoyed by Americans' faith that education is the best approach to most social problems. That faith is best redeemed, American leaders say, in schools that are common to all, respectful to all, and equal in their treatment of all children. Despite the cultural cost involved in having a common public-school system, and despite the public schools' manifest failure to treat children equally, Americans widely share a belief in fairness and cohesion through common schools, a belief that is the core of the cosmopolitan solution. (Kaestle 1983, 221–22)

The victory of the common-school reformers in the middle of the nineteenth century did not end controversy about the governance and quality of American schools. In virtually every subsequent decade, vociferous critics pointed out failures of American schools. Nonetheless, public schools survived, in large measure because they provided public benefits critical to a diverse, pluralistic society.

Different perceptions of the failures of public schools sustained a relatively small but vibrant set of nonpublic schools. Generations of Catholic parents, the vast majority of them working class, have sent their children to Catholic schools, in many cases because they felt that their children were not treated fairly in public schools or because public schools did not support their religious beliefs. In 1950 more than 90 percent of students attending nonpublic schools were enrolled in Catholic schools. Wealthy parents sent their children to expensive private schools, not because their children were treated unequally but because they wanted unequal treatment, that is, a superior education to that available in public schools.

One could argue that today's debate about the role of markets in the delivery of schooling to American children is no more serious a challenge to the public schools than previous challenges were. This may prove to be the case. However, a recent U.S. Supreme Court decision may open the doors to new roles for private schools. This decision, in the Zelman v. Simmons-Harris (536 U.S. 639 [2002]) case, affirms the constitutionality of the use of public funds to provide vouchers to low-income families to pay for their children's education in church-run nonpublic schools in Cleveland. Another indication of growing concern about the education provided in public schools is the rising number of parents choosing to educate their children at home. The number of American children being educated at home has increased markedly over the past two decades, and today, almost 3 percent of American children are home-schooled. While parents have different motivations for schooling their children at home, the most common reason appears to be that they believe their children's moral and religious needs will not be met in public or currently available private schools (Reich 2002).

Sources of Concern

Perhaps the most widely cited evidence that American schools are in need of significant reform are studies showing that American students score lower than students in many other countries on comparable tests of math and science, as illustrated in table 6.1. Eighth-grade students in the United States scored significantly below the cross-national mean on the Third International Mathematics and Science Study tests taken by students in many Organization for Economic Cooperation and Development countries in 1999. These score differentials, which date back to the first international test score comparisons of the 1960s, appear to reflect differences in the skills and knowledge of eighth graders in different countries rather than anomalies of sample design.

To the authors of "A Nation at Risk," the lagging test score performance was an indication of a serious public problem. In the words of the report,

> Knowledge, learning, information, and skilled intelligence are the new raw materials of international commerce and are today spreading throughout the world as vigorously as miracle drugs, synthetic fertilizers, and blue jeans did earlier. If only to keep and improve on the slim competitive edge we still retain in world markets, we must dedicate ourselves to the reform of our educational system for the benefit of all—old and young alike, affluent and poor, majority and minority. Learning is the indispensable investment required for success in the "information age" we are entering. (National Commission on Excellence in Education 1983, 7)

TABLE 6.1 *Eighth-Grade Mean Scale Scores on the Third International Math and Science Study, 1999 by Country*

	Mathematics	Science
Korea	587	549
Japan	579	550
Belgium	558	535
Netherlands	540	545
Hungary	532	552
Canada	531	533
Australia	525	540
Czech Republic	520	539
United States	502	515
England	496	538
New Zealand	491	510
Italy	485	498
Country mean	529	534

Source: Data from Centre for Educational Research and Innovation (2001, 309, chart F1.2).

The dimensions of the problem were not seen as just economic:

> Our concern, however, goes well beyond matters such as industry and commerce. It also includes the intellectual, moral, and spiritual strengths of our people which knit together the very fabric of our society. The people of the United States need to know that individuals in our society who do not possess the levels of skill, literacy, and training essential to this new era will be effectively disenfranchised, not simply from the material rewards that accompany competent performance, but also from the chance to participate fully in our national life. A high level of shared education is essential to a free, democratic society and to the fostering of a common culture, especially in a country that prides itself on pluralism and individual freedom. (National Commission on Excellence in Education 1983, 7)

Of special concern is the enormous overrepresentation of students of color in this "disenfranchised" group. The National Assessment of Educational Progress, often referred to as the "nation's report card," shows that in the year 2000 as many as 69 percent of African American high school seniors and 56 percent of Hispanic seventeen-year-olds (compared with 26 percent of non-Hispanic white students) were unable to demonstrate basic mathematical skills (National Center for Education Statistics 2001). Students of color are also much more likely than non-Hispanic white students to drop out of American schools before graduation. This is especially true in large urban school districts that serve almost exclusively students of color. Many urban high schools have dropout rates exceeding 50 percent (Balfanz and Legters 2001). As the earnings figures in table 6.2 attest, school dropouts face dismal economic prospects.

The relatively low cognitive skills of students of color and their relatively high dropout rates pose alarming equity concerns. The primary ethical defense of an economic system in which labor market earnings determine family incomes is that all Americans are entitled to a free public education that effectively develops their skills and talents. This commitment is explicit in the constitutions of most states. Yet the evidence from the National Assessment

TABLE 6.2   *Median Annual Earnings for Americans Aged Twenty-Five Years and Older, 2000, by Educational Attainment (Dollars)*

	Less than Ninth Grade	High School Dropout	High School Graduate	Four-Year College Graduate
Males	17,658	21,365	30,665	50,441
Females	11,370	12,736	18,393	32,163

Source: Data from U.S. Bureau of the Census (2001).

of Educational Progress indicates that this commitment is not honored for a great many children, especially children of color living in big cities.

Added to the equity concerns are economic considerations because increasingly the American labor force will consist of workers of color and workers born outside the United States. While these groups made up less than 30 percent of the U.S. labor force in the year 2000, they will constitute more than half of the labor force by the year 2020 (Ellwood 2001). Consequently, the productivity of the nation's labor force (and the viability of the social security system) will increasingly be determined by workers who left American schools with weak cognitive skills.

In summary, the large percentage of young people of color who enter adulthood without the skills to earn a middle-class living and to support the next generation of children poses the nation's greatest educational problem. This is very much a public problem that threatens the nation. Because 40 percent of U.S. children of color attend school in one of the nation's fifty largest school districts, the greatest challenge is to improve the quality of education provided in big cities.[2] Moreover, much of the new evidence on the consequences of market-based educational initiatives comes from experiments in large cities. For these reasons I pay particular attention in this chapter to the implications for urban children of greater dependence on market-based initiatives for delivering K–12 educational services in the United States.

Many students in urban schools come to school with handicaps, including inadequate nutrition, mental or physical impairments, or a lack of knowledge of English. The parents of a large percentage of urban children have limited education and low incomes and lack the resources to supplement the instruction their children receive in school. Low-income families also are particularly likely to change residences frequently, resulting in disruptions of children's schooling. Developing strong skills in this student clientele is an enormously difficult challenge.

Peer group effects make the challenge more difficult. Children tend to learn less in classes in which a large proportion of students have relatively low skill levels than in classes in which their peers have higher achievement (Hoxby 2000b). They also learn less when they are in classes in which a large number of their classmates are mobile, either entering or leaving the school during the school year (Hanushek, Kain, and Rivkin 2001). The role of peer group effects in urban schools is exacerbated by the decisions middle-class parents make. To maximize the quality of their own children's education, they either move to suburbs or send their children to private schools, thereby increasing the percentage of low-income students with special needs in urban public schools. These decisions also leave urban schools without the voices of well-educated parents to make the case for high academic standards.

Another factor contributing to the low achievement of students leaving urban schools is the inability of public sector school bureaucracies to focus resources on improving student achievement.[3] Regulations designed to protect the interests of students with special needs, such as learning disabilities or a lack of English proficiency, place constraints on resource allocation decisions. Relevant federal legislation and court decisions include the 1975 Education for All Handicapped Children Act and the U.S. Supreme Court's 1974 decision in the bilingual case, Lau v. Nichols (414 U.S. 563 [1974]). The children covered by these laws and court decisions do need special attention. The difficulty is that the laws provide parents of eligible children with legal rights not available to other children. In urban districts in which large numbers of students fall under the provisions of the regulations, compliance complicates the resource allocation process and increases costs.[4]

There is little question that all these factors—the special needs of urban children, peer group effects, the inefficiency of government service provision, and legislative constraints on resource allocation—contribute to the low skills of students leaving urban schools. However, there is considerable disagreement on the relative importance of these factors. The most compelling case for the greater use of markets rests on the assumption that inefficiency in government service provision is the core problem, that private sector providers will be more efficient, and that competition will result in improvements in the performance of public schools.

The Roles of Markets in American K–12 Education

Throughout the nation's history, some parents have sent their children to private schools. Approximately 10 percent of American children attend nonpublic elementary or secondary schools today, a percentage that has remained remarkably stable over the past century.

Some analysts argue that the most effective way to improve the quality of education for children of color and children from low-income families is to allow them to attend nonpublic schools funded by tax revenues. The collection of information in the past twenty years on the cognitive skills and educational attainment of students attending public schools and Catholic schools allows comparisons of the effectiveness of these institutions. While the comparisons are fraught with potential for selectivity bias, the most carefully conducted studies show that students living in big cities who attend Catholic schools have higher academic achievement and are more likely to go on to college than are similar students attending urban public schools (Neal 1997). At the same time, there appears to be little difference in educational outcomes between students attending Catholic schools and students attending suburban public schools. Unfortunately, there is virtually no research examining the effectiveness of non-Catholic private schools. This is troubling since the percentage of students enrolled in private schools that are not

Catholic schools has increased from 10 percent in 1950 to more than 50 percent today.

Parents' choosing to send their children to private schools is not the only way that markets play a role in K–12 education in the United States. American public education is primarily a local affair, with fifteen thousand local school districts setting their own budgets and salaries, hiring their own teachers, and writing their own curriculums.[5] In most districts, individual schools serve children living in particular neighborhoods, and the quality of education varies markedly from district to district and even from school to school within districts. Given this governance structure, the dominant way families obtain the education they want for their children is by buying or renting housing in the attendance area of a public school they find attractive. Families pay premiums for housing in school districts and neighborhoods served by schools with high student achievement scores (Black 1999). Thus housing choices are a critical way in which markets influence the allocation of K–12 education services in the United States.

Historically, local control of public education has served the nation well. During the past century, American literacy rates and educational attainment rose rapidly, overtaking those in most European countries (Goldin 2001). The human capital created by formal schooling fueled economic growth throughout the twentieth century and contributed to rising incomes (Goldin and Katz 1999).

Recent research also indicates that competition among locally controlled public school districts contributes to improvements in student performance. Caroline Hoxby (2000a) finds that the more competition school districts face, the more successful they are in enhancing students' achievement. Using data in Texas, Eric Hanushek and Steven Rivkin (2003) find that the more competition school districts face, the better the quality of instructors they provide. At the same time, local control has also resulted in great variation in the quality of education provided, with children of color and children from low-income families especially likely to attend low-quality schools.

In summary, while the vast majority of children in the United States attend public schools, residential housing markets and markets for nonpublic schools currently play significant roles in determining the quality of education American children receive. These markets operate within a particular legal framework, elements of which include that access to public schools is tied to residential location, that (most) public schools cannot deny admission to students living within their attendance boundaries, and that parents can deduct property taxes from their incomes in computing federal tax liability but cannot deduct private school tuition payments. Changes in elements of this legal framework would alter the influence of markets on the quality distribution of K–12 education.

For parents to use market mechanisms to gain access to particular schools for their children, they must use personal income to secure housing in appropriate neighborhoods or pay private school tuition. Consequently, market mechanisms are currently available primarily to families with significant financial resources.

New Roles for Markets in Education?

Over the past forty years a number of individuals and organizations have pushed for a greater role for markets in the provision of K–12 education. One argument, made by Milton Friedman (1962) and by E. G. West (1965), is that public schools restrict the freedom of American parents to choose the education that would best serve their children. A second argument, often made in conjunction with the first, is that competition among providers of educational services would improve the quality of American education (West 1965; Friedman and Friedman 1980). Advocates of these arguments have found support in James Coleman, Thomas Hoffer, and Sally Kilgore's (1982) *High School Achievement,* which argues that Catholic schools and other private schools are more effective than public schools in educating children.

In the past decade a number of government and private initiatives have aimed at increasing schooling choices, especially for families that lack the funds either to pay for private schools or to secure housing in neighborhoods with strong public schools. The basic argument underlying these programs, which include both vouchers and charter schools, is that while government should pay for schooling, government should not be the sole provider of government-funded education. Instead, traditional public schools should compete with other providers of educational services. The U.S. Supreme Court's 2002 decision in Zelman v. Simmons-Harris provides support to advocates of this position.

The recent voucher and charter school initiatives are market based in the sense that they facilitate schooling choice by eligible families and potentially increase the competition conventional public schools face in obtaining funding. However, the initiatives are quite different from the two-party markets described in economics textbooks. They introduce a third party to the transaction—the organization, usually a unit of government, that pays for the schooling. Inevitably, this third party plays a regulatory role, making and enforcing decisions about a great many issues, including funding rules and the obligations of participating schools. Systems under which a variety of organizations may provide educational services funded by government do not entirely eliminate government bureaucracies. They do change the nature of the regulatory regime, and these changes may significantly alter the distribution of student achievement and the cost of schooling. I emphasize this to draw attention to the details of school choice systems.

In describing recent use of choice-based initiatives, I focus on the following questions:

- Did the market-based initiative provide new schooling options for students from low-income families?
- Did the program result in improved schooling outcomes for children from low-income families?
- Did the program affect the quality of public schools?
- Did the program affect the extent to which schools are segregated by race and class?

Vouchers

The idea that government might pay for educational services but not provide them is an old one. As an alternative to building high schools, many rural communities have provided vouchers for families to use to pay for their children to attend either private schools or public schools in neighboring communities (Coons and Sugarman 1978). In 1962 Milton Friedman advocated that government provide educational vouchers to parents that they could use to pay for their children's education at the private or public schools of their choice. Friedman saw vouchers as a way to stimulate innovation and improve efficiency (Friedman 1962).

In the late 1960s the federal Office of Economic Opportunity commissioned Christopher Jencks and his Harvard colleagues to design a voucher plan that would improve educational options for students from low-income families. The government attempted to test Jencks's regulated compensatory voucher model in Alum Rock, California, in the early 1970s. However, political opposition constrained the options to public schools and effectively eliminated competitive pressures (Stern, DeLone, and Murnane 1975).

During the decade in which Friedman and Jencks were writing, the quality of public education was an issue, though considerably less important than it is today because the economy at that time provided a great many manufacturing jobs that paid quite good wages to workers carrying out routine tasks. Since then, changes in the economy have dramatically reduced earnings prospects for individuals who leave school with weak cognitive skills and thereby increased the importance of providing all Americans with strong skills. These economic changes contributed to the reawakening of interest in vouchers in the 1990s, this time as a means of providing school options to children of low-income parents living in large cities.

Beginning in 1990, the Milwaukee Parental Choice Program provided vouchers that would pay for private schools for some Milwaukee children. The enabling legislation was quite restrictive, granting eligibility only to children whose family income was less than 175 percent of the federal poverty line, limiting the amount of each voucher to $2,500, restricting participation to a maximum of 1 percent of the Milwaukee public school population, and allowing participants to enroll only in secular private schools—and only in those that would accept the voucher as the full school cost to families. In 1995 new legislation relaxed the enrollment cap to 15 percent of the Milwaukee school population and allowed participants to enroll in religious schools. The value of the vouchers also increased, rising to a maximum for $5,100 for the 1999 to 2000 school year.[6] Initially, enrollment in the program was modest, with 337 students attending seven private schools in the 1990 to 1991 school year. In the 2003 to 2004 school year, more than 13,000 students participated in the Milwaukee voucher program (Carr 2004).

In 1995 Ohio passed legislation creating a voucher program for low-income students in the Cleveland public school district that was similar in design to the Milwaukee Parental Choice Program. Restrictions included a limitation to children whose family income was less than 200 percent of the poverty line and a maximum voucher value of $2,250. By the 1998 to 1999 school year, the number of students enrolled in private schools under the Cleveland voucher program had risen to 3,744 attending 59 private schools. It is the constitutionality of this program that the U.S. Supreme Court upheld in its June 2002 Zelman v. Simmons-Harris decision.

While state governments funded the voucher programs in Milwaukee and Cleveland, private groups provided funding for voucher (or scholarship) programs in New York City, Washington, D.C., and Dayton, Ohio. Under these programs, students from low-income families were provided scholarships that paid up to 60 percent of private school tuition, with maximum values ranging from $1,200 (Dayton) to $1,700 (Washington, D.C.). Eighty-five percent of the students who enrolled in private schools under the program attended religious schools, the vast majority of which were Catholic schools. Lotteries were used to determine which eligible families would be awarded scholarships, a process that facilitated research on the outcomes of the programs (Howell et al. 2002). Research on the recent voucher and scholarship programs has increased understanding of the consequences of small-scale voucher programs aimed at increasing schooling options for low-income children. It should not be surprising that the findings are complex, providing ammunition to both advocates and opponents of voucher systems.

Did these market-based programs provide new schooling options for students from low-income families? Many children from low-income families did enroll in private schools under the voucher and scholarship programs, even though the values of the vouchers and scholarships were modest. This suggests that well-designed small-scale choice plans can provide new schooling options for children from low-income families.

At the same time, the limited evidence suggests that both supply and demand are quite sensitive to the value of the vouchers. Hope Schools, the primary not-for-profit recipient of the Cleveland vouchers, withdrew from the program and turned its schools into charter schools, since the latter received greater funding (Hess 2002). Fewer than half of the students who applied for and received scholarships under the privately funded Washington, D.C., scholarship programs attended private school in both of the first two years of the program.[7] In a nationwide survey of parents who were given educational vouchers, the modal reason (45 percent) parents gave for not using the vouchers was that they could not afford to pay the remaining costs of private school attendance (Peterson, Campbell, and West 2002).

Did the voucher programs result in improved schooling outcomes for participating children from low-income families? Here, too, the evidence is complex. Participation in the Milwaukee Parental Choice Program raised math scores between 1.5 and 2 percent per year, though reading scores were not improved by participation (Rouse 1998). Black children enrolled in private elementary schools under the private scholarship programs had higher reading and math scores than did similar children in public schools, with the effects concentrated on children in the fifth grade. However, the results are highly sensitive to decisions about treatment of cases with missing baseline test scores (Krueger and Zhu 2003). In what is a major puzzle, there were no differences in achievement for Hispanic students, and the explanation does not appear to be related to proficiency in English (Howell et al. 2002).

Did the programs affect the quality of public education? Hoxby (2003) reports that achievement in those Milwaukee public schools that served the largest percentage of students eligible for the Milwaukee Parental Choice Program rose more than that in other Milwaukee public schools or in a comparison group of schools in another community. She sees this as a direct consequence of the threat of enrollment and funding loss that the plan provided. In contrast, Frederick Hess (2002) argues that the Milwaukee Parental Choice Program did not have a significant impact on the quality of public schools.

Did the programs affect the extent to which schools are segregated by race and class? Only children from low-income families attending highly segregated urban public schools were eligible for these voucher and scholarship programs. As a result, these programs could not have resulted in increased or decreased segregation.

Charter Schools

In 1991 Minnesota passed the first legislation authorizing the creation of charter schools. The basic idea behind these schools, which are public schools in the sense that they do not charge tuition and core funding comes from government, is that they are not subject to many of the regulations that constrain traditional public schools. In return, charter schools are held responsible by the chartering authority for fulfilling the conditions of their charter. Those that do not may be closed.[8] Over the past twelve years, forty-one states have passed charter school–enabling legislation. The rules governing charter schools differ markedly from state to state, in the requirements to obtain a charter, in funding levels, in the number of schools that may receive charters, and in accountability provisions. As a result, the number of charter schools varies widely from state to state. Of the approximately 2,990 charter schools in operation in January 2004, 491 were located in Arizona, 500 in California, 258 in Florida, 241 in Texas, 210 in Michigan, and 147 in Wisconsin. Total enrollment in the nation's charter schools in January 2004 was approximately 698,000 students.[9]

Evaluating the effectiveness of charter schools in increasing students' academic achievement is difficult because enrolled students are a self-selected population. Charter schools may enroll more motivated students; on the other hand, they may enroll students who have not fared well in public schools. Consequently, it is difficult to construct a good estimate of the "counterfactual" against which to compare the achievement of charter school students— that is, an estimate of what the achievement trend of charter school students would have been had they remained in public schools. It is also difficult to evaluate the effect that competition from charter schools has on the effectiveness of public schools. The key problem is that charter schools may start up either in the attendance areas of chronically ineffective public schools or near public schools that are experiencing a temporary lapse in performance. Again, the difficulty lies in developing a credible estimate of what the achievement trend would have been for public schools located near charter schools had the charter schools not existed.

Researchers have developed a variety of creative strategies to identify charter school effects. Unfortunately, the results appear to be extremely sensitive to methodological choices. This is particularly evident in research on Michigan charter schools.

Did the charter schools provide new schooling options for students from low-income families? The growth in the number of charter schools over the past decade is striking, suggesting that many educational entrepreneurs have figured out how to overcome start-up costs associated with finding space, hiring staff, and creating curriculum. Charter schools in Michigan are particularly likely to attract students who have not been achieving well in public schools. Charter schools in California serve about the same percentages of low-income and minority students as public schools do. Thus the evidence from these two states containing many charter schools is that they do provide new schooling options for many students, including those from low-income families and minority groups. A notable exception, however, are students with disabilities. The proportion of such students in California charter schools (7.6 percent) is only half that in public schools (16.5 percent) (Zimmer et al. 2003, 25).

Did the charter schools result in improved schooling outcomes for children from low-income families? Two studies report that test scores of students in Michigan charter schools are no higher than those of observationally similar students in public schools. However, both studies point out that results are sensitive to methodological details (Bettinger 2002; Eberts and Hollenbeck 2001).

Did the charter schools affect the quality of traditional public education? Hoxby (2003) reports that public schools that experienced the greatest competition from charter schools made more progress in improving student achievement than did public schools experiencing less competition. Eric Bettinger (2002), using a different strategy for identifying the effect of competition, reaches the opposite conclusion, as do Randall Eberts and Kevin Hollenbeck (2001). One possible explanation for the difference in results concerns the length of time public schools have to respond to competition from charter schools. Hoxby's data permits a longer-run response than do the data used in the other studies.

Did the charter schools affect the extent to which schools are segregated by race and class? To date there is little data assessing the extent of such influence. It is notable that charter schools do not appear to attract a disproportionate share of high-achieving students from public schools. In fact, the opposite appears to be the case.

In summary, the last decade's experiences with vouchers and charter schools indicate that many parents, including those with low income, want new schooling options for their children. Parents whose children are not faring well in traditional public schools are particularly likely to take advantage of new schooling options. The growth in enrollment in the Milwaukee Parental Choice Program and in the number of students attending charter schools indicates that supply is relatively elastic at the current scale. A closer look, however, suggests that supply is quite sensitive to funding levels (Hess 2002). The evidence on whether students achieve higher test scores in private schools under voucher programs or under charter schools is less clear cut, with variation by racial group and by subject area. There is also disagreement on the extent to which competition from voucher programs or charter schools led to improvements in the performances of neighboring public schools. A clearer picture must await collection of data on longer-run outcomes, such as school graduation rates and college enrollment rates.

Large-Scale Choice Programs

The choice programs developed in the 1990s in the United States were relatively small in scale. In the 2001 to 2002 school year, enrollment in the Milwaukee Parental Choice Program was only 10 percent of the total enrollment in the Milwaukee public schools. Enrollment in Arizona charter schools was only 7 percent of total enrollment in conventional public schools in the state, and the percentage in other states was lower still. A larger-scale system of choice involving nonpublic schools raises a host of questions. How will the mix of private schools change as seats in Catholic schools, the dominant supplier of private schools in the past, fill up? Will new providers prove as effective as Catholic schools have been? Will large-scale programs lead to sorting by race or socioeconomic status, as parents seek to place their children in schools that serve high-achieving children? Given peer group effects, will schools seek to recruit high-achieving children, denying admission to children not perceived as providing beneficial impacts on their classmates? These are only a sample of the important questions about the consequences of large-scale choice plans. Of course, the consequences will depend on program design. To obtain information on the consequences of large-scale choice programs, one must look to the experiences of other countries.

The Netherlands

As reported in table 6.1, students in the Netherlands achieved considerably higher average scores on eighth-grade math and science exams than did U.S. students. In the Netherlands, most students attend nonpublic schools, with government paying almost all costs. However, the Dutch choice plan looks very different from the choice plans currently advocated in the United States. Private schools in the Netherlands are highly regulated by the government. Government determines how many teachers each private and public school is entitled to and pays all teachers, using a single national scale. Government imposes rigid restrictions on the ability of schools to fire teachers, and layoffs are determined strictly by seniority. All schools must follow a uniform curriculum, which specifies the number of hours spent on each required subject each year. The net effect of these regulations, coupled with the relatively small size of private schools, is that teacher costs and the costs of facilities are estimated to be 10 to 20 percent higher than they would be in a monolithic public school system (James 1986). The Dutch choice plan is directed primarily at solving problems related to religious diversity; its focus is not to improve efficiency through competition. One must look to other countries for examples of school choice systems introduced to spur competition.

New Zealand

In 1991 New Zealand introduced a nationwide system of school choice with the intent of promoting efficiency through competition. One element of the system includes block grants to schools based on total enrollment. The financing system does not pay additional funds to schools that enroll students with learning handicaps, who are expensive to serve. Parents may enroll their children in any school. However, oversubscribed schools may decide which applicants to accept (Fiske and Ladd 2000).

New Zealand does not have a system of common examinations, so there is no information on the extent to which the school choice system results in improved student achievement. However, there is evidence that the system has resulted in increased stratification of schools based on socioeconomic status (Fiske and Ladd 2000).

Chile

In 1980 the Chilean national government radically decentralized education and began financing it with education vouchers. Under this system, funding for public schools and participating private schools is determined month to month by student enrollments. Since the introduction of vouchers, enrollment in private for-profit schools that accept vouchers has grown rapidly; such schools currently enroll 21 percent of elementary school students in Chile. Catholic schools that accept vouchers enroll another 10 percent (McEwan and Carnoy 2000). In the Chilean choice system, the value of the voucher is not dependent on student characteristics, and schools are free to select their students.

Chile does have a data system that supports research on the skills of students attending different types of schools and on cost differences. Patrick McEwan and Martin Carnoy find that, net of socioeconomic status, students enrolled in private, for-profit voucher schools—the schools that have experienced the greatest growth under the choice system—have slightly lower achievement than students enrolled in public schools, and the achievement difference is larger for schools outside of the capital city, Santiago. At the same time, the for-profit schools have 13 to 17 percent lower costs than public schools. In contrast, students attending Catholic schools have higher achievement, on average, than similar students attending public schools. However, the Catholic schools also have higher costs than the public schools (McEwan and Carnoy 2000).

McEwan and Carnoy also explored whether competition improved the effectiveness of Chilean public schools. They report a small positive impact on the effectiveness of public schools located in Santiago (where competition is presumably greatest) but no effects on the achievement of students in public schools outside the capital city.

A final question concerns the impact of the Chilean choice system on segregation by socioeconomic status. Chang-Tai Hsieh and Miguel Urquiola (2001) report that the choice system resulted in an increase in sorting of students among schools, with the "best" public school students switching to the private sector.

In summary, the recent evidence from Chile and New Zealand suggests that large-scale voucher systems that do not provide extra resources for students who are relatively expensive to educate and who are perceived as less attractive classmates result in significant student sorting, with disadvantaged students relegated to the least attractive schools. This is not a surprise to economists, who have predicted that this would occur in systems that provide all students with vouchers of the same value (Epple and Romano 1998; Manski 1992). Peer group effects matter (Hoxby 2000b); parents are aware of this, and those with resources seek to place their children in schools with high-achieving peers. On the supply side, schools that seek to attract high-achieving students have incentives to exclude low-achieving children unless these students bring with them higher-valued vouchers. Since academic achievement is strongly correlated with socioeconomic status and race in most countries, sorting by academic achievement results in sorting by socioeconomic status and race. Consequently, choice systems like those operating in Chile and New Zealand would not contribute to solving the most critical educational problem facing the United States: the extremely low skills with which urban students, most of whom are young people of color from low-income families, leave school.

This does not mean that increasing the role of family choice in allocating educational resources could not improve outcomes for children of color and children from low-income families. The choice system in Milwaukee and the private scholarship plans in New York and other cities have resulted in increased student achievement for some children and have increased parental satisfaction levels. A recent National Research Council Committee on financing American schools concludes that it would be valuable to conduct relatively large-scale voucher experiments to learn more about their likely impacts on the distribution of student outcomes in U.S. settings (Ladd and Hansen 1999, 273). Of course, the difficult questions concern the design of these experiments.

Voucher Experiments: Design Issues

As explained earlier in this chapter, four factors contribute to the inadequacy of the skills with which most students leave urban schools: the handicaps these students bring to school, peer group effects, the inefficiency of government service delivery, and the resource complications introduced by regulations aimed at protecting children with special needs. The basic argument for greater use of markets in allocating educational services is that government inefficiency is the most important reason students leave urban public schools with low skills and that competition will result in improvements in the performances of urban public schools. It follows from this logic that voucher experiments should be designed to maximize the likelihood that urban public schools will respond positively to the spur of competition. One implication is that the design should minimize the likelihood that the public schools are left with a disproportionate share of students who are especially expensive to educate or who are perceived as negative influences on the learning of their classmates. Providing such children with higher-valued vouchers seems like a promising strategy to achieve this end. But how would the values of the vouchers for different children be determined?

Caroline Hoxby (2001) offers a creative proposal under which a market-based pricing system would determine the values of vouchers for individual children in a manner that would "internalize" the externality posed by children perceived as exhibiting a negative influence on their classmates' achievement. Whether Hoxby's proposal is politically feasible remains to be seen, as are the consequences if it were made a part of a large-scale voucher system.

Another issue concerns the impact of regulations; for example, every child designated as disabled is entitled to an individual education plan that provides a relatively open-ended entitlement to "free appropriate public education" individualized to the needs of the child. The services and programs required to meet this mandate can greatly increase the cost of educating these students. Satisfying the regulations for appropriate bilingual education also increases costs. It is possible that a school choice system that provided higher-valued vouchers for children who are expensive to educate or who pose negative externalities on the learning of other children would solve the difficult problem of providing all children with access to a good education. This is an important question to examine in a large-scale voucher demonstration.

In a voucher system in which the values of vouchers do not reflect the cost of educating children with special needs or the negative externalities that some children exert on the learning of their classmates, all schools aiming to produce high-achieving graduates have incentives to discourage the admission of such children. This creates a tension for the design of a large-scale voucher system. If the goal of a large-scale voucher demonstration is to learn whether it can catalyze improved performance of public schools, it seems important that all participating schools, public and nonpublic alike, should be obligated by the same regulations regarding admission and treatment of disabled children, children who lack fluency in English, and children seen as exerting negative externalities. However, if these rules are highly restrictive, as they currently are for public schools, the likely outcome is that participating nonpublic schools will be hampered in allocating resources, just as public schools are today.

Yet another issue concerns information. For parents to make good decisions about schooling for their children, they need to know the skills children are learning in different schools. One way to provide such information is to require that students in all public and nonpublic schools take the same examinations that most states are putting in place as part of standards-based educational reforms. However, here, too, there is a tension in design. Requiring all schools participating in a voucher system to administer the same exams makes it easier to compare schools, but it is likely to hamper schools' efforts to develop innovative curriculums that parents may want for their children even if the curriculum does not lead to high scores on state-mandated exams.

Another difficult set of design issues concerns funding level and duration of a voucher experiment. While educating children who come to school with significant disadvantages is difficult, it is not impossible. Recent evidence from Community District 2 (Elmore 2004) in New York City provides guidance on what it takes:

- an unwavering focus on improving literacy and math, the core skills needed to learn efficiently
- detailed ongoing assessment of the skills of every child
- teachers who understand well the subjects they are teaching
- intense professional development aimed at increasing the capacity to improve instruction
- strong leadership

The District 2 experience shows that real progress is not just a matter of getting the incentives right. The central challenge is building capacity, and this takes time and resources—considerably more resources than those provided in the Milwaukee and Cleveland voucher programs. For these reasons it is important that a voucher experiment have a minimum duration of five years and provide participating schools with the resources needed to meet the significant educational needs of urban children.

Given the controversy surrounding the voucher concept, it seems likely that the political compromises necessary to obtain legislative support for a large-scale voucher experiment would include keeping the funding level modest and the duration relatively brief. Such compromises in design would dramatically reduce the likelihood that the experiment would provide reliable evidence on the extent to which market-based educational initiatives can improve the quality of education provided to urban children.

In many respects the design of a voucher plan that has the greatest promise for improving the education of urban children—differentially valued vouchers, the same participation rules for public and private schools, provisions for collecting and disseminating information on student outcomes, adequate funding, and a minimum length of five years—is similar to the "regulated compensatory voucher plan" that Christopher Jencks and his colleagues designed in the late 1960s. At that time, the Office of Economic Opportunity was unable to find a community willing to give this voucher model a chance.[10]

Other disheartening evidence about the political viability of a large-scale voucher plan that would provide low-income urban parents with attractive schooling options comes from California. In 1991 Berkeley law professor Jack

Coons and his colleague Stephen Sugarman initiated a ballot drive to put school vouchers on the California ballot. They designed a plan with a $5,000 basic voucher with a significant dollar premium for disabled children. Their plan also provided a number of provisions designed to ensure that children from low-income families obtained real schooling choices: No participating school could charge low-income families more than the value of the voucher. The value of the voucher was adjusted to cover transportation costs for low-income children. Oversubscribed schools had to reserve 20 percent of their seats for low-income children (Murnane and Levy 1996, 210–13).

To obtain the requisite number of signatures to put vouchers on the ballot, Coons and Sugarman needed the support of groups with different priorities. As the petition deadline neared, they lost control of their coalition. Proposition 174, the initiative that did appear on the California ballot in 1993, was very different from the plan Coons and Sugarman advocated. The value of the voucher was only $2,600, not enough to provide a good education, especially not for urban children with great needs. The plan provided no transportation funding for low-income children, nor any head start in learning to use vouchers, nor any higher-valued voucher to make low-income children or disabled children more attractive to schools. Proposition 174 was so far from Coons and Sugarman's vision of a voucher plan that would improve schooling options for low-income children that they voted against it (Murnane and Levy 1996). The question remains whether there is political support for a voucher system that would improve schooling options for low-income children.

It is possible that concerns about the inadequate skills of students leaving urban school districts are sufficiently great today that a case could be made politically for a regulated compensatory voucher experiment. However, this remains to be seen. The evidence from Chile and New Zealand suggests that only a system that provides higher-valued vouchers for children with special needs and children perceived as unattractive classmates has the potential to improve schooling options for urban children.

The rapid growth in the number of charter schools in many states provides some natural experiments about the consequences of certain kinds of educational choices. However, the rules regarding the terms on which charter schools are established and the terms on which they compete with public schools vary from state to state. Paying attention to these rules is critical in assessing the lessons from the charter school experiments (Gill et al. 2001).

Summing Up

Markets have always played a role in determining the quality of education American children receive. Residential housing markets have enabled a great many families to "buy" the local public schooling they want for their children.

Other families have provided for the education of their children by paying for private schools. While this mixed system has contributed to the development of the United States as a nation and to its economic growth, it has also left many low-income families, particularly those in big cities, without access to good schooling. The low skill levels of children leaving urban schools is especially problematic today as a result of both changes in the economy and increases in the proportion of the nation's students who are children of color from low-income families.

One proposed solution to the urban education problem is to provide low-income families with improved schooling options through the use of vouchers or charter schools. Providing families who lack resources with educational choices makes sense. The consequences of attempting to do this through a large-scale voucher or charter school system are unknown. Carefully designed experiments could provide critical knowledge. However, it is important to get beyond deceptive rhetoric about replacing government monopoly with markets. Markets have played a role in American education and will continue to do so. The critical questions concern the design of a regulatory system that introduces a third party—the organization that pays the bill—into markets characterized by significant peer group effects. The outcomes that matter include not only the distribution of student achievement scores but also a range of public goods, such as the degree of support for democratic institutions. Such public outcomes are difficult to measure. However, they are just as important today in evaluating our educational institutions as they were when the founding fathers envisioned education as a critical vehicle for building the new nation.

Notes

1. This section is based primarily on Carl Kaestle's (1983) *Pillars of the Republic.*
2. In this calculation I restrict "children of color" to African American and Hispanic children. The calculation makes use of data from Beth Young (2001, tables 5 and 9) and *Digest of Educational Statistics* (2001, table 98).
3. Thoughtful descriptions of the problems of "government failure" are found in John Chubb and Terry Moe (1990), Frederick Hess (2002), and Charles Wolf (1988).
4. For an illustration of the resistance public school districts encounter in attempting to improve efficiency in delivering special education services, see David Pierson, "Parents Fight Changes in Special Ed," *Los Angeles Times,* September 16, 2002, California Metro section, p. 1.
5. Before World War II, the number of local school districts in the U.S. exceeded one hundred thousand.
6. The information in this paragraph is taken from Hess (2002). Hoxby (2003) points out that implementation of the provisions in the 1995 legislation were held up for several years owing to legal challenges.

7. The corresponding numbers for the New York and Dayton scholarship programs are 21 percent and 40 percent. All of these numbers are taken from Howell et al. (2002, 204, table 6).
8. This description is taken from Hess (2001).
9. The data on charter schools is taken from a chart labeled "Charter School Laws" in Center for Education Reform (2002).
10. The voucher demonstration in Alum Rock, California, was so constrained that it provided little information about the consequences of a large-scale voucher system (Stern, DeLone, and Murnane 1975).

References

Balfanz, Robert, and Nettie Legters. 2001. "How Many Central City High Schools Have A Severe Dropout Problem, Where Are They Located, and Who Attends Them? Initial Estimates Using the Common Core of Data." Paper presented at the Civil Rights Project forum, Dropouts in America. Harvard University Graduate School of Education (January 13).

Bettinger, Eric P. 2002. "The Effect of Charter Schools on Charter Students and Public Schools." Working paper. Cleveland: Case Western Reserve University (January).

Black, Sandra E. 1999. "Do Better Schools Matter? Parental Valuation of Elementary Education." *Quarterly Journal of Economics* 114(2, May): 577–99.

Carr, Sarah. 2004. "Doyle Plan Demands More Choice of Schools: Proposal Would Raise Enrollment Cap, Require Testing." *Milwaukee Journal Sentinel* (March 7): n.p. Available at: http://www.jsonline.com/news/metro/mar04/213077.asp (accessed November 30, 2004).

Center for Education Reform. 2002. "Charter School Laws." Available at: www.edreform.com (accessed November 19, 2004).

Centre for Educational Research and Innovation. 2001. *Education at a Glance: OECD Indicators.* Paris: Organization for Economic Cooperation and Development.

Chubb, John E., and Terry M. Moe. 1990. *Politics, Markets and America's Schools.* Washington, D.C.: Brookings Institution Press.

Coleman, James S., Thomas Hoffer, and Sally Kilgore. 1982. *High School Achievement.* New York: Basic Books.

Coons, John E., and Stephen D. Sugarman. 1978. *Education by Choice: The Case for Family Control.* Berkeley: University of California Press.

Digest of Educational Statistics. 2001. Washington: U.S. Department of Education, National Center for Education Statistics.

Eberts, Randall W., and Kevin Hollenbeck. 2001. "An Examination of Student Achievement in Michigan Charter Schools." Staff Working Paper 01-68. Ypsilanti, Mich.: Upjohn Institute (March).

Ellwood, David T. 2001. "The Sputtering Labor Force of the 21st Century: Can Social Policy Help?" Working Paper 8321. Cambridge, Mass.: National Bureau of Economic Research (June).

Elmore, Richard F. 2004. *School Reform from the Inside Out: Policy Practice and Performance.* Cambridge, Mass.: Harvard Education Press.

Epple, Dennis, and Richard E. Romano. 1998. "Competition Between Private and Public Schools: Vouchers and Peer Group Effects." *American Economic Review* 88(1): 33–62.

Fiske, Edward B., and Helen F. Ladd. 2000. *When Schools Compete: A Cautionary Tail.* Washington, D.C.: Brookings Institution Press.

Friedman, Milton. 1962. *Capitalism and Freedom.* Chicago: University of Chicago Press.

Friedman, Milton, and Rose D. Friedman. 1980. *Free to Choose.* New York: Harcourt Brace Jovanovich.

Gill, Brian P., P. Michael Timpane, Karen E. Ross, and Dominic J. Brewer. 2001. *Rhetoric Versus Reality: What We Know and What We Need to Know about Vouchers and Charter Schools.* Santa Monica, Calif.: Rand.

Goldin, Claudia. 2001. "The Human Capital Century and American Leadership: Virtues of the Past." Working Paper 8239. Cambridge, Mass.: National Bureau of Economic Research (April).

Goldin, Claudia, and Lawrence F. Katz. 1999. "The Returns to Skill in the United States Across the Twentieth Century." Working Paper 7126. Cambridge, Mass.: National Bureau of Economic Research (May).

Hanushek, Eric A., John F. Kain, and Steven G. Rivkin. 2001. "Disruption versus Tiebout Improvement: The Costs and Benefits of Switching Schools." Working Paper 8479. Cambridge, Mass.: National Bureau of Economic Research (September).

Hanushek, Eric A., and Steven G. Rivkin. 2003. "Does Public School Competition Affect Teacher Quality?" In *The Economics of School Choice,* edited by Caroline M. Hoxby. Chicago: University of Chicago Press.

Hess, Frederick M. 2001. "Whaddya Mean You Want to Close My School? The Politics of Regulatory Accountability in Charter Schooling." *Education and Urban Society* 33(2): 141–56.

———. 2002. *Revolutions at the Margins.* Washington, D.C.: Brookings Institution Press.

Howell, William G., Patrick J. Wolf, David E. Campbell, and Paul E. Peterson. 2002. "School Vouchers and Academic Performance: Results from Three Randomized Field Trials." *Journal of Policy Analysis and Management* 21(2): 191–217.

Hoxby, Caroline M. 2000a. "Does Competition Among Public Schools Benefit Students and Taxpayers?" *American Economic Review* 90(5): 1209–38.

———. 2000b. "Peer Effects in the Classroom: Learning from Gender and Race Variation." Working Paper 7867. Cambridge, Mass.: National Bureau of Economic Research (August).

———. 2001. "Ideal Vouchers." Unpublished manuscript. Harvard University.

———. 2003. "School Choice and School Productivity (or Could School Choice be a Tide that Lifts All Boats?)." In *The Economics of School Choice*, edited by Caroline M. Hoxby. Chicago: University of Chicago Press.

Hsieh, Chang-Tai, and Miguel Urquiola. 2001. "When Schools Compete, How Do They Compete?" Working paper. Cornell University.

James, Estelle. 1986. "Public Subsidies for Private and Public Education: The Dutch Case." In *Private Education: Studies in Choice and Public Policy,* edited by D. C. Levy. New York: Oxford University Press.

Kaestle, Carl F. 1983. *Pillars of the Republic: Common Schools and American Society, 1780–1860.* New York: Hill and Wang.

Krueger, Alan, and Pei Zhu. 2003. "Another Look at the New York City School Voucher Experiment." Working Paper 9418. Cambridge, Mass.: National Bureau of Economic Research (January).

Ladd, Helen F., and Janet S. Hansen, eds. 1999. *Making Money Matter: Financing America's Schools.* Washington: National Academies Press.

Manski, Charles F. 1992. "Educational Choice (Vouchers) and Social Mobility." *Economics of Education Review* 11(4): 351–69.

McEwan, Patrick J., and Martin Carnoy. 2000. "The Effectiveness and Efficiency of Private Schools in Chile's Voucher System." *Educational Evaluation and Policy Analysis* 22(3): 213–39.

Murnane, Richard J., and Frank Levy. 1996. *Teaching the New Basic Skills.* New York: Free Press.

National Center for Education Statistics. 2001. *National Assessment of Educational Progress: 2000 Mathematics Assessment.* Washington: U.S. Department of Education.

National Commission on Excellence in Education. 1983. "A Nation at Risk: The Imperative for Educational Reform." Report. Washington: U.S. Department of Education.

Neal, Derek. 1997. "The Effects of Catholic Secondary Schooling on Educational Achievement." *Journal of Labor Economics* 15(1): 98–123.

Peterson, Paul E., David E. Campbell, and Martin R. West. 2002. "Who Chooses? Who Uses? Participation in a National School Voucher Program." In *Choice with Equity,* edited by Paul T. Hill. Stanford, Calif.: Hoover Institution Press.

Reich, Rob. 2002. "Testing the Boundaries of Parental Authority over Education: The Case of Home Schooling." In *Political and Moral Education, NOMOS XLIII,* edited by Stephen Macedo and Yael Tamir. New York: New York University Press.

Rouse, Cecilia E. 1998. "Private School Vouchers and Student Achievement: An Evaluation of the Milwaukee Parental Choice Program." *Quarterly Journal of Economics* 113(2): 553–602.

Stern, David, Richard DeLone, and Richard J. Murnane. 1975. "Evolution at Alum Rock." *Review of Education* 1(3, August): 309–18.

U.S. Bureau of the Census. 2001. "Educational Attainment—People 25 Years Old and Over, by Total Money Earnings in 2000, Work Experience in 2000, Age, Race, Hispanic Origin and Sex." Current Population Survey, P-60. *Annual Demographic Survey* (March supplement), table PINC-03. Available at: ferret.bls.census.gov/macro/032001/perinc/new03_000.htm.

West, E. G. 1965. *Education and the State.* 1st ed. Indianapolis: Liberty Fund.

Wolf, Charles. 1988. *Markets or Governments?* Cambridge, Mass.: MIT Press.

Young, Beth Aronstamm. 2001. "Characteristics of the 100 Largest Public Elementary and Secondary School Districts in the United States, 1999-2000." National Center for Education Statistics. Washington: U.S. Department of Education, Office of Educational Research and Improvement.

Zimmer, Ron, Richard Buddin, Derrick Chau, Brian Gill, Cassandra Guarino, Laura Hamilton, Cathy Krop, Dan McCaffrey, Melinda Sandler, and Dominic Brewer. 2003. *Charter School Operations and Performance: Evidence from California.* Santa Monica, Calif.: Rand.

7

EARLY CHILDHOOD EDUCATION AND CARE

Sheila B. Kamerman and Jane Waldfogel

C HILD care and child rearing may still be viewed as primarily the responsibility of families, but the conventional wisdom that emerged in the mid-nineteenth century regarding mothers' exclusive responsibility for the care and education of their preschool-age children at home has largely disappeared. In effect, the middle- and late-nineteenth-century triangle of family, economy, and education that led to the growth of the public education system in the United States is now being played out in another series of role disputes. Just as the public schools expanded in large part in the nineteenth century by assuming tasks that the family no longer could accomplish (the socialization and control of youth) and the economy no longer needed (the labor of young adolescents), an early childhood education and care system may now be assuming the roles of education, care, and socialization of three- and four-year-olds in response to new knowledge about how children learn and in order to facilitate or support their mothers' labor force participation (Smelser and Halpern 1978). Questions still remain, however: where should the care and education be provided, who should pay for it, and what should be done about the one- and two-year-olds?

One major factor driving current developments is the increased participation of mothers of young children in the labor market, reducing their availability as full-time providers of care and education for their young children. Another major factor has been the increased recognition that, whether or not their mothers are working, children can benefit from experiences in group settings such as preschools before their entry into formal school. These benefits can be especially large for children who would otherwise start school at a disadvantage owing to disability, learning problems, inadequate cognitive stimulation, and so on.

The trend toward the greater involvement of nonfamily resources in early childhood education and care has been observed in all industrialized countries.

Where countries have diverged is in who takes responsibility. In the United States, policy in this area, as in other areas, has tended to look first to the family and private sector and to look to government only in the event that the market fails or when there are compelling reasons of public interest for the government to get involved. In European countries, in contrast, policy has tended to look first to the government, and the role of the private sector in the provision of early childhood care and education has been minimal.

Our view is that just as government had the primary role in the development of the public primary and secondary school education system in the United States, so should it have that role in preschool. The private sector may have a role in the delivery of early childhood education and care (ECEC) programs in the United States and internationally, and it certainly has had, both historically and at present.[1] But we would argue that the private sector should not have the dominant role because there are larger public interests involved, such as equality of access and opportunity, and because there are good reasons to believe that markets in this area will fail—in particular, with regard to the quality of care provided in general and the supply and quality of infant and toddler care. In normal markets, as pointed out in chapter 8 in this volume with regard to health care, consumer demand supposedly drives what producers supply; but demand is sometimes induced by producers and suppliers and sometimes by experts and professionals. If the level of consumer demand leads to an inadequate supply, as in the case of infant care in the United States, or to a supply of poor quality care (as in the case of most early childhood education and care programs), or to a price that is beyond what many parents can pay, the result is interpreted as market failure. What the market generates in the way of supply and quality may not be adequate to provide all the things that society needs and values. Alertness to these needs and values requires some kind of capacity within either government or the private sector.

As provision of care and education of young children increasingly shifts from families to providers outside the family, two major policy questions arise. The first is to what extent government should subsidize the costs of care and education for children under compulsory school age. In the United States, some child care for low-income working parents has been subsidized, and some educationally oriented programs such as Head Start have been provided free of charge to low-income families, but coverage is far from universal. There are also some subsidies for middle- and upper-income parents, but the amounts involved tend to be small. Other countries, in contrast, tend to cover a much larger share of the costs of early childhood care and education, and not just for low-income families. Should we be spending more on early childhood education and care, and if so, for which children and for what purposes? Although spending more money on early childhood education and care may be controversial, there is already a good deal of movement in the United States toward acceptance of the idea that government ought to fund universal preschool education for four-year-olds and, in some jurisdictions, three-year-olds. This position has been adopted by governors in forty-three states and has been endorsed by a leading business group, the Committee for Economic Development (2002).

A second question concerns government's role in the provision of early childhood education and care services. Funding aside, is there a reason to prefer public over privately delivered care for young children? To put it another way, if government were to expand its funding for early childhood education and care, whether for low-income children or for all children, should government provide its own early childhood education and care, or should it instead support care delivered by the private sector (nonprofit or for-profit), as it mainly does now? Here, we are agnostic. We see no compelling reason to prefer public over private provision; the main issues here are choice, quality, and access (see Cleveland and Krashinsky 2003). If the private sector can support consumer choice, deliver as high-quality care as the public sector does, and provide equal access, then there is no reason to prefer public sector provision. There are challenges to supporting consumer choice, improving quality, and promoting equal access, in both the public and private sectors.

Historical Perspectives

Early childhood education and care programs in the United States and other advanced industrialized countries have evolved out of remarkably similar historical streams including child protection, early childhood education, services for children with special needs, and services to facilitate mothers' labor force participation. As a result, ECEC programs have multiple goals: to provide support to struggling families, to help prepare children for primary school, to provide early identification and treatment for disabilities and special needs, and to provide care for the children of working parents.

In all these countries, an overarching theme is the movement from private charity, beginning in the early and middle nineteenth century, to public responsibility, evolving largely after World War II. The extent of public responsibility varies, however, across countries. The relative emphasis given in public policy to custodial care of poor and disadvantaged children of working mothers, on the one hand, and education and socialization of all children, on the other, appears to be one of the most distinguishing variations.[2] A second variation has to do with the age group the policies are aimed at, in particular, the differences between those policies aimed at children under the age of two or three and those designed to address the needs of children from the age of two or three to compulsory school entry at the age of five, six, or seven. A third variation has to do with the significant differences in the extent to which relevant policies stress the role of government (in delivering and funding these programs), private philanthropy and the voluntary (nonprofit) sector, the family, and the private (for-profit) sector.

Historical Roots

The "official" history of ECEC in the United States begins with two developments: day nurseries (child care centers), first established in the 1830s under voluntary auspices and designed to care for the "unfortunate" children of working mothers, and nursery schools, developed from the early education programs in Massachusetts of the 1830s and the later "kindergarten" programs based on the work of Friedrich Froebel. The first day nursery was established in 1838 in Boston to care for the children of seamen's wives and widows (Steinfels 1973). Day nurseries subsequently expanded in response to pressures created by the rapid industrialization and massive immigration that took place in the latter part of the century and the need to ensure protection of vulnerable children reared in unfortunate circumstances. These day nurseries drew on extensive developments in France and England from the beginning of the nineteenth century, under the auspices of private charities or private in-home or out-of-home arrangements. They were custodial in nature, focusing primarily on basic care and supervision of the children. By the end of the century, a National Federation of Day Nurseries had been established in the United States. During war times—the Civil War, World War I, and World War II—these programs increased in number, only to decline again when war ended.

Paralleling the history of day care or day nurseries, Barbara Beatty (1995, ix) launches her study of early childhood education by pointing out that "Americans have used different forms of extra-familial preschool education since the colonists arrived on this continent in the early 17th century. Families often employed neighborhood women to run informal dame schools. Private and public infant schools were started in the early 19th century." Kindergartens and nursery schools expanded slowly during the nineteenth century and experienced a significant increase only during the 1920s, as a form of enriched experience for middle-class children. Beatty argues that in the latter half of the twentieth century one of the greatest changes in modern American education policy, kindergarten, became so accepted that it has now become a universal experience for five-year-olds, basically making kindergarten a public responsibility, but that concern has not yet been extended to early education and care for younger children.

Little public support developed in the United States for either program type until the mid-1960s and early 1970s, when a confluence of factors led to the significant expansion of both. The dramatic expansion in the numbers of ECEC programs, both day care centers and nursery schools, both reflected and contributed to a resurgence of national interest in early childhood development. The War on Poverty included attention to cognitively deprived and otherwise disadvantaged children and the development of compensatory education programs as a response. Researchers stressed the importance of early education as a strategy for both better preparation for school and ensuring access to health care and improved nutrition. Head Start was established first as a summer program and then as a year-round program. Paralleling these developments, the rising welfare caseload stimulated interest in providing federal funds for child care for women receiving social assistance as well as those who had received aid earlier and those who were viewed as at risk of receipt. The increase in rates of female labor force participation by middle-class mothers raised the issue of the need for decent-quality out-of-home care for children generally. Middle-class parents, regardless of their employment status, increasingly viewed preschool as a valuable experience for their children and essential for facilitating an easier transition to school.

In 1971 Congress enacted the first national comprehensive child care legislation, but President Richard Nixon vetoed it on grounds that such a program would constitute an effort at "communalizing" child rearing (Kamerman and Kahn 1976). Conservatives mounted a massive campaign throughout the 1970s to block any federal child care initiative; only in the early 1980s did they begin to acknowledge the need for such services, albeit under private auspices (employers or the market). In subsequent years these diverse streams have continued to expand: care for poor or neglected children, care for the children of working parents, compensatory education, and early education to enhance the development of young children. In testimony before the House Committee on Ways and Means on March 12, 2002, Tommy Thompson, the secretary of the Department of Health and Human Services, stated unequivocally the importance of child care, noting the Bush administration's "enthusiastic support" for maintaining a historically high level of funding for child care and emphasizing the role of child care in achieving child well-being as well as a "vital work support" and a strategy for attaining literacy skills.

Although ECEC scholars and advocates are increasingly convinced of the need to integrate all the different program types, categorical funding, coupled with diverse societal values, continues to support the differences. More resources are needed to expand the supply and improve the quality of ECEC services. The result is a fragmented system of wide-ranging quality and with skewed access but with some movement in recent years toward the integration of early childhood education and care (OECD 2000; 2001a; 2001b).

In Britain, as in the United States, infant schools stressing education were established in the early nineteenth century, expanded rapidly, and then largely disappeared to be replaced later by part-day kindergartens. They provided an "inferior" form of care and education to the children of poor working women and in 1851 covered 20 percent of three-year-olds and 40 percent of four-year-olds. By 1901, 43 percent of two- to five-year-olds were attending these schools, and Britain seemed well on the way to providing a voluntary but free educational service for all young children from the age of two or three, if parents chose to avail themselves of it. Scholars state that the main need appeared to be improvement in the quality of care (Pringle and Naidoo 1975; Tizard, Moss, and Perry 1976). In contrast, middle- and upper-class children were cared for at home by nannies or their equivalent (in-home market care), supplemented increasingly, beginning in the last quarter of the nineteenth century, by private, nonprofit kindergartens organized on the model of the German early childhood specialist, Friedrich Froebel.

The failure to improve the quality of infant schools for children of the working class, or to integrate these programs with the new educational philosophy of the kindergarten and the inclusion of five-year-olds in primary schools, contributed to the decline in the popularity of nursery education in twentieth-century Britain. At the same time, compulsory schooling beginning at the age of five led to increased coverage for four- and five-year-olds, thus providing a substitute for some part of what is nursery education elsewhere, but reinforced the assumption that infant and toddler care were still the responsibility of the family. One other result was the continuation of a pattern of fragmentation between early education as an enrichment program and day care as a "protective" service. It took almost another century for there to be a significant increase in coverage and a renewed effort at integrating the two parallel streams. Only under the New Labour government has a new thrust emerged, with a stated goal of full coverage for three- and four-year-olds, the establishment of an integrated care and education program, and a significant increase in coverage of children under the age of three, a largely underserved group until recently.

In France and Italy, developments began with nineteenth-century charitable institutions for poor, deprived, often abandoned children (David and Lezine 1975; Pistillo 1989). In France the programs serving three- to five-year-olds were taken over by the Ministry of Education in 1836 and integrated into the public school system in 1886. Since World War II, and especially since the mid-1950s, growing pressure from middle-class families to expand the programs to include their children as well has led to a substantial expansion. The objective was largely to provide a socialization and educational experience for children from the age of two or three and to prepare them for primary school. Current coverage includes just about all children aged three, four, and five and half the two-year-olds in France, in a free and voluntary preschool program (Kamerman and Kahn 1994; Cooper 1999). Provision for younger children emerged later and grew more slowly, designed initially for protective purposes, to minimize the spread of contagious diseases, and thus with no attention to education. Coverage of younger children is still limited in Italy (less than 10 percent of children under the age of three) but much more extensive in France (close to 30 percent of children under the age of three, including two-year-olds in the preschool program). Subsequently, the focus has been on providing care to the children of working parents, and the goals have been broadened. In France, support for family day care as well as center care and in-home care was also provided.

The Italian developments were similar to the French but were totally dominated by the Catholic Church until national legislation was enacted in the late 1960s and early 1970s, dramatically increasing the role of government (Pistillo 1989). Begun in the nineteenth century as institutions for poor abandoned children, ECEC programs were recognized for their educational and socialization benefits only after World War II. Legislation assigning the national government and the Ministry of Education the major role in financing the establishment and operation of preschools for all three- to six-year-olds and greatly expanding the supply was enacted in 1968. Soon afterward, a law was passed in 1971 that required the national government to contribute to the funding of child care services for children under the age of three, as well, but required regional and local governments to assume responsibility for their operation. Working mothers have priority for places in these facilities. The 1968 legislation led to a rapid and extensive expansion of preschool programs throughout the country, under the auspices of the Ministry of Education. With little national government financial support mandated by the 1971 law, centers for the very young saw only modest growth. Differences in investment across regions led to wide variations in the supply of services for the very young; there are also differences in administrative auspice, with some of the regions (especially those with more extensive coverage) maintaining these programs under education departments.

In Sweden, too, kindergartens began in the mid-nineteenth century, largely under nonprofit, voluntary social welfare auspices (Berfenstam and William-Olssen 1973; Hwang and Broberg 1992). Compulsory schooling was limited to children aged seven and older. Government funding was not prevalent until after World War II, and the growth in demand for preschool programs was closely linked to rising rates of labor force participation of women with young children. Established as a universal program heavily subsidized for all, albeit with income-related fees to cover part of the costs, the program was designed for a middle-class population. As a result, a stress on quality was built into the system from the beginning. In the middle and late 1990s, Sweden guaranteed a place for all children of working parents and students from the age of one year and shifted the administration of its ECEC program from the National Board of Health and Welfare to the Ministry of Education. In the early twenty-first century, Sweden set a maximum fee for ECEC programs for all children at no more than 2 to 3 percent of family income and guaranteed a place for all four- to five-year-olds even if their parents were not in the labor force.

In short, the roots of ECEC policies and programs in the countries of the Organization for Economic Cooperation and Development can be found in nineteenth-century developments in preschool education and in the care of the children of working mothers. Over time, education became dominant for three- to five-year-olds in France and Italy, as well as in many of the other continental European countries, because of national policies and public priorities. Day care emerged as the dominant mode for children under the age of three in these countries and for infants to six-year-olds in Sweden and other Nordic countries, also as a result of national policies, public priorities, and pressure, but in response to demographic trends as well, especially trends in female labor force participation. In the Anglo-American countries, the two parallel streams continued, in part because of the absence early on of a national policy supporting early childhood education and in part, perhaps, because of the continued ambivalence about where primary responsibility for child rearing and socialization should lie.[3]

Variation by the Age of the Children

The age of the children served also makes a difference in how child care is viewed. Care for infants and toddlers is viewed differently from care for older preschoolers, and a different set of considerations with regard to the role of the family, markets, and government comes into play when parental or other care for infants and toddlers is considered as distinct from educationally oriented programs for older preschoolers. A host of evidence indicates that educationally oriented programs based in schools or centers are beneficial for older preschoolers (those aged three and older) (see recent reviews in Shonkoff and Phillips 2000; Smolensky and Gootman 2003; Meyers et al. 2004). For children under three, findings regarding the cognitive benefits of center- or school-based programs are more variable and seem to depend on program quality. High-quality intensive interventions for disadvantaged children beginning as early as the first year of life have been found to have large and often lasting benefits (Barnett 1995; Karoly et al. 1998; Currie 2001; Waldfogel 2002). However, it is less clear whether run-of-the-mill day care centers for infants and toddlers provide a substantial cognitive benefit when compared with individual or smaller-group providers, who may provide more one-on-one attention or more sensitive care.

The history of ECEC programs underscores the variations by age of the children served. Most of the developments in services have targeted the older group, the children from two and one-half or three to the age of compulsory school entry. In most of the continental European countries, a separate system was established for these children, under the auspices of the ministries of education, and they followed the pattern of primary school by being publicly funded and publicly delivered. Even the Nordic and other countries that began with freestanding ECEC programs or programs under social welfare auspices (Sweden, Scotland, Spain, northern Italy) are now moving toward education auspices, driven by more extensive public support for an educational component in the early childhood program and support for education in general. There is some evidence that this may be occurring in the United States as well. These countries are moving toward a universal and free (for the core education program) or heavily subsidized (for supplementary out-of-school services) system. There may be some program developments that remain under religious or other nonprofit auspices, but most are public and secular, including those in Italy and Spain. Another policy regime has emerged with regard to infant or infant and toddler care, and that is a cash benefit, either linked with a job-protected leave following childbirth or adoption (a maternity or parental leave and benefit) or a wage substitute (a child-rearing grant).

The Historic Role of the Private Sector in ECEC Programs

Early childhood care and education has been a mixed delivery system in the United States from its beginnings in the nineteenth century, including publicly operated infant schools in New England, private nonprofit philanthropic day nurseries in New York, and private market care provided by domestic servants throughout the country. A more explicit movement toward a government role occurred during the Great Depression, when the Works Progress Administration established ECEC programs as a strategy for creating jobs for women, and World War II, when women's needed participation in the paid workforce spurred extensive public interest in the provision of child care. This interest diminished sharply after the war, as women were encouraged to return to at-home roles in child care and child rearing.

Beginning in the 1960s, a federal role in funding ECEC programs emerged in relation to compensatory education for young children (Head Start) and welfare (Aid to Families with Dependent Children) to make paid work a more viable option for poor single mothers and in response to the dramatically rising labor force participation of women generally and married women with young children in particular. The numbers of nonprofit providers increased during the 1970s and 1980s, following federal legislation enacted in 1967 permitting public agencies to purchase private nonprofit (voluntary agency) services with public money. For-profit ECEC programs emerged during the same years, when federal tax legislation made it possible for parents to obtain a tax credit to offset some of the cost of ECEC services and thus to purchase services from for-profit providers. At the same time, with the dramatic rise in labor force participation rates of women with young children, demand for the services increased significantly. During these same years, the public role in delivering these services initially expanded (for day care and kindergarten) but then leveled off and even declined over time (for child care); but the government's role may now be increasing again with regard to the growing numbers of prekindergarten programs, often publicly funded.

At the present time, the public role is particularly significant with regard to financing ECEC, through the Child Care and Development Fund, Temporary Assistance for Needy Families and related funds, and the child and dependent care tax credit. Many state governments also provide ECEC funds, but the dominant funding source is the federal government. The delivery system includes some public programs (kindergarten and prekindergarten), but given that most government subsidies for low-income working families are vouchers, and tax credits are the primary subsidy benefiting middle- and upper-income families, current public policy emphasizes demand subsidies and thus favors private delivery.

Although European ECEC programs began in a similar way to those in the United States, with support from the private philanthropic sector, in many of these countries a significant role for government emerged earlier than in the United States. In Italy, for example, legislation enacted in 1968 assigned responsibility for preschool education for three- to six-year-olds to the Ministry of Education, leading to a significant expansion in both the supply and the quality of these programs, almost all publicly funded and most publicly delivered and secular, as well. In contrast, the 1971 legislation, targeting services for children under three, left responsibility for funding and regulation with the regions (and, arguably, ended up with great diversity in coverage, quality, and supply).

In France, the Ministry of Education assumed (or was assigned) responsibility for the preschool programs as early as the late nineteenth century. In Sweden, it was during the post–World War II expansion of ECEC programs that government emerged as the major funder and provider of such services. Britain, like the United States, ended up with a mixed system but is now attempting to design a more coherent and integrated system, with a closer link to education. In effect, only the Anglo-American countries maintained a dual system of welfare-related services for the poor, funded by government, and preschool education for the middle class (and, in the United States, a compensatory education program as well), funded by a mixture of government funds (through tax benefits) and parent fees. These programs are part of a largely private system (both for profit and nonprofit) that is only now beginning to move toward an integrated system, but only for three- and four-year-olds (with five-year-olds already in kindergartens, under publicly funded education auspices).

There does not appear to be any general disagreement about the importance of the ECEC service, at the very least as a service for children of working parents, for children of parents leaving welfare for work, or to prepare children for school. There remains disagreement with regard to other issues, such as the following:

- who should pay for this service, how, and how much
- how the service should be delivered, and by whom

- whether, how, and by whom the service should be regulated
- whether the existing supply of services is adequate
- whether quality matters, and, if so, how much, and how the desire for adequate quality should be balanced with reasonable cost

Other issues also requiring attention include the difference between public funding and public delivery (military base ECEC, public kindergarten, prekindergarten, Head Start), public funding and private delivery (contracting, vouchers, tax subsidies), private funding and private delivery (commercial, for-profit nursery schools), and the difference between private nonprofit and private for-profit sectors. It is clear from this diversity of types of arrangements that government support does not imply that government provides the services directly and that involvement of the private sector does not necessarily mean involving the for-profit sector.

In short, countries that adopted an educational framework or model for their ECEC programs, in particular for the programs serving children from age two or three to age five, six, or seven, followed a pattern of public provision or funding and voluntary agency (religious or secular) delivery (with a subsidy emerging in recent years for family care for infants). Countries that adopted a social welfare framework with policies driven by pressures from rising female labor force participation (in particular, middle-class married mothers and organized labor) also followed a model dominated by public provision and funding, with some supplementation by private nonprofit providers. Even family day care providers are largely publicly funded and regulated in these countries. Countries that developed their ECEC programs in the context of social assistance (welfare, in U.S. terms) and child protection are more likely to have a fragmented delivery system with mixed public and private funding (both nonprofit and for-profit) and with some services under education auspices and some under social welfare auspices. In the international context, the private sector plays a very small role, with commercial (for-profit) providers limited to family day care providers (but only in a few countries and, even then, publicly regulated) and large for-profit chains (such as KinderCare or Bright Horizons) limited to the Anglo-American countries.

Arguments For and Against More Government Funding for ECEC

As noted earlier, the federal government, rather than the states or localities, is the major source of public funding for ECEC in the United States. The 1990s saw a significant increase in federal funds, both through the Child Care and Development Block Grant, as amended and transformed into the Child Care and Development Fund, and under the 1996 Personal Responsibility and Work Opportunities Reconciliation Act. Moreover, during this same period, there has been a significant increase in state-level support for child care for women leaving welfare and support for prekindergarten programs as well. Early childhood education and care is a big industry today. Federal expenditures in FY 2002 constituted more than $7 billion in direct funding ($3.7 billion from Temporary Assistance for Needy Families and $3.9 billion from the Child Care and Development Fund)—in contrast to $2.1 billion as recently as in 1997—in addition to about $2.7 billion through the child care tax credit (U.S. House of Representatives 2004).

Yet in spite of the large amount of money being spent on the ECEC sector, there is general agreement that the quality of care being provided to preschool-age children is probably inadequate (Shonkoff and Phillips 2000; Smolensky and Gootman 2003). National studies have repeatedly found that a disconcertingly large share of American children are in care that is of poor or only mediocre quality (see, for instance, Helburn 1995; NICHD Early Child Care Research Network and Duncan 2003). Moreover, low- and moderate-income families report that child care is so expensive that they are either unable to afford care or unable to afford care of the quality they would like.

Should the government be spending more on ECEC? The standard economic perspective illuminates several important reasons for government involvement in this area. The classical response from economists is that government should be involved (or should increase its involvement) only in the event of a market failure. As Richard Nelson argues in his introduction to this volume, it is possible to take a wider view on this question.

Several potential market failures have been identified in the area of ECEC (for useful discussions, see Gormley 1995; Blau 2001). Some of the same arguments with regard to market failures in K–12 education and health care apply to ECEC as well (see chapters 6 and 8 in this volume). These include the problems of limited information, imperfect capital markets, and the issue of externalities.

Some parents are kept from purchasing high-quality ECEC for their children because they do not have the requisite information, either because they do not know what high-quality care consists of or because they do not know how to tell which providers offer it. There is a fair amount of evidence of this problem (see, for example, Blau 2001; Cleveland and Krashinsky 2003), but there is not general agreement as to how to rectify it. After all, if the problem is limited information, spending more money on care is not the most obvious solution. Spending money on improved resource and referral services, or on educating parents, might well be more effective.

If parents do value high-quality care, know what it is and where to purchase it, and would gladly borrow against their own or their child's future earnings to finance it but are unable to do so, then imperfect capital markets are an issue. But again, it is not clear that government should spend more money on ECEC. Instead, government could set up viable credit markets to allow parents to borrow against future earnings.

The discussion of limited information and imperfect capital markets has assumed that parents and their children are the only beneficiaries of investments in ECEC and thus the only ones whose interests need to be taken into account. But arguably society as a whole would benefit if children were in higher-quality ECEC, as these children would enter school prepared to be better learners and, in the long run, better citizens. If there are such externalities, or benefits that accrue to people outside the child's immediate family, then it might well be worth government's investing more money to improve the quality of care that children receive. How much government should invest, and in which children, would depend on the cost of those investments and their likely benefits. There is some evidence on these points regarding early childhood interventions such as Perry Preschool (see Karoly et al. 1998) but less evidence regarding improvements in child care and ECEC programs more generally.

The preceding discussion considers the improvements that might be made in terms of efficiency if government were to invest more in ECEC. The case that government should invest more because of limitations of information or imperfections in the capital market is weak. (These problems are real, but their solutions lie elsewhere.) The case is much stronger, we think, that government should be investing more because of the positive externalities that would accrue to society if the quality of ECEC were improved. Because such externalities do not enter into families' decision making, families' investments in ECEC are suboptimal, from a social perspective, and society could potentially be better off if government invested wisely in high-quality ECEC.

Increased government spending may also be justified on equity grounds. That is, even if increased spending on ECEC did not improve efficiency but did increase equity, such spending would be justified (if equity is valued). We would argue that equality of access in ECEC is a valuable end in and of itself but is also important as it relates to promoting equality of readiness for school.[4]

Ninety-four percent of American five-year-olds attended kindergarten in 1999. In effect, kindergarten has become universal. It is no longer the major transition from home to school that it was in the past. Instead, preschool provides that transition for many children in the United States (and most children in many other countries). Thus a preschool experience is increasingly essential if school readiness is a goal. But direct funding of preschool providers has declined significantly at the same time as demand subsidies have increased. Some of the large providers have vacancies because low-income parents cannot afford the fees that some of these chains claim they must charge to survive.

The costs of ECEC have increased significantly over the past two decades. In constant 1995 dollars, ECEC costs rose from $59 per week in 1985 to $85 in 1995 (Bureau of the Census 1987; Smith 2000; 2002). Moreover, poor families who paid for child care spent about $75 a week for child care, 35 percent of their income in contrast to the nonpoor's 6 percent (Bureau of the Census 2002, table 11A). In effect, poor families spent more than five times as much as the nonpoor on ECEC services.

Children of affluent families and children in families with highly educated parents are far more likely to be enrolled in ECEC than poor children or those with parents with limited education. Fifty-eight percent of three- and four-year-olds from families with incomes of $40,000 or more attended preschool in 1999 compared with 41 percent of those from families with incomes less than $20,000 (Jamieson, Curry, and Martinez 2001). Two-thirds of the children of women college graduates were enrolled, double the proportion of children whose mothers did not complete high school (34 percent). Most of the children under the age of five enrolled in preschool in 1999 were white non-Hispanics (66 percent). Proportionately more whites were enrolled (55 percent) than African Americans (50 percent) or Hispanics (32 percent) (Jamieson, Curry, and Martinez 2001).

Barriers to child care services for low-income families include a limited supply of subsidies and high copayment requirements; strict eligibility criteria for qualifying for subsidies; too few providers, especially in rural and inner-city communities; an inadequate supply of services providing care during non-traditional hours, care for children with special needs, and care for ill children; a limited supply of out-of-school programs; low reimbursement rates, which can dissuade providers from delivering services to low-income families; and poor quality of services that are affordable (Layzer and Collins 2000).

Furthermore, when left to the market, access to decent-quality programs is a problem for other reasons, too. For example, many of the large chains will not locate their services in low-income neighborhoods on the assumption that there will not be enough consumers in these communities to support such an enterprise. And low-income parents, like most parents, do not want to use services outside their own neighborhoods.

A recent report by the Committee for Economic Development (2002, 1) underscores the extent to which a consensus seems to have emerged regarding the importance of ECEC and the need to advance public policy with regard to these services. The report notes that "all children deserve the opportunity to start school ready to learn. . . . We believe that it is time for the United States to acknowledge society's stake in and responsibility for early education as it long has for older children by making publicly funded pre-kindergarten available to all children aged 3 and over whose parents want them to participate."

The federal government has long recognized this in its Head Start program, but this program still does not reach all eligible three- and four-year-olds and reaches only a tiny share (about 6 percent in 2002) of children under the age of three, with the new Early Head Start component (U.S. DHHS 2002). Moreover, as a primarily part-day and part-year program, Head Start does not adequately serve working parents who need child care for longer hours and often more flexible hours. While funding for low-income child care has greatly expanded with the welfare reforms of the 1990s, these vouchers reach only a small minority of eligible families (12 percent in 1999). Perhaps as a result, the child care usage patterns of low-income families continue to look very different from those of moderate-income and affluent families, with greater reliance on informal care and less use of educationally oriented center-based care. As evidence continues to mount that center-based care is associated with better school readiness (see, for example, NICHD Early Child Care Research Network and Duncan 2003), spending more money to subsidize quality ECEC for low-income families seems a worthwhile investment.

In short, if ECEC is viewed as an important and increasingly essential service, what Suzanne Helburn and Barbara Bergmann (2002) and others have called a merit good, there is an obvious problem of inequitable access. Leaving ECEC to the market will not redress that problem, since without government intervention only the more affluent families will be able to afford high-quality care. A further concern is that the private sector or the voluntary agencies may siphon off the more affluent consumers or the more able children while compromising access and quality for the poor by leaving the more difficult cases in the hands of an underfunded voluntary sector or an understaffed public sector.

In addition to the problems of efficiency and equity, there may also be a broader set of reasons for the government to be involved in this particular area. We have looked at the issue from the viewpoint of standard economic theory, highlighting problems of both efficiency and equity. But as Nelson argues in his introduction to this volume, it is also possible to make what he calls a more positive case for government intervention. In this area, for instance, many European countries see child care as an important experience for children because it provides opportunities for early education as well as opportunities for socialization, development, and enjoyment. This perspective, in which access to high-quality child care is viewed as a right or as a merit good that all children in the community should receive, is part of the explanation for why European countries have more expansive, and publicly supported, child care systems than the United States.

Arguments For and Against a Private Sector Role

In the United States, the ECEC industry is made up of for-profit providers (large national or regional commercial chains), small commercial "mom-and-pop" providers (centers, individual family day care providers, or family day care systems), in-home nonrelative caregivers (domestic servants, nannies), nonprofit voluntary agency providers (centers, often under religious auspices), and public providers (programs sponsored and operated by the military, programs based in public schools, some Head Start programs, some family day care systems in some jurisdictions). These ECEC providers supplement the care provided by families, who remain the single largest source of care for preschool children. Of the 19.3 million children under the age of five in the United States in 1995, half were cared for by relatives (grandparent or parent), 30 percent in organized facilities (center, nursery school, preschool, Head Start), 22 percent in family day care homes, and 9 percent by nonrelatives in the child's own home (Smith 2000).[5] (The overlap is the result of multiple forms of care, usually by relatives [grandparent or parent] providing supplementary care.) Fifty percent of three- and four-year-olds, but only 19 percent of infants, were cared for in organized facilities (and almost two-thirds of infant care is provided by relatives).

The high rates of grandparent and other relative care of infants may have to do with parents' difficulty in obtaining infant care, their inability to afford the high costs of infant care even if available, or their preference for more homelike care (Smith 2000). In contrast, as children get older, school readiness may be a more important factor in choosing center or preschool programs.

Although family members remain the most common type of caregiver for preschool-age children, they do not provide the largest number of hours of care. In 1995 preschoolers spent more time in the care of nonrelatives than in the care of relatives during their parents' work or school hours (thirty-three and twenty-four hours per week, respectively) and also during their parents nonwork or nonschool hours (twenty and twelve hours per week, respectively), suggesting that relative care has become a supplement rather than a primary form of care for many families.

As noted in an earlier analysis by one of the authors (Kamerman and Kahn 1989, 236), child care services constitute the prototypical illustration of privatization and a stress on the private market as an explicit social service policy. The child care industry in the United States has always been a mixed economy, in that privately funded and operated programs have always coexisted with totally public programs. Publicly funded but privately delivered child care services came to dominate the child care market as the supply of services increased during the 1970s and 1980s, in response to federal regulations that permitted public funds to be used to purchase services from private nonprofit providers and the child and dependent care tax credit, which permitted working parents to purchase services from for-profit providers and still benefit from the tax credit. The Reagan administration was committed to making child care even more of a market operation by reducing federal expenditures for child care services, stressing a policy of subsidizing demand rather than supply, eliminating the federal role in setting minimum standards for federally funded child care, and stressing the role of informal rather than formal care. Subsidizing demand created an incentive for parents to purchase care in the open market and encouraged private sector providers to produce and deliver services.

The private sector in the United States consists of more for-profit providers, and fewer nonprofit providers, than is the case in other countries. There has been a long-standing debate in the child care literature as to whether for-profit providers operate differently from nonprofit providers and, in particular, whether, on average, they offer lower-quality care. Although generalizations are hard to draw, given the range of quality in both settings, the weight of the evidence suggests that these providers do operate differently and that, on average, for-profit providers do offer lower quality care (see, for example, Gormley 1995; Cleveland and Krashinsky 2003; Smolensky and Gootman 2003).

The standard arguments in favor of a private sector role in ECEC include the likelihood that the private market will produce a larger supply; freedom of choice for consumers; the greater efficiency among for-profit providers; support for individual over societal choices; and the greater responsiveness of the private market to consumer preferences. The major arguments against a role for the private sector, or limiting its role, include the inadequate supply of ECEC services produced by the private market; inequitable access to ECEC services; and the inadequate quality of ECEC services produced by the private market.

Supply

Economists tell us that when consumers have greater purchasing power, there is an increase in effective demand, and the market responds by expanding supply. Economists also tell us that if regulations are reduced, the number of providers as well as the number of services available will increase (Rose-Ackerman 1983; 1986; Helburn 1995). Certainly, the supply of ECEC programs has increased over the past two decades, especially programs serving three- to five-year-olds, but it is not clear that quality has been sustained. Moreover, with the enactment of Temporary Assistance for Needy Families legislation and the work requirement imposed on recipients, including those with infants and toddlers, the limited subsidy level as well as restricted access to subsidies and low take-up rates (only 12 to 15 percent of those who qualify actually obtain subsidies), reports of waiting lists for child care centers continue, and big shortages remain with regard to infant and toddler care.

Consumer Choice

Choice is a central issue in this domain and one that has been emphasized by many analysts (see, for instance, Young and Nelson 1973; Phillips and Adams 2001). For more than two decades now, federal policy has stressed the importance of supporting consumer choice (Hayes, Palmer, and Zaslow 1990; Thompson 2002) and therefore increasing demand subsidies (tax credits or vouchers). For those with incomes high enough to take advantage of the child and dependent care tax, the policy has provided modest support for parental choice. Although there are no data on how parents spend their tax subsidy, it can be spent on far more varied forms of care than a grant given directly to a child care provider (for example, it can offset some of the costs of in-home-care, family day care, center care, nursery school, or prekindergarten). For those receiving benefits from Temporary Assistance for Needy Families or the Child Care and Development Fund in the form of vouchers, the policy in principle supports choice, but in fact choice is limited in that welfare-related subsidies do not cover current market costs, are difficult to obtain, and are not accepted by all providers. Thus although choice is a compelling argument in favor of a role for the private sector, or mixed private-public provision, this is more true for moderate-income and affluent families than for low-income families, for whom affordability problems currently preclude a full set of choices.

Cost Effectiveness

The conventional wisdom is that the private sector is more efficient than the public sector and would lead to an increased supply of services at lower costs. We address the issue of supply earlier in this chapter. Per child costs of publicly subsidized care have been reduced as a consequence of increased private delivery and decreased public provision. But there has been a concomitant decline in quality as for-profit providers substitute for public and nonprofit providers (Gormley 1995).[6]

Quality of Care, Regulations, and Standards

The issue of what constitutes quality includes what is known about the impact of child care on child development and the ways to measure and improve quality. The discussion about quality began with a debate about the Federal Inter-Agency Day Care Requirements in the 1970s, the enactment of standards in 1980, and the subsequent elimination of federal standards under Ronald Reagan, when the 1981 Social Services Block Grant (under Title XX of the Social Security Act) superseded the earlier legislation. About 55 percent of the children receiving ECEC services through the Child Care and Development Fund are in licensed care. Licensing may be a necessary but not sufficient device for ensuring quality. Eighty-seven percent of the centers in the "Cost, Quality, and Child Outcomes" study (Helburn 1995, 72) provided mediocre or poor-quality services. Indeed, there is widespread agreement that "the average quality of child care in the United States is probably too low relative to the social optimum" (Blau 2001, 11; see also Shonkoff and Phillips 2000; Phillips and Adams 2001; Smolensky and Gootman 2003).

The literature suggests a positive link between child care quality and a child's daily experiences, school readiness, and later academic achievements and social interactions (Shonkoff and Phillips 2000; Vandell and Wolfe 2000; Smolensky and Gootman 2003). Other researchers have found that low-income women view child care quality and reliability as more important than cost, but nevertheless they are more likely to receive low-quality care (Helburn 1995). Children participating in good quality care are less likely to be held back a grade or be placed in special education programs (Basile, Henderson, and Henry 1998). Children in high-quality child care demonstrate greater language development, greater mathematical skills, greater thinking and attention skills, and fewer behavioral problems in school than children attending poorer quality child care (Shonkoff and Phillips 2000; Kamerman et al. 2003). There is also emerging evidence that child care quality has larger impacts on cognitive test scores for children whose scores are low to start with (NICHD Early Child Care Research Network and Duncan 2003).

Probably the best evidence on quality differences between nonprofit and for-profit providers comes from comparisons of for-profit and nonprofit centers in the "Cost, Quality, and Outcomes" study (Helburn 1995). That study finds that structural elements of quality (staff-to-child ratio, group size, staff qualifications and training) varied with profit status and were significantly higher in nonprofit than in for-profit centers. Furthermore, staff turnover rates were lower in nonprofit centers, and staff had longer tenure. However, process quality (teacher observations, caregiver interactions with children) was comparable in nonprofit and for-profit centers in states with adequate to high regulations but very poor in for-profit centers in states with lax regulations (Helburn 1995, 54–55). The study also finds "evidence of inadequate consumer knowledge which creates market imperfections and reduces incentives for some centers to provide good quality care" (Helburn 1995, 66). This "inadequate consumer knowledge" arises because parents simply do not have the information, lack the ability to evaluate quality, or do not understand that differences in quality make a difference in the impact on their children.

In the United States as well as other countries, public education is now taken for granted as the dominant form of compulsory education, albeit with some provision of private nonprofit education. For-profit schools play a role in vocational training in the United States but are largely invisible in elementary and secondary education. In other countries, however, public programs (publicly funded or delivered services) are dominant in preschool programs as well, either because they are defined as "education," and thus treated the same as primary and secondary school education, or because of a strong conviction about the importance of government's role in ensuring equitable access, quality, and other desirable attributes. In contrast, more than half the providers of ECEC in the United States are private, and they operate largely for profit.

The tension in the United States between public and private provision can be seen in the area of prekindergarten programs. As states move to providing universal prekindergarten programming for four-year-olds and even, in some instances, three-year-olds, they face choices about whether to provide these programs under public, private, or mixed auspices. In Georgia, for example, the first state with a fully implemented statewide universal prekindergarten program, which covered about 80 percent of four-year-olds in the state in 2001, 57 percent of the classes are run by private providers (Raden 1999). In Oklahoma, most prekindergarten programs are located in public schools. New York has a mixed system. In still another state, for-profit providers blocked an effort by the state superintendent of education to establish a universal, statewide program for four-year-olds in the public education system because of so-called "unfair competition" presented by the public schools.

In principle, government can influence the quality of care provided by the private sector through the standards it sets for that care with regulations. However, regulations are not very effective if they are not monitored (Phillips and Mekos 1993), and monitoring is costly (Gormley 1995). There is also a lot of debate about whether the aspects of child care that can be regulated relate to the aspects of child care that have to do with quality and with child outcomes: regulations tend to focus on measurable quantities, like number of children, size of group, staff-to-child ratios, and the like, whereas process quality has more to do with staff interactions with children. However, some regulations—of group size and teacher training, for instance—do seem to be associated with better outcomes for children (Vandell and Wolfe 2000; Blau 2001). There is also evidence that child care programs are generally of higher quality in states with tougher regulations and that children in those programs have better developmental outcomes (NICHD Early Child Care Research Network 2003). For this reason, many child care analysts (such as David M. Blau [2001] and Helburn and Bergmann [2002]) recommend sticking with mixed public and private sector provision and using increased information for parents, along with increased regulation, to improve the quality of care offered in both public and private sectors. Using private programs offers many advantages: it enhances consumer choice, may offer improved quality, and may well be cheaper than locating programs in public facilities. At the same time, however, private programs may be more diverse in terms of quality and more inequitably distributed. If so, children might well receive more equitable ECEC in public programs. We have not seen any direct evidence on this question but view it as very important, as it will come up again and again as the United States moves toward earlier enrollment of children in ECEC programs.

The Role of the Family

In the United States, and internationally, the family has the primary responsibility for children and their support but not the exclusive responsibility. Family law in all the industrialized countries stresses this (Kamerman and Kahn 1997). Although historically parents were responsible for the financial support of their parents and siblings, as well as their children, filial responsibility has been eliminated in most of the industrialized countries, and parental responsibility is limited to children. Society has assumed collective responsibility for the elderly (through old-age insurance benefits) and for the disabled. In many countries, collective responsibility has been assumed, at least in part, for children as well, albeit not in the United States. For example, several countries (Netherlands, Australia, New Zealand) once provided a "family wage" set at a level that would support a man, woman, and two children. The concept was that with a family wage, families with children would need only one wage earner to provide adequate support; the second adult could concentrate on child care and rearing. That model no longer exists. Most wives have entered the labor market to compensate for the economic inadequacy of the traditional family model in current times.

A child or family allowance, a cash benefit provided to families based on the presence of a child and the number and, sometimes, age and ordinal position of children, is another device for supplementing earned income for families with children (Kamerman and Gatenio 2002; Kamerman et al. 2003; Kamerman, forthcoming). Eighty-eight countries provide such a benefit to compensate for the additional costs of bearing and rearing children. The United States provides a tax benefit for modest-income working families with children and another tax benefit for families with incomes above the tax threshold where children are present. But the United States has not provided a universal cash benefit, nor does it have any other fully universal child benefit. The provision of the earned income tax credit and the child tax credit offer some evidence that the United States acknowledges some level of responsibility for ensuring adequate income to families with children, but it is only partial, at a limited level, and only for some families with children. The U.S. family benefit package provided through the tax system is nowhere near as generous as the comparable tax and cash benefit packages provided by many other countries (Kamerman and Gatenio 2002).

The United States has clearly assumed that parents will carry responsibility for the provision of an adequate standard of living and that they will achieve this primarily through the workings of the market.[7] U.S. policies toward ECEC follow a similar pattern. The United States provides free primary and secondary public school education for children aged six to sixteen and kindergarten for most five-year-olds, but it does not provide the equivalent for younger children. Nor does it ensure universal, let alone equitable, access to ECEC. In contrast, several countries guarantee children a place in ECEC programs when they reach a certain age (one year in Denmark and Sweden, two and a half in France and Belgium, three in Germany and Italy). In the United States, families continue to bear most of the responsibility for early childhood care and education. In the late 1990s, half of the 19 million children in the United States under the age of five were cared for by a relative, usually a grandparent or a parent.

Working parents often choose to work different shifts to ensure parental care for their young children. Most of the care provided by family members is unpaid, but this does not mean it comes without costs. Parents pay for the care they themselves provide by forgoing current earnings from the labor market and by reducing their likely future earnings; they often "pay" for the care provided by other family members by trading goods or services. These costs can be substantial and should be taken into account when thinking about the resources expended in this sector (Young and Nelson 1973).

When they do purchase child care, poor and near-poor parents in the United States pay a disproportionate share of their income for these services (35 percent and 17 percent, respectively). In contrast, Sweden, for example, has recently announced a policy setting the maximum fee for ECEC programs for all children at no more than 2 to 3 percent of family income. Parents in the United States pay a significantly higher proportion of ECEC operating costs than parents in other countries.

What the European countries have done to support family care, where they believe it is especially important, is to enact policies that subsidize the family in carrying out its caring tasks. Child or family allowances constitute one form of such support. In addition, in recent decades most of these countries have enacted paid and job-protected parental, child-rearing, or child care leaves following childbirth or adoption. The paid leaves, which last from one to three years, are in some cases limited to working parents and in others are available to all parents, fully or partially replacing wages forgone while they are on leave (Kamerman 2000a, 2000b; Waldfogel, 2001). The objective is to make it possible for parents to take care of their infants at home instead of placing them in out-of-home care, without being subject to a substantial economic penalty. With regard to such policies, again, the United States follows a different path, stressing family responsibility without providing societal support.

Most of the financial, time, and emotional burdens of rearing children (and the pleasures) are borne by parents, sometimes aided by other relatives. But an increasing share is provided outside the family, either purchased in the market, provided or funded by government, or provided by the family but with the help of government.

Conclusion

The pressure to expand the supply, quality, and access to ECEC programs continues. With 65 percent of women with children under the age of six in the labor force in 2002, the need for extrafamilial child care is large and still growing. Concern with school readiness, as well as a growing body of research that documents the value of these programs for child development, points to the importance of quality as well as access. Kindergarten attendance has become universal, with almost all five-year-olds already enrolled or in first grade. In contrast, only about half of the nation's three- and four-year-olds are enrolled in a preschool program, a lower proportion than in almost any other major industrialized countries. Because these programs are predominantly private in the United States, the cost of attending may be prohibitive for some families. The gap in enrollment between low-income and middle- to high-income families is substantial, as is the gap in share of family income expended for child care, with low-income families paying a disproportionately large share of income.

There is no longer a debate about whether a child's development is better enhanced if cared for at home. Indeed, higher-income families and families with highly educated mothers are more likely to enroll their young children in preschool programs than low-income families or those with less-educated mothers. Early childhood care and education programs are becoming a normative experience, at least for three- and four-year-olds. Given adequate quality, those children who are not enrolled are seen as deprived or disadvantaged (Kamerman et al. 2003; Meyers et al. 2004).

Whether ECEC services are contracted, subsidized by vouchers or tax credits, or delivered directly, however important, is not the issue here. Nor is it whether the services are publicly delivered or delivered through a private for-profit or nonprofit organization. The ultimate issues are the adequacy of the resources provided (largely requiring public funds); recognition of the value of these programs to society and therefore provision of equitable access regardless of income; a recognition of differential "quality" and the need for good management and accountability to ensure quality; and an acknowledgment of the importance of government support to families in their parenting roles. If society values ECEC services, and if quality matters, either government will provide the services, or it will provide the resources and ensure adequate quality, or the private sector will provide the services and government will have to subsidize access and regulate those services.

The role of the family in early childhood education and care is obviously important. But the family can no longer do the job by itself, meaning that government or the market must step in, because if decent-quality ECEC services are not available for preschool-age children, children, schools, and society will suffer.

The United States continues to lag behind other countries in its policies and to stress the role of the market or of families alone, without recognizing the negative consequences for children. History shows us that when families cannot meet the education and socialization needs of their children, the government has stepped in, as it did when establishing public primary schools. Experience has shown that when families cannot meet the care and education needs of their preschool-age children on their own, the private sector alone will not do an adequate job. Government must play a role, whether as a provider of services directly or as a funder and regulator of services provided by the private sectors.

Notes

1. Early childhood education and care programs include nonrelative in-home and out-of-home care services, kindergarten, prekindergarten, nursery school, child care and day care centers, and family day care homes.
2. Compulsory education for primary school was enacted in Sweden in 1842, in Italy in 1860, in Britain in the 1870s, in France in 1882, and in Germany in the 1870s and 1880s. The first compulsory public primary school in the United States was established in Massachusetts in 1852. By 1870 most American cities offered eight years of graded public elementary school, and public secondary schools were being established. By the end of the nineteenth century, primary school enrollment was universal, typically for five years.
3. As in several other countries, one other factor is the division of responsibilities between federal and state governments and the allocation of responsibility for education to state governments.
4. For recent evidence on this point for the United States, see Magnuson, Ruhm, and Waldfogel (2004); and Magnuson et al. (2004). French research also underscores the role of preschool education in ensuring school readiness and reducing school problems; for a summary of this research, see Kamerman et al. (2003).
5. The 30 percent in organized care is up from 23 percent in 1985; the 9 percent cared for in-home by nonrelatives and the 22 percent in family day care is down from 37 percent in 1985.
6. In thinking about cost effectiveness, it is also important to be clear about what the objectives are. Historically, many of the efforts in this domain in the United States have had as their goal increasing the employment of low-income women, particularly welfare recipients. If this is seen as the goal of ECEC policy, then a cost-effective policy will try to provide child care for the largest number of families

possible so as to yield the largest possible employment effect. However, if the goal of ECEC policy is to promote child development, then a cost-effective policy would emphasize quality over quantity.

7.   For instance, the United States provides access to health care for all poor children, through Medicaid, for children under the age of six in families with incomes up to 133 percent of poverty, and for some children in families with somewhat higher incomes as well but not as a universal entitlement for all children regardless of family income. The United States has a policy of trying to enforce the financial obligations of noncustodial parents in supporting their children but does not provide a guaranteed minimum child support benefit, ensuring children of financial support even when their noncustodial parent fails to pay support or pays it irregularly or at an inadequate level.

References

Barnett, W. Steven. 1995. "Long-term Effects of Early Childhood Programs on Cognitive and School Outcomes." *Future of Children* 5(3): 25–50.

Basile, Kathleen C., Laura W. Henderson, and Gary T. Henry. 1998. *Pre-Kindergarten Longitudinal Study 1996–97 School Year.* Report. Georgia State University, School of Policy Studies, Applied Research Center.

Beatty, Barbara. 1995. *Preschool Education in America.* New Haven, Conn.: Yale University Press.

Berfenstam, Ragnar, and I. William-Olssen. 1973. *Early Child Care in Sweden.* New York: Gordon and Breach.

Blau, David M. 2001. *The Child Care Problem: An Economic Analysis.* New York: Russell Sage Foundation.

Cleveland, Gordon, and Michael Krashinsky. 2003. *Financing ECEC Services in OECD Countries.* Discussion paper. Paris: Organization for Economic Cooperation and Development.

Committee for Economic Development. 2002. *Preschool for All: Investing in a Productive and Just Society.* New York: Committee for Economic Development.

Cooper, Candy. 1999. *Ready to Learn: The French System of Early Education and Care.* New York: French American Foundation.

Currie, Janet. 2001. "Early Childhood Intervention Programs: What Do We Know?" *Journal of Economic Perspectives* 15(2): 213–38.

David, Miriam, and Irene Lezine. 1975. *Early Child Care in France.* New York: Gordon and Breach.

Gormley, William T., Jr. 1995. *Everybody's Children: Child Care as a Public Problem.* Washington, D.C.: Brookings Institution Press.

Hayes, Cheryl D., John L. Palmer, and Martha J. Zaslow, eds. 1990. *Who Cares for America's Children: Child Care Policy for the 1990s.* Washington: National Academy Press.

Helburn, Suzanne, ed. 1995. *Cost, Quality, and Child Outcomes in Child Care Centers.* Denver: University of Colorado.

Helburn, Suzanne, and Barbara Bergmann. 2002. *America's Child Care Problem: The Way Out.* New York: Palgrave.

Hwang, Carl-Philip, and Anders G. Broberg. 1992. "The History and Social Context of Child Care in Sweden." In *Child Care in Context,* edited by Michael Lamb, Kathleen Sternberg, Carl-Philip Hwang, and Anders G. Broberg. Hillsdale, N.J.: Lawrence Erlbaum.

Jamieson, Amie, Andrea Curry, and Gladys Martinez. 2001. "School Enrollment in the United States: Social and Economic Characteristics of Students." *Current Population Reports,* P20-533. Washington: U.S. Bureau of the Census.

Kamerman, Sheila B. 2000a. "From Maternity to Parenting Policies: Women's Health, Employment, and Child and Family Well-Being." *Journal of the American Women's Medical Association* 55(2): 96–99.

———. 2000b. "Parental Leave Policies: An Essential Ingredient in Early Childhood Education and Care Policies." *Social Policy Report* 14(2): 3–15.

———. Forthcoming. "Europe Advanced While the U.S. Lagged." In *Work, Family, and Democracy,* edited by Jody Heyman. New York: New Press.

Kamerman, Sheila B., and Shirley Gatenio. 2002. "Tax Day: How Do America's Child Benefits Compare?" Issue brief. Clearinghouse on International Developments in Child, Youth, and Family Policies (April). Available at: www.childpolicyintl.org (accessed November 30, 2004).

Kamerman, Sheila B., and Alfred J. Kahn. 1976. *Social Services in the United States.* Philadelphia: Temple University Press.

———, eds. 1989. *Privatization and the Welfare State.* Princeton, N.J.: Princeton University Press.

———. 1994. *A Welcome for Every Child Care, Education, and Family Support.* Washington, D.C.: Zero to Three.

———. 1997. *Family Change and Family Policies in Great Britain, Canada, New Zealand, and the U.S.* Oxford, U.K.: Oxford University Press.

Kamerman, Sheila B., Michelle Neuman, Jane Waldfogel, and Jeanne Brooks-Gunn. 2003. "Social Policies, Family Types, and Child Outcomes: A Review of the Literature." Working paper 6. Social Employment and Migration. Paris: Organization for Economic Cooperation and Development.

Karoly, Lynn A., Peter W. Greenwood, Susan S. Everingham, Jill Houbé, M. Rebecca Kilburn, C. Peter Rydell, Mathew Sanders, and James Chiesa. 1998. *Investing in Our Children: What We Do and Don't Know About the Costs and Benefits of Early Childhood Interventions.* Santa Monica, Calif.: Rand.

Layzer, Jean, and Ann Collins. 2000. *National Study of Child Care for Low-Income Families: State and Community Substudy.* Interim Report. Cambridge, Mass.: Abt Associates.

Magnuson, Katherine A., Marcia Meyers, Christopher Ruhm, and Jane Waldfogel. 2004. "Inequality in Preschool Education and School Readiness." *American Educational Research Journal* 41(1): 115–57.

Magnuson, Katherine A., Christopher Ruhm, and Jane Waldfogel. 2004. "Does Prekindergarten Improve School Preparation and Performance?" Working Paper 10452. Cambridge, Mass.: National Bureau of Economic Research (April).

Meyers, Marcia K., Dan Rosenbaum, Christopher Ruhm, and Jane Waldfogel. 2004. "Inequality in Early Childhood Education and Care: What Do We Know?"

In *Social Inequality,* edited by Kathryn Neckerman. New York: Russell Sage Foundation.

National Institutes of Child Health and Human Development (NICHD) Early Child Care Research Network. 2002. "Child Care Structure → Process → Outcome: Direct and Indirect Effects of Child Care Quality in Young Children's Development." *Psychological Science* 13: 976–1005.

National Institutes of Child Health and Human Development (NICHD) Early Child Care Research Network and Greg Duncan. 2003. "Modeling the Impacts of Child Care Quality on Children's Preschool Cognitive Development." *Child Development* 74: 1454–75.

Organization for Economic Cooperation and Development (OECD). 2000. "Twelve-Country Thematic Review of Early Childhood Education and Care Policy." In *Country Background Reports.* Paris: OECD.

———. 2001a. *Starting Strong: Early Childhood Education and Care.* Paris: OECD.

———. 2001b. "Twelve-Country Thematic Review of Early Childhood Education and Care Policy." In *Country Notes.* Paris: OECD.

Phillips, Deborah, and Gina Adams. 2001. "Child Care and Our Youngest Children." *Future of Children* 11(1): 35–52.

Phillips, Deborah, and Debra Mekos. 1993. "The Myth of Child Care Regulations: Rates of Compliance in Center-Based Child Care Settings." Paper presented at the annual research conference of the Association for Public Policy Analysis and Management. Washington, D.C. (October 28–30).

Pistillo, Filomena. 1989. "Pre-Primary Education and Care in Italy." In *How Nations Serve Young Children,* edited by Patricia Olmsted and David Weikart. Ypsilanti, Mich.: High Scope.

Pringle, Mia, and Sandhya Naidoo. 1975. *Early Child Care in Britain.* New York: Gordon and Breach.

Raden, Anthony. 1999. *Universal Prekindergarten in Georgia: A Case Study of Georgia's Lottery-Funded Pre-K Program.* New York: Foundation for Child Development.

Rose-Ackerman, Susan. 1983. "Unintended Consequences: Regulating the Quality of Subsidized Care." *Journal of Policy and Analysis and Management* 3(1): 14–30.

———. 1986. "Altruistic Nonprofit Firms in Competitive Markets." *Journal of Consumer Policy* 9: 291–310.

Shonkoff, Jack P., and Deborah A. Phillips. 2000. *From Neurons to Neighborhoods: The Science of Early Childhood Development.* Washington: National Academy Press.

Smelser, Neil, and Sydney Halpern. 1978. "The Historical Triangulation of Family, Economy, and Education." In *Turning Points,* edited by John Demos and S. Spencer Bookcock. Chicago: University of Chicago Press.

Smith, Kristin. 2000. "Who's Minding the Kids? Child Care Arrangements, Fall, 1995." *Current Population Reports,* P70-70. Washington: U.S. Bureau of the Census.

———. 2002. "Who's Minding the Kids? Child Care Arrangements, Fall, 1997." *Current Population Reports,* P70-86. Washington: U.S. Bureau of the Census.

Smolensky, Eugene, and Jennifer A. Gootman, eds. 2003. *Working Families and Growing Kids: Caring for Children and Adolescents.* Washington: National Academies Press.

Steinfels, Margaret O'Brien. 1973. *Who's Minding the Children? The History and Politics of Day Care in America.* New York: Simon & Schuster.

Thompson, Tommy. 2002. Testimony before the U.S. House of Representatives Committee on Ways and Means. *Hearing on the President's Plan to Build on the Success of Welfare Reform* (March 12, 2002).

Tizard, Jack, Peter Moss, and Jane Perry. 1976. *All Our Children: Preschool Services in a Changing Society.* London: Maurice Temple Smith.

U.S. Bureau of the Census. 1987. "Who's Minding the Kids? Child Care Arrangements, Winter, 1984–85." *Current Population Reports,* P70-9. Washington: U.S. Government Printing Office

———. 2002. *Survey of Income and Program Participation.* Washington: U.S. Bureau of the Census.

U.S. Department of Health and Human Services (DHHS). 2002. "Head Start: Promoting Early Childhood Development." Available at: www.hhs.gov/news/press/2002/pres/headstart.html (accessed May 17, 2002).

U.S. House of Representatives. 2004. Committee on Ways and Means. *The Green Book 2004.* Washington: U.S. Government Printing Office. Available at: waysandmeans.house.gov/Documents.asp?section=813 (accessed November 29, 2004).

Vandell, Deborah L., and Barbara Wolfe. 2000. *Child Care Quality: Does It Matter and Does It Need to Be Improved?* Madison: University of Wisconsin, Institute for Research on Poverty.

Waldfogel, Jane. 2001. "What Other Nations Do: International Policies Toward Parental Leave and Child Care." *Future of Children* 11(1): 99–111.

———. 2002. "Child Care, Women's Employment and Child Outcomes." *Journal of Population Economics* 15(3): 527–48.

Young, Dennis R., and Richard R. Nelson. 1973. *Public Policy for Day Care of Young Children: Organization, Finance, and Planning.* Lexington, Mass.: Lexington Books.

8

MARKET VERSUS STATE IN HEALTH CARE AND HEALTH INSURANCE: FALSE DICHOTOMY

Dahlia K. Remler, Lawrence D. Brown, and Sherry A. Glied

E VEN A cursory glance around the developed world suggests that there are many ways to organize a health care system. The degree of institutional variation across developed countries is perhaps greater in this sector than in virtually any other domain of social policy. There are no purely market health care systems, and few remaining systems are purely governmental. In most countries, both sectors play a role. The tremendous importance of health insurance and the intertwining of health insurance and health care services make it hard even to describe what a pure market for health care would be. Would it be a system of competing health maintenance organizations that use bureaucratic measures when dealing with providers? Would it be a system of medical savings accounts that patients use to buy services directly from doctors and hospitals? Would it be no third-party payment at all, with or without indemnity insurance? Here we explore the sources of the interdependence between markets and government and what they mean for earnest but empty efforts to ascribe distinctive virtues and vices to each sector and then prescribe how to "choose between" them.

The Indispensable State

Controversy about the proper size and scope of governments' and markets' roles in health care rests on four basic issues. The first, and perhaps most fundamental, is the proper amount of redistribution from rich to poor for health care provision. The inequities between services consumed by the rich and the poor that arise in relatively pure markets, such as those for toys or cars, are, to most people, unacceptable in health care (for an exception, see Epstein 1997). In consequence, the role of governments in providing health care to the poor is long-standing. Otto von Bismarck started the first national health insurance program in Germany in the late nineteenth century; and as early as

1928, 14 percent of U.S. health care expenditures were paid by governments (Somers and Somers 1961). Today, even while 40 million Americans lack coverage, government supplies nearly half the dollars in the health care system. There is almost universal agreement that the widespread lack of health insurance in the United States is a major problem. On the other hand, there is wide disagreement within the United States—and elsewhere—about what degree of redistribution to the poor or those with moderate income is merited in the area of health care.

The second issue is what roles the government should play—as regulator, financier, or provider—in health care for the nonpoor. There is variation in health system design—across countries and over time—in the role of government in financing, regulating, and providing care to the nonpoor in addition to the poor. Economists have long recognized that informational asymmetries in health care services necessitate a role for government, even without any redistribution (Arrow 1963).

Governments have the universal responsibility of regulating the provision of health care services. Health care providers, particularly physicians, have far more information than their patients. Quack doctors and quack drugs appear through history; and, particularly in the period since their legitimate counterparts have provided scientifically proven effective therapies, governments have had the role of rooting them out. Information asymmetries between providers and patients provide a compelling and widely accepted case for government to act as regulator of doctors and other health care providers, hospitals, and drugs. The informational advantages of providers over the entire rest of society, whether government or private sector, implies that professional societies must play a role in ensuring the quality of health care. Professionalism itself also plays a critical role (Mechanic 1996).

Economists also recognize selection in insurance markets as necessitating a role for government. Selection is a problem because competition among insurers results in incentives to avoid those insurees that are more likely to cost more, and therefore market competition fails to achieve socially desirable redistribution among nonpoor people who differ in health status. The extreme skewness of health care expenditures, with the costliest 1 percent of individuals consuming 27 percent of all medical expenditures in the United States today (Berk and Monheit 2001), makes the financial rewards of selection frighteningly large. Government must play a role in addressing selection.

The third issue about the proper roles of government and markets in health care concerns the extent to which services financed by the government can still be provided through markets. For example, equity can, in principle, be addressed by distributing health care–specific vouchers with no further government involvement (Tobin 1970). For this issue, the debate is similar to that in several other sectors discussed in this book, such as education and early childhood care; but in health care, the issue is further complicated because one decision can be made for health insurance while another is made for health care services. Traditional Medicare is government-provided insurance used to purchase privately provided health care services. Medicare risk contracts are government-purchased but privately provided insurance. The Veterans Affairs Health Care system is government-provided insurance and health care. Recently, there has been debate about whether the proper role of government is as provider or simply as financier of potential pharmaceutical coverage for Medicare beneficiaries.

The fourth issue is whether governments should play a role in containing the aggregate costs of health care. The existence of health insurance—highly desirable for reasons described later—has its own bad side effects: because, when choosing medical treatments, people are spending other people's money, they do not consider the costs of the care. Such insensitivity to costs—the moral hazard problem—pervades health care services covered through insurance. The tremendous skewness of health care expenditures results in the need to pool large groups of people together in order to truly diversify risk. Efforts to control moral hazard must be transmitted from the large group that pools risk down to the individual level at which treatment decisions are made. Such efforts bring large transaction costs. That the transaction costs in health care so far exceed those in education or other areas is explained by the extremely high variance of expenditures and clinical idiosyncrasy (Glied and Remler 2002). The need to address moral hazard means that private health care markets lose many of the traditional advantages of markets over government, making the choice between markets and government moot for many purposes.

The presence of rapid, cost-increasing technological change in health care complicates redistribution and means that the government's role in cost containment is strongly linked to its interest in redistribution (Glied 1997; Glied and Remler 2002). If we allow wealthy people to spend as much as they want on their health care, maintaining equity becomes an extremely, and perhaps prohibitively, expensive proposition. A market-based rationing that allows people to choose more-expensive options will carry financial incentives to develop new technologies that offer great improvements in health at prices the wealthy will willingly pay. Once those technologies are invented, however, if we do not fund the redistribution to cover them for everyone, equity suffers. While in principle equity can be addressed through health care–specific vouchers, as costs rise the cost of achieving a given degree of equity also rises. If equity is greatly valued, the least costly way of attaining it may be to limit private spending (Lindsay 1969).

These concerns imply that the degree of government involvement in the health care system for the nonpoor and the means of providing coverage to the poor are connected to the degree that redistribution both among the nonpoor (that is, across health status) and between the poor and nonpoor is viewed as desirable. However, the extent of government involvement also rests on the empirical question of the seriousness of selection problems in health insurance and how effectively governments and markets control costs. This debate has been the fulcrum of U.S. health policy over the past three decades, and more recently it has come to influence, though not dominate, policy debate in some other Western nations.[1]

Since the 1970s, the United States, like other Western nations, has worried continually over health care costs that are commonly said to be too high, rising too fast, and producing too little value for the money. One set of analysts has urged expansion of public regulation, in particular, firmer limits on payments to providers and on expansion of health care facilities, as the logical corrective. Others, however, insist that market forces—cost consciousness among consumers, incentives within organizations for efficient production, and competition among "firms"—deter or dispel these problems in other "industries" and that they can do so in health care, as well (for example, Goodman and Musgrave 1994). Weary of protracted political battles with providers, beleaguered by conservative critiques of bumbling "big" government, and intrigued by the assurances that a bracing infusion of market forces could shape up the sector, many policy makers have embraced proposals to restore normal market forces to health care.

This experiment in expanding the role of markets in health care has provided new information to inform the debate about the proper roles of government and markets. Our assessment of the results of that experiment suggests that market enthusiasts overstate their case. Many of the problems of concern to society and policy makers cannot be solved through purely market mechanisms; substantial government action is needed. The strategic dichotomy between markets and governments is fundamentally false: the strategic tool kits available to market-based and government-based approaches and available to public and private insurers differ less than ideology may suggest. Sound policy consists not in choosing between markets and government but rather in artfully integrating these pervasively interdependent sectors.

The Retreat and Return of Health Care Markets

Although the United States is atypical in not providing universal health coverage, the interplay between markets and government forces in this nation well illustrate the larger issues. Not so long ago, health care was a fairly normal market, at least for people who could afford to pay for it themselves. Well into the twentieth century, consumers mainly paid for the services of medical providers (physicians and hospitals) as they did for other goods and services, that is, out of pocket and without much, if any, help from insurance. Government regulation of providers, meanwhile, did not extend far beyond licensure.

The Great Depression left a sizable share of the population unable to afford medical care, along with other goods and services. In consequence, providers invented health insurance programs (specifically, Blue Cross for hospitals and Blue Shield for physicians) that would stabilize their revenues.

Starting around World War II, medical science spawned innovations that finally made it likely that a medical encounter would do a patient more good than harm and made the hospital a site for saving lives rather than a place one went to die. Growing and accelerating medical efficacy brought in its wake rising popular demand for access to these benefits, which, in turn, brought surging demand for health insurance. Health insurance provides financial protection for those who obtain such costly care and, even more important, offers access to care to some who might otherwise not be able to obtain it at all (Nyman 2003).

Spurred by a federal decision in wartime to exclude employer-purchased health coverage from taxable income, the nonprofit Blue Cross and Blue Shield plans grew rapidly in numbers and membership. They soon found themselves facing commercial (for-profit) competitors seeking their share of this big new market.

The rise of commercial competitors to Blue Cross altered the existing system of redistribution among the nonpoor. Blue Cross and Blue Shield had been community-rated plans. Their commercial competitors offered coverage on an experience-rated basis. Healthy people now paid less than sick people for the same insurance. Insurers began to compete by manipulating the risk pool, offering plans that were more likely to appeal to the lower risks (such as plans with higher cost-sharing but much lower premiums). A large empirical literature documents that selection of this type is significant in practice as well as in theory (for example, Price and Mays 1985).

A number of business and labor groups voiced principled objection to this method of buying cheaper coverage, arguing that the only way to eliminate it was to implement national health insurance. Economic theory suggests that selection is a strong argument for restricting choice in health insurance markets (Diamond 1992). Mandatory pooling of everyone into a single insurance group, as in a single-payer system or national health insurance, eliminates the problem. But history suggests that for many groups competitive insurance systems functioned reasonably without everyone being pooled into one group. For example, employment-based health insurance in the United States appears to address effectively most problems of adverse selection for those who can join large employer groups. But employer-sponsored coverage in large groups is unavailable to many people. Furthermore, the possibility of job loss or job change means that even people with employer-sponsored coverage do not have health care "security" over time.

The problem of maintaining secure coverage over time complicates the standard analysis of selection. After insurance became nonuniversal and experience rated, people with chronic, obvious health conditions could no longer buy or retain coverage except at very high prices. This not only seemed inequitable, it also meant that even initially healthy people were not truly insured over time. Real, meaningful insurance would incorporate coverage both for immediate risks and against the risk of developing health risks in the future, including the risk of a rise in one's actuarially fair premium (Cochrane 1995). Such insurance would have to run over time and even, to cover congenital conditions, start before conception. Private, unregulated markets do not appear to be capable of generating such contracts.

The difficulties in having private markets provide coverage to people who were outside employer-sponsored coverage and already at high risk of ill-health was one motivating factor in the passage of Medicare, the first large expansion of government financing beyond the poor. The enactment of Medicare in 1965 gave the federal government a huge new role in the health care system. At the same time, the growing value of health care coverage pushed equity issues ever higher on the public agenda. The contemporaneous introduction of Medicaid addressed equity concerns by substituting insurance coverage for traditional government funding of indigent care and provided additional benefits to unemployed lower-income people and their children.

Between 1945 and 1965, medical innovation continued to raise the value of health insurance, and employer-based health insurance continued to expand. The expectation that third parties should and would pay for care became the norm. With the arrival of Medicare and Medicaid, roughly 85 percent of the U.S. population had health insurance, and the rising costs of public programs drove home what private payers had been saying for some time: all this progress and coverage do not come cheaply. Somehow, through premiums, taxes, or some other source, the true costs of care must be covered—there is no free lunch. By 1970, almost everyone agreed that the nation faced a "health cost crisis," and a search for solutions was in full swing.

The expansion of health insurance in the thirty years preceding 1970 made the health care cost crisis different from other increases in the costs of private goods or publicly provided services. The near omnipresence of insurance in health care means that health care consumers are essentially spending other people's money and may not consider the full cost of their decisions. The normal market relationship between price and demand—the basis of most arguments for market efficiency—is attenuated. This moral hazard effect means that even in principle, the outcomes of the free market in health care might not have been socially optimal.

Government responded to the cost crisis accordingly, promulgating regulations to address the apparent overutilization generated by insurance. New variations on old public regulation themes came quickly on line: the federal government promoted utilization review (professional standards review organizations), capital expenditure reviews by the states (certificate-of-need laws), health planning (health systems agencies), and prospective setting of hospital rates (which states could elect to adopt under authority created by the feds in 1972). Critics, however, insisted that the imposition of new public rules on providers was largely beside the point: fee-for-service medicine coupled with third-party coverage guaranteed the exemption of health care from the healthy discipline of market forces and made excessive cost growth inevitable. A growing corps of economists and health service researchers began diligently pondering how well a "market approach" fits, or can be made to fit, the particular properties of the health care sector.

In essence, the debate between proponents of markets and regulation in responding to the health care cost crisis focused on which institution was better suited to address the problems of moral hazard. Moral hazard itself is an inevitable consequence of all forms of insurance, whether public or private. And despite the intensity of the debate, private insurers and publicly run health care delivery systems must rely on the same set of imperfect tools—consumer cost-sharing, incentives for providers, direct control of treatment decisions, and restriction of supply—for allocating services among consumers (Remler 1994).

Historically, health insurance contracts coped with moral hazard by shifting some of the burden of paying for health care expenditures—and some of the associated financial risk—back to the user of services through cost-sharing. Even a small copayment at the point of purchase, which shifts relatively little risk onto the consumer of services, can significantly reduce health care expenditures (Newhouse and the Health Insurance Experiment Group 1993). Consumer cost-sharing exists in most U.S. insurance contracts, including most health maintenance organizations, and in many public systems. For example, the Swedish health care system charges a copayment of around SK 140 (approximately US$14) for a physician visit (World Health Organization 1996).

Many economists focused on the incentives of consumers (beneficiaries) to use more care and consequently urged greater cost-sharing as the best approach to addressing moral hazard and limiting cost escalation in health care. The highly skewed nature of health care spending, however, limits the extent to which consumer cost-sharing can be used as an exclusive rationing tool, even in theory (Remler and Atherly 2003). A pure cost-sharing system would impose substantial financial burdens on patients with serious health conditions, and most advocates of enhanced cost-sharing put substantial limits on it. John Goodman and Gerald Musgrave (1994), like most advocates of medical savings accounts, couple them with high deductible policies that would still leave much health care spending out of the free-enterprise, cost-consciousness instilling system they propose. Cost-sharing also has political limitations, since consumers are also citizens (and voters), and substantial cost-sharing is already built into Medicare, which covers people with unusually great needs.

Providers were a more appealing target. Left and right converged on the contention that provider dominance and professional sovereignty were the roots of extravagant health care spending, but the two persuasions parted on causes and correctives. Liberals argued that providers reigned because government did not constrain physicians and hospitals with sufficient force. Retrospective reimbursement of actual costs and charges were widely derided as blank checks that invited misuse of services and resources. The liberal answers were direct government action to restrict supply factors and to impose price controls (fee schedules).

Conservatives, by contrast, insisted that providers were dominant because purchasers of health services declined to behave as they would and should in a normal market. By allowing suppliers of medical care to define demand, they acquiesced in the illogical incentives intrinsic to the conjunction of fee-for-service medicine and third-party payment. The more providers do, the more money they make, and so long as the parties of the first and second parts (consumers and providers) go unconstrained, the parties of the third and fourth parts (insurers and purchasers of coverage) will foot the escalating bill. The implicit argument was to introduce market forces at the service level, but clear discussion of how to do that in the context of health insurance was lacking.

Following this logic, both private and public systems sought ways to change the ways they paid providers. In a fee-for-service payment system in which reimbursement exceeds costs, the more services doctors provide the more they earn (Pauly 1970). But under a capitation or salary system, health care providers operate under "supplier cost-sharing" and have incentives to limit the availability of care (Ellis and McGuire 1993).

In the public system, Medicare adopted the logic of reducing costs by changing payment mechanisms in its implementation of the prospective payment system (diagnosis-related groups) for per case hospital payment in 1983. Following a somewhat similar logic, the British National Health Service uses a per patient capitation mechanism to compensate some primary care providers.

Changing payment incentives outside hospitals and outside the public system, however, required a more radical overhaul of health insurance. At a critical juncture, Dr. Paul Ellwood persuaded health officials in the Nixon administration that organizational innovations—integrating insurance and delivery in prepaid group practices—would allow the development of plans that could instill correct incentives. Choice and market forces at the plan level would translate into market forces for lower costs (and possibly higher quality) at the service level. Ellwood explained that the Kaiser-Permanente Health Plan (which had huge memberships in Northern and Southern California) was a living, breathing model of this rational approach and proposed that prepaid group practice (rechristened as "health maintenance organizations" [HMOs]) be used to get Medicare costs down. He suggested that the federal government should seek to launch flexible versions of prepaid group practices, embody the

HMO option in a new Part C in Medicare, get as many elderly as possible into HMOs, and let competition go to work.

Congress showed little enthusiasm for HMOs in Medicare, and the HMO development legislation signed in December 1973 aimed mainly to implant new organizational infrastructure into the private health insurance system. Many health economists applauded the new commitment to market forces in health care, and "managed care," as it would come to be called, was off and running (Brown 1983).

In the first decade of the federal program, HMOs were slow to catch on. Consumers worried about loss of freedom in choosing providers. The strength of market systems is supposed to stem from choice, but consumers seem to care less about their plan options than about choice of provider at the time of treatment. Corporate purchasers knew little about HMOs and were reluctant to rock the benefits boat by pressuring workers to join them. Insurers viewed HMOs as a formidable managerial challenge and feared losing their shirts by investing in them too heavily. Providers continued to obstruct the growth of these detested ventures in what was viewed as corporate medicine.

By the mid-1980s, however, the tide had turned. Organizational innovation within the HMO industry produced more casually run plans that reassured consumers who feared that aggressive gatekeeping and limited panels of providers would reduce choice at the time of treatment. Heads of firms had grown more anxious about health costs, more leery of government "solutions" (such as Jimmy Carter's proposal for a national hospital rate-setting system, which died in 1979), and more impressed by the proselytizing of market-minded health economists. Insurers had gained experience with HMOs and recognized that large profits might be made from shifts from inpatient to outpatient care and from specialist to generalist services—recognition that triggered large infusions of equity capital into this increasingly for-profit industry. Providers made an uneasy peace with HMOs, resignedly concluding that if they could not beat them they might as well join, run, or even own them. By 1990, managed care had replaced indemnity coverage in the mainstream of the U.S. health insurance system.

The growth of managed care, however, led to a quite predictable backlash. Supplier cost-sharing—at the plan level or at the service level—encourages providers to limit care. If patients are ill informed, or too docile, as they often are, capitation or salary payment can lead to underprovision of services, just as fee-for-service payment can lead to overprovision (Blomqvist 1991).

Capitation or salary payments also give providers incentives to avoid costly cases. This problem of selection under capitated payment is well documented in the U.S. Medicare HMO program (Newhouse 1996). The same problem arises in systems with fixed budgets. In Canada, for example, hospitals that were paid fixed budgets used "bed blockers"—long-stay, low-intensity patients—to reduce hospital costs (Evans et al. 1989; Newhouse

1996). Increased incentives for selection leave high-cost patients at risk of higher costs and worse access to care, intensifying concerns about equity, even among people who are not poor.

Financial incentives at both the consumer and provider levels generated undesirable side effects within the health care system, leading both governments and private insurers to adopt nonfinancial means of regulating service use. One approach, adopted by both public and private payers, is to place restrictions on the behavior of providers and consumers. These limits can take the form of restrictions on the types of providers a patient may see (for example, through gatekeeping programs) and on the types of services a patient may receive (for example, through utilization management programs).

Requirements that patients see a primary care gatekeeper before seeking care from a specialist have been used, with mixed success, by U.S. HMOs. Countries with public health insurance systems also sometimes use gatekeeping programs. Gatekeepers may have financial incentives to restrict use (as under the general practitioner [GP] fund-holding program in the United Kingdom), but in other cases (Canada, for example), they do not face incentives to limit referrals. Direct review of utilization, especially inpatient utilization, is now common in U.S. private health insurance programs and is practiced in Medicare by federally authorized peer review organizations. The significant transactions costs of utilization review, popularly depicted as seemingly endless phone tag, undermine to some extent its cost-containment effects.

A related, alternative strategy for containing costs is to restrict the supply of factors needed to provide care, such as personnel, buildings, or equipment. Publicly run health care systems may limit the number of hospital beds available, the number of physicians who may practice in a given jurisdiction, and the types of technology available. Private health insurers that limit coverage to a prespecified list of providers (selective contracting) can also curb supply in these ways. Restricting supply factors can result in rationing by waiting time, physical distance, or severity of need.

Utilization review, gatekeeping, provider restrictions, and supply limits have proved unpopular with both providers and consumers. Direct restrictions on access have generated the so-called managed care backlash. Many plans have responded to the backlash, possibly reacting to threats that members will exit to other plans with looser and looser options, such as point-of-service plans and an end to gatekeeping. As it happens, many of these tools are exactly what plans use to control costs, and so loosening raises costs. Therefore, plans must also respond by making clear that such changes will increase costs. The right balance among access, quality, and cost presupposes a degree of precision in the sending and reading of signals within and between complex formal organizations that may not be attainable in the real world.

The managed care backlash both reflected and reinforced the determination of consumer and provider groups to enlist the power of government to constrain managed care organizations. The federal government debated a national patients' "bill of rights." State after state passed legislation that enabled "any willing provider" to join managed care organizations, required managed care organizations to offer point-of-service options to members who wanted to seek care outside the plans' provider panels, obliged plans to speed up payment of providers' bills, entitled plan members to direct access to certain specialists, fashioned rules for external review of members' complaints against plans, and sought to detect and forestall financial problems that could drive plans into insolvency. Today, government increasingly constrains the management of both the internal operations of managed care organizations and the external competition among them.

Managed Competition: Combining Strategies

The difficulties involved in using individual means of addressing moral hazard led market enthusiasts to argue that only an optimal combination of strategies, carefully managed by government, could yield effective cost containment. In an appropriately structured market, competition among insurers gives them an incentive to control costs. If they can decrease the cost of care, and thus premiums, without reducing the quality of care (at least not by much), then they should be able to gain market share and drive out their less efficient competitors. Following this logic, Alain Enthoven (1980) suggested a system of competition between health plans that would integrate the roles of insurance and health care delivery. Such integration would provide the right incentives, and the plans would then presumably adopt the optimal mix and level of rationing tools.

Enthoven's vision incorporated HMOs but also a substantial government superstructure that would address problems of selection. He proposed that competition among managed care plans be managed by the government, that is, enfolded in and constrained by rules that defined standard benefit packages, required open enrollment, defined allowable variations in premiums, and more. Later analysts added to the model by urging that managed competition requirements include a system of explicit redistributional side payments—a risk adjustment system—that would pay insurers enough to cover an individual's expected costs. Many systems that offer multiple competing health plans now use risk adjustment, including Medicare+Choice in the United States and a similar arrangement in the German health insurance system. Risk adjustment systems of this type extend the domain of government redistributional activity well beyond redistribution from the rich to the poor.

Throughout the 1980s, interest in Ellwood and Enthoven's managed competition vision—a market solution that would address selection and equity concerns and give firms the right incentives to tackle moral hazard—had grown among analysts. Such an intricate interfusion of market forces and government rules contained far too much of the latter to appeal to the Reagan or first Bush administrations. As a New Democrat, however, Bill Clinton sought "market alternatives" to the traditional liberal strategies of taxing, spending, and regulating. Casting their fate with managed competition (Glied 1997), the Clinton reformers fashioned a plan under which newly concentrated purchasers would shop and choose among managed care plans that could stay competitive only by controlling the providers who worked for them.

The New Democrats labored heroically to honor market forces while averting the undesirable side effects of market imperfections. One key challenge was to avoid the problems of selection that everyone expects in a genuinely competitive insurance market. Another worry was how to get purchasers to live up to their weighty responsibilities as sources of demand for high quality and low price in a newly normal market. The Clinton reformers answered by proposing that employees who worked in firms of five thousand or fewer workers be obliged to join individual purchasers in federally designed health insurance purchasing cooperatives, also known as regional health alliances. They understood that the healthier, if not forced to pool with the less healthy, will opt out for their own lower-cost plans, leaving those unfortunates with chronic disease stuck without affordable insurance. To the surprise and dismay of the reformers, the mandatory alliances were branded as another layer of government bureaucracy into which innocent citizens would be forced. The alliances, and the Clinton plan's artful synthesis of market forces and government rules, soon vanished into political oblivion.

Following the demise of national health reform, the system returned to the status quo ante, namely, unmanaged competition among managed care organizations. This competition slowed the rate of growth of costs, at least for a few years, but as discontent spread with the methods managed care organizations used to try to influence treatment decisions, a backlash against managed care arose. People discovered that market forces push managed care organizations to use the same array of highly imperfect tools available to government health care systems, resulting in bureaucracy, lack of choice, and rationing.

This is not surprising. Both the presence of moral hazard and the tools available to address it are essentially the same for government and private insurers. The similarities between government and privately operated health insurance systems will, thus, tend to be more important than the differences. Bureaucracy will be a characteristic of both private and public health insurance.

Markets may have some advantages. If people have heterogeneous tastes about rationing tools, well-informed (and well-heeled) consumers may prefer to be rationed using price mechanisms that allow them considerable choice at the point of service. Less informed (and less affluent) consumers might prefer rationing mechanisms that do not emphasize choice at the point of service. Competing forms of health insurance permit the expression of this heterogeneity.

Yet a strong case also exists that government is better able than markets to combat moral hazard. One advantage of a government-operated system is that, as a monopolist, government may be better able to limit supply factors than market actors can. A second advantage is that government-operated systems may be able to ration care more equitably. If society believes that health care is a right, the inevitable inequities that arise when markets try to address moral hazard may be unpalatable.

Market and Government in Europe

Observers on the left of center have long urged that the United States abandon its insular pretensions and draw lessons from other Western nations, all of which manage to insure virtually their whole citizenry while spending 10 percent or less of gross domestic product in the process. The dynamics of health policy in Europe in the 1990s presented these cosmopolites with a discordant datum, however: many nations were looking to the United States for lessons on how to infuse market forces into their national health insurance systems. In fact, despite the major differences between Europe and the United States, particularly Europe's greater commitment to redistribution, cross-national policies exhibit many of the same take-home messages as the U.S. experience.

The sources of the European interest in market forces were not obscure: health care costs in other nations chronically exceeded budget makers' expectations and preferences. (That these nations spent less than the United States on health care was irrelevant to the central political issue, to wit, rising health spending rates that complicated their own internal budget balancing.) By long-standing political agreement, governments obliged providers to bargain over price (through fee schedules and negotiated rates); in exchange, governments mostly stayed away from clinical decisions. But cost, after all, equals price times volume, and volume is mainly assailable by clinical micro-management. Moreover, experts in these nations had digested accumulated studies contending that health systems housed huge amounts of waste (inappropriate care, unnecessary utilization, duplicative facilities, and all the rest). The implication was that costs could be brought to more defensible levels if (and perhaps only if) these systems somehow learned to "manage care."

In countries, like Germany, with multiple sickness (health insurance) funds, a first and relatively easy step was to belabor the funds, which employed many thousands of workers who surely ought to be more proactive in shaping the care patterns they funded. Executives of the sickness funds replied that they lacked the levers with which to manage care and could get them only if governments summoned the courage to write such authority into law. Influential analysts, however, warned that the lethargic condition of the sickness funds was but a symptom of the deeper problem, namely, the absence of competition in systems in which market forces had for too long been unfairly anathematized. European policy makers, unanimous in rejecting the unmanaged competition that was sweeping the United States, sought to institute competitive regimes so adroitly managed that they posed no threat to the solidarity and equity of national systems, the managed competition that had eluded the United States.

In the 1990s Great Britain, Germany, Netherlands, Sweden, and Israel adopted reforms that sought to tilt their systems toward managed competition. Unlike the United States, all of these countries were already committed to universal coverage. Although these schemes differed in detail, they all wrestled with four additional preconditions for managed competition: a basic benefits package, choice by citizens among sickness funds, risk-adjusted payments to the competing funds, and the power of funds to contract with providers selectively. These elements serve to enhance competition, and the inclusion of mandatory risk adjustment means that these plans incorporate substantial explicit redistribution among the nonpoor.

While these elements were seen as critical for making competition effective in reaching social goals, they all were also difficult to implement. Basic benefits packages might replace implicit rationing of services with explicit (and, needless to say, "hard") choices about coverage, but such lists were difficult to draw and make stick. Citizens might be allowed to choose among funds, but the funds were often confused about how (and why) they should compete. Risk adjustment methods were (allegedly) crucial to the preservation of solidarity and equity in these national systems: if funds were not paid enough to cover those likely to cost more, they would compete by discouraging them. However, methods that reliably captured the consequences for use of services of variables beyond age and sex were elusive. Selective contracting, particularly the closed panels key to American managed care, would end the decades-old understanding that any provider working in the national health insurance system could treat any citizen who sought his or her services.

At the close of the 1990s, researchers tended to agree that these competitive stirrings had not been for naught: providers, nervous about what market forces might do to their market shares, grew more diligent at scrutinizing (or, at any rate, documenting) their practice patterns and clinical choices. None of these societies had met all the preconditions noted, however. Some observers urged governments in search of new management efficiencies in the health care system to cut to the chase by wielding the political and financial power of the state more aggressively and directly in negotiations with providers, not by adding an intervening variable, the well-managed competitive health care market, which entailed too many complexities, contingencies, and institutional implausibilities to yield efficiencies efficiently.

However great the European commitment to redistribution, market forces are needed to exert incentives for restraining costs. But market forces bring a need for a greater government role in addressing selection, and private health plans share with public plans the same imperfect tool kit for addressing moral hazard.

Market and State: A False Dichotomy

The peculiar characteristics of health care limit the traditional advantages of markets over government-run systems. Information asymmetries mean that government must regulate providers, so providers will have more power than in normal markets. The advantages of markets in addressing heterogeneity of tastes are limited by the potential for adverse selection. Selection means that choice must be restricted if people are to be meaningfully insured over time and that government must play some role in ensuring redistribution across health status. Risk adjustment is one form of government intervention that can allow health care to benefit from market competition.

Many problems of the health services market stem from the existence of insurance, which is a necessity in a world of high and uncertain medical costs. Moral hazard means that rationing of health care services by price alone cannot simultaneously provide adequate insurance and eliminate wasteful overconsumption. Private and public insurers have essentially the same tool kit, however, including substantial bureaucratic, non-price-rationing elements. Thus even an entirely market-based health system will never look like other markets. In some cases, government can better deploy the necessary tools; in others, markets have the upper hand.

Government-run systems are not immune from market failures, either. Governments cannot erase the informational asymmetries between providers and patients, nor can they eliminate the excess utilization owing to moral hazard. Governments can limit adverse selection by forcing everyone into a single plan, but even a public system encounters selection problems once patients, or providers, have choices about where to go or whom to treat. The overlap between the problems of government and market contributes to the constant policy oscillation between them.

Given widespread concern about equity in health care (substantially beyond concern about it in any other realm), a government role in redistribution to maintain equity is essential, even if the extent of commitment to equity varies within and between countries. The issue is further complicated because redistribution may imply limits on private spending. The costs of maintaining equity, with respect to both income and health status, rise as costs rise. Even in a market-dominated system, government cannot be indifferent to the cost of care.

Although distinct in origin and evolution, the American and European systems suggest one broad lesson. In health affairs, government and market are not "either or" choices between strategic alternatives, but rather "both and," complementary and interdependent social sectors. American attempts to reach affordable universal coverage show that the more one wants from market forces, the more one needs from government, the source of the all-important framework well-functioning markets require. The strivings of national health insurance systems in Europe signal the converse: the larger the role of government, particularly as redistributor, the deeper the need for market forces to address health care costs.

Today, no developed country operates either a purely public or a purely private system of health care. All governments play some role as financier for the poor and as regulator of both health care services and health insurance. Some governments also play the role of provider of health insurance or health care services. Yet neither is there today a system without substantial use of market forces, particularly for health care services. A combination of government and market forces is essential to the realization of many policy goals.

The authors thank Hank Levin, Richard Murnane, Richard Nelson, Michael Sparer, and participants in the two Russell Sage conferences, The Complexities and Limits of Market Organization, for discussions and comments on earlier drafts.

Note

1. In addition to the debate on the role of government in health care and health insurance, there is some debate about and attention to the roles of not-for-profit and for-profit institutions. The charitable origins of health care institutions and some norms have lead to a substantial role for not-for-profits in hospitals and insurance, although not in physician practice. However, empirical evidence about behavioral differences between for-profits and not-for-profits is mixed, with frequent findings of no difference (Sloan 1998; Rosenau and Linder 2003).

References

Arrow, Kenneth J. 1963. "Uncertainty and the Welfare Economics of Medical Care." *American Economic Review* 53(5): 941–73.

Berk, M. L., and A. C. Monheit. 2001. "The Concentration of Health Care Expenditures, Revisited." *Health Affairs* 20(2): 9–18.

Blomqvist, Ake. 1991. "The doctor as double agent: Information asymmetry, health insurance, and medical care." *Journal of Health Economics* 10(4): 411–32.

Brown, Lawrence. 1983. *Politics and Health Care Organizations: HMOs as Federal Policy.* Washington, D.C.: Brookings Institution Press.

Cochrane, John H. 1995. "Time Consistent Health Insurance." *Journal of Political Economy* 103(3): 445–73.

Diamond, Peter. 1992. "Organizing the Health Care Market." *Econometrica* 60(6): 1233–54.

Ellis, Randall P., and Thomas G. McGuire. 1993. "Supply-side and Demand-side Cost Sharing in Health Care." *Journal of Economic Perspectives* 7(4): 135–51.

Enthoven, Alain. 1980. *Health Plan: The Only Practical Solution to the Soaring Cost of Medical Care.* Reading, Mass.: Addison-Wesley.

Epstein, Richard Allen. 1997. *Mortal Peril: Our Inalienable Right to Health Care?* Reading, Mass.: Addison-Wesley.

Evans, R. G., M. L. Barer, C. Hertzman, G. M. Anderson, I. R. Pulcins, and J. Lomas. 1989. "The long good-bye: the great transformation of the British Columbia hospital system." *Health Services Research* 24(4): 435–59.

Glied, Sherry. 1997. *Chronic Condition: Why Health Reform Fails.* Cambridge, Mass.: Harvard University Press.

Glied, Sherry A., and Dahlia K. Remler. 2002. "What Every Public Finance Economist Should Know about Health Economics: Recent Advances and Unresolved Questions." *National Tax Journal* 55(4): 771–88.

Goodman, John C., and Gerald L. Musgrave. 1994. *Patient Power: The Free-enterprise Alternative to Clinton's Health Plan.* Washington, D.C.: Cato Institute.

Lindsay, Cotton M. 1969. "Medical Care and the Economics of Sharing." *Economica* 144(November): 351–62.

Mechanic, David. 1996. "Changing Medical Organization and the Erosion of Trust." *Milbank Quarterly* 74(2): 171–89.

Newhouse, Joseph P. 1996. "Reimbursing Health Plans and Health Providers: Efficiency in Production versus Selection." *Journal of Economic Literature* 34(3): 1236–63.

Newhouse, Joseph P., and the Health Insurance Experiment Group. 1993. *Free for All? Lessons from the RAND Health Insurance Experiment.* Cambridge, Mass.: Harvard University Press.

Nyman, John A. 2003. *The Theory of Demand for Health Insurance.* Stanford, Calif.: Stanford University Press.

Pauly, Mark V. 1970. "Efficiency, Incentives and Reimbursement for Health Care." *Inquiry* 7(1): 115–31.

Price, James R., and James W. Mays. 1985. "Biased Selection in the Federal Employee Health Benefits Program." *Inquiry* 22(1): 67–77.

Remler, Dahlia K. 1994. "Intruding on Medical Treatment." *Challenge* 37(5): 52–55.

Remler, Dahlia K., and Adam J. Atherly. 2003. "Health Status and the Heterogeneity of Cost Sharing Responsiveness: How Do Sick People Respond to Cost-Sharing?" *Health Economics* 12(4): 269–80.

Rosenau, Pauline Vaillancourt, and Stephen H. Linder. 2003. "Two Decades of Research Comparing For-Profit and Nonprofit Health Provider Performance in the United States." *Social Science Quarterly* 84(2): 219–41.

Sloan, Frank A. 1998. "Commercialism in Non-profit Hospitals." *Journal of Policy Analysis and Management* 17(2): 234–52.

Somers, Herman M., and Anne R. Somers. 1961. *Doctors, Patients, and Health Insurance.* Washington, D.C.: Brookings Institution Press.

Tobin, James. 1970. "On Limiting the Domain of Inequality." *Journal of Law and Economics* 13(2): 263–77.

World Health Organization. 1996. "Health Care Systems in Transition: Sweden." Copenhagen: World Health Organization Regional Office for Europe. Available at: www.euro.who.int/document/e72481.pdf (accessed November 11, 2004).

Part III

SCIENCE AND TECHNOLOGY

A WIDE variety of activities and institutions are involved in the advance of science and technology. Public funding plays an important role in parts of the system but a limited role in other parts. Market elements are important in various activities but seldom in the raw form depicted in the economics textbooks. Large parts of the system are regulated. The chapters in part III are concerned with various aspects of this "mixed" system. In all three of the sectors studied here, one sees increasing use of markets in the governing structures. The question is whether this is a positive or a negative development.

The enterprise of basic research has long grounded its claim for public support, combined with a good deal of freedom to pursue leads that scientists themselves deem interesting and promising, on a threefold argument. First, the long-run payoffs from the support of basic research, in terms of economic progress, improved medical care, and a variety of other aspects of practical value to society, are enormous. Second, the particular practical results that come from basic research are difficult to predict in detail and should be regarded as, to a large extent, serendipitous; accordingly, the expectation of large payoff is maximized when scientists are free to do what they think is good science. Third, scientific knowledge is nonrivalrous in use, and hence its value is maximized if there are no financial or other bars for potential users. This package of arguments in effect has kept basic research largely a non-market activity, on the demand side funded by government and on the supply side conducted largely in universities and public laboratories.

In recent years, several developments have brought change to the system. First of all, there is growing recognition that basic research is indeed targetable, and in fact has long been targeted, and that while particular practical results generally are not predictable, the broad area of application of results, should the research be successful, is quite predictable. Major companies in the electrical equipment and electronics industries, and in the chemical and pharmaceutical industries, have funded a certain amount of basic research based exactly on that understanding. A second important development is that, as a result of decisions of the U.S. Patent and Trademark Office and the U.S. courts, in several fields of science the results of research are often patentable. Third, universities and public laboratories doing research in these fields now are active patenters. As a result of all these changes, there is much more "market" in the governance of basic research than there used to be. There are many questions as to what the consequence of this will be for the long-run advancement of science and for technical progress.

Many important technologies were nurtured in their early years by government agencies seeking greater capabilities to deal with the tasks and problems facing them. A striking recent example is the Internet. In its early days, the principal funder of the research and technical experimentation that led to the Internet was the U.S. Department of Defense. Later, the National Science Foundation became a major supporter of this work. The commercial value of the Internet, so obvious today, was not apparent in the early days; and until recently, there was little private money going into these efforts.

The early uses of the Internet were almost exclusively governmental or scientific. The governing structure that emerged in the early days reflected this. As commercial uses became evident, for-profit companies began to use the Internet, and total use began to expand rapidly. As that happened, developing the software, and hardware, for the Internet came to be perceived as a highly profitable business. Indeed, the economic boom of the late 1990s was to a considerable extent driven by these developments. As the commercialism of the Internet has increased, so have the role and power of commercial interests in its governance. The question of intellectual property rights has become more prominent. Clearly, the Internet governing structure is in transition, and there are serious questions regarding how much market and nonmarket mechanism there should be in the structure that is coming into existence.

Satellites are another complex of technologies brought into existence through government programs. One of the important uses satellites have found is in collecting and distributing to interested users a vast amount of information about the earth's surface and its atmosphere. These uses range from very practical crop yield and weather forecasts to a variety of scientific uses. In the early days, the design, development, and operation of the relevant satellites was a government function. So, too, was the distribution of data gathered by the satellite system.

In recent years, with definite urging, commercial interests have entered all of these activities, and government has withdrawn from many. The collection and distribution of data by satellites has become increasingly market governed. The following chapters address some of the questions regarding whether this is appropriate.

9

BASIC SCIENTIFIC RESEARCH

Richard R. Nelson

MODERN capitalism has proved a remarkably powerful engine of technological progress. Most of the attention to its workings has focused on the business firms and entrepreneurs operating in a market setting, who are the central actors in developing and introducing new products and processes. At the same time, it is widely recognized that the power of market-stimulated and market-guided invention and innovation are often dependent on the strength of the science base from which they draw (Nelson 1993; Mowery and Nelson 1999). This science base largely is the product of publicly funded research, and the knowledge produced by that research is largely open and available for potential innovators to use. That is, the market part of the capitalist engine rests on a publicly supported scientific commons.

The message of this chapter is that the scientific commons is becoming privatized, in the sense that intellectual property rights are being established and enforced on important new parts of it. While the privatization of the scientific commons up to now has been relatively limited, there are real dangers that, unless it is halted soon, important portions of future scientific knowledge will be private property and fall outside the public domain, and that could be bad news for both the future progress of science and for technological progress. The erosion of the scientific commons will not be easy to stop.

A number of influential philosophers and sociologists of science have put forth a set of views, a theory, about the scientific enterprise that until recently has served well to protect the scientific commons. However, this theory no longer is adequate to the task because the way it characterizes the nature of the scientific enterprise does not fit modern perceptions and the present reality. Under this theory, it is hard to understand why privatization and markets are encroaching on the commons, and, if they are, what is the matter with that. It is important, therefore, to scrutinize that theory.

A key element of the theory is that, outside of industry, the work of scientists is and should be motivated by the search for understanding and that the practical payoffs that often come from successful research are largely unpredictable. Vannevar Bush (1945) is one among many proponents of public support of science who put forth this theme. Bush argues that it would be a mistake to look to likely practical payoffs as a guide to where scientific funds should be allocated. Serendipity is the reason why scientific research often has practical payoff, and the chances of serendipity are greatest when bright and dedicated scientists are free to attack what they see as the most challenging scientific problems in the way they think most promising.

For this reason, decisions regarding what questions to explore, and the evaluation of the performance of individual scientists and broad research programs, should mostly be in the hands of the working scientists. Indeed, for the government or the market to intrude too much into how scientific research resources are allocated would be to kill the goose that lays the golden egg. In the terms used by Michael Polanyi (1967), society should appreciate and protect the "Republic of Science."

An associated belief or ideal is that the results of scientific research should be published and otherwise laid open for all to use and evaluate. As Robert Merton (1973) argues, the spirit of science is "communitarian" regarding access to the knowledge and technique it creates. All scientists are free to test the results of their fellows, to find them valid or not, and to build on these results in their own work. Because the results of scientific research are laid in the public domain for testing and further development, the bulk of scientific knowledge accepted by the community is reliable (as John Ziman [1978] has emphasized), and scientific knowledge is cumulative. These are basic reasons why the scientific enterprise has been so effective as an engine of discovery. Economists often have argued that keeping science open is the most effective policy for enabling the public to draw practical benefits from it.

My argument here is that the part of the theory about good science that stresses the value of open science is basically correct but is in danger of being forgotten or denied. As originally put forth, this part seemed a natural consequence of the other aspects of the theory: that the practical payoffs from scientific research were not predictable but largely came about through serendipity and that the allocation of scientific resources should be guided not by anticipation of particular practical payoffs but rather by the informed judgments of scientists regarding the most important problems to work on. Keeping scientific findings in the public domain, with reward to the scientist being tied to the acclaim of his or her fellows along with public funding of research based on peer review of the scientific promise of the proposal and the scientist, then, would seem an important part of an incentive and control system for fostering productive science (for a discussion along these lines, see Dasgupta and David 1994).

However, the notion that academic scientists have no idea and do not care about the practical problems their research might illuminate has never been fully true. In this era of biotechnology, it is obvious, if it was not before, that both the funders and the undertakers of research often have well in mind the possible social and economic payoffs from what they are doing. If, in fact, much of scientific research is consciously aimed, at least broadly, at problems the solution to which can have major and broadly predictable practical value, what is the case against harnessing market incentives to the undertaking of research and to the use of research results? In particular, why should the privatization of these kinds of research results be viewed as a problem?

The case for open scientific knowledge clearly needs to be reconstructed to recognize explicitly that much of scientific research is, in fact, oriented toward providing knowledge useful for the solution of practical problems, that the applications of new scientific findings often are broadly predictable, and that this is why control over scientific findings in some cases is financially valuable property. There is a case for keeping basic scientific knowledge open, even under these conditions. To privatize basic knowledge is a danger both for the advance of science and for the advance of technology.

The role of serendipity notwithstanding, for the most part science is valuable as an input to technological change these days because much of scientific research is in fields oriented to providing knowledge that is of use in particular areas. These are the scientific fields in which, as Donald Stokes (1996) notes in *Pasteur's Quadrant,* the research aims for deep understanding but the field itself is oriented toward achieving practical objectives, such as improving health, achieving better understanding of the properties of materials, or achieving a powerful theory of computing.

However, even where the scientific base is strong, it almost never is clear what will be the most fruitful paths to the solution of practical problems. There are great advantages to society in having a number of different parties engaged in the efforts to advance a technology, with winners and losers being determined in ex post competition rather than through ex ante agreement to focus efforts on one particular tack rather than another. A strong base of scientific knowledge should be understood as making more powerful the innately evolutionary processes involved in the advance of technology rather than as eliminating the need for multiple competitive sources of innovation. To restrict access to basic science is to cut down significantly on the number of parties who can effectively invent in a field.

Ideological and political debates that occurred after World War II led to broad consensus regarding the value of public support of open autonomous science. That rhetoric stressed that the payoffs from science were almost completely unpredictable, and thus the allocation of funds to science should not be influenced by perceptions of social needs. The publicly supported science system that actually developed was, in fact, much more oriented to making progress on important practical problems than that rhetoric allowed, and this is now obvious.

I do not want to argue that most academic researchers working in, for example, the biomedical sciences define their goals in terms of particular diseases. Much of the most important work in such fields is quite fundamental in nature, in that it explores basic processes and phenomena without a clearly defined specific practical objective in mind. However, the fundamental questions and appealing lines of scientific research noted in *Pasteur's Quadrant* (Stokes 1996) are strongly influenced by perceptions of what kind of knowledge is relevant to problem solving in a field. Thus one of the reasons why cell biology is now such a fashionable field is the belief that basic understanding won here just might unlock the cancer puzzle or enable us to understand better how receptors work. This perception of how the modern science system actually operates has eroded the notion that it is important to keep science open.

While perceptions of possible applications of research are not as vague as proposed in the earlier rhetoric about serendipity, the actual paths to application of apparently promising scientific discoveries are, in fact, uncertain. Understandings that come from science seldom lead immediately or directly to the solution of practical problems. Rather, they provide the knowledge and the tools to wrestle with practical problems more effectively. For just this reason—that the findings of basic science set the stage for follow-on applications work—for society to get maximal benefit from its support of basic science requires that there be open access to scientific research results. Open access permits many potential inventors to work with new knowledge. Privatization restricts access to only those whom the "owner" allows to make use of that knowledge. This is why some of the recent developments are so worrisome.

The Coevolution of Practice and Understanding

Virtually everybody these days appreciates that the power of modern technological innovation depends to a considerable extent on its ability to draw from modern science. But there is little general understanding, and some quite wrong beliefs, about the nature of the science-technology links. Understanding these correctly is a precondition, I believe, for having an effective discussion about what public policy toward science ought to be. This certainly is so regarding the current controversies about patenting in science.

Technologies need to be understood as involving both a body of practice, manifest in the artifacts and techniques that are produced and used, and a body of understanding, which supports, surrounds, and rationalizes the former. For technologies that are well established, an important part of the body of understanding supporting practice is generally grounded in the empirical experience of practitioners regarding what works and what does not, things that sometimes go wrong, reliable problem-solving methods, and so on. However, in recent times, virtually all powerful technologies have strong connections with particular fields of science. These connections, of course, are central in the discussion of this chapter.

There is a widespread belief that modern fields of technology are, in effect, applied science, in that practice is directly drawn from scientific understanding and advancing technology is essentially a task of applying scientific knowledge to achieve better products and processes. This task requires scientific expertise but in most cases is relatively routine once the target is specified. Indeed, in his *Capitalism, Socialism, and Democracy,* Joseph Schumpeter (1942) argues that by the mid-twentieth century that was largely the case, and the kind of competition among firms that had over the prior century made capitalism such a powerful engine of progress was no longer necessary. With strong science, technological advance could be planned. Schumpeter's views were in accord with those of many prominent scientists of his day, and today as well. Yet careful studies of how technological advance actually proceeds in this modern era clearly show that the process remains resistant to planning in any detail, and competitive exploration of multiple paths remains an essential part of it (see, for example, Nelson and Winter 1982; Rosenberg 1996).

Virtually all empirically oriented scholarly accounts of how technology progresses (for example, Constant 1980; Nelson and Winter 1982; Basalla 1988; Dosi 1988; Mokyr 1990; Vincenti 1990; Petroski 1992; Ziman 2000) observe that the process is evolutionary in the following senses: First, at any time there generally are a wide variety of efforts going on to improve prevailing technology or to supersede it with something radically better. These efforts generally are in competition with one another and with prevailing practice. To a considerable extent, the winners and losers in this competition are determined through an ex post selection processes. Second, today's efforts to advance a technology are to a considerable extent informed by and take off from the successes and failures of earlier efforts. While there are occasional major leaps that radically transform best practice, for the most part technological advance is cumulative. Scholars of technological advance also have generally stressed that the advanced technologies of a given era almost always are the result of the work of many inventors and developers. Technological advance is a collective, cultural, evolutionary process.

The proposition that technological advance is an evolutionary process in no way denies, or plays down, the often extremely powerful body of understanding and technique used to guide the efforts of those who seek to advance it, at least in modern times. A strong body of scientific understanding of a technology serves to enlarge and extend the area within which an inventor or problem solver can see relatively clearly and thus make informed judgments regarding what particular paths are promising as solutions and which ones are likely to be dead ends. Moreover, the sciences and engineering disciplines provide powerful ways of experimenting and testing new departures, so that a person or organization who commands these can explore the merit of designs without going to full-scale operational versions. Thus strong science enables the process of designing and inventing to be more productive and powerful than it would be were the science base weaker.

However, it does not change the fact that the process of advancing the technology remains evolutionary. Strong science provides tools for problem solving, but usually in itself it does not solve practical problems. If anything, strong science increases the advantages to society of having many competent actors striving to improve the art.

The connections between the "body of practice" aspect of a technology and the "body of understanding" part need to be understood in this context. Virtually all modern technologies are supported by a strong body of science or sciencelike understanding that illuminates how the artifacts and techniques employed work, provides insight into the factors that constrain performance, and provides clues as to promising pathways toward improvement. At the same time, much of practice in most fields remains only partially understood, and much of engineering design practice involves solutions to problems that professional engineers have learned "work," without any particularly sophisticated understanding of why. Medical scientists still lack good understanding of just why and how certain effective pharmaceuticals do their work, and theories about that can change from time to time.

Technological practice and understanding tend to coevolve, with advance of understanding sometimes leading to effective efforts to improve practice, and advance in practice sometimes leading to effective efforts to advance understanding. Thus the germ theory of disease developed by Louis Pasteur and Robert Koch, by pointing clearly to a certain kind of cause, led to successful efforts to get certain diseases (now known to be caused by external living agents) under control. James Clerk Maxwell's theory of electromagnetism led to investigations by Heinrich Hertz and Guglielmo Marconi and the invention of the radio. But in many cases advances in practice come first and lead to efforts to understand scientifically. Thus the discovery by William Shockley and his team at Bell Laboratories that a semiconducting device they had built as an amplifier worked, but not in the way they had predicted, led Shockley to understand that there was something wrong, or incomplete, about the theory in physics regarding the electrical characteristics of semiconductors, which, in turn, led to his own theoretical work and a Nobel Prize. Nathan Rosenberg (1996) has argued that a number of the most challenging puzzles science has had to face have been created or made visible by new technologies, as well as the puzzles of why they work as they do.

Much of the development of modern science should be understood as the result of institutionalized responses to these challenges and opportunities. Quite often, specialized fields of applied science or engineering have developed out of the experience of more generally trained scientists working on the problems of a particular technology or industry. Thus the field of metallurgy came into existence as chemists worked on problems of quality control in the rapidly growing steel industry (Rosenberg 1998). As the industries producing chemical products expanded, chemical engineering developed as a field of research, as well as teaching. The physics of mechanical forces had long been useful for civil engineers designing buildings and bridges; but with the new physics of electricity and magnetism, a whole new set of science-based industries was launched. As complex electrical "systems" came into place, the new field of electrical engineering grew up. Later on, the invention of the modern computer would spawn the field of computer science. Stronger knowledge in chemistry and biology led to the development of a collection of specialized fields involved in agricultural research. Pathology, immunology, and cardiology emerged as fields for study and research at medical schools.

All of these fields of science are in Pasteur's Quadrant. Research done in these fields often probes for quite deep understanding. But the field as a whole, and broad programs of research in the field, are dedicated quite explicitly to solving particular kinds of practical problems and advancing bodies of practical technology. I have developed this story at considerable length because in much of the writings on science, and the institutions governing science, these applied sciences tend to be ignored. However, in the United States, Western Europe, and Japan, they account for most of the resources going into the support of science.

Karl Popper (1989), Donald Campbell (1974), John Ziman (1978), Philip Kitcher (1993), and other scholars of the advancement of science have stressed that science is a system of knowledge. The test that guides whether new reported findings or theories are accepted into the corpus of accepted knowledge is "Is it valid? Is it true?" Popper and his followers have argued that there can be no firm positive answer to that question. The ability of findings or theories to stand up under attempts at refutation, or (probably more commonly) for apparent implications to hold up when they are explored, may be the best available outcome. But in any case, from this philosophical perspective, the quest in science is for understanding in its own right. And there certainly is a lot of truth to this position as a characterization of the nature of scientific debates.

On the other hand, as Walter Vincenti and others who have reflected on the similarities and differences between technological and scientific knowledge have argued, the central test for technological knowledge is "Is it useful?" Technological knowledge is part of a cultural system that is concerned with achieving practical ends rather than knowledge for its own sake. The objective is to get something that works, or works better, and understanding is important only in so far as it helps in that effort.

However, the selection criteria for new science and for new technology cannot be kept sharply separate for sciences in Pasteur's Quadrant. In these fields, an important and often stringent testing ground for science is provided by those who think they see how it might be applied in practice. And failure to understand why something works is a strong motivation for scientific research.

Most modern scientific research, including research done at universities, is in fields in which practical application is central in the definition of a field. Not surprisingly, these are the fields on which efforts to advance technology mostly draw. Two recent surveys (Klevorick et al. 1995; Cohen, Nelson, and Walsh 2002) asked industrial research and development (R&D) executives to identify the fields of academic research that have contributed most to their successes in R&D. The fields they listed were exactly those previously discussed in this chapter.

The most recent of these studies (Cohen, Nelson, and Walsh 2002) also asked about the kind of research output that was most valuable to industry and the most important pathways through which industry gained access. Contrary to much of the current discussion, it was not prototype technologies that were rated an important output of academic research for most industries (biotechnology is an exception) but rather general research results and research techniques (and even in biotechnology, these kinds of research outputs were rated as useful much more often than prototypes). Relatedly, in most industries the respondents reported that the most frequent use of university research results was in problem solving in projects rather than in triggering the initiation of projects.

In most industries, the respondents said that the most important pathway through which people in industry learned of and gained access to what was coming out of public research was through publications and open conferences. Put another way, industry today gets most of its benefit from academic science through open channels. In their more narrowly focused but more detailed study of the pathways through which research results from the departments of mechanical and electrical engineering at the Massachusetts Institute of Technology get to industry, Ajay Agrawal and Rebecca Henderson (2002) arrive at a similar conclusion.

In all the fields of technology that have been studied in any detail, including those in which the background science is very strong, technological advance remains an evolutionary process. Strong science makes that process more powerful but does not reduce the great advantages of having multiple paths explored by a number of different actors. From this perspective, that most of scientific knowledge is open, and available through open channels, is extremely important. This enables there to be at any time a significant number of individuals and firms who possess and can use the scientific knowledge they need to compete intelligently in this evolutionary process. The "communitarianism" of scientific knowledge is an important factor contributing to its productivity in downstream efforts to advance technology.

The Governance of Public Science

World War II and the period just after it marked something of a watershed in broad public and political recognition of the important role that public science plays in technological progress, particularly in the United States and the United Kingdom. To be sure, many earlier visionaries like Francis Bacon had argued for support of science as a means through which societies could progress materially. Scholars like Don Price (1962), David Hart (1998), and David Guston (2000) have described the earlier history of debate about science policy in the United States. But it was the World War II experience, in which government-supported and government-focused R&D was so successful, both in the development of weapons that won the war and in the development of medical capabilities that greatly reduced casualties from wounds and infectious diseases compared with earlier wartime experiences, that gripped the public attention. The title of the Vannevar Bush report (1945) advocating a major postwar program of support of science in the United States caught the spirit: "Science, the Endless Frontier."

In both the United States and the United Kingdom, the discussion about the appropriate postwar role of public science was structured and constrained, for the most part, by recognition of the central role of companies with their own R&D capabilities in the process of technological advance; the point of view there was implicitly Schumpeterian. While there were exceptions, the discussion was not about contesting that role. Rather, the focus was on the system of public science, done in universities and public laboratories, that was separate from the corporate system but strongly complementary and needed public support. The argument of those who advocated stronger government support was that this would make the overall system of innovation more powerful.

In both the United Kingdom and the United States, the debate about the governance of public science squared off along much the same lines. In the United Kingdom, the distinguished physicist, and socialist, J. D. Bernal (1939) argued for a government program in which the allocation of public funds to science would be strongly guided by the weighing of social needs, and the support program as a whole would be closely monitored by the government. To this point of view, Michael Polanyi, a distinguished philosopher of science, took strong exception, advocating a largely self-governing "Republic of Science" (1967), which would be publicly funded but in which the scientific community itself would set priorities and decide on what was good science.

In the United States, Vannevar Bush's manifesto, "Science, the Endless Frontier," also argued strongly for a self-governing scientific community but one in which national priorities played a role in setting broad research directions, at least in certain areas. In particular, national security and health were singled out as areas in which the overall research budget and broad research priorities needed to be made through political and governmental processes. Given the funding within those broad areas, however, scientists themselves were to have basic discretion for devising the research programs they thought most appropriate. Government nonscientists were not to meddle in this. Regarding the role of public science in supporting economic progress more broadly, Bush saw the government's role as supporting basic research, with the science system being self-governing with respect to both identification of the broad fields of greatest promise and the details of allocating funds and carrying out research.

There is no question but that, like Polanyi's response to Bernal, Bush's articulation of a basically self-governing community of science was put forth in good part to counter, and block, proposals for a postwar publicly supported science system that would involve much more political and government control of the allocation of resources. In the United States, Senator Harley Kilgore took much the same position as did J. D. Bernal in the United Kingdom. Bush believed that this would destroy the creativity and power of science and that it would be far better to have the top scientists running the show.

There also is no question but that Polanyi and Bush felt it of extreme importance that government support fields, such as theoretical physics and mathematics, in which perceptions of potential practical payoff have little to do with the way the fields unfold yet which provided important knowledge and technique that helped to win the war. Hence the emphasis on serendipity and the unpredictability of areas of potential payoff. It is almost certain that both men knew well that much of scientific research was not of this kind but rather was in fields in which perceptions of practical problems played a significant role in defining the broad agenda, if not the short-run priorities of resource allocation. However, the rhetoric of Polanyi and Bush obscured the fact that most of science is in Pasteur's Quadrant.

It is not surprising, therefore, that in both the United States and the United Kingdom it turned out that mission-oriented agencies became the primary government supporters of basic research. Thus in the United States the Department of Defense funded basic work in computer and materials science and in electrical engineering. The Department of Energy (previously, the Atomic Energy Commission) has had principal responsibility for funding high-energy physics. The National Institutes of Health (NIH) became the primary funder of university research in the biomedical sciences. The National Science Foundation, the only significant research funding agency in the United States without a mission other than support of science, has always been a small supporter relative to the mission-oriented agencies. The lion's share of the research done in the United States, funded by government and undertaken in universities and public laboratories, is in fields in Pasteur's Quadrant.

This fact both removes the puzzle of why science has contributed so much to technological advance and enables one to understand better why Vannevar Bush (and most of his science-trained followers writing about science policy) had such strong faith in the ability of the scientific community to steer its efforts in socially productive directions. But this recognition also signals that the lines between basic science and applied science are fuzzy, not sharp. It also raises the question of where the publicly supported "Republic of Science" ought to leave off and the market begin. It is fair to say that for the most part the postwar debates were somewhat ad hoc about this. Thus Bush recognized a central role for market-organized and market-induced R&D and saw public science as providing inputs to that market system but saw the roles of government and markets as being separate. He provided little in the way of coherent argument, however, about where one stopped and the other began. Indeed, despite its obvious importance, outside of economics this question has aroused little analytical interest.

Economists have grappled with the question of the appropriate spheres of government activity in the science and technology system using two theoretical concepts: externalities and public goods. The externalities concept is about benefits (and costs) of private economic activity that those who make the relevant decisions do not see as benefits (or costs) to them. Here economists have highlighted the "spillovers" from industrial R&D, information and capabilities created by a firm's efforts to create better products and processes that it cannot fully capture and hence benefit other firms, including competitors. In general, the analyses by economists oriented toward the externalities from R&D have served as a base not for arguments for a domain of public science but rather for arguments that industrial R&D in some instances should be encouraged by favorable tax treatment and perhaps subsidies of various kinds to reduce private costs. Indeed, the policy discussion proceeding under the conception that research yields externalities naturally tends to be pulled toward devising policies that will make the results of R&D more proprietary, less public. An important part of the current policy discussion, in fact, is oriented in just this way.

The public good concept of economists is much more directly relevant to analysis of the appropriate domain of public science, or at least the range where "communitarianism of knowledge" should apply. For our purposes here, the most salient aspect of the economists' public good concept is that a public good is nonrivalrous in use: unlike a standard economic good, like a peanut butter sandwich, which either you or I can eat but not both (although we can split it), a public good can be used by all of us at the same time without eroding the quality for any of us.

Knowledge is a canonical case of something that is nonrivalrous in use in this sense, and this is not a proposition conjured up by economists. The notion that I can tell you what I know, and then you will know it, and I will too, almost surely has been widely understood by sophisticated persons for a long time. There is no "tragedy of the commons" for a pure public good like knowledge. To deny access, or to ration it, can result in those denied doing far less well than they could if they had access. In the case in point, if access to certain bodies of scientific knowledge or technique can be withheld from certain researchers, they may be effectively barred from doing productive R&D in a field.

That something is nonrivalrous in use does not mean that its use cannot be restricted. However, until relatively recently it was broadly assumed that it was difficult to restrict access to scientific knowledge. Certainly, scientific knowledge could not be patented. This effectively took science outside the domain in which market incentives could work. Indeed, the presumption that the returns to scientific research could not be appropriated was a central part of the argument that public funding was necessary.

However, over the past quarter century two key developments have challenged this view of basic science. First, the courts have ruled that at least some of the results of basic research can be patented. About the same time that the implications of these rulings were becoming evident, Congress passed the Bayh-Dole act of 1980, which strongly encouraged universities to take out patents on their research results where they could, on the basis of a (not well-supported) argument that this would enable firms that could make practical use of the results to do so under a protective license (for a detailed account, see Eisenberg 1996). The first of these developments significantly increased the incentives for for-profit firms to engage in the areas of basic research where the results can be patented and to try to make their living licensing patented research results to other firms that can make use of them. The second has brought about profound changes in the way universities give access to their research results. As a result, important areas of science are now much more under the sway of market mechanisms than used to be the case. In particular, in some important fields of science important bodies of scientific understanding and technique now are private property rather than part of the commons.

So what is the problem with that? There is a strong presumption these days that if market organization can and will do a job, that obviously is a good thing. From this point of view, the main argument that needs to be made for government support of basic research is that the long-run benefits to society are high and that for-profit firms have little incentive to do much of it because of the difficulties in establishing property rights and the long time lags and uncertainties involved in moving from research results to commercial product. If these barriers to market organization are lowered for some reason, let the market move in.

Knowledge of an effective product design or a production process, what customarily is considered as technological knowledge, shares with scientific knowledge the property of being nonrivalrous in use. Yet society relies largely on the market to induce R&D aimed at creating new products and production processes, and there is little dispute that granting patents on product and process inventions is reasonable social and economic policy. So why not allow patents on the stuff of basic science, if that will induce the market to move in?

My response is that the outputs of scientific research almost never themselves are final products, or even close, but have their principal use in further research, some of it aimed to advance the science further, some to follow leads that may enable a useful product or process to be found and developed. In both cases, there is considerable uncertainty about the best paths to pursue. Progress calls for a number of paths to be explored. My concern is not with patents on the outputs of scientific research that are directly useful or close to that, so long as the scope of the patent is limited to that particular use. It is about not hindering the ability of the scientific community, both that part interested in advancing the science further and that part interested in trying to use knowledge in the search for useful products, to work freely with and from new scientific findings.

I do not know of a field of science in which knowledge has increased cumulatively, and, through cumulative advance, dramatically, that has not been basically open. It is easy to argue that scientists have never fully followed the canons of science identified and laid out by Robert Merton: universalism, communitarianism, disinterestedness, and organized skepticism. Scientists are well known to keep their work secret until they are ready to publish. Certainly, a lot of self-interest, opportunism, hostility, and downright deviousness and lying can be observed in the histories of the progressive sciences. A scientific paradigm held by the elite in a field can hold intellectual tyranny. It is valuable to bring new organizations into the basic research scene, and in some cases for-profit business firms have explored paths that the academic community snubbed.

On the other hand, a careful reading of important scientific controversies— for example, the argument about the nature of combustion at the start of the nineteenth century, or the nature of the genetic code, or whether the expansion of the universe is decelerating or accelerating—shows the importance and the power of a public science system in which by and large all participants have access to much the same facts and the debates about whether new proposed facts or theories are valid are open to all working in a field. One cannot come away from reading Horace Judson's (1996) *The Eighth Day of Creation,* a history of the development of molecular biology as a field of science, without respecting the power of open science to progress.

This is equally true for sciences that are strongly in Pasteur's Quadrant. Roy Porter's (1997) history of medical knowledge and practice, *The Greatest Benefit to Mankind,* gives case after case of progress being made through a system in which researchers were free to try to replicate or refute the arguments and findings of others.

While my argument focuses on the advantages of an open science for the advancement of science, much of the discussion that follows is concerned with developing a case for the importance of open science to technological progress. These arguments, of course, are mutually reinforcing. Keeping the body of scientific knowledge largely open for all to use, in the attempt to advance science and in the attempt to advance technology, is in my view an extremely important matter. Its importance is not recognized adequately in the current discussions.

I conclude this section by putting forth three views on what should be done about the encroachment of proprietary property claims into what had been the domain of public science. The first is to cede the contested turf. If research findings can be patented, we should accept and embrace that. If universities can patent their results, and limit access to the highest bidder, fine. We should welcome the presence of private firms motivated to do research by the lure of patents, and with it control of subsequent work in a field, or royalty incomes. Indeed, these developments diminish or even eliminate the need for public funding of certain fields of science.

The second is to coexist and compete on the contested terrain. This is pretty much the policy that developed regarding research on the human genome. The argument here is that publicly supported research, with the results of that research kept open, provides useful competition to private research, even if some private firms do not like the competition (Eisenberg and Nelson 2002).

A third position is to resist and try to roll back the invasion of privatization. This point of view sees that invasion not only as probably undesirable but also as something that is occurring under a given set of policies, which can be changed. Thus if the movement of patentability upstream into the sciences, together with the expectations under the Bayh-Dole act, leads for-profit companies to engage in research to identify the genetic code, and to the patenting of that code by them and by universities operating under public funding, maybe patent law and practice, and Bayh-Dole, need to be revised.

I have given my reasons for rejecting the first position. My position on the issue is a combination of the second and third. I believe it important to preserve as much of the commons as possible. However, doing so will not be easy.

The Importance of Protecting the Scientific Commons

The major expansion of patents into what used to be the realm of science is well documented. I am persuaded that there is enough of a potential problem here to call the alarm. However, I confess that the evidence that there already is a problem, that access to scientific research results having high promise of enabling the solution of important practical problems is being sharply limited by patent holders, presently is limited. The most detailed study is by John Walsh, Ashish Arora and Wesley Cohen (2002). This study asked researchers in the biomedical field whether their research had been hindered by patent rights that blocked access to certain paths they wanted to explore.

Scholars studying this potential problem have identified at least two different kinds of situations in which the presence of patents can hinder research (for a general discussion, see Merges and Nelson 1990). One of these is the problem caused by patents on "research tools" (see National Research Council 1997), whereby research techniques of widespread use in a field, materials that are inputs to a wide range of research endeavors, or key pathways for research (like the use of a particular receptor) are patented, and the patent holder aggressively prosecutes unlicensed use or reserves exclusive rights to further research using the tool. The second, highlighted recently by Michael Heller and Rebecca Eisenberg (1998), is focused on contexts in which development of or advance toward a useful product or technique may involve transgressing on several patents held by different parties.

The latter problem, that of the need to assemble a large number of permissions or licenses before being able to go forward, was found by the Walsh, Arora, Cohen (2002) interviews and case studies to be not particularly important, as of yet. Regarding research tools, a number of the more important general-purpose ones are available to all who will pay the price, and while in some cases there were complaints about the price, at least they were available.

On the other hand, the study did identify a number of instances in which the holder of a patent on an input or a pathway that was important in a particular field of exploration did not widely license use, and in some cases sought to preserve a monopoly on use rights. It is clear that in a number of the cases, the patented finding had been achieved through research at least partially funded by the government. This policy may well have been reasonable from the point of view of the patent holders. But it is not good from the point of view of society seeking to maximize the benefits of publicly funded research.

The authors of the study take a cautious position regarding the implications of their findings. I find them sufficient evidence to indicate that there is a real problem here, or there will be soon, and it is time to think about what can be done to contain it.

Two broad policy arenas bear on this issue, to which I want to call attention here. One is intellectual property rights law. The second is the policies of universities and public laboratories regarding their research findings and government policy regarding the university research it funds. The following discussion is oriented to what is needed, in my view, to preserve an appropriately wide area of public scientific knowledge.

Can We Protect the Republic of Science Through Patent Law?

Many people are puzzled when they learn that patents are being taken out on genes or gene codes or more generally are intruding into the realm of science. There is a widespread belief that scientific facts or principles or natural phenomena are not patentable. Indeed, the courts have endorsed this position strongly, as a general philosophical principle.

But the lines between natural substances and principles and man-made ones are blurry, not sharp. Nearly a century ago, a landmark patent law case was concerned with whether purified human adrenalin was a natural substance, and hence not patentable (although the process for purification certainly was patentable), or whether the fact that adrenalin never was pure in its natural state meant that the purified substance was man-made and hence patentable. The Court decided the latter, and while it can be argued that the decision was unfortunate, one certainly can see the logic supporting it (Parke-Davis & Co. v. H. K. Mulford & Co. [1911]). In any case, the precedent set here has held through the years. Recent patents on purified proteins and isolated genes and receptors are couched in terms that highlight something that man has created or modified from its natural state.

A recent article by Avital Bar-Shalom and Robert Cook-Deegan (2002) is concerned with the consequences of a patent granted on a monoclonal antibody (antibodies are natural substances, but particular antibodies cloned by a particular process have been judged not to be natural) that binds to a particular antigen (a natural substance) on the outer surface of stem cells and hence is capable of recognizing such cells and serving as a basis for processes that would isolate stem cells The patent also claimed "other antibodies" that can recognize and pick out that antigen. The latter part of the claim in effect establishes ownership of the antigen. Bar-Shalom and Cook-Deegan argue, correctly in my view, that the inclusion in the patent claims of all "other antibodies" meant that the patent was unreasonably broad and should have been pruned back by the patent office and the courts. However, one can clearly see the blurry lines here between the natural and the artificial. The patentee could well argue that the "invention" was a method of recognizing a particular antigen (such a method would seem to fall within the bounds of patentability) and the particular antibody actually used was just an exemplar. In the case in question, this patent was licensed exclusively to a particular company and, in turn, was later effectively used to close down another company that had achieved a process capable of isolating stem cells earlier than the licensee, using a method judged to infringe.

The issue of undue patent scope aside for the moment, the problem of determining the patentability of a research output whose future use is largely in further research seems almost inevitable for research in Pasteur's Quadrant, for obvious reasons. The original work in question was done by an oncologist at Johns Hopkins University. The research clearly was fundamental, and at the same time was aiming for understandings and techniques that would be useful in dealing with cancer.

The problem becomes even more complicated in scientific fields that are concerned with advancing understandings of technologies, fields like computer science and aeronautical engineering. Thus Vincenti (1990) describes at some length the research done at Stanford during the 1920s that aimed to develop good engineering principles (reliable if rough "laws") that would guide the design of aircraft propellers. The results of this research were laid open to the general aviation design community and were not patented. Had the researchers had the motivation, they probably could have posed their results in terms of processes useful in propeller design, which might have been patentable then and quite likely would be today. A significant portion of the work within the modern field of computer science is concerned with developing concepts and principles that can help improve design. Up until recently, at least, little of this work seems to have been patented, but portions of it clearly could have been.

In each of these cases, the research outputs were at once important inputs to a flow of future research and useful inputs for those focused on solving practical problems. In much of this chapter, I have been arguing that, because of the latter, there are major general economic advantages if those understandings and techniques are made part of the general tool kit available to all those working to advance practice in the area. The obvious objection is that the ability of the discoverer or developer of these understandings and techniques to control their use is an important incentive for the research that creates them. I would reply that, at least in the case of government-funded research at universities, this usually is not the case.

I am not optimistic about how much of the problem can be dealt with by patent law. The focus here is on patent law on research outputs that provide tools for advancing a science or technology, as contrasted with a final product or process per se. Here, one can urge several things of the patent office and the courts, though the problem of innately blurry lines will remain.

First, one can urge more care not to grant patents on discoveries that largely are of natural phenomena by requiring a strong case that the subject matter of the patent application or patent is "artificial" and by limiting the scope of the patent to elements that are artificial. Linda Demaine and Aaron Fellmeth (2003) make a similar argument that patents should be allowed only on outputs of research that are a "substantial transformation" from the natural; the lines here are blurry. But the slope clearly is slippery, and a strong argument can be made that the dividing line has been let slip too far, and thus leaning hard in the other direction is warranted. In the case of purified natural substances, this would call for a greater proclivity to limit the patent to the process and not allow the purified product per se to be patented.

Second, one can urge a relatively strict interpretation of the meaning of "utility" or usefulness. This issue is particularly important for patent applications and patents that argue very broadly that the research result in question can be useful in efforts to achieve something obviously useful—a case for usefulness once removed. The problem here is that the direct usefulness then is as an input or a focus of research, and this is the kind of generic knowledge and capability I argue is important to keep open and in the public domain. A stricter interpretation here would require a more compelling demonstration of significant progress toward a particular practical solution than seems presently required, particularly if combined with the suggestion (which follows) about reining in patent scope, and would be a major contribution to protecting the commons.

Third, there is the issue of the allowed patent scope. There is a strong tendency of patent applicants to claim practical application far wider than they actually have achieved. The claim covering "all antibodies" that identify a particular substance is a case in point. While there are obvious advantages to the patentee of being able to control a wide range of possible substitutes to what has actually been achieved, there are great advantages to society as a whole to disallowing such broad blocking of potential competitive efforts. I believe that getting the Patent Office and the courts to understand the real economic costs of granting too broad patents is of the highest priority.

I have argued the special importance of not allowing patents to interfere with broad participation in research going on in a field. One way to further this objective would be to build some kind of an explicit research exemption, analogous to the fair-use exemptions in copyright law, into patent law. Indeed, there is a long history of statements by judges to the effect that use in pure research is not a violation of a patent. Universities clearly have been clinging to this theory to justify their freedom of research.

A recent decision of the Federal Circuit Court (Madey v. Duke, 2002) has changed the situation. In a ruling on an infringement suit against Duke University, the court argued that doing research, basic or applied, was part of the central business of a university and that the university benefited in terms of funding as well as prestige from the research it did. Thus university interests, not simply scientific curiosity, were at stake in the research. Therefore, it was quite reasonable under the law for a patent holder to require that the university take out a license before using patented material in research. After this ruling, it is highly likely that patent holders will act more aggressively when they believe that university researchers may be infringing on their patents. While there is a chance that the Supreme Court will reverse the decision, that is not a good bet. It now looks as if an exemption for use in basic research will come into place only if there is new law.

However, under current university policies, a case for such new law is not easy to make. Among other things, there clearly is a problem of how to delineate basic research. As I have been highlighting, much of university research is in Pasteur's Quadrant, where in many cases there are practical objectives as well as the goal of advancing basic understanding. In recent years, universities have been patenting their research results.

Discussions with industry executives suggest that, until recently, industry often gave university researchers a de facto research exemption. However, now they are often reluctant to do so. In many cases, they see university researchers as direct competitors to their own research efforts aimed to achieve a practical result that is patentable. They feel themselves burdened by the requirement to take out licenses to use university research results that are patented and see no reason why they should not make the same demands on universities. In my view, the obstacles to a serious research exemption are largely the result of university policies.

Of the several proposals for a research exemption that have circulated recently, I find one of the most interesting to be that put forth by Rochelle Dreyfuss (2002). In what follows, I amend it slightly. Under the Dreyfuss proposal, a university or nonprofit research organization (under one version of her proposal, any research organization) would be immune from prosecution for using patented materials in research if those materials were not available on reasonable terms (my amendment) and if the university or other research organization agreed not to patent anything that came out of the research (or if they did patent, to allow use on a nonexclusive royalty free basis—my amendment). Certainly, there could be some difficulty in determining, if the matter arose, whether the patented material was available at reasonable terms, or just what "reasonable" means, but in many of the most problematic cases this proposal is designed to fix, the answer is that the patents are not available at all. In some cases it would not be easy to determine whether a patent emanated from a particular research project or from some other activity. These problems do not seem unusually difficult compared with other matters often litigated. It is likely that, for the most part, if a research organization proceeded under this law, there would not be much litigation, and there would be much reduced fear of such.

Since the Duke decision, the road to a university research exemption almost surely must go through Congress. The advantage of a proposal like Dreyfuss's is that it would trade open access to research results for university researchers for agreement of university researchers not themselves to add to the problem of patents in science. The principal obstacle to such a deal, I believe, is the universities themselves.

Will Universities Come to the Defense of the Scientific Commons?

I believe the key to ensuring that a large portion of what comes out of future scientific research will be placed in the commons is staunch defense of the commons by universities. Universities almost certainly will continue to do the bulk of basic scientific research. If they have policies of laying their research results largely open, most of science will continue to be in the commons. However, universities are not, in general, supporting the idea of a scientific commons, except in terms of their own rights to do research. In the era since Bayh-Dole, universities have become a major part of the problem, avidly defending their rights to patent their research results and license as they choose.

Derek Bok (2003) has argued persuasively that the strong interest of universities in patenting is part and parcel of trends that have led universities to embrace commercial activities in a variety of areas—athletics, for example, as well as science. Earlier in this chapter, I proposed that Bayh-Dole, and the enhanced interest in universities for patenting, should be regarded as one aspect of a broad increased public acceptance of the importance of intellectual property rights. But these factors do not make the problem any less significant, only harder to deal with.

The current zeal of universities for patenting represents a major shift from the universities' traditional support of open science. This does not mean that traditionally university research was largely distanced from practical applications. There long have been many university research programs designed to contribute to economic development (see Mowery and Rosenberg 1989; Rosenberg and Nelson 1994). Since the late nineteenth century, university research has played a major role in the development of American agricultural technology. The hybrid seed revolution, which was key to the dramatic increases in productivity made during the half century after 1930 in corn and other grain production, was made possible by work at agricultural experimentation stations that explored basic concepts and techniques of hybridization. These basic techniques were made public knowledge. Universities also made available on generous terms the pure lines of seeds the universities developed to serve as the basis for commercial efforts to design and produce hybrids. University-based research on plant nutrition and plant diseases and pests helped companies identify and design effective fertilizers and insecticides. Little of this university research was patented.

American engineering schools and departments have a long tradition of doing research to help industry. Earlier, I noted the development of chemical and electrical engineering as scientific fields largely within universities and Stanford's role in developing principles of propeller design. Several universities played key roles in developing the early electronic computers. Some patenting of devices came out of university engineering research but also an apparent continuing commitment to contribute to the advancement of basic engineering understanding as the common property of the professions.

American medical schools also have long been contributors to technical advance in medicine and the enhanced ability of doctors to deal with human illness. Medical schools occasionally have been the sources of particular new medical devices and new pharmaceuticals, although this was not common before the rise of biotechnology and modern electronics. While patents were sometimes taken out on particular products (streptomycin, identified by a team led by a Rutgers University scientist, is a good example), by and large until the 1980s there was little patenting, and many medical schools had an articulated policy of dedicating research results to the public commons.

The sea change, or the schizophrenia, began to emerge as a result of several developments (see Mowery et al. 2001). First, during the 1970s and 1980s there was a broad general ideological change in the United States in attitudes toward patents, from general hostility in the 1930s and the early postwar years to a belief that patents were almost always necessary to stimulate invention and innovation. Actually, several empirical studies provide evidence that in many industries patents are relatively unimportant as a stimulus to R&D (see Cohen, Nelson, and Walsh 2000). However, much of the argument for Bayh-Dole concentrated on pharmaceuticals, and patent protection was and continues to be important for pharmaceuticals companies.

Second, there was the rise of molecular biology as a field of science and the development of the principal techniques of biotechnology, which for a variety of reasons made university biomedical research a much more likely locus of work leading to pharmaceuticals or potential pharmaceuticals and of techniques that could be used in such work. Third, as noted, several key court decisions made many of these developments patentable. The apparent possibility of substantial income from university research clearly attracted some university officials and university scientists. The patenting of the Cohen-Boyer gene-splicing process, and the quick flow of revenues to the two universities that held the rights, provided a strong signal that substantial money could now be brought in from the licensing of university inventions.

The Cohen-Boyer patent was granted before the passage of Bayh-Dole. Bayh-Dole legitimated, even warranted, university patenting; and universities have not been slow in adopting policies whereby patenting anything that can be patented is the rule.

In my view, there is nothing wrong per se with universities patenting what they can from their research output. In some cases such patenting may actually facilitate technology transfer, although in many cases it is a good bet that rather than technological transfer being enhanced the university is simply earning money from what it used to make available for free (see the case studies in Colyvas et al. 2002). The cases that worry me are those in which the university is licensing exclusively or narrowly a development that is potentially of wide use and those in which the university is limiting the right to take a particular development further to one or a few companies when there still is sufficient uncertainty regarding how best to proceed to make participation by a number of companies in that endeavor socially desirable. The argument that if an exclusive license is not given no one will try to advance seems particularly dubious for research tools of wide application or for findings that appear to open up possibilities for new research attacks on diseases, for which a successful remedy clearly would find a large market. The Cohen-Boyer patent was licensed to all comers, and there were plenty of them. The report by Jeannette Colyvas and colleagues (2002) gives several examples showing the willingness of pharmaceuticals companies to work from university research findings that appeared to point toward promising treatments without receiving an exclusive license.

I do not see a major problem if access to certain parts of the commons require a small fee. What I want to see happen is that universities recognize that if they patent research results of these sorts, they have an obligation to license them at reasonable fees to all who want to use them. (Similarly, with respect to "research tools" created by industry research and patented, my difficulty is not so much with those for which use is open to users who pay a fee, provided the fee is not too high, but with those that are not made widely available.) Bok (2003), recognizing the problem I am discussing here, proposes that the major universities come to an agreement to license widely and easily, not grant exclusive licenses, research results that basically are inputs to further research. However, a policy of open licensing of research results of certain kinds is not likely to be adopted voluntarily by universities because this practice will not always be seen as maximizing expected revenues from intellectual property. And that is what many universities are aiming for now.

A recent report signed jointly by a number of university presidents and chancellors and foundation presidents (Atkinson et al. 2003) shows the tension here. The authors clearly recognize the problem that can, and has, been caused by university patents (their focus is the field of agricultural research) that block or cause high transaction costs for downstream research to advance agricultural technologies. They propose the establishment of a "public sector intellectual property resource for agriculture," which would make access easier. But the authors stop far short of agreeing to a general policy of open licensing of university research results that can set the stage for downstream applied R&D.

Universities will not give up the right to earn as much as they can from the patents they hold unless public policy pushes them hard in that direction. I see the key as reforming Bayh-Dole. The objective here, it seems to me, is not to eliminate university patenting but to establish a presumption that university research results, patented or not, should, as a general rule, be made available to all who want to use them, at low transaction costs and reasonable financial costs. This would not be to foreclose exclusive or narrow licensing in those circumstances in which it is necessary to gain effective technology transfer. Rather, it would be to establish the presumption that such cases are the exception rather than the rule.

There is nothing in Bayh-Dole that explicitly encourages exclusive or narrow licensing, but neither does anything discourage it, and the rhetoric associated with the legislation pushed the theory that generally dedicating research results to the public commons does not encourage use. There is nothing in the legislation that says universities should use their patenting and licensing power to maximize university income, but there is little in the language that discourages that. What is needed, I believe, is language that recognizes much better than the current language that much of what comes out of university research is most effectively disseminated to users if placed in the public domain and that exclusive or restricted licensing may deter widespread use, at considerable economic and social cost.

The act as currently written does include a clause stating that its objective is "to ensure that inventions made by nonprofit organizations . . . are used in a manner to promote free competition and enterprise without unduly encumbering future research and discovery" (quoted from Bayh-Dole act of 1980). However, presently this clause appears to have no teeth. My proposal is that this statement of objective be highlighted and supplemented by the proposition that in general this objective calls for licensing that will achieve the widest possible use. Exclusive or narrow licensing by a university should require an explicit rationale. Willingness of firms to take up university research results without an exclusive license should be regarded as evidence that an exclusive license is not appropriate.

Such language would encourage universities to move in the right direction on their own, by strengthening the hand of those at universities who believe that universities should be contributing to the scientific and technological commons. At the present time, such university researchers and administrators seem to be bucking the law as well as internal interests. It also would provide legitimacy to government agencies funding university research to press for licensing that gives broad access. The recent tussle between the NIH and the University of Wisconsin regarding stem cell patents illustrates the value of such an amended Bayh-Dole. In this case, the university originally had in mind arranging an exclusive license for a firm, and that would have been very profitable for the university. The NIH in effect indicated that unless the university licensed widely and liberally, it would consider the university's licensing policies when evaluating research proposals. The university then went along with the license policies advocated by the National Institutes of Health. Several legal scholars have proposed that, under the current law, the NIH in this case was skating on thin ice. There is nothing in the law that explicitly calls for open licensing. Had the NIH been forced to follow its bark with a bite, it might well have been taken to court. Arti Rai and Rebecca Eisenberg (2001) make a similar argument for amendment of Bayh-Dole.

Consider how the case analyzed by Bar-Shalom and Cook-Deegan (2002) might have gone had the amendment I am proposing been in place. It is likely that the NIH recognized quite early in the game the value of allowing more than one company to work with the new technique for identifying stem cells, and of having widespread research use allowed, and would have balked at the exclusive license that was given had it felt itself on a firm footing in doing so. Later in the game, the NIH was asked to open use of the patented technique, under the "march in" provisions of Bayh-Dole, but did not do so because the way the legislation is written, such a step clearly is exceptional. It would have been in a far stronger position to accede to the request to open up use if the language I propose were in the legislation.

Many university administrators and researchers certainly would resist such an amendment on the grounds that it would diminish their ability to maximize financial returns from their patent portfolio. As noted earlier, the principal support for university patenting with freedom to license as they wish now comes from universities and is based on their perception of their own financial interests; the case for it on grounds that this facilitates technology transfer is no longer credible. If pressed hard, the case that the current policy is against the public interest should carry the day. If universities were so constrained in their licensing policies, their resistance to a research exemption of the sort proposed by Dreyfuss might be dampened, since the financial costs to them of agreeing not to patent or not to charge for licenses would be diminished.

The theme of this chapter is that our scientific commons is in danger, that the costs of further erosion are likely to be high, and that we ought to move to protect it. What I have proposed is a strategy for protecting the commons.

The author wishes to thank John Burton, Wesley Cohen, Paul David, Rochelle Dreyfuss, Nathan Rosenberg, Bhaven Sampat, Marie Thursby, and Eric von Hippel for helpful comments and suggestions on earlier drafts. He hastens to add that none of the above necessarily agrees with all of the positions espoused here.

References

Agrawal, Ajay, and Rebecca Henderson. 2002. "Putting Patents in Context: Exploring Knowledge Transfer at MIT." *Management Science* 48(1): 44–60.

Atkinson, Richard, Roger Beachy, Gordon Conway, France Cordova, Marye Anne Fox, Karen Holbrook, Daniel Klessig, Richard L. McCormick, Peter McPherson, Hunter Rawlings III, Rip Rapson, Larry Vanderhoef, John Wiley, and Charles Young. 2003. "Public Sector Collaboration for Agricultural Management." *Science* 301(5630): 174–75.

Bar-Shalom, Avital, and Robert Cook-Deegan. 2002. "Patents and Innovation in Cancer Therapeutics: Lessons from CellPro." *Milbank Quarterly* 80(4): 637–76.

Basalla, George. 1988. *The Evolution of Technology.* Cambridge, U.K.: Cambridge University Press.

Bernal, J. D. 1939. *The Social Functions of Science.* London: Routledge and Kegan Paul.

Bok, Derek. 2003. *Universities and the Marketplace.* Princeton, N.J.: Princeton University Press.

Bush, Vannevar. 1945. *Science, the Endless Frontier.* Washington: National Science Foundation.

Campbell, Donald. 1974. "Evolutionary Epistemology." In *The Philosophy of Karl Popper,* edited by P. A. Schelpp. LaSalle, Ind.: Open Court.

Cohen, Wesley, Richard Nelson, and John Walsh. 2000. "Patenting Their Intellectual Assets: Appropriability Conditions and Why U.S. Manufacturing Firms Patent or Not." Working Paper 7522. Cambridge, Mass.: National Bureau of Economic Research.

———. 2002. "Links and Impacts: The Influence of Public Research on Industrial R and D." *Management Science* 48(1): 1–23.

Colyvas, Jeannette, Michael Crow, Annetine Gelijns, Roberto Mazzoleni, Richard Nelson, Nathan Rosenberg, and Bhaven Sampat. 2002. "How Do University Inventions Get Into Practice?" *Management Science* 48(1): 61–72.

Constant, Edward. 1980. *The Origins of the Turbojet Revolution.* Baltimore: Johns Hopkins University Press.

Dasgupta, Partha, and Paul A. David. 1994. "Towards a New Economics of Science." *Research Policy* 23(5): 487–521.

Demaine, Linda, and Aaron Fellmeth. 2003. "Natural Substances and Patentable Inventions." *Science* 300(5624): 1375–76.

Dosi, Giovanni. 1988. "Sources, Procedures, and Microeconomic Effects of Innovation." *Journal of Economic Literature* 26(3): 1120–71.

Dreyfuss, Rochelle. 2002. Untitled. Unpublished manuscript.

Eisenberg, Rebecca. 1996. "Public Research and Private Investment: Patents and Technology Transfer in Government Sponsored Research." *Virginia Law Review* 82: 1663–83.

Eisenberg, Rebecca, and Richard Nelson. 2002. "Public vs. Proprietary Science: A Useful Tension?" *Daedalus* 131(2): 89–101.

Guston, David. 2000. *Between Politics and Science.* Cambridge, U.K.: Cambridge University Press.

Hart, David. 1998. *Forged Consensus.* Princeton, N.J.: Princeton University Press.

Heller, Michael, and Rebecca Eisenberg. 1998. "Can Patents Deter Innovation? The Anticommons in Biomedical Research." *Science* 280(5364): 698–701.

Judson, Horace. 1996. *The Eighth Day of Creation.* Cold Spring Harbor, N.Y.: Cold Spring Harbor Press.

Kitcher, Philip. 1993. *The Advancement of Science.* New York: Oxford University Press.

Klevorick, Alvin K., Richard C. Levin, Richard Nelson, and Sidney Winter. 1995. "Sources and Significance of Inter-industry Differences in Technological Opportunities." *Research Policy* 24(2): 185–205.

Merges, Robert, and Richard Nelson. 1990. "The Complex Economics of Patent Scope." *Columbia Law Review* 90(4): 839–916.

Merton, Robert. 1973. *The Sociology of Science: Theoretical and Empirical Investigations.* Chicago: University of Chicago Press.

Mokyr, Joel. 1990. *The Lever of Riches.* Oxford, U.K.: Oxford University Press.

Mowery, David, and Richard Nelson. 1999.*The Sources of Industrial Leadership.* Cambridge, U.K.: Cambridge University Press.

Mowery, David C., Richard R. Nelson, Bhaven N. Sampat, and Arvids A. Ziedonis. 2001. "The Growth of Patenting and Licensing by American Universities." *Research Policy* 30(1): 99–119.

Mowery, David C., and Nathan Rosenberg. 1989. *Technology and the Pursuit of Economic Growth.* Cambridge, U.K.: Cambridge University Press.

National Research Council. 1997. *Intellectual Property Rights and Research Tools in Molecular Biology.* Washington: National Academy of Sciences Press.

Nelson, Richard. 1993. *National Innovation Systems.* Oxford, U.K.: Oxford University Press.

Nelson, Richard, and Sidney Winter. 1982. *An Evolutionary Theory of Economic Change.* Cambridge, Mass.: Harvard University Press.

Petroski, Henny. 1992. *The Evolution of Useful Things.* New York: Alfred Knopf.

Polanyi, Michael. 1967. "The Republic of Science." *Minerva* 1(1): 54–74.

Popper, Karl. 1989. *The Logic of Scientific Discovery.* New York: Basic Books.

Porter, Roy. 1997. *The Greatest Benefit to Mankind.* New York: W. W. Norton.

Price, Don. 1962. *Government and Science.* Oxford, U.K.: Oxford University Press.

Rai, Arti, and Rebecca Eisenberg. 2001. "The Public and Private in Bio Pharmaceutical Research." Mimeo. *Law and Contemporary Problems* 66(winter/spring): 289.

Rosenberg, Nathan. 1996. "Uncertainty and Technological Change." In *The Mosaic of Economic Growth,* edited by Ralph Landau, Timothy Taylor, and Gavin Wright. Stanford, Calif.: Stanford University Press.

———. 1998. "Technological Change in Chemicals." In *Chemicals and Long-Term Economic Growth,* edited by Ashish Arora, Ralph Landau, and Nathan Rosenberg. New York: John Wiley.

Rosenberg, Nathan, and Richard Nelson. 1994. "American Universities and Technical Progress in Industry." *Research Policy* 23(3): 323–48.

Schumpeter, Joseph. 1942. *Capitalism, Socialism, and Democracy.* New York: Harper and Row.

Stokes, Donald. 1996. *Pasteur's Quadrant: Basic Science and Technological Innovation.* Washington, D.C.: Brookings Institution Press.

Vincenti, Walter. 1990. *What Engineers Know and How They Know It.* Baltimore: Johns Hopkins University Press.

Walsh, John, Ashish Arora, and Wesley Cohen. 2002. "The Patenting and Licensing of Research Tools and Biomedical Innovation." Paper prepared for the Science, Technology, and Economic Policy (STEP) Board of the National Academy of Sciences.

Ziman, John. 1978. *Reliable Knowledge.* Cambridge, U.K.: Cambridge University Press.

———. 2000. *Technological Innovation as an Evolutionary Process.* Cambridge, U.K.: Cambridge University Press.

10

THE INTERNET

David C. Mowery and Timothy Simcoe

T HE INTERNET is a vast "network of networks" that has enjoyed rapid growth in users and applications since the early 1990s, and its growth shows few signs of abating. Partly because of its fast growth, the expanding realm of Internet applications is not always easily accommodated by the technical and quasi-regulatory architectures that underpin the Internet, creating significant challenges to governance. This chapter discusses the roles of public and private sector institutions in the development, adoption, and governance of the Internet and examines some of the "hybrid" governance structures that have emerged to help manage its rapid growth.

The Internet's growth has relied on innovations in information technology and organization that stretch back to the 1960s. Both public and private institutions and actors have played important roles in the Internet's development and its current operation. On the one hand, the Internet grew out of publicly funded research; its earliest users were large public institutions; and governments continue to regulate many elements of the network infrastructure and content. On the other hand, most of the network infrastructure is managed by private firms; use of the network now extends far beyond the early public sector adopters; private investment funds the majority of new Internet applications and content development; and a highly competitive Internet service provider industry is critical to the growth and diffusion of the network.

The Internet is not an industry, a market, or a single technology but rather a collection of computer networks that utilize a common infrastructure to run a wide variety of applications. Indeed, one of the defining features of the Internet is the flexibility of its underlying architecture, which allows two computers to share data with each other, regardless of either one's hardware, operating system, or even the physical characteristics of their network connections. The only necessary conditions for participation in this loose confederation of networks are that a computer has a connection, or more precisely an Internet address, and that it utilizes a software protocol known as TCP/IP (Transmission Control Protocol/Internet Protocol). As a result, the Internet's "common infrastructure" is characterized by considerable technical heterogeneity.

The Internet's diverse network infrastructure reflects the "open" nature of the TCP/IP standard and the limited role that the original designers envisioned for the network. By placing the core protocols in the public domain, the inventors of these protocols encouraged their adaptation to a wide range of different hardware and software platforms. The TCP/IP protocols deliver information from one network address to another, independent of the content of messages or the underlying transport technology. By placing all the responsibility for processing and interpreting data in the terminals attached to the edges of the network, the architects of the Internet created a "platform" that was application independent. But the Internet's open architecture has several drawbacks that have become more apparent over time. These weaknesses include security flaws, such as the vulnerability of websites to "denial-of-service" attacks, and the network's poor performance in applications that require time-sensitive data delivery, such as voice or video.

Software developers have gravitated to the Internet because of its flexibility, openness, and huge installed base. The earliest applications of the Internet included email, FTP (file transfer protocol, a program for transmitting files), and Telnet (a program for logging onto a remote machine). The invention of the World Wide Web in the early 1990s led, in turn, to new applications, such as search engines and software for secure processing of financial transactions, and to the innovative repackaging and distribution of a vast amount of information. More recently, "browsing" of the vast collection of interlinked documents that constitute the World Wide Web has emerged as the most popular use of the network, and other new applications, including instant text messaging and voice communication, are growing in popularity and importance. Because the Internet is flexible with respect to use as well as technology, several authors have described it as a "commons" for software innovation (for example, Lessig 2001).

The importance of today's network can be measured in part by the size and diversity of the current user population. Although the flexible and distributed nature of the Internet's architecture makes it difficult to count users or characterize their use of the network, one measure of its size is the number of Internet addresses that have been assigned. As of early 2003, more than 160 million Internet addresses were in use.[1] The owners of these addresses included individuals as well as public and private sector institutions from almost every corner of the globe, and the number of active addresses grew by 34 percent between July 2001 and July 2002.

Internet users can connect to the global "network of networks" in a variety of different ways. Although many users continue to connect through networks operated by the public sector institutions that were the original adopters, a larger number now do so through corporate networks or by using the telephone network to connect to an Internet service provider (ISP). Internet service providers are the primary owners and operators of the Internet infrastructure. Large firms and institutions purchase Internet access from ISPs, who provide high-speed connections over dedicated fiber-optic lines. Individual users purchase accounts from ISPs that are accessible through the telephone network, cable television network, or wireless and satellite connections. The ISPs' internal infrastructures closely resemble those of traditional telecommunications networks, and major telecommunications providers such as AT&T and MCI/WorldCom are among the largest ISPs. Most ISPs in the United States and Europe are private firms, but the dominant service provider in many industrializing countries continues to be either the state or an incumbent telecommunications monopolist.

Internet service providers provide Internet access to any other computer attached to the global network, regardless of the other machine's ISP. Interconnection among ISPs, however, is a necessary but not sufficient condition for the operation of the Internet. A second essential component of the network is the administration of the Internet name and address space, the tables used to route information between computers. Much of the Internet's architectural flexibility comes from its delegation of many of these administrative tasks to the operators of particular subnetworks, but it is still necessary to maintain certain "top-level" names and numbers in a set of publicly accessible tables. The organization created to oversee this responsibility on a global basis is the Internet Corporation for Assigned Names and Numbers (ICANN). The corporation was created in 1998 to consolidate a variety of high-level coordination activities that were previously carried out primarily by the U.S. government, government contractors, or ad hoc groups of engineers from the community that developed the Internet. ICANN assigns the unique IP numbers used to address particular computers or networks; oversees the operation of the domain name system that maps these numbers onto domain names; and assigns and maintains a number of other technical parameters used by various standards to operate the network. From its inception, ICANN has been plagued by controversies over such issues as the fairness of its domain name allocation policy, the selection of its members, and its relationship to national governments.

The Internet as of 2004 operates within (and sometimes around) a complex mix of public and private sector institutions that oversee different aspects of its development, deployment, and operation. The history of the Internet also highlights the interplay between public and private institutions and between infrastructure and applications. The U.S. public sector (primarily the federal government) influenced the development of the Internet through financial support for research and development (R&D), oversight of standard setting, and "traditional" regulatory activities in the fields of telecommunications policy, antitrust and (more recently) intellectual property, and consumer protection.

Public investment in and influence over the technical development of the Internet in the United States were at their zenith from 1960 to 1980, although federally sponsored R&D remains important to the technical development of the Internet. During the 1980s and 1990s, however, private sources of investment supplanted public funding in supporting the development and especially the commercial deployment and exploitation of the Internet. U.S. telecommunications regulatory policy was another important impetus to the rapid adoption of the Internet in this nation.[2]

Both public and private sector institutions also have affected the governance of the technical standard–setting process, a critical influence on the Internet's evolution. The institutions of Internet "self-governance" that emerged during the 1980s to coordinate technical decision making, such as the Internet Engineering Task Force (IETF) and the World Wide Web Consortium (W3C), were initially organized and funded by the public sector. But these organizations also encouraged private sector participation in overseeing a variety of other issues, and their decisions were often influenced by developments within industry. Since 1995, the growing commercial importance of the Internet has increased the workload of many of these organizations, and critics have demanded that government play a larger role in standard setting and oversight. Indeed, as the Internet's economic significance has expanded (in part because of increased private sector investment in the development of Internet applications), a growing chorus of voices from consumers and industry has argued that in some cases the Internet is "too important for the market"— that is, private governance must be supplemented with public oversight or regulation.

Finally, governance of the Internet has been influenced by national and historical circumstances. The development of the institutions of Internet governance, no less than other important economic institutions, is at least as much a product of "path dependence" as it is the result of a design motivated primarily by considerations of efficiency. This observation applies as well to the technical architecture of the Internet, which reflects the focus of its designers on low-cost (and often low-quality), flexible, "end-to-end" communications within a small technical community. The rapid growth of the Internet, however, means that such path dependence raises a number of vexing questions. There is still considerable uncertainty surrounding the application and commercial prospects of many Internet-based technologies, and public policy makers therefore are reluctant to commit to new regulations or governing institutions that might be difficult to undo. But waiting also creates risks, since the emergence of market- or industry-based self-regulation may limit the set of regulatory alternatives available in the future.

Our description of the Internet's development and the diverse set of organizations that coordinate its operations highlights the fact that the Internet is both public and private and is overseen by both market and nonmarket institutions. A variety of public, private, and hybrid organizations govern different aspects of the development and use of the public "network of networks." Some of these organizations operate in competitive markets, while others derive their authority from government or through the mutual consent of those concerned with the evolution and operation of the network. Many of these organizations were founded in the United States, but other national governments exert considerable control over both network access and applications, at times in direct opposition to private sector governance organizations. Will the Internet's ability to bypass national or regional obstacles to access or restrictions on content force greater global harmonization of policies? Can the norms and principles of design and use that emerged during the development of the network be sustained in the face of the Internet's commercialization? This chapter cannot answer these questions, but our discussion of them sheds light on the enduring tensions between markets and governments in the development and management of complex technical systems.

A Brief History of the Internet's Development

The Internet's development within the United States spans three phases from 1960 to 2002. During the first phase (1960 to 1985), computer scientists and engineers in the public and private sectors contributed to the theoretical and technical innovations that laid the foundations for data networking and the Internet, which was a loosely organized computer network used largely by the U.S. research community. As the number of hosts, users, and applications grew, however, the technical and organizational challenges of developing and deploying a wide-area network were supplanted by the complex tasks of managing the expansion of the core infrastructure and establishing a framework for connectivity that could accommodate rapid growth. The second phase of the Internet's development (1985 to 1995) was profoundly influenced by the management and policy decisions of the National Science Foundation (NSF), operator of a major national Internet "backbone" (NSFNET).[3] During this period, the governance of several major components of the network infrastructure shifted from public to private hands, and ISPs were founded to link the growing user base to computer networks.

The third phase in the evolution of the Internet began in 1995 with the privatization of NSFNET and the initial public offering of Netscape, the developer of one of the earliest browsers, based on the HTML and HTTP software protocols that are the core technology of the World Wide Web. The introduction and rapid diffusion of the Web attracted many companies into the development of commercial content and applications for the growing network. The intensity of these activities has receded with the collapse of the dot-com "bubble" in the U.S. stock market, but the development of Internet applications and extensions as of 2003 remains dominated by private investment in commercial applications and extensions.

From 1960 to 1985: Early Computer Networks

Research on computer networking began in the early 1960s, roughly fifteen years after the invention of the modern computer. Most of the U.S. research in this field during the 1960s was funded by the U.S. Department of Defense to develop technologies that could support shared use of the scarce computing resources located at a small number of U.S. academic and industrial research centers. Although the Department of Defense sought to exploit a variety of new computer-related technologies in defense applications, it supported "generic" research and the development of a substantial infrastructure in academia and industry for this research, in the expectation that a viable computer industry capable of supplying defense needs would require civilian markets as well (Langlois and Mowery 1996).

During the early 1960s, several researchers, including Leonard Kleinrock at the Massachusetts Institute of Technology, Paul Baran of Rand, and Donald Davies at the National Physical Laboratories in the United Kingdom, developed the theory of packet switching.[4] Digital packet switching offered performance and reliability advantages over analog networks for data communications and could support a communications network that was less vulnerable to a targeted attack than the centrally switched telephone network (Brand 2001). To realize these advantages, however, computer science researchers had to develop communication protocols and devices that did not use the circuit-switched infrastructure operated by established telecommunications companies.[5]

By the late 1960s, the theoretical work and experiments of Baran, Kleinrock, Davies, and others led the Defense Advanced Research Projects Agency (DARPA) of the Department of Defense to fund the construction of the ARPANET, widely recognized as the earliest forerunner of the Internet.[6] The first "killer application" developed for ARPANET was electronic mail (email), released in 1972. A 1973 DARPA study showed that within one year of its introduction, email generated 73 percent of all ARPANET traffic (Zakon 2000). E-mail was the first example of an application that unexpectedly soared in popularity on the network and caused a surge in network usage, a pattern repeated several times in the history of the Internet. By 1975, as universities and other major defense research sites were linked to the network, ARPANET had grown to more than one hundred nodes.

In 1974 two DARPA-funded engineers, Robert Kahn and Vinton Cerf, published the first version of the TCP/IP protocol suite.[7] A key intellectual advance contained in the standard was its conception of a "network of networks" that separated the transmission of information from physical aspects of the network design.[8] The new data-networking protocol allowed physically distinct networks to interconnect with one another as "peers" and exchange packets through special hardware, called a gateway. Although TCP/IP is now technologically synonymous with the Internet, its emergence as a dominant standard was uncertain for more than a decade following its introduction. By publishing TCP/IP and placing the standard in the public domain, Kahn, Cerf, and their collaborators strengthened its position in a two-decade competition among a variety of networking protocols, including proprietary standards such as IBM's SNA (Systems Network Architecture) and Digital Equipment's DECNET, open alternatives such as Datagram (UDP [User Datagram Protocol]) networking and the Unix to Unix Copy protocol (UUCP), and standards supported by established telecommunications firms, such as X.25 and Open Standard Interconnect.

The TCP/IP protocol also benefited from good timing. Its development coincided with the emergence of a common computing platform within the computer science research community (IBM or DEC hardware running the Unix operating system).[9] The TCP/IP protocol became an integral part of this de facto standard, particularly after it was incorporated into the 4.2 BSD version of Unix. The "free" nature of TCP/IP made it especially attractive to the academic developers of BSD/Unix. A growing developer community refined and extended TCP/IP in a process that resembled the development of contemporary "open-source" software such as the Linux operating system.

In addition to technological innovations, diffusion of the Internet benefited from the creation of a set of flexible and responsive technical governance institutions. These institutions trace their origins to an informal correspondence process called Request for Comments, which was started in 1969 by Steve Crocker, a computer science graduate student at the University of California at Los Angeles. The use of Requests for Comments grew quickly, and in 1970 another UCLA student named Jon Postel became the editor of what became a series of technical documents, an influential post that he held for many years. Requests for Comments were distributed over the nascent computer network and quickly became the standard forum where ARPANET's growing technical user community gathered to propose and debate new ideas. Requests for Comments combined open dissemination and peer review, features characteristic of academic journals, with the speed and informality characteristic of an e-mail discussion list.[10] The documents were used to propose specifications for important new applications such as Telnet and FTP as well as to refine networking protocols such as TCP/IP.

The Internet's first formal governance organizations began to appear in the United States during the early 1980s, a period of rapid expansion in the network. Efforts to rationalize the resources of several U.S. networking initiatives operated by the National Aeronautics and Space Administration (NASA), the

Department of Energy, and the NSF led to the creation of a set of organizations, funded by the NSF and DARPA, to oversee the standardization of the network on TCP/IP. The Internet Configuration Control Board was established in 1979 by Vinton Cerf, then serving as the director of the DARPA network. The Board and its successors drew their leadership from the ranks of the computer scientists and engineers who did much of the early government-funded networking research, but membership in the organization was open to the broader community of Internet users and included many participants from private sector organizations. In 1983, when ARPANET switched over to TCP/IP, the Internet Configuration Control Board was reorganized as the Internet Architecture Board, incorporating the influential IETF that continues to manage the Internet's architectural standard-setting process. In 1992 the Internet Society was founded with funding from a variety of private and public sector sources to coordinate the activities of a number of loosely affiliated institutions, including the Internet Assigned Numbers Authority and the IETF (Cerf et al. 2000). Centralized governance emerged more slowly within the European computer-networking community; the first notable organization formed to coordinate the diffusion of TCP/IP was Reseaux IP Européen, founded in 1989.

From 1985 to 1995: Infrastructure Development and Growth

The number of Internet users and network traffic volume grew significantly from 1985 to 1995. Growth was accompanied by consolidation and privatization of the network infrastructure and by increased use of the Internet for commercial applications. Rapid growth in user numbers was fueled by a confluence of technical developments in data networking and deregulatory telecommunications policies that reduced prices and encouraged access to the public communications infrastructure.

The first steps toward privatization of the U.S. network infrastructure were taken in 1983, when DARPA split the ARPANET into two parallel networks—ARPANET and MILNET. The latter network was used exclusively for military applications, and ARPANET linked research computers in industry, academia, and government research facilities. Following the DARPA-MILNET split, several federal government agencies continued to manage the backbone of the nonmilitary network.

A critical decision in this second stage of the Internet's development was the National Science Foundation's 1985 directive that any university receiving NSF funding for an Internet connection must use TCP/IP on its network and NSFNET as the backbone and must provide access to all "qualified users." The NSF requirement strengthened the position of TCP/IP as the dominant network protocol, and its extensive deployment in academic computing created a large pool of university-trained computer scientists and engineers skilled in its use. In the same year, all of the federal agencies then operating networks—DARPA, the NSF, the Department of Energy, and NASA—established the federal Internet exchange, a common connection point that allowed them to share their backbone infrastructure. The "peer-to-peer" model for exchanging traffic represented by the federal Internet exchange became a fundamental feature of the core Internet infrastructure. The original ARPANET was decommissioned in 1990, and its users and hosts were transferred to the new NSFNET.[11]

Although a growing population of users could access NSFNET by 1990, applications of the network were constrained by the NSF's acceptable use policy, which prohibited the use of NSFNET for "commercial purposes." At the time, demand for commercial networking services was growing, fueled by an expansion in corporate local-area networking that began in the late 1970s (Bresnahan and Chopra 1990). Growth in the number, size, and scope of corporate networks was driven by the expanding installed base of Unix workstations and microcomputers, the creation of "killer applications" such as document processing and spreadsheets, and the spread of the client-server architecture, in which a series of smaller "client" computers were linked by a local network to one or more large "servers." Increased corporate networking encouraged private sector research and investment in networking technology and expanded the installed base of users seeking a connection to the NSF's "network of networks."

The growth in corporate networking also intensified tensions between public infrastructure governance and private applications development that eventually produced changes in the governance of the Internet. In spite of the acceptable use policy, commercial users continued to attach to NSFNET (often in partnership with academic institutions), and efforts to circumvent the policy led to the creation of the commercial Internet exchange, an interexchange point for service providers selling access to long-haul networking for commercial use. Intense lobbying led the NSF to abandon the policy in 1991 and accelerated the transfer of control of the core network infrastructure into private hands. In 1995 control over NSFNET's four major network access points was transferred to Sprint, Ameritech, MFS, and Pacific Bell. Growing commercial investment and interest in Internet applications thus triggered a shift from public to private, market-based governance of the network.

Growth in regional networks and the NSFNET backbone in the late 1980s relied on a series of incremental improvements and innovations that cumulatively improved the performance of the Internet by orders of magnitude.[12] One technology that facilitated the growth of the Internet infrastructure was the domain name server, introduced in 1984. A domain name server maps Internet domain names (for example, haas.berkeley.edu) to the numerical network address scheme utilized by TCP/IP, providing a real-time concordance between machine-readable and humanly recognizable Internet addresses. Another important technological contribution was the creation of a hierarchical classification scheme for subnetworks. The creation of this classification system prevented saturation of the IP address space, a critical constraint on the growth of the Internet. Together, the domain name server and the associated system for allocating subnetwork addresses replaced the centralized coordination previously provided by the telecommunications monopoly; these technologies were indispensable to the eventual growth of the World Wide Web.

Simultaneously with the rapid growth and consolidation of the NSFNET infrastructure, a new innovation placed computer networking within reach of individuals as well as institutional users. The first commercial "bulletin board" service was launched by CompuServe in 1979 and rapidly gained thousands of subscribers. Several companies followed CompuServe into this market, and the entire group became known as online service providers. The three largest online service providers, Prodigy, CompuServe, and America Online (AOL), became household names. Prodigy, a joint venture among IBM, Sears, and CBS Television, was launched in 1984; AOL was founded in 1985. Online service providers' networks initially were independent of the NSFNET infrastructure, but by the early 1990s they were competing with a host of regional ISPs that offered dial-up Internet connections.[13] As had occurred repeatedly in the development of the Internet, applications developed in public research institutions continued to diffuse into the private sector; these regional ISPs often adopted methods developed by academic "modem pools." They quickly discovered that a minimum efficient scale of operations required no more than a few hundred customers, enough to fund a modem pool and high-speed Internet connection (Greenstein 2000).[14]

The final major event in this second stage of the Internet's development was the invention and diffusion of the World Wide Web. In May 1991 Tim Berners-Lee and Robert Cailliau, two physicists working at the CERN (European Particle Physics Laboratory) in Switzerland, released a new document format called hyper-text markup language (HTML) and an accompanying document retrieval protocol called hyper-text transfer protocol (HTTP).[15] Together, HTML and HTTP turned the Internet into a vast cross-referenced collection of multimedia documents. The collaborators named their invention the World Wide Web (WWW), which proved to be another "killer application" that accelerated growth in Internet usage.

To use the Web, users needed a connection to the Internet and application software, known as a "browser," to retrieve and display HTML documents. Although it was not the first Internet browser, the program that launched the World Wide Web was a free browser named Mosaic, written by a graduate student named Marc Andreesen, who was working at the National Center for Supercomputing Applications at the University of Illinois.[16] During 1993, the first year that Mosaic was available, HTTP traffic on the Internet grew by a factor of 3,416. By 1996 HTTP traffic was generating more Internet traffic than any other application.

From 1995 to 2002:
Internet Commercialization

The invention of the World Wide Web catalyzed the development of commercial applications by simplifying the Internet and providing a set of standard protocols for delivering content to almost any desktop computer. The manic commercialization of the Internet arguably began with the initial public offering of Netscape in August 1995. Netscape hoped to commercialize a version of the Mosaic browser, but at the time of its initial public offering it had few assets other than Andreesen and a rapidly growing installed base of users. Nevertheless, the financial success of the stock offering sparked a surge in Internet-related entrepreneurial activity, much of which focused on implementing uses of the Internet that facilitated commercial transactions (e-commerce).

The speed and magnitude of the shift in the Internet from a research network to a commercial opportunity is highlighted by changes in the distribution of top-level domain names during the second half of the 1990s.[17] In 1996 the commercial ".com" and ".net" top-level domains contained roughly 1.8 times as many registered host computers as the educational ".edu" domain. By 2000 the term "dot-com" had become a popular expression for fledgling Internet businesses, and the .com and .net domains accounted for more than six times as many registered hosts as the .edu domain. Consumer-oriented e-commerce markets, such as online retailing, content delivery, and auctions, generated high visibility and a number of recognizable Internet brands such as Yahoo!, Amazon.com, and eBay, but the use of the Internet for intermediary or business-to-business transactions appears to have grown even more rapidly.[18]

Financial markets in the United States played a central role in the commercialization of the Internet during the 1990s by ensuring a robust supply of equity and venture capital financing for new firms (Gompers and Lerner 1999). Venture capitalists historically have been major sources of financing in both information technology and biomedical ventures, but their role in the commercialization of the Internet during the 1990s appears to have outstripped their importance in biotechnology during the 1980s and in other information technology sectors during earlier periods. Figure 10.1 highlights the divergence between venture capital investments in information technology and healthcare (including biotechnology) from 1995 to 2002, underscoring the rapid growth in both the number of investments and the size of overall venture capital funding in information technologies, many of which were focused on the Internet and related applications. Indeed, the market-driven boom-and-bust

FIGURE 10.1   *Venture Capital Investment in Information Technology and Health Care, 1995 to 2002*

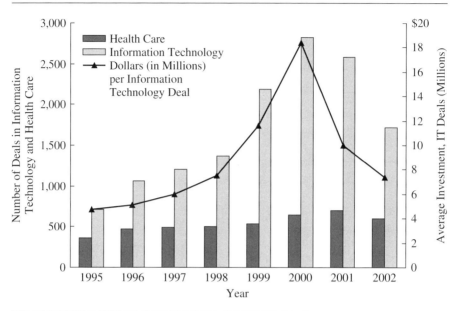

Source: Data from Pricewaterhouse Coopers (2003).

cycle associated with Internet commercialization during the period is reminiscent of the "swarming" of entrepreneurs described by Joseph Schumpeter (1932) in *The Theory of Economic Development.* Although the sharp decline in the share prices of most Internet-based start-ups that began in 2000 signaled the end of the investment euphoria, these large investments in commercial applications of the Internet will have economic effects for years to come.

Sources of Innovation

Throughout its history, the development of the Internet and its underlying technologies has drawn on the investment funds and innovative energies of the public and private sectors. Public funds supported the development of many of the technological advances that fueled the Internet's early development. The decision by DARPA, a leading source of public R&D funding for computer-networking technologies during this period, to place many of these contributions, such as TCP/IP, e-mail, and FTP, in the public domain and encourage their commercial application had a lasting impact on the network's development. Many private sector innovations, such as the Ethernet protocol and the Unix computer operating system, also ended up in the public domain. Equally important were the private sector investments in computer-networking technology that accelerated the adoption of the local area networks that were an important component of the "network of networks." Although both public and private funding were essential to the early development of Internet-related technologies, the sources of funding for R&D shifted in favor of private funding during the second and third phases of the Internet's development, and the Internet's future development and deployment are likely to be dominated by private investment.

Public R&D Investment

In the wake of World War II, defense-related federal R&D spending played an important role in the creation of the U.S. information technology industries, including semiconductors, computers, and computer software (see Markiewicz and Mowery 2003). The Internet's development drew on the technologies, R&D infrastructure, and firms that played central roles in the creation of all of these industries. Internet-related projects funded through the Department of Defense include the foundational work on packet switching, creation of the ARPANET, and research on a variety of protocols, including TCP/IP. Federal R&D investments strengthened U.S. universities' research capabilities in computer science, facilitated the formation of university "spin-offs," and trained a large cohort of technical experts who aided in the development, adoption, and commercialization of the Internet.

Although reliable estimates of the total federal investment in Internet-related R&D do not exist, federal investments in academic computer science research and training infrastructure during the postwar period were substantial. According to a report from the National Research Council's Computer Science and Telecommunications Board, federal investments in computer science research increased fivefold from 1976 to 1995, from $190 million in 1976 to slightly more than $1 billion in 1995 in constant (1996) dollars (National Research Council 1999, 53). Richard Langlois and David Mowery (1996) have compiled data from a variety of sources that indicate that between 1956 and 1980 the cumulative NSF funding for research in "software and related areas" amounted to more than $411 million (1996 dollars). According to Vinton Cerf and his colleagues (2000), the NSF spent roughly $200 million to expand NSFNET between 1986 and 1995. The Defense Advanced Research Projects Agency and the NSF almost certainly accounted for a majority of federal Internet-related R&D funding.

Inasmuch as the U.S. government was not the only national government supporting domestic R&D in computer networking during the 1960s and

1970s, the benefits of government-sponsored R&D in the United States flowed as much from the scale and structure of these programs as from any first-mover advantages. The success of the United States' R&D programs in this field reflected several factors. Public support for such early-stage R&D supported relatively liberal dissemination of the underlying ideas. Such broad dissemination reflected the interests of the Department of Defense's information technology program managers in the creation of a broad national research infrastructure in computer science that was accessible to both civilian and defense-related firms and applications (Rees 1982, 110–11; Flamm 1988, 224–26). Classified R&D was important, but a great deal of U.S. defense-related R&D consisted of long-term research that was conducted in universities, which by their nature are relatively open institutions.

The Department of Defense's procurement policy complemented DARPA's broad-based approach to R&D funding.[19] Contracts were often awarded to small firms, and this policy fostered entry by new firms into the emerging Internet industry, supporting competition and innovation. The NSF's subsequent support for the development of its NSFNET infrastructure also emphasized university-industry collaboration. The diversity of the federal Internet R&D portfolio reflected the fact that federal R&D investments were not coordinated by any central agency (even within the Department of Defense) but were distributed among several agencies with distinct yet overlapping agendas. The Department of Defense and NASA, for example, each pursued networking initiatives during the 1970s. In an environment of technological uncertainty, this diversified and pluralistic program structure, however inefficient, appears to have been beneficial.

The success of federally funded programs in the United States, especially when compared with many similar programs in Western Europe, suggests that the organization of publicly funded research is at least as important as the level of such investment. The United States' public R&D investment in information technology and computer networking was loosely coordinated, broadly distributed, and tolerated a certain amount of duplication and redundancy, all characteristics that appear to have aided network development and growth. Other factors in the success of R&D programs in the United States were their neutrality with respect to specific commercial applications and the ability to avoid excessive pressure for early commercialization. The Defense Advanced Research Projects Agency, for example, was willing to fund projects such as TCP/IP that made current networking standards obsolete, despite the absence at the time of a clear military or commercial application for the technology. In addition, U.S. R&D programs benefited from their large scale and their extension from technology development into deployment of networking technology.

The commercialization of the Internet within the United States also benefited from scale effects of a different sort. The enormous domestic installed base of desktop computers and a large population of technically sophisticated users were important to the rapid development of new applications. Firms and entrepreneurs in the United States also demonstrated considerable facility in adopting and exploiting foreign inventions.

Private-Sector Investment in R&D and Deployment

The contributions of publicly funded R&D infrastructure and technical innovations to the Internet's development were complemented by a stream of privately funded innovations that accelerated during the second and third phases of the Internet's development. Industry invested huge sums in computer-networking and related technologies that propelled the adoption of the Internet during the 1980s and 1990s. In 1970 investment in software and information technology amounted to $8.31 billion (in 1996 dollars), 24 percent of total U.S. private fixed investment; by 1999 investment in these items had grown to $542.2 billion (1996 dollars), 47 percent of private fixed investment (data on "private fixed investment by type" compiled by U.S. Department of Commerce 2001).

The large domestic installed base of computing and networking hardware, much of it based on the Wintel (Windows operating system and Intel microprocessor) architecture, made it easy for many U.S. companies to connect to the Internet. In many cases, adoption of the Internet involved little more than establishing a connection to an existing network and "turning on" TCP/IP for the host computers. This large privately financed investment in information technology created a huge domestic platform in the United States for the rapid adoption of the Internet and for user-led innovation in Internet services and technologies. But the ability of markets to coordinate this rapid development and adoption of the Internet benefited from earlier decisions by the Department of Defense and the NSF to support a single, open standard for Internet architectures.

The advances in Internet capacity and speed that accelerated its adoption resulted from innovations in the networking hardware and software products whose markets grew exponentially throughout the 1990s. The firms that eventually came to dominate the networking equipment market were not large incumbents such as IBM or Digital Equipment. Instead, a group of smaller firms, most of which were founded in the late 1980s, rose to prominence by selling multiprotocol products that were tailored to the open platform represented by TCP/IP and Ethernet.[20] Cisco, Bay Networks, and 3Com, along with a host of other start-ups that eventually were acquired by industry incumbents, developed new products that were based on this open network architecture. The rapid growth of the U.S. network created a large domestic market for these firms and aided their dominance of the global networking equipment market, just as U.S.-packaged computer software firms had benefited from the burgeoning U.S. domestic personal computer market during the 1980s (Mowery 1996).

The source of HTML and HTTP, the inventions that triggered the mid-1990s surge in consumer Internet adoption, was a publicly funded European physics laboratory. But decades of federal and private sector investments in R&D and infrastructure within the United States supported the rapid exploitation of these inventions by U.S. entrepreneurs and accelerated the adoption of the Internet following the introduction of browsers. By the early 1990s, the basic protocols governing the operation of the Internet had been in use for more than twenty years, and their stability and robustness had improved considerably from this lengthy period of gestation and refinement (Greenstein 2000). Although the key inventions underpinning the Web originated outside the United States, its rapid diffusion and commercialization in this country occurred largely through the efforts of private organizations.[21] Private investment complemented and responded to the incentives created by public policies and larger market forces. Private sector funding supported the emergence of the networking hardware companies focusing on the open standards architecture of TCP/IP and the huge investments in e-commerce that followed the diffusion of HTML and the World Wide Web.

The sources of funding for R&D and infrastructure investment have shifted from the public to private sectors during the forty-year development of the Internet. New firms, many financed by venture capital, along with existing firms, the savings of individuals, and other sources, have played a key role in commercialization and adoption of the Internet. In this and other respects, the development of the Internet closely resembles the development of other components of the electronics and information technology sector, such as semiconductors or computer hardware. Although the private sector now dominates investment in Internet development and deployment, public funding continues to support a large university-based R&D infrastructure that is important to both technical training and innovation. But the growth in private sector investment and the higher commercial stakes that now surround decisions on Internet governance, particularly in the area of technical standards, have created strong pressures for increased public oversight. Paradoxically, continued growth in the private sector investments in the Internet that contributed to its "privatization" by the NSF in 1995 now appears to be increasing pressure for public oversight of standard setting and related activities.

Regulation and Technical Coordination

The development of the "network of networks" that became known as the Internet relied on a set of governance institutions in the public and private sectors. As we noted at the beginning of this chapter, there is little doubt that federal telecommunications regulatory policies (which, by the 1980s, focused on deregulation) provided a powerful impetus to domestic development and adoption of the Internet in the United States. But the very nature of the Internet as a network of networks meant that the development of protocols and technical standards to promote interoperability among a huge array of systems and components also was essential. Our discussion of the governance of technical standard-setting highlights the extent to which change in the sources of financing for the Internet and the dramatically increased commercial stakes involved in decisions on such standards have begun to change the character of these governance institutions.

U.S. Telecommunications Policy and the Internet

The design of the TCP/IP protocol separates the medium through which data is delivered from a computer's ability to use the Internet. From its inception, therefore, the fundamental design advance that underpinned the Internet tended to weaken the market power of incumbent telecommunications service providers in the United States.[22] In practice, however, the vast majority of Internet traffic flows over the fiber-optic cables and copper wires of the traditional telephone network.[23] The market-opening effects of this technological advance thus were substantially enhanced by the deregulation of telecommunications markets, particularly in the United States. Public regulation of telecommunications services, along with other policies affecting the evolution of the structure of the U.S. telecommunications services industry, accelerated the adoption of computer networking in general and the Internet in particular.

   Throughout the postwar period, AT&T's involvement in the development of computer networking was restricted by a 1956 consent decree in a federal antitrust case against the telecommunications firm that led it to focus its energies on its existing lines of business. Meanwhile, the Federal Communications Commission's hearings, Computer I and Computer II (decided in 1971 and 1976, respectively), declared that computing lay outside the boundary of AT&T's regulated monopoly (Weinhaus and Oettinger 1988). In addition to preventing AT&T from aggressively pursuing the commercial data–networking market, these judicial and regulatory decisions led to the licensing of several of Bell Laboratories' major innovations in information technology, including the transistor and related semiconductor technologies as well as Unix and the C programming language. The liberal terms on which these technologies were licensed promoted their extensive diffusion and incorporation into a suite of open standards technologies that eventually included TCP/IP.

   The second federal antitrust suit of the postwar era against AT&T culminated with the 1984 modified final judgment, which inaugurated a sweeping restructuring of the U.S. domestic telecommunications industry. By separating the regional Bell operating companies (or "Baby Bells") from AT&T, the modified final judgment increased competition in markets for telecommuni-

FIGURE 10.2   *Access Charges and Internet Penetration in OECD Countries, 1998*

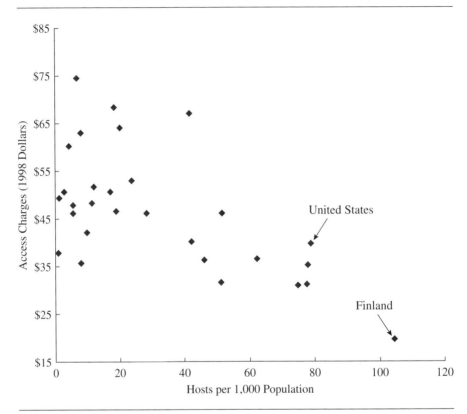

Source: OECD (1999).

cations services and infrastructure for large clients. Competition lowered prices for leased lines, which were used within the academic and commercial networking community to connect local area networks to "interexchange" points, linking them to long-haul carriers and to one another. Commercial ISPs relied on low-cost leased lines in creating the commercial Internet exchange in 1991, underscoring the importance of low-cost access to the telecommunications network as a key factor in the rapid adoption of Internet applications by enterprises and households.

The importance of low-cost infrastructure access and the early U.S. commitment to telecommunications deregulation is apparent in figure 10.2, which illustrates the relationship between the price of Internet access and Internet penetration among member nations of the Organization for Economic Cooperation and Development (OECD). The United States ranks among the lowest in access charges and is second only to Finland in market penetration. The United States was among the first governments to deregulate domestic telecommunications service during the 1980s, but Internet adoption in the United States also benefited from a decades-old feature of U.S. telecommunications regulation. Since the 1920s, the Federal Communications Commission had mandated unmetered pricing of local telephone service. The agency's regulators extended this policy to the Internet by classifying ISPs as "enhanced service providers," thereby allowing them to establish their modem banks within the local loop and provide flat-rate Internet access.[24] As a result of U.S. telecommunications policy and complementary factors that included a large domestic market, an extensive academic network operating on a common platform, large private investments in computing infrastructure, and a strong domestic base of network equipment manufacturers, a domestic ISP industry appeared first in the United States.[25]

The 1996 Telecommunications Act sought to reinforce competition in the market for broadband access. The results of the 1996 act, however, illustrate the complexities of market governance and the difficulty of designing regulatory policy for an industry undergoing rapid technological change (see chapter 3, this volume). For example, current regulatory policy mandates that telecommunications firms using their own network infrastructure to offer broadband Internet service must allow other ISPs to utilize this infrastructure to sell competing services. No comparable requirement has been imposed on cable firms, however, which creates considerable potential for cable-based broadband service providers to offer differentiated products, such as enhanced quality of service for particular content providers. The Internet's underlying architecture, developed to provide the broadest possible access across heterogeneous networks, also imposes a ceiling on attainable quality of service and therefore impedes such "differentiated quality of service" offerings (for example, voice communications and animation). But any substantial shift toward such differentiation could erode one of the Internet's most attractive features, its ability to connect users to a vast portfolio of products, information, and other services. There is a real tension between the vast "commons" for innovation created by the Internet's "end-to-end" architecture and the immanent demand for differentiated quality of service (David 2001). Although this tension is embedded in the Internet's architecture, recent telecommunications regulatory policy decisions have intensified it.

Technical Coordination

The rapid diffusion of the Internet and the World Wide Web relied on a set of robust, scalable networking standards, such as HTML, HTTP, Ethernet, and the TCP/IP protocol suite.[26] These important technical standards were complemented by a host of less well known standards for tasks such as encryption, email, the transmission of music and images, and acquiring an IP address.

The economic literature on standard setting distinguishes between the de facto standards that emerge from a process of diffusion and technology adoption and the de jure standards that are developed and often enforced by standard-setting organizations (David and Greenstein 1990). Although the development of the Internet has included several major market-driven battles over proprietary standards, such as the "browser wars" between Microsoft and Netscape, many of the technical standards that remain critical to the Internet's infrastructure relied on a standard-setting process that combined elements of de facto and de jure standard setting under shared public and private governance. In the case of the Internet, these processes were unusual in their structure and performance, frequently combining openness and consensus decision making with the relatively rapid development of technical standards.

Beginning shortly after the creation of the ARPANET, the Request for Comments process, characterized by open deliberations within the technical community building the network, emerged as the major forum for technical decision making on the operation and architecture of the Internet. This voluntary process produced open standards in a relatively timely fashion, using the new network to facilitate communication within a widely distributed research community and to provide continuous documentation on the evolution of the network. From its inception, participation in the Request for Comments process was open to any interested participant and drew on public and private sector researchers. All of the early standards published through the Request for Comments process, such as e-mail, FTP, and TCP/IP, entered the public domain, and the authors of these standards encouraged independent implementations and further research on them.

As the network grew rapidly from 1979 to 1982 and connected more commercial users, the Internet Configuration Control Board, founded in 1979, provided a more formal nonmarket structure for Internet self-governance. The process of making important management decisions about the Internet was further institutionalized through the creation of organizations such as the Internet Assigned Names and Numbers Authority to oversee the allocation of addresses and domain names among users. Infrastructure management and technical standardization were coordinated by the Internet Architecture Board. The Internet Configuration Control Board, the Internet Assigned Names and Numbers Authority, and the Internet Architecture Board were initially funded by the federal government, and only in 1992 did the official Internet standard-setting bodies (principally the IETF, the Internet Assigned Numbers Authority, and the Internet Architecture Board) begin to rely on private sector funding through the Internet Society, a professional society organized to help coordinate infrastructure development.

During the Internet's transition to more formal governance structures and private funding, the commitment to open standards within the technical community remained strong. The IETF, which remains open to any interested individual and does not allow institutional membership, is characteristic of the technical communities that built and managed the Internet infrastructure. The IETF does not take roll-call votes, favoring a decision-making process based on "rough consensus and running code" that encourages experimentation and independent implementation of any proposed protocols. The organization rebelled against the growing authority of the Internet Architecture Board during the early 1990s, and the IETF maintains the relatively informal Request for Comments process as its forum for "official" technical communications.[27]

The effectiveness of the IETF's standard-setting process is indicated by the fact that many of its open standards were widely adopted in the face of alternatives developed by private companies and public agencies during the 1980s and 1990s. Perhaps the best example is the emergence of TCP/IP as a de facto standard. The protocol was formalized as a de jure Internet standard as early as 1974 but gained widespread acceptance as the de facto standard for internetworking during the 1980s and early 1990s in the face of competition from technical guidelines proposed by the global telecommunications industry (X.25), the computer industry (Open Standard Interconnect protocols), and private companies such as Digital (DecNet) and IBM (SNA).

Ironically, by paving the way for the rapid commercialization of the Internet, TCP/IP and the other early IETF standards helped create the current high-stakes environment in which the historically open, collaborative, self-organized institutions such as the IETF may not suffice for effective governance of the standard-setting process. One sign of the challenges posed to this process by Internet commercialization was the creation of the World Wide Web Consortium in 1994 to deal with the proliferation of browsers and extensions to the HTML standard. The W3C was founded by Tim Berners-Lee in 1994, with funding from CERN, DARPA, and the European Union.[28] Its organization reflected the higher economic stakes created by the competition between Netscape and Microsoft, the rapid pace of commercialization for web-related innovations, and Berners-Lee's concern that the IETF could not move rapidly enough to adapt to the privately financed development of browsers, following his invention of HTML and HTTP.[29]

Although their internal structures appear to be similar, a major difference between the W3C and the IETF is the requirement that participants in the W3C be sponsored by a member organization, typically their employer. The W3C currently has five hundred member organizations that each pay $50,000 ($5,000 for nonprofits) for representation on the W3C Advisory Committee and on W3C technical working groups. The W3C successfully managed the standards-related aspects of the competitive battle during the mid-1990s between Microsoft and Netscape over their respective browser technologies,

FIGURE 10.3   *Privatization of the IETF, 1991 to 2004*

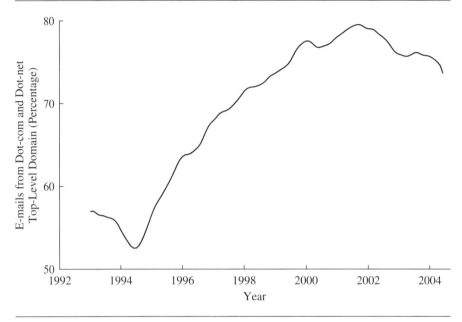

Source: Data from Simcoe (2004).

preserving a common standard for HTML (Cusumano and Yoffie 1998). Since then, the consortium has continued to develop and support a set of technical specifications for the Web's software infrastructure that promote openness, interoperability, and a smooth evolution for the HTML standard.

The changing composition of the IETF is another indicator of the diffi-cult task faced by Internet self-governance institutions in an increasingly com-mercial environment. The data in figure 10.3 illustrate the growth of private-sector participation in the IETF during the 1991 to 2004 period by tracing the growing percentage of emails sent to IETF Working Group discussion lists from participants with a top-level domain of ".net" or ".com." Commercial participation in IETF email discussions, a reflection of the changing compo-sition of the networking research community, grew from about 57 percent of the messages in early 1993 to a September 2001 peak of 79.5 percent, declin-ing (in the wake of the collapse of the "dot-com" bubble) to 73.7 percent by June 2004.[30] The growing economic stakes associated with IETF decisions in-dicated by the changing affiliations of participants in these debates are re-flected in the intensified struggles within the IETF over internal rules and structure. For example, in 1996 the IETF changed its intellectual property policy from a requirement that technical proposals place all standards-related IP in the public domain to a requirement for licensing of any standards-related IP on reasonable and non-discriminatory terms. This decision by the IETF launched an internal debate between technology vendors and open-source developers that continues to simmer.[31] These and other examples of growing internal tensions underscore the risk that the historic nonmarket norms, institutions, and conventions of the Internet community may no longer suffice for effective governance in standard setting.

The most recent sign of the stress placed on the standards process by Internet commercialization is the controversy surrounding the reorganization of the Internet Assigned Numbers Authority into the Internet Corporation for Assigned Names and Numbers.[32] The dramatic growth of the World Wide Web has sparked a number of controversies over ownership of the "virtual real estate" inherent in Internet domain names (for example, www.mcdonalds.com) and numerous national and international disputes over name and trademark ownership. The corporation was organized in 1998 as a private sector, nonprofit institution recognized by the United States and other governments as "the global consensus entity to coordinate the technical management of the Internet's domain name system" (ICANN 2003, 1). In principle, this means that ICANN has the power to resolve domain name disputes. In reality, however, the organization, composed of members from the private sector and the "Internet community," has encountered lengthy delays in decision making, and its actions have generated criticism from the Internet community and industry alike for being opaque and unresponsive. A recent proposal by ICANN's president to replace representatives from the Internet community with representatives from national governments generated an outcry among Internet users (Lynn 2002). The controversy over ICANN illustrates the difficulties of bringing the consensus-driven approach to governance that proved so successful in creating many Internet technical standards into an area that is characterized by high commercial stakes and conflict.[33]

The creation and adoption of the key Internet protocols weakened the centralized control over network architectures formerly exercised by private and state-controlled telecommunications monopolists. But these protocols do not themselves provide a solution to the inevitable trade-off between the ability of a centralized authority to promote efficiency in coordinated decision making and the rent seeking or abuse of power that often follows the creation of a central authority. Moreover, as noted earlier, these protocols have created other challenges to the Internet's continued evolution as an open network of networks. In the case of the Internet, the decline of AT&T's control over its circuit-switched network architecture created a need for the domain name system and an IP address hierarchy to facilitate widespread use of a decentralized network. The commercialization of the network has intensified criticism by various groups of the organizations managing the domain name system and IP address space.

The Internet has relied on hybrid forms of public and private governance for the creation of an infrastructure based on open standards that has accommodated rapid growth in the network. Some credit for this success undoubtedly goes to the farsighted individuals who designed an informal process that utilized the technology itself to encourage collaborative development within a research community open to any interested participant. But the effectiveness of the process also owes much to the fact that these open standards developed in an environment free of the pressures of standard setting for proprietary technologies. Although the open alternatives created by organizations such as the IETF prevailed over privately developed proprietary alternatives and standards designed by industry consortiums, the recent experiences of ICANN, the W3C, and the IETF itself suggest that the "open model" is being challenged by the pressures of commercialization.

Private incentives are a powerful force for solving problems of coordination, but they may shape the self-governing nonmarket institutions that seek to facilitate coordination, such as the ICANN and W3C, in unexpected ways. Indeed, the higher economic stakes have led to demands for greater transparency, accountability, and oversight of many parts of the standard-setting process, culminating in calls for government representation on ICANN. Even if they retain their quasi-private status, ICANN and other organizations will continue to be influenced in significant ways by public policy in intellectual property, antitrust, and other areas, and the field of standard setting will be overseen by a complex mix of public and private actors and incentives.

Governing Internet Applications: Regulation and Markets

Much of the Internet's success as a de facto networking standard can be attributed to the fact that its core protocols were placed in the public domain. This created an "innovation commons" for software developers that led to a proliferation of novel applications. At the same time, many Internet applications raise difficult policy questions in areas such as the governance of intellectual property, the regulation of content (such as pornography or "hate material"), competition policy in communications industries, and the protection of consumer privacy. Several authors have written extensively on particular issues, such as Lawrence Lessig (1999, 2001) on intellectual property, and Dennis Yao (2003) on the interplay among the courts, federal regulatory agencies (particularly the Federal Trade Commission), and industry self-regulators in the United States. Each of these discussions illustrates the limits and complexities of both market and nonmarket governance and regulation of the Internet, and a thorough accounting extends well beyond the scope of this chapter.

Because the Internet serves as a platform for distributing a wide variety of content and applications, Internet regulation has received little attention. Instead, diffusion of the Internet has sparked a series of debates over regulatory or other responses to specific Internet applications. A central theme in these debates is the question of whether new legal and regulatory frameworks are needed to respond to the capabilities and limitations imposed by the Internet in a specific application.

One example of these debates is the controversy over Internet privacy. Broadly defined, Internet privacy encompasses the legality of encryption, the appropriate use of monitoring technologies, the collection of personal information, and the control of unwanted solicitation, or "spam." During the mid-1990s, encryption and surveillance were the most prominent subjects in the privacy debate. Much of the interest in these two issues was triggered by federal proposals for restrictions on the export of software containing "strong encryption" and by the "Clipper Chip" proposal.[34] These restrictions limited U.S. companies' ability to sell products incorporating advanced cryptography in foreign markets, forcing many firms to produce different versions of the same product for foreign and domestic consumption. In addition, concern within the U.S. law enforcement community over potential limits to surveillance of criminal activity created by strong cryptographic protection of Internet-based communications resulted in the inclusion within the Clipper Chip proposal of a mandate for a "backdoor" for government wiretaps in all electronic communications. Both of these policy initiatives were ultimately unsuccessful. The export restrictions were lifted in 2000 after intense lobbying from an unusual alliance between the software industry and civil libertarians, and the Clipper Chip proposal was never implemented. One reason for the failure of these initiatives was the fact that strong public-domain encryption protocols had been available for Internet download since 1991, through a program called Pretty Good Privacy written by U.S. programmer Phil Zimmerman. Ultimately, the widespread dissemination of encryption technologies through the Internet seriously undermined the credibility of law enforcement efforts to limit their application on the Internet.

During the late 1990s, the commercialization of the Internet shifted the focus of the privacy debate from questions of encryption to the issue of user monitoring and data collection. A survey conducted by the Federal Trade Commission in 1999 indicated that more than 90 percent of websites collected some type of user information (Bernstein 2000). Many websites require users to submit personal information before allowing access to a service. Others use so-called cookie technologies that place a file on the user's computer to keep track of their web browsing and use. Such monitoring of consumer behavior and the collection of personal data raised questions about the rights of consumers to prevent "personal" information from being aggregated, sold, or used in other ways they find objectionable.

Advertisers and content providers have argued that market forces and self-regulation will solve the problem. Indeed, industry self-regulation has developed rapidly, managed by industry associations such as the Direct Marketing Association and independent initiatives such as Trust-e and the Network Advertising Initiative. Critics of these efforts, however, argue that they are voluntary and generally favor business interests by limiting verification or enforcement and placing the burden on consumers to elect "opt-out" provisions rather than the more protective "opt-in" alternative. Some well-publicized perceived corporate abuses, such as efforts by the online advertising company DoubleClick to merge personal information collected from offline sources with its web databases, have strengthened the arguments of critics. The Federal Trade Commission has adopted a wait-and-see approach to this issue, but the European Union's 1995 Privacy Directive gives consumers a great deal of control over the use of personal information. It remains to be seen how and when these two approaches may be reconciled.

The growth of spam has recently assumed a prominent role in the Internet privacy debate. These e-mail solicitations are merely the latest (electronic) manifestation of such direct-marketing perennials as "junk" mail or telephone solicitation, but the low cost of automating bulk e-mail and the fact that senders' access charges are relatively low (especially on a per message basis) has produced rapid growth in spam and intense criticism by consumers. One consulting firm marketing its services to corporations seeking to manage the spam problem (and, accordingly, a source with an interest in a high estimate of the costs of spam) has estimated the costs of spam for U.S. corporations alone to have exceeded $10 billion in 2003 (Ferris Research 2003). Many companies report that the volume of inbound spam-related e-mail creates significant hardware and software costs in addition to opportunity costs for the end user (Wagner 2003).

Several congressional bills aimed at fighting spam have failed to pass, and they may be unenforceable in any event because of the ease with which senders can disguise the source of a message or move their origin outside of a given legal jurisdiction. The end-to-end nature of the Internet's architecture thus renders the "network of networks" particularly vulnerable to this type of abuse. Recent congressional debates over regulation of spam also have attracted the opposition of critics who are concerned about the potentially chilling effects of such restrictions on free speech through the Internet. These critics instead support technological solutions such as filters, which have become increasingly popular, or measures by network administrators to block specific originating addresses as a means of isolating the network service providers that shelter flagrantly abusive spam originators.

A particular difficulty associated with the issue of Internet privacy is the speed with which its contours change in a rapidly evolving technological landscape. Indeed, the growth of the Internet itself complicates regulatory efforts. The growing availability of cryptographic technology through the Internet essentially overtook and rendered moot the policy debate over encryption technologies during the 1990s, and the technologists of 2003 are seeking to develop tools that can protect users against unwanted monitoring or solicitation.

In addition, of course, there is a legitimate debate as to whether the "privacy issue" is a problem. Do consumers have "rights" to control private use of information gathered by firms or to prevent unwanted solicitation through this open communications medium? If so, are these rights stronger or weaker than those traditionally allowed to commercial entities that gather consumer information through other means? At least some of the emotion and vehemence of the debate over Internet privacy reflects the medium rather than the activity of monitoring itself. It remains unclear how to delineate those rights in a way that protects consumers and legitimate commercial interests and takes account of the changing technological landscape.

Proponents of the free market argue that some types of privacy protection will emerge in response to consumer demand; and private regulatory initiatives have indeed surfaced in several cases. Yet consumer advocates argue that these initiatives lack teeth and rarely go far enough toward a true remedy. In many cases, technological solutions to the privacy problem are at least as effective as any regulatory actions. Some privacy technologies, such as ad-filtering tools that alert a user when information is being shared, or free alternate e-mail accounts, are already widely available. Other privacy tools, such as strong cryptography or anonymous re-mailers, raise a variety of questions—particularly within the law enforcement community. The ability of the Internet to spawn "vigilantism" against abusive marketers (for example, denial-of-service attacks on their websites) creates still other problems.

As the Internet matures, a number of technologies for managing online identities, facilitating payments, and managing personal information may become available. While these may solve some of the problems of privacy that pervade today's Internet, they are likely to raise a number of new issues about database and registry ownership. Like the standard-setting process, the growth of new, profitable Internet applications has intensified public concern over the consequences of unfettered private sector exploitation of data collected on consumer behavior, leading to calls for increased public sector oversight or outright prohibition of some commercial practices. The rapid growth of these applications has also triggered an effort by industry to self-regulate various practices and applications. The ultimate outcome of the privacy debate is impossible to forecast at present, but there seems no doubt that a complex interaction between public and private oversight and proposals for regulation will characterize this debate in the United States and other industrial economies for the foreseeable future.

Conclusion

Who governs the Internet? Both private and public governance have played important roles in the development of the network. The roles of public and private entities have varied over time, however, and their influence over different elements of the Internet also has varied. Public funding remains important for information technology R&D and the support of the large university infrastructure that trains engineers and computer scientists. Meanwhile, funding for Internet deployment and applications has shifted from public to private sources, and the growing commercial potential of the Internet led to its "privatization" in the United States in the 1990s. The U.S. telecommunications infrastructure that underpins the Internet has moved toward a deregulated, competitive structure, but public and private regulation of the organizations that govern Internet standardization and technical infrastructure management has expanded. Indeed, the very growth of the Internet and related opportunities for investment and profit from its commercial applications are influencing demands for greater public involvement in its oversight, and new Internet applications continue to trigger public debates over the merits of public regulation versus market governance of these activities. As the comparison of Internet privatization in 1995 and the current pressure for growing public oversight of its evolving architecture suggest, the relationship among commercialization, governance, and the technological evolution of the Internet is a complex one that may more closely resemble a pendulum than a linear progression.

A host of current and potential future applications of the Internet pose complex dilemmas about network regulation and governance. The use of public data by private firms, the collection of personal data over the Internet, and the marketing practices used by Internet firms all have raised concern among consumers, and the federal government has been engaged for years in a debate with privacy advocates over the use of Internet encryption technologies. As more consumers acquire high-speed broadband connections to the Internet, antitrust and telecommunications regulators will have to confront difficult questions about common-carriage rules regulating infrastructure access and the level of competition provided by alternative access technologies. The growth of Internet-based business opportunities also has forced the U.S. Patent and Trademark Office to make difficult determinations about the application of established intellectual property rights standards to "business methods" and other novel artifacts (see Graham and Mowery 2001).

In all of these areas, the interaction between public and private institutions is complicated by "path dependence"; new issues are often handled by organizations, agencies, and bureaucracies created to address other issues; and the economic and political stakes in these new issues often reflect the legacy of previous political, regulatory, and economic decisions and policies. Such path dependence is apparent in the regulatory apparatus that oversees the Internet's growth at present in the United States. The Federal Communications Commission, the primary regulatory overseer, has assumed this responsibility by default as a result of its historical involvement in telecommunications regulation.

Path dependence is apparent as well in the unusual challenges created by the growing burdens placed on the original Internet protocols by consumer demands for higher levels of security, differentiated quality of service, and privacy protection. The Internet's original architecture, as Paul David (2001) and others have pointed out, was designed to support interaction within the relatively small, homogeneous international community of researchers that was responsible for many of the technical and governance innovations that followed. The explosion of new applications and users on the Internet since the early 1990s, however, has radically transformed the size and characteristics of users, a fact that is partially responsible for the increased demands for public governance.

The history of the Internet is best understood as the result of a complex interaction between the public and private sectors. Private industry in the United States responded quickly to the opportunities created by the publicly funded development of an early network infrastructure. In contrast to technology development, however, our discussion of the development of computer networking and the Internet suggests that the ability of markets to substitute for regulation is limited. Typically, the introduction of a market (such as the market for domain names) or the creation of bureaucracy (such as ICANN) has unintended consequences that result from its interaction with the changing economic environment that surrounds it. Indeed, the brief history of commercial exploitation of the Internet suggests that the explosion in market applications and profits has triggered intensified public pressure for public intervention. The controversies in technical standards, intellectual property rights, and privacy all suggest that the distributional and other consequences of market governance may trigger a public sector response that can result in regulatory intervention. The design of institutions to govern this global network of networks will challenge the ingenuity of public policy makers, technical experts, and industry.

Research for this paper was supported by the Alfred P. Sloan Foundation and the Andrew W. Mellon Foundation.

Notes

1. The widespread adoption of technologies for sharing or temporarily allocating IP addresses means that this measure almost certainly understates the number of users and computers attached to the network.

2. Considerable evidence suggests that differences among the Organization for Economic Cooperation and Development economies in their telecommunications regulatory policies have powerfully influenced the differential growth of Internet usage among those economies.

3. The term "backbone" generally refers to the high-speed long-distance connections between major interconnection points located in different cities. These connections are generally leased from long-distance telecommunications providers, with the cost shared among several networks.

4. Packet switching is fundamentally different from circuit switching, the technology that connects ordinary telephone calls. On a packet-switched network, information is broken up into a series of discrete "packets" that are sent individually and reassembled into a complete message on the receiving end. A single circuit may carry packets from multiple connections, and the packets for a single communication may take different routes from source to destination.

5. The researchers did, however, lease the long-distance phone lines used to carry their data from AT&T.

6. Donald Davies completed a prototype data network in 1969, and a French network, CYCLADES, was demonstrated in 1972. U.S. researchers were among the pioneers in computer networking but did not dominate early developments in the field.

7. "Transmission Control Protocol (TCP)" (1974); "Transmission Control Protocol (TCP)," in the *IEEE Transactions on Communication* (Cerf and Kahn 1974).

8. In software development, standards refer primarily to the specification of an interface—a set of commands that can be used by other programmers to write new software. These interfaces simplify the complex task of writing a program from scratch. With open standards, the developer of an interface places the set of commands—and, generally, the source code used to create them—into the public domain. This allows other developers to improve and extend the interface and encourages programmers to adopt the commands contained in it as a true industry standard.

9. The Unix operating system was invented by Kenneth Thompson and Dennis Ritchie of Bell Laboratories in 1969. Its evolution illustrates the power of an open standard as well as the difficulties in maintaining technical compatibility within an "unsponsored," open standard. AT&T originally licensed the Unix source code to universities for a nominal fee because of a 1956 consent decree that restrained them from competing in the computer industry and mandated the licensing of patented technology. The licensing policy had several offsetting effects. Research users, including computer scientists at the University of California at Berkeley, developed modifications that significantly improved the operating system (including the bundling of TCP/IP) but developed several incompatible versions of the program. AT&T's subsequent efforts to exploit Unix

commercially failed in the presence of free and arguably superior, albeit incompatible, competing versions of the operating system.

10. Indeed, the Request for Comments process of widely distributed problem-solving individuals and teams that discovered and fixed technical flaws in the network technology anticipated some of the key features of open-source software development, an activity that depends on the communications and interactions made possible by the Internet (see Lee and Cole 2000; Kuan 2000).

11. International connections also started to be established in large numbers around this time, as in 1988 networks from Canada, Denmark, Finland, France, Iceland, Norway, and Sweden connected to the NSFNET. Australia, Germany, Israel, Italy, Japan, Mexico, Netherlands, New Zealand, and the United Kingdom followed one year later.

12. The speed of the NSFNET backbone was upgraded from 56K (57,600 bits per second) in 1985 to T1 (1.5 million bits per second) in 1988 and to T3 (46.1 million bits per second) in 1991.

13. The first true ISP was world.std.com, which began offering dial-up Internet access to customers in the greater Boston metropolitan area in 1990.

14. Although scale-related entry barriers were not prohibitive, neither were scale-related limits to growth: the largest nationwide providers, such as AOL, grew to enormous size.

15. The development of these important technical advances was motivated by Berners-Lee and Cailliau's interest in helping physicists archive and search the large volume of technical material being transmitted over the Internet. Like the TCP/IP protocol, however, these software innovations were placed in the public domain and were available at no cost to other innovators.

16. The National Center for Supercomputing Applications was an NSF-funded facility devoted to research on supercomputing architecture and applications. By the early 1990s, networking technologies and powerful desktop computers had reduced academic researchers' need for access to supercomputers. As a result, Andreesen and colleagues focused on developing new technologies to support expanded use of computer networking (Abbate 1999, 216). Federally funded "excess capacity" in the research computing infrastructure thus contributed to an important innovation in networking.

17. Top-level domains are the uppermost level in the hierarchical classification established by the Internet's domain name system. They commonly refer to the last part of an email addresses, such as .com or .edu.

18. The U.S. Bureau of the Census estimates that 94 percent of electronic commerce is business-to-business (B2B). These estimates are based on the rough assumption that manufacturing and wholesale e-commerce is entirely B2B, while retail and service e-commerce is entirely B2C (business-to-consumer) (U.S. Department of Commerce 2002).

19. DARPA was strictly a defense R&D agency and did not engage in large-scale procurement.

20. Ethernet was developed in 1972 by Robert Metcalfe at the Xerox Palo Alto Research Center. Unlike TCP/IP, which operates through gateways to connect different networks, it governs a set of computers attached to a single network. As

the most widely used local-area-networks protocol on the Internet, Ethernet represents another "open standards" success story.

21. Berners-Lee claims that his efforts in 1991 to encourage a French research group at the INRIA ("Institut National de Recherche en Informatique et en Automatique," see Berners-Lee 2000, 243) laboratory to commercialize an application that could have been the first commercial browser met with failure because of the researchers' concern that gaining funding from the European Union Commission to undertake the necessary integration tasks would take too long (Berners-Lee 2000, 44–45).

22. Many incumbent telecommunications service providers were slow to adopt data-networking innovations, such as packet switching, within their own infrastructures, even as the rapidly growing ISPs incorporated these innovations into theirs into the early 1990s.

23. As of this writing in 2003, however, private wireless networking appears to be eroding the traditional dominance of Internet traffic by cables and wires.

24. This classification was reaffirmed in the Federal Communications Commission's May 1997 "Access Reform Order," which ensured that ISPs did not have to pay the same per minute access charges that long-distance companies pay to local telephone companies for use of the network.

25. However, many of the formal institutions, such as Reseaux IP Européen, an ISP consortium and interconnection point for Western Europe, were founded around the same time as their U.S. counterparts, in this case, the commercial Internet exchange.

26. HTML and HTTP themselves are derived from a long-established standard for document formatting called SGML (standard generalized markup language).

27. These characteristics are apparent in other important Internet institutions founded during the late 1980s and early 1990s, including the commercial Internet exchange and the Reseaux IP Européen that was discussed earlier.

28. The institutional sponsors of the W3C now include the Massachusetts Institute of Technology in the United States, INRIA in France, and Keio University in Japan.

29. Berners-Lee (2000, 76) states in his memoir that "I did not want to form a standards body per se, but some kind of organization that could help developers of servers and browsers reach consensus on how the Web should operate. With Mosaic picking up the ball and running single-handedly for the goal line, and more and more gopher users considering the Web, evidence was mounting that 'the Web' could splinter into various factions—some commercial, some academic; some free, some not. This would defeat the very purpose of the Web: to be a single, universal, accessible hypertext medium for sharing information." He further notes in his discussion of the founding of W3C, "I wanted the consortium to run on an open process like that of the IETF's, but one that was quicker and more efficient, because we would have to move fast" (92).

30. These data are taken from an analysis of more than 600,000 archived email messages from IETF groups (Simcoe 2004). The results are similar when participation is measured based on messages, unique users (that is, email addresses), or participating institutions. Common email addresses such as "yahoo.com" and

"hotmail.com" were excluded, and a number of precautions were taken to exclude unsolicited spam and bulk commercial email.

31. A sample of the debate can be read online at www.ietf.org/mail-archive/working-groups/ipr-wg/current/maillist.html (accessed November 22, 2004). Mark Lemley (2002) documents the wide variety of IP rules and practices within technical standard–setting organizations.

32. Originally known as the Internet Assigned Numbers Authority and occasionally referred to as the Internet Assigned Names and Numbers Authority.

33. In view of the strong similarities between the standard-setting process that historically has operated within the Internet and the structure of innovative activity in such important innovations in "open source" as the Linux operating system, an innovation that has attracted increased commercial interest and investment, it is tempting to predict that similar tensions and possibly pressure for public oversight could arise there as well.

34. Strong encryption algorithms use keys with a length greater than 128 bits.

References

Abbate, Janet. 1999. *Inventing the Internet.* Cambridge, Mass.: MIT Press.

Berners-Lee, Tim. 2000. *Weaving the Web.* New York: HarperCollins.

Bernstein, Jodie. 2000. "Online Profiling: Benefits and Concerns." Prepared statement of Jodie Bernstein, director of the FTC Bureau of Consumer Protection, before the U.S. Senate Committee on Commerce, Science, and Transportation, 106th Congress, 2nd Session, June 13.

Brand, Stewart. 2001. "Founding Father: An Interview with Paul Baran." *Wired Magazine* 9(3): 144–53.

Bresnahan, Timothy F., and Amit Chopra. 1990. "The Development of the Local Area Network Market as Determined by User Needs." *Economics of Innovation and New Technology* 1(1–2): 97–110.

Cerf, Vinton G., and Robert Kahn. 1974. "A Protocol for Packet Network Intercommunication." *IEEE Transactions on Communication* C-20(5): 637–48.

Cerf, Vinton G., Barry M. Leiner, David D. Clark, Robert E. Kahn, Leonard Kleinrock, Daniel C. Lynch, Jon Postel, Larry G. Roberts, and Stephen Wolff. 2000. "A Brief History of the Internet." Internet Society. Available at: www.isoc.org/internet/history/ (accessed November 22, 2004).

Cusumano, Michael, and David B. Yoffie. 1998. *Competing on Internet Time: Lessons from Netscape and Its Battle with Microsoft.* New York: Free Press.

David, Paul A. 2001. "The Evolving Accidental Information Super-Highway." *Oxford Review of Economic Policy* 17(2): 159–87.

David, Paul A., and Shane Greenstein. 1990. "The Economics of Compatibility Standards: An Introduction to Recent Research." *Economics of Innovation and New Technology* 1(1): 3–41.

Ferris Research. 2003. "Research Focus: Spam." Available at: www.ferris.com/url/spam.html (accessed September 2003).

Flamm, Kenneth. 1988. *Creating the Computer.* Washington, D.C.: Brookings Institution Press.

Gompers, Samuel, and Josh Lerner. 1999. *The Venture Capital Cycle.* Cambridge, Mass.: MIT Press.

Graham, Stuart, and David C. Mowery. 2001. "Intellectual Property Protection in the Software Industry." Paper presented at the National Research Council conference, "Intellectual Property and Policy." Washington, D.C. (October 15).

Greenstein, Shane. 2000. "Framing Empirical Work on the Evolving Structure of Commercial Internet Markets." In *Understanding the Digital Economy,* edited by Erik Brynjolffson and Brian Kahin. Cambridge, Mass.: MIT Press.

Internet Corporation for Assigned Names and Numbers (ICANN). 2003. "ICANN and the Global Internet." Report to International Telecommunications Union, prepared for Workshop on Member States' Experiences with ccTLD, Geneva (March 3–4). Available at: http://www.icann.org/cctlds/icann-and-the-global-internet-25feb03.pdf (accessed November 22, 2004).

Kuan, Jennifer. 2000. "Open-Source Software as Consumer Integration into Production." Unpublished manuscript. University of California at Berkeley, Haas School of Business.

Langlois, Richard N., and David C. Mowery. 1996. "The Federal Government Role in the Development of the U.S. Software Industry." In *The International Computer Software Industry: A Comparative Study of Industry Evolution and Structure,* edited by David C. Mowery. New York: Oxford University Press.

Lee, Gwendolyn K., and Robert E. Cole. 2000. "The Linux Kernel Development as a Model of Open Source Knowledge Creation." Unpublished manuscript. University of California at Berkeley, Haas School of Business.

Lemley, Mark A. 2002. "Intellectual Property Rights and Standard-Setting Organizations." *California Law Review* 90(6): 1889–1980.

Lessig, Lawrence. 1999. *CODE: and Other Laws of Cyberspace.* New York: Basic Books.

———. 2001. *The Future of Ideas: The Fate of the Commons in a Connected World.* New York: Random House.

Lynn, S. 2002. "President's Report ICANN–The Case for Reform." Internet Corporation for Assigned Names and Numbers. Available at: www.icann.org/general/lynn-reform-proposal-24feb02.htm (accessed November 22, 2004).

Markiewicz, Kira, and David C. Mowery. 2003. "The Federal Role in Financing Major Innovations: Information Technology during the Postwar Period." Paper presented at the Social Science Research Council (SSRC) conference, Financing Innovation. Irvine, California (March 22).

Mowery, David C. 1996. *The International Computer Software Industry: A Comparative Study of Industry Evolution and Structure.* New York: Oxford University Press.

National Research Council. 1999. *Funding a Revolution: Government Support for Computing Research.* Washington: National Academies Press.

OECD. 1999. *OECD Communications Outlook 1999.* Paris: OECD.

PricewaterhouseCoopers. 2003. "PricewaterhouseCoopers/Thomson Venture Economics/National Venture Capital Association MoneyTree Survey (Investments by

Industry Table)." Available at: www.pwcmoneytree.com/moneytree/index.jsp (accessed November 22, 2004).

Rees, M. 1982. "The Computing Program of the Office of Naval Research, 1946–53." *Annals of the History of Computing* 4(2): 102–20.

Schumpeter, Joseph A. 1932. *Theory of Economic Development: An Inquiry into Profits, Capital, Credit, Interest, and the Business Cycle.* Cambridge, Mass.: Harvard University Press.

Simcoe, Timothy. 2004. "Committees and the Creation of Technical Standards." Working paper. University of Toronto. Available at: www.rotman.utoronto.ca/timothy.simcoe (accessed November 22, 2004).

"Transmission Control Protocol (TCP)." 1974. Request for Comments 0675. Available at: www.faqs.org/rfcs (accessed November 22, 2004).

U.S. Department of Commerce. 2001. Bureau of Economic Analysis. "National Income and Product Accounts." Available at: www.bea.doc.gov/bea/dn/nipaweb/ (accessed November 22, 2004).

———. 2002. "E-Stats." Available at: www.census.gov/estats (accessed September 2003).

Wagner, M. 2003. "Spam Costs $11.9 Billion; Users Favor Legal Ban." *InternetWeek* (January 2). Available at: www.internetweek.com (accessed September 2003).

Weinhaus, Carol L., and Anthony G. Oettinger. 1988. *Behind the Telephone Debates.* Westport, Conn.: Ablex.

Yao, Dennis A. 2003. "Non-market Strategies and Regulation in the U.S." In *The Global Internet Economy,* edited by Bruce Kogut. Cambridge, Mass.: MIT Press.

Zakon, Robert H. 2000. "Hobbes' Internet Timeline v5.1." Available at: www.isoc.org/guest/zakon/Internet/History/HIT.html (accessed September 2003).

11

SATELLITE DATA

Roberta Balstad

WHEN CONGRESS passed the Commercial Space Act in 1998, it was reaffirming its interest and that of the U.S. government in a strong private sector role in remote sensing and earth observation satellites. Although the field had traditionally been dominated by government agencies and public priorities, there had been interest in commercial provision of remote sensing data and in the development of a robust private sector remote sensing industry as early as the Carter administration. Stimulated by the model of commercially successful communication satellites, U.S. government policy makers over several decades envisioned the growth of a private sector remote sensing industry that would provide data and technology for a broad range of both nonmilitary and national security applications. However, aside from the implementation of operational uses of remote sensing for such traditionally governmental responsibilities as weather monitoring and prediction, most of the civil applications of satellite remote sensing data that had developed over the previous twenty-five years were scientific in nature. For this reason, the commercialization of satellite remote sensing necessarily involved commercialization of what had become a basic source of data for many types of scientific research.

Federal policy toward land remote sensing in the United States has moved from a model in which the federal government supported the collection of satellite remote sensing data that were provided to scientists for research at little or no cost to one in which new types of satellite data for scientific research must be purchased from a private sector firm in a commercial market. My focus in this chapter is not on the commercial viability of satellite remote sensing but on the desirability of a policy of relying on the commercial or market sector for research data. At issue is whether the commercialization of this significant source of basic research data in the earth sciences will provide scientists with the data they need and how the implementation of a commercial model for data is likely to affect basic research in the earth sciences.

The underlying purpose of this inquiry is to examine what Richard Nelson (2001; this volume, chap. 9) calls the "encroachment of proprietary property claims into what had been the domain of public science." The more recent federal policy has had an impact on the mix of market and nonmarket mechanisms in satellite remote sensing. After several decades of promoting a larger role for the private sector in remote sensing, there are three operational, fully commercial earth observation satellites in the United States, but the industry itself is not healthy. If the firms in this industry do not survive, as many observers fear, not only will scientists be without a source of what has become valuable research data, but the development of replacement or backup satellites by the government will take many years.

Remote Sensing and the Public and Private Sectors

Overall, the commercial satellite industry appears to be thriving and extremely profitable. Space is the locus for significant economic activity related to the construction, launch, and operation of satellites and related services, and space technology industries annually earn about $125 billion in profit. Some observers have estimated that by 2010, the cumulative U.S investment (public and private) in space could equal current U.S. investments in Europe (Krepon 2001). A closer look at the economics of space reveals, however, that there are three distinct commercial space sectors: space communications, satellite navigation or global positioning, and earth observation or remote sensing. (A fourth commercial activity is space transportation, which is concerned with launch capabilities. Because the commercial market for these services is limited to the space industry and affects science only indirectly, it is not considered here.)

Most of the private sector revenue generation in the industry is related to the use of space for communications. This is also the space industry that has been in operation the longest. Space communications encompasses the use of space satellites for telephone communications and television and radio transmission. Many of the satellites for this purpose are privately owned and operated; others are operated under public-private sector and multilateral agreements. COMSAT, the earliest private sector communications satellite system, was initiated with financial support from the U.S. government in 1963 and now has annual revenues of more than $600 million. However, other firms, such as Hughes Electronics, which supplies satellite communications services for entertainment and business and has annual sales in space communication of more than $7 billion, and EchoStar Communications, with annual space sales of close to $3 billion, dwarf COMSAT's revenues (SpaceNews 2002).

The most rapidly growing commercial sector related to space is space navigation or global positioning. Built on the military positioning capability developed during the cold war and publicly released by the Department of Defense in the early 1990s, the Navigation Satellite Timing and Ranging (NAVSTAR) Global Positioning System is operated by the U.S. government. By 1998, the selective availability of the global positioning system was deactivated, providing civilian and commercial users with significant increases in accuracy in positioning data. The European Union is currently developing plans for a competitor system, Galileo, which could be complete by 2015 (Braunschvig, Garwin, and Maxwell 2003). Global positioning data provides a capacity for determining locational coordinates that are accurate from meters to centimeters worldwide. The private sector industry that has developed around this technology is not based on sales of data. It is based on the commercial development of instruments that are capable of downloading freely provided global positioning data from government satellites and obtaining locational coordinates. This industry is expected to earn about $16 billion in profit in 2003 (Krepon 2001).

The third commercial sector in space is remote sensing or earth observation. Most simply, remote sensing from space involves the use of airborne or satellite-mounted sensors for purposes of obtaining reliable data from the electromagnetic spectrum that can be digitally or visually processed to obtain information (Jensen 2000). Passive sensors receive and measure reflected solar or earth radiation; active sensors provide their own energy sources for purposes of measurement. Passive sensors include such instruments as imaging radiometers, which provide pictures of the sensed objects, and atmospheric sounders, which obtain profiles of water vapor, transpiration, and some gases such as carbon dioxide in the atmosphere. Active sensors include such instruments as scatterometers, which transmit pulses of energy and measure their return from earth's surface and atmosphere; lidar, which times the return of a pulse of light reflected from the surface of the earth; and radar altimetry, which is similar in operation to lidar but involves microwave energy instead of light (U.S. Congress 1994; Jensen 2000). Although passive microwave can see through some cloud cover, radar has the advantage of being able to provide surface data through heavier precipitation. All these capabilities were initially developed by scientists and have grown into operational applications.

Private sector firms have been involved in remote sensing in various ways for as long as they have been involved in either space communications or global positioning, yet the commercial remote sensing industry is still considerably smaller than space communications, and the commercial market for remote sensing data has grown much more slowly than that for global positioning data. The limited commercial success thus far of remote sensing relative to other private sector enterprises in space is not the result of a lack of interest in potential markets or in the commercial advantages of remote sensing. On the contrary, since its earliest days, satellite remote sensing has been viewed by some U.S. policy makers and by many in the private sector not only as a technology for obtaining critical scientific, weather, and atmospheric data but also as a potentially profitable industry for providing commercially produced data to both the public and the private sectors. The intersection of these two visions of the future of remote sensing, that is, remote sensing as a public good and as a market driver, is the focus of this chapter.

The Development of Satellite Remote Sensing

Earth observation from space is not a recent phenomenon. Yet despite its long history, reaching back to attempts to mount cameras on kites, balloons, and even carrier pigeons, most of the early applications of remote sensing were military rather than civilian in purpose (Colwell 1984). Civilian earth observation grew directly from the use of aerial observation technologies for photo reconnaissance in World War I. Following the war and throughout the 1920s and 1930s, demobilized photogrammetrists initially trained by the military founded a large number of small commercial firms to provide airborne photography, photointerpretation, and photogrammetric services to local governments for mapping and cadastral purposes (Jensen 2000). Although these were commercial endeavors, the scale of these enterprises was small and their markets were localized.

World War II and the cold war that followed it gave another boost to the use of airborne sensors and the development of new technologies such as rocket photography for earth observation (McLucas 1991). However, it was in the postwar period, with the launch of TIROS, a low-altitude, earth-orbiting weather satellite, in 1960 that the U.S. government initiated what became an expanding program of satellite remote sensing for civilian purposes. TIROS, an acronym for the Television and Infrared Observation Satellite, initially provided observations of the atmosphere only in subpolar regions from its sun-synchronous orbit five hundred miles above the earth. By 1965, however, it was extended into polar orbit and provided daily global coverage with data on a two-thousand-mile swath of the earth's surface. TIROS was followed by a geo-synchronous satellite in 1974 called the Geostationary Operational Environmental Satellite that provided continual data on a single region of the earth rather than orbiting the globe. These satellites and their successors continue to be operated by the National Oceanographic and Atmospheric Administration (NOAA) and provide valuable information on atmospheric moisture, temperature, winds, and clouds for weather prediction and monitoring.

In 1972 the National Aeronautics and Space Administration (NASA) launched a civil land observation satellite, the Earth Resources Technology Satellite, later renamed Landsat 1. This was the first in a series of what has now been seven satellites launched as part of the Landsat system. Landsat 6 did not achieve orbit and dropped into the ocean in 1993. However, NASA successfully launched Landsat 7 in 1999 while Landsats 4 and 5 were still in operation, providing data continuity within the Landsat time series. In May 2003, Landsat 7 developed a problem in orbit, and at this writing data are no longer available. At this point it is not clear whether the satellite is recoverable. The space agency is planning for what it calls the Landsat Follow-On (rather than Landsat 8), although it is likely to be years before the satellite is operational. Beginning with the launch of Landsat 1, the sensors used in the Landsat system provided multispectral data with better resolution than the weather satellites and more spectral bands than aerial photography.[1] In general, Landsat data cover a 185-kilometer swath of earth's surface, although Landsat 7 was designed to provide data at 15 meters and up to 60 meters, depending upon what bands in the electromagnetic spectrum were used. The satellite had a repeat cycle of sixteen days (that is, it provided data on the same spot on earth's surface every sixteen days). Landsat's spectral breadth and frequent repeat cycle, together with its focus on land surfaces instead of clouds, opened new possibilities for both applied and scientific uses of remotely sensed data.

From the start, NASA saw its role as both providing the technology for satellite remote sensing and fostering use of the data. This meant that the agency supported demonstration projects based on Landsat data and made the data available for research and applications at low cost (Mack 1990). Early on, the agency established a Technology Transfer Division within the Office of Space and Terrestrial Applications and gave it the responsibility of fostering the use of Landsat data among all potential users, commercial, public sector, and scientific (OAO 1981).

Scientific and Other Uses of Satellite Remote Sensing Data

One of the initial applications of Landsat was based on a mix of foreign and domestic policy concerns. The Large Area Crop Inventory Experiment was established to forecast crop yields using remote sensing data (NRC 1985; Mack 1990). The program, which began in 1974 as a collaboration among NASA, NOAA, the U.S. Department of Agriculture, and several universities, was intended to provide information for agricultural policy. However, it was also related to the U.S. commercial and strategic interest in identifying agricultural capacity in other countries, particularly in the Soviet Union. One of its goals was to provide information so that the United States could avoid a repetition of its experience in 1972, when President Richard Nixon concluded a major sale of surplus grain to the Soviet Union without full knowledge of the agricultural crisis it was facing. Private sector firms claimed they lost money in the grain sale because they had little knowledge of the extent of the Soviet grain failure, information that could have been provided by Landsat (Christian Johannson, pers. comm., April 18, 2002; see also Mack [1990]).

The Large Area Crop Inventory Experiment was a response to this concern. Landsat was able to provide other types of information for foreign policy, as well. For example, in 1985 data produced by Landsat 5 were used to monitor the Russian nuclear power plant disaster at Chernobyl, and after the Gulf war, Landsat data were used to monitor burning oil wells (Dehqanzada and Florini 2000; NRC 2001).

Landsat data have been widely used over the succeeding three decades for civil public and commercial uses, such as mapping; resource exploration and extraction in the petroleum industry; identifying changes in coastal channels; studying land cover, including agriculture, soils, vegetation, minerals, and rock formations; observing settlement patterns; and identifying land use patterns (Mack 1990). They have also been used for site selection, groundwater identification, and mineral prospecting. The U.S. Agency for International Development used remote sensing in the early 1970s for monitoring and assessing natural hazards, environmental change, agriculture, and irrigation patterns in developing countries (Reining 1980; OAO 1981). The agency saw remote sensing as an instrument to foster economic development overseas and supported centers that provided technical training in remote sensing for individuals from many parts of the world.

In addition to these practical and policy applications of the data, however, remote sensing data from Landsat and other sensors were from the start used extensively by earth scientists for geophysical research and interdisciplinary research on environmental and global change. The field of environmental and global change research, which has grown rapidly over the past two decades, is crucially dependent on access to satellite data over multiple time points. At the present time, scientists have access to thirty years of Landsat data, which provides an incomparable database for tracking change on the earth's surface. Scientists have, for example, used remote sensing data to understand the impacts of vegetation and other types of land cover and land use on climate and the interactions of ecosystem type and change with climate in boreal, temperate, and tropical ecosystems (NRC 1999). Other scientists have used remote sensing data to measure the extent and the pace of deforestation in Brazil (Skole and Tucker 1993; Wood and Skole 1998). Among the more widely recognized results of atmospheric research using remote sensing data is its role in identifying and measuring the hole in the ozone layer over Antarctica, which was initially demonstrated in 1985 with data from Nimbus-7 Total Ozone Mapper. Oceanographers use remote sensing to obtain data on sea surface temperature and phytoplankton abundance, and earth observation data are also being used for coastal, hydrological, and natural hazards research (NRC 2002). Even social scientists in such fields as demography and anthropology are beginning to use remote sensing data in their research. For example, Francesca Pozzi, Christopher Small, and Gregory Yetman (2003) have used nighttime satellite images together with gridded census data to model the distribution of human populations on a global scale, and Barbara Entwistle and her colleagues (Entwistle et al. 1998) have studied land use in Thailand using both surveys and satellite data.

New Remote Sensing Capabilities

By the late 1980s, NASA was making plans to launch new satellites with significantly improved sensors. The agency committed itself to building a system of satellites, called the Earth Observing System, over a fifteen-year period. These satellites were intended to provide new types of data at a scale and frequency previously unavailable for scientific research on global environmental change. The first major satellite in the program was TERRA, successfully launched in 1999.

In the private sector, other systems were initiated during the 1990s. Among these was a public-private partnership formed by NASA and Orbital Sciences Corporation to build the Sea-viewing Wide Field-of-view Sensor (SeaWiFS) to obtain ocean color data for both scientific and commercial purposes (NRC 2002). During the same period, several firms in the private sector developed plans for high-resolution satellites that were funded, launched, and operated wholly in the private sector. In 1999, on its second attempt, Space Imaging successfully launched IKONOS, a satellite that provided imagery with one-meter resolution for commercial sales. A second commercial satellite, Quick Bird, was successfully launched by DigitalGlobe in 2001 and a third, Orbview 3, was launched in June 2003.

The United States is not the only country with satellite earth observation capabilities. The Russians preceded the United States into space in 1957 and gained a commercial remote sensing capacity with the establishment of Sovinform-sputnik in 1995, a firm that sells imagery with two-meter resolution. The French established a public-private partnership in remote sensing with the establishment of the Systeme pour l'Observation de la Terre (SPOT), a Landsat-like satellite initially launched in 1986. The system was developed by the French government and has never fully separated public and private sector remote sensing activities. Data sales for SPOT are managed by SPOT Image, a public-private sector partnership. Japan, Canada, India, the European Space Agency, and a number of other countries also operate remote sensing programs. There is even a remote sensing satellite, built by Stellenbosch University, in South Africa.[2]

National Policy for Civilian Remote Sensing

The commercial operation of civil remote sensing satellites has been a recurring theme in U.S. space policy since the time of Landsat 1. Even before the satellite was launched, the Landsat contractor, General Electric, approached

NASA about the possibility of selling similar satellites to other countries and to the private sector for proprietary uses of remote sensing data. NASA responded that the production of proprietary private sector data was in conflict with U.S. policy to provide open access to civil satellite data (Mack 1990). Some developing countries had raised questions about the legality of obtaining remote sensing data on their countries without their consent and the uses to which these data would be put. The U.S. government wanted to provide open access to the civil remote sensing data to avoid foreign policy problems (and possibly to draw attention away from national security satellite data). In fact, when the Landsat data were made publicly available in the early 1970s, the response from a number of developing countries, such as Thailand, Mali, Brazil, Egypt, and Ghana, was to endorse the utility of the new technology (Logsdon 1998, 262–63). As a result, there was less concern about potential objections by foreign governments with the launch of Landsats 2 and 3 in 1975.

However, despite their objections to the proposal by General Electric that it sell satellite systems in other countries, the U.S. government was not opposed to either commercial ownership or commercial management of land remote sensing. The space program was experiencing budget cuts in the 1970s, and the Office of Management and Budget was concerned about undertaking the expense of a continuing series of land observation satellites. In 1977, after Landsats 2 and 3 had been launched, scientists and engineers began planning for Landsats 4 and 5 but encountered objections from the White House Office of Science and Technology Policy. The National Aeronautics and Space Administration argued that the satellite program would not cost the government money in the long run because the usefulness of the data would create a market for it and would lead to commercialization of the program, just as the private sector had assumed responsibility for communications satellites. In short, NASA chose a market model to justify to the Office of Management and Budget the expense of building the Landsat system (NRC 1995). There seemed to be little consideration of the impact on science of using private sector market mechanisms to supply data for research.

The formal policy foundation for commercialization of earth observation was laid in a series of presidential decision directives and acts of Congress, beginning with a directive by President Jimmy Carter (PDD-37) that encouraged the commercial exploitation of space. Carter had been emphasizing the need to reduce federal government expenditures, and land remote sensing appeared to be a strong candidate for the transfer of a function from the public sector to the private sector. In 1978, the same year as Carter's directive, Senator Harrison Schmidt of New Mexico introduced legislation in the Senate that would require creation of an Earth Resources Information Satellite Corporation that was modeled on COMSAT, the private sector corporation that managed communications satellites (Mack 1998). The legislation was never put to a vote, however. In PDD-37 President Carter did not intend to give the private sector full independence of government control. Rather, he maintained that the U.S. government must authorize and regulate commercial remote sensing. Later that year, the Carter administration also committed the United States to providing data continuity in land remote sensing satellites through the 1980s at a minimum and in 1979 transferred responsibility for Landsat operations to NOAA (NRC 1985, 2002). That agency already had responsibility for operational support of satellites used for meteorology, ocean observing, and climate prediction and now added Landsat data continuity through the 1980s to its mandate. The agency was instructed to ensure that there would be two additional Landsat satellites (Landsats 4 and 5). The agency was also directed to examine whether land remote sensing satellites could be operated by the private sector. After this transfer of operational responsibility to NOAA, NASA increasingly focused its attention on scientific remote sensing and technological innovation in earth observation satellites.

The Carter commitment to commercial exploitation of remote sensing technologies was enthusiastically advanced by the Reagan administration in the early 1980s, when private sector assumption of what had previously been considered government responsibilities was actively encouraged in a number of areas. The Reagan administration did not, however, maintain the government's commitment under President Carter to Landsat data continuity.[3] The Cabinet Council on Commerce and Trade, chaired by the secretary of commerce, was asked in 1981 to examine whether both Landsat and the country's weather satellites could be transferred to the private sector (NRC 1985). In response to the administration's enthusiasm for privatizing government satellites, COMSAT offered to assume responsibility for both Landsat and the government's weather satellites. The proposed transfer of the nation's weather satellites to the private sector was opposed by both houses of Congress, which held a series of hearings in 1983 on this issue (U.S. House of Representatives 1983). Members of Congress had previously been, and continued to be, willing to consider transfer of earth observation satellites to the private sector. However, under the leadership of Don Fuqua, a congressman from Florida, Congress decisively rejected the proposal to privatize the weather satellites and passed concurrent resolutions in both houses expressing their belief that operation of the meteorological satellites should remain the responsibility of the government (NRC 1985; Mack and Williamson 1998). The argument for maintaining government responsibility for meteorological satellites was that it was in the public interest for the federal government to continue to provide information on the weather. Members of Congress pointed out that it had long been the responsibility of the federal government to protect property and public safety and that weather forecasts and warnings of severe weather events were essential to the public safety. They believed that it was not in the public interest to sell the satellites that made these forecasts possible (Logsdon 1998, 321–29).

Both the Congress and the Reagan administration also recognized that the policy dispute about meteorological satellites was threatening to derail the plan to transfer land observation satellites to the private sector. COMSAT and the government weather data model presented two opposing models of how to manage civil land remote sensing, one private and one public. Unlinking the privatization of meteorological satellites from the privatization of land satellites and abandonment of the plan to privatize the weather satellites made it possible for the Reagan administration to move ahead on its plans to privatize the civil land remote sensing system. Arguments for the transfer of these satellites to the private sector were rooted in a desire to reduce federal government expenditures, confidence in the existence of a viable private sector market for remote sensing images, and a pervasive belief that private sector operations were inherently more efficient than government operations. In addition, there was a widely held belief that the United States needed a strong private sector capability in remote sensing operations to be competitive with other nations, particularly the French, who were about to launch SPOT as a commercial satellite.

The Reagan administration eliminated funding for planning Landsats 6 and 7 in its revised 1982 budget on the assumption that continuity of the Landsat system and these two satellites would be supported by the private sector. In 1984, the policy dispute about weather satellites settled, Congress passed the Land Remote-Sensing Commercialization Act of 1984, which established a process for commercialization of Landsat data sales and gave the secretary of commerce responsibility for the process. The legislation specifically prohibited transfer of weather satellites to the private sector, but it declared that "competitive, market-driven private sector involvement in land remote sensing is in the national interest of the United States" (*Land Remote-Sensing Commercialization Act of 1984,* n.p.). The legislation also emphasized that although the private sector was "best suited to develop land remote-sensing data markets," there should be cooperation between the federal government and private industry to build subsequent satellites that would provide Landsat data continuity.

Shortly thereafter, in 1985, NOAA awarded a competitive contract to the Earth Observation Satellite Company (EOSAT), a joint venture of Hughes Aircraft and RCA, that allowed it to sell data from both Landsat 4 (which had been launched in 1982) and Landsat 5 (which was launched by NASA in 1985) in the commercial market. Under the 1984 act, the federal government was to continue to support operations of the system to allow EOSAT to develop a private market for the data (Mack and Williamson 1998). The company was expected to create a data market large enough to support future Landsat satellite operations. Agreement on a plan to capitalize the construction of future Landsat satellites was difficult to achieve, and eventually the government decided to support the construction of only one more satellite,

Landsat 6. This decision meant that the United States had no provision for land satellites beyond the launch of Landsat 6 in 1992. However, the extensive use of French SPOT data in 1991 during the Gulf war, together with the growing interest in Landsat data for global change research and recognition that, without any Landsat capability beyond Landsat 6, the French would dominate the international market for land remote sensing data, persuaded U.S. policy makers to reconsider this stance. In 1992, declaring that the basic purposes of Landsat data were research and national security, Congress transferred control of Landsat to the Department of Defense and NASA (U.S. Congress 1994).

The Land Remote-Sensing Policy Act of 1992 was in part a response to what had been a growing concern in the research community about the high cost of Landsat data in the private sector (Morain 1998). Scientists found that the cost of Landsat images had increased by a factor of ten, and the growing scientific use of land remote sensing data had declined. The 1992 legislation specifically noted that "the cost of Landsat data has impeded the use of such data for scientific purposes, such as for global environmental change research, as well as for other public sector applications" (*Land Remote-Sensing Policy Act of 1992,* n.p.).

Yet even before responsibility for Landsat 4 data sales was transferred to the private sector, NOAA had been instructed to recover the operating costs of the satellite through data sales. To do this, the agency tripled the price of the data. As a result, sales declined substantially, and consequently there was no increase in revenue (NRC 1985). When EOSAT assumed responsibility for marketing Landsat data and attempted to recover its operating costs, it encountered the same problem. Landsat data that had previously cost the user $400 now cost $4,400. Although there were some government and commercial data purchases, scientific use of Landsat 4 and Landsat 5 data declined rapidly because of the high cost of the data. This was widely perceived to be a consequence of turning data sales over to the private sector, but it was, in fact, a consequence of the attempt to recover costs by charging for data, whether by the private or the public sector.

After the failed launch of Landsat 6 in 1993, EOSAT and the U.S. government concluded a new agreement on the cost and right to reproduce Landsats 4 and 5 data purchased by the government and affiliated nonprofit users, including educational institutions and scientists conducting research related to global change (Sheffner 1999). Under this agreement, new images would cost government and affiliated users no more than $2,500, and images archived at the U.S. Geological Service's EROS Data Center (named after the Earth Resources Observation System, an early Department of Interior program for obtaining information on natural resources by satellite) would cost $425. In 1994 a presidential decision directive spread Landsat responsibility across three federal agencies, assigning formal responsibility for the construction and launch of Landsat 7 to NASA, management of the spacecraft and ground systems to NOAA, and Landsat 7 data archiving and distribution to the EROS Data Center in Sioux Falls, South Dakota.

The Commercial Role in Remote Sensing

There are a number of ways that commercial firms can be and have been involved in civil satellite remote sensing since the launch of Landsat in 1972. They include government construction and satellite operation contracts; data distribution and sales; value-added services; and, most recently, vehicle launch and operation, with sales or licensing of the data obtained from the satellites. From its start, civil remote sensing, like military remote sensing, has involved a high degree of collaboration between the public and private sectors. Private sector aerospace contractors have been involved in both the planning and construction of satellites for the government. Landsat 1, which was put into orbit by NASA in 1972, was actually built by General Electric under a NASA contract and was launched by NASA at Vandenburg Air Force Base (Specht 2002). The satellite's sensor, the MultiSpectral Scanner, was developed by another private sector firm, Hughes Aircraft Company (McDougall 1985). Private sector firms continue to play a major role in earth observation satellite and sensor construction. A second form of commercialization is the operation and sale of data from satellites built by the government. An example of this type of commercialization, more appropriately called "privatization," is the sale of Landsat 4 and Landsat 5 to EOSAT in 1984 and the commercial sale of Landsat data by EOSAT after that time. A third type of commercialization is through private sector value-added reseller firms that provide data products to customers. These firms obtain, process, and analyze data from multiple sources, including airborne sensors and both government and commercial remote sensing satellites. Like the airborne remote sensing firms that initially appeared in the interwar period, many of these value-added firms are small and serve local markets.

In the 1990s, however, the term "commercialization" increasingly came to be used to refer to private ownership and operation of remote sensing systems or to public-private partnerships. Enabled by Title II of the Land Remote-Sensing Policy Act of 1992 and a new presidential decision directive (PDD-23) that provided for the licensing and operation of private remote sensing systems in 1994, the Department of Commerce, through NOAA, began to issue licenses to private sector firms for satellite operations (Williamson 1997). To date, almost twenty licenses have been issued. They include licenses to Space Imaging and EarthWatch (now DigitalGlobe), private sector firms that now operate satellites and sell high-resolution data commercially to public, academic, and private sector customers. Earlier, a license was issued to OrbImage, a subsidiary of Orbital Sciences, for the Sea-viewing Wide

Field-of-view Sensor, a satellite built under a public-private partnership agreement that enables the private sector partner to sell satellite data commercially as they are obtained and, after a fourteen-day period, to provide the data through NASA to scientists at no cost.

Although commercial remote sensing firms are fully funded through private sector investments, they are still subject to government policies and regulations through the licensing process, which imposes conditions on the operation of commercial remote sensing firms. These firms are subject to government shutter control if it is deemed necessary for purposes of national security. There had initially been a prohibition against the production of civil remote sensing data at one-meter resolution because of the possibility that these data could be used for military or security purposes. President Bill Clinton decided to relax that prohibition when it became clear that high-resolution data were already being produced in other countries and that the United States' reluctance to make high-resolution data publicly available worldwide was limiting both its competitiveness and the market for its data. Beginning in 2001, NOAA issued licenses to private sector firms to produce data at even finer resolution (0.5 meters) for the commercial market. The capacity to produce and license high-resolution data worldwide opened up multiple markets—both civil and military—to potential private sector remote sensing firms. To protect national security, however, the federal government also imposed a shutter control policy on commercial remote sensing firms. Under this policy, the U.S. government can prohibit the distribution of remote sensing images during a national emergency or crisis in order to protect the government's exclusive access to data and to prevent potential enemies or other governments from gaining access to the data. Thus although the federal government restricts access to sensitive information through its licensing authority, it has not attempted to interfere in the market for the data except for reasons of national security. More specifically, it has not intervened to impose more liberal access practices for scientific research, even though that research can have demonstrable public benefits.

A second issue that arose with the establishment of private sector, high-resolution land remote sensing was related to the creation of markets for data. Despite the brave assertion in the Land Remote-Sensing Commercialization Act of 1984 that the private sector was best able to create a market for remote sensing data, there was increasing discussion of the influence of the federal government on private sector markets for remote sensing data. In the mid-1990s, according to a report of the National Research Council's Space Studies Board (NRC 1995, 127), the market for remote sensing data was "mixed but is currently dominated by governmental needs. The aggregate investment in governmental earth observations for research and operational needs vastly exceeds any commercial activity at present, or any likely in the immediate future." As NASA began to emphasize the development of smaller satellites for research data, many in the private sector complained that it was competing with them. In 1994 a report to the Congress by its Office of Technology Assessment suggested that Congress might consider encouraging NASA to purchase data on the private market. "Such a mechanism," the report went on, "has the advantage of providing the government with needed data while assisting private firms in developing new earth observation systems" (U.S. Congress 1994, 17). However, the advantages to be gained in the private sector, it increasingly appeared, required the financial support of the public sector to be realized. Moreover, NASA had two fundamental earth science missions: to support research and to advance the technology of satellite remote sensing. The agency's purchase of privately produced remote sensing data for research left it without a means to meet its second mission, advancing earth observation technologies and planning higher-risk satellite programs to improve the technology of earth observation.

At present, three privately funded and operated satellites have been successfully launched, two of which have been selling data commercially for several years. However, the data from these satellites are not sold, as the term is conventionally used. Rather, data are "licensed" to users, who pay for the privilege of using the data but are restricted from redistributing them. This restriction negatively affects scientific use of the data. Although the presumption behind the concept of a "market" for commercial remote sensing data in the scientific community is based on the idea that scientists will purchase a license to use a specific image (at commercial prices) for their research, the most significant financial investment in commercially produced data for use by scientists has been by the U.S. government. The Science Data Purchase Program, more commonly known as the Science Data Buy, was created by Congress essentially as a market stimulation program that would also provide scientists with commercially produced data. Through its 1997 appropriation, Congress instructed NASA to spend $50 million on commercially produced remote sensing data for scientific research (NRC 2002).

Science is not the only arena in which the federal government has attempted to stimulate the market for privately produced remote sensing data. In 2002 the Central Intelligence Agency instructed its agencies to use more commercial satellite data, and in May 2003 President George W. Bush, in a major space policy statement, ordered federal agencies to expand their use of satellite images produced in the private sector (Eric Lichtblau, "U.S. to Rely More on Private Companies' Satellite Images," *New York Times,* May 13, 2003, p. A-26).

Remote Sensing Data for Scientific Research

Since the launch of Landsat 1 in the early 1970s, complex interactions among technological, economic, institutional, and political forces have resulted in the establishment of a series of remote sensing systems and the availability of a steady stream of civil satellite data and information. As the U.S. government was trying to work out a satisfactory balance between public and private sector responsibilities in civil satellite remote sensing, the scientific community was becoming increasingly dependent upon earth observation satellites for research data. By 1994, the Office of Technology Assessment found that scientists and universities were among the primary users of civil remote sensing data (U.S. Congress 1994).

Traditionally, scientists have obtained research data in a variety of ways, each of which raises slightly different data policy issues. Scientists collect data or observations for their research through direct observations or experiments, obtain and adapt data initially collected by government or other institutions for administrative or other operational purposes, or obtain data from community data resources that are explicitly intended to be used by large numbers of scientists. In the first model, data requirements are determined by individual investigators, and data collection is treated as a routine part of a research project. The observations and measurements obtained are defined by the requirements of a specific analytic problem. In this model, scientists base their research on their data and devote significant portions of their careers to data collection. Nor surprisingly, they often take a proprietary stance in regard to sharing their data with other scientists. Although the argument for refusing to share the data is rarely couched in terms of intellectual property, there is an operating assumption that any data collected by a scientist for a specific research purpose belong to that scientist and his or her research assistants. Other scientists are able to evaluate and use the data only in the context of scientific publications.

A different data model exists in some research areas of the social sciences. In such disciplines as sociology, political science, history, and economics, data obtained by the government (and occasionally the private sector) for administrative and statistical purposes (such as the decennial census of the United States and local records of vital statistics) can be used in research. The federal government also obtains information on income, employment status, and family expenditures for economic and social policy purposes. In the United States, these publicly collected statistics are available to potential data users, including social scientists, without charge or for minimal cost.

Still a third approach to obtaining research data is to create major research databases that are designed from the start to serve as a resource for scientists across the research community. In the social sciences, the National Science Foundation has supported the collection of research data, such as the American National Election Studies and the General Social Survey, for widespread use in the research community (NRC 1982).

The earth sciences have a long tradition of developing community data resources for use by many scientists. As early as the 1880s, scientists working under the auspices of the International Polar Commission established forty observing stations to provide data on the two polar regions and certain areas in temperate latitudes. Fifty years later, a similar data collection effort was undertaken as part of the Second Polar Year (the first effort was retroactively named the First Polar Year) in which scientists from forty countries obtained research data. The third, and most ambitious effort, took place in 1957, when the third international effort to obtain earth science observations was established. This was the International Geophysical Year. Instead of the polar focus of the first two international efforts, this project was intended to provide coordinated scientific observations on geophysical phenomena on the earth and the earth's atmosphere over an eighteen-month period, beginning on July 1, 1957 (Miller and Jacobson 1991). The timing of the International Geophysical Year was related to the expected intensification of solar activity and the desire to obtain solar data.

The International Geophysical Year was considered to be highly successful. Although its most well known result was the Soviet launch of Sputnik, the first orbital satellite, the International Geophysical Year also produced earth science data on a scale previously unknown. The U.S. Antarctic station, for example, produced seventeen tons of records. Scientific research on the aurora borealis, cosmic rays, geomagnetism, glaciology, gravity, ionospheric physics, and a number of other fields was enriched with International Geophysical Year data. One outgrowth of this program was the establishment of the World Data Center Program by the International Council of Scientific Unions. One of the principal purposes of the World Data Centers was to promote international access to scientific data and, in particular, to ensure that scientific data collected under the auspices of the International Geophysical Year was freely available to scientists on both sides of the Iron Curtain (ICSU 1996). Since the International Geophysical Year, data from civil earth observation satellites have been widely used in scientific research. Both NASA and NOAA have built and launched a number of satellites that provide data for scientific research, and both agencies maintain a number of data centers and services to make the data available to the research community (Zygielbaum 1993).[4]

Impacts of the Commercialization of Remote Sensing on Science

The major remote sensing data policy issues for scientists are data continuity, access to heritage or legacy data, free and open access to current data, and the capacity to redistribute data used in research. Some of the issues that limit scientists' use of commercial remote sensing data are related to the limitations on the right to reproduce and disseminate the data to other scientists, the lack of open access archiving of legacy or heritage data to measure change over time, the cost of obtaining data, and the speed of data delivery. These issues have an immediate effect on science data use. For example, the principle that research data should be shared and redistributed within the scientific community is now widely recognized by scientists and enforced by research funding agencies in the federal government. However, commercial data-licensing restrictions prohibit redistribution of data that are obtained by commercial satellites. This is a case in which the market-driven demands of the industry to recover investment and make a profit for investors through repeated licensing of the same data undermine the consensus in the science community that there should be free and open access to research data. Scientific research data, which was previously considered a public good, has become the intellectual property of private sector firms. The contradiction in U.S. government policy, which simultaneously supports policies to encourage free and open access to research data and to commercialize research data, is ignored.

Because of the accumulation of three decades of civil remote sensing images, satellite data can be used to do new types of scientific research. Scientists interested in the analysis of environmental and global changes over time have thirty years of earth observation images to use in detecting patterns of change over time. This type of research will be more difficult, or even impossible, if the principal source of scientific data is available only commercially. Both the cost of the data to scientists and the coverage provided by the private sector are problems. Unlike government satellite operations, commercial data producers do not routinely obtain global coverage or even periodically repeated coverage of specific parts of earth's surface. Although private sector satellites are continuously in orbit, the shutters of the sensors are opened to obtain data only when firms have an order for a particular image. Even assuming that all images procured by private sector remote sensing firms are archived for later use by scientists and others, this biases the data significantly. In a few years, there may well be a commercial remote sensing archive, but the images it holds will be those that have been ordered by clients of the commercial firm. There will be no continuous land observations over earth's surface for scientific analysis and comparisons of change over time. Although the federal government has purchased commercial data for specific global data sets, the cost of contracting with private sector firms for continuous or even periodic global coverage would be too expensive for routine monitoring or data collection.

Speed of data delivery was initially a problem for scientists obtaining data from commercial satellite remote sensing firms under the Science Data Buy. The time between placing an order and obtaining data is always dependent upon orbit, cloud cover, and processing time. However, under the Science Data Buy, timely data delivery to scientists was often slow. There is some anecdotal evidence that now that two firms are competing to provide high-resolution data to the same markets, the speed of delivery has improved.

However, in addition to those issues that directly influence scientists' acquisition and use of research data, other issues related to the commercialization of earth observation remote sensing could affect the earth science research enterprise. When scientific data are produced as a result of a national industrial strategy rather than a scientific research strategy, commercially appropriate but scientifically problematic changes in the technical requirements, management, and availability of the data could be implemented. For example, when the production of new satellites for scientific data was the responsibility of government science agencies such as NASA or NOAA, scientific requirements defined the technological requirements, and science data needs drove the data requirements of the system. Under a private sector system, in which data are produced for an anticipated commercial market, data and system requirements are determined by estimates of the size of anticipated markets, principal user requirements, and capacity to pay. Initial predictions for the market for commercial satellite remote sensing data in the 1990s emphasized the central importance of government markets and generally ignored the science market (Fritz 1996).

Not all the impacts are negative. The three commercial satellites in orbit today produce data at significantly higher resolution than most government satellites. Initially, some scientists responded to the availability of these data by arguing that although the high resolution might be useful for a few types of research, the narrow swath width of the data was a problem, particularly for global change research.[5] Other scientists, participating in a workshop sponsored by the National Research Council, argued that scientific research had been adapted to government-produced low-resolution data because they were available and that commercial high-resolution data could open up new types of scientific research. Moreover, the high-resolution data available through the private sector could be used to calibrate the low-resolution, wide-swath data and make it more useful (NRC 2002).

If scientists become more dependent upon commercially produced research data than on government-produced data in the future, however, new problems may arise. Data gaps owing to the bias imposed by commercial sales is one. Another is related to the potential loss of access to earth observation data because of the federal government's exercise of shutter control in cases of war, national emergency, or foreign policy needs. This has not been a problem thus far, but it could become one in the future, although this may be no different from inevitable curtailment of access to earth observation images in a time or site of war or national emergency.

There is also a concern within the scientific community that existing private sector remote sensing firms will not be able to create a sufficiently large commercial market for their data and hence will not survive. If this were to happen, there could be an abrupt end to the availability of high-resolution data for research unless the government assumed responsibility for the private sector satellites. Such a hiatus in remote sensing capability, were it to occur, would have an impact on scientific research similar to the hiatus in the supply of remote sensing images for research caused by the increase in prices for Landsat images in the 1980s.

There are at least two other models for public-private roles in space that encourage the development of private sector enterprises and at the same time could also provide inexpensive, widespread data for scientific research. The first is exemplified by weather satellites and the second by global positioning satellites. In both cases, the federal government builds, launches, and operates the satellites that provide data. In the case of meteorological or weather satellites, the private sector then uses the information produced by public sector satellites as the basis of profitable businesses. In the case of global positioning satellites, a viable and growing private sector industry has developed to provide devices for downloading and using positioning data.

Private sector or commercial remote sensing is based on a different model, one in which financial support for the entire satellite enterprise is assumed by the private sector. The initial expenses of satellite construction, launch, and operations are high, but the marginal costs of producing a specific image are low. To reduce the impact of the high initial costs, the federal government has provided some financial incentives to the industry through guaranteed purchases of data for both operational and scientific purposes. However, it is still not clear whether this model is financially viable. There is a valid question as to whether the heavy initial investment in satellite design and launch is actually recoverable through commercial transactions.

As long as there is a strong government interest in earth observation data for scientific research (to say nothing of mapping, national security, and other governmental uses of the data), it may be more practical for the federal government to guarantee its continuing access to high-resolution earth observation data by constructing and launching high-resolution satellites itself and licensing private sector firms for commercial uses of the data. An alternative is for the federal government to develop long-term contracts with private satellite companies for the collection and open dissemination of data for scientific research. Either effort could be advised and financially supported by a coalition of government remote sensing data users (including science agencies that are not involved in satellite remote sensing). This approach would be similar to the cooperation of the Department of Defense, NOAA, and NASA in building the National Polar Orbiting Operational Environmental Satellite System. Multiagency collaboration in civil remote sensing was tried with Landsat, but the division of labor among collaborating agencies was strictly functional, and strategic planning and collaboration across agencies was limited. Moreover, when attempts at cost recovery through commercial sales were implemented in the 1980s, both operational and data user experience with civil earth observation satellites was in its infancy. The community of remote sensing data users was small, and there was not a sufficiently large market to support the industry. The effort is widely judged to have failed.

A second, related question is whether the supply of civil high-resolution data should be controlled or governed by the private sector. Although a government license is required for commercial remote sensing data production, the licensing process is focused on data resolution, shutter control policies, and ultimate disposition of the data. It does not attempt to influence or regulate commercial market activities. Broader government regulation of the satellite remote sensing industry, in addition to the initial licensing process, might provide a way for scientists in nonprofit institutions such as universities to obtain access to high-resolution commercial data for their research and ensure that widely accepted scientific practices such as redistribution of research data are not violated under intellectual property or licensing restrictions imposed by the need of data producers to turn a profit.

If the federal government continues its policy of encouraging the development of a private sector remote sensing industry, there are other approaches to improving data access for scientists and increasing the market for commercial data products. The commercial sector could change its approach to scientific data provision. Instead of viewing scientists as a market segment of potential (paying) data customers, private sector data producers could segment the use of remote sensing data by scientists in nonprofit institutions like universities and, with federal help, subsidize their access to commercially produced data in exchange for their conducting research on remote sensing applications and training the remote sensing workforce. The argument for this approach is that the industry will obtain more benefit from widespread scientific use of data than from limited direct data sales to scientists.

This approach would encourage scientists to contribute directly to expansion of the commercial market for remote sensing data in at least two important ways. First, their research could contribute to the development of new capabilities and applications of remote sensing data, enlarging the potential market for commercial remote sensing images. This is particularly vital as the private sector assumes what was previously NASA's role in providing data for scientific research. As federal roles in earth observation evolved over the past two decades, NASA emerged with a dual responsibility: to provide data for scientific research and to advance the technology of remote sensing. The private sector is assuming only one of these responsibilities, data provision. Unless the increasing need for ways to promote technological innovation in remote sensing is addressed, the United States may find itself losing its technological lead. In the current policy environment, university scientists can play a larger role in technological innovation—if they have the open access to data and funding for technological innovation that encourages them to design research and engineering projects using remote sensing.

A second function of university scientists that could contribute to a more effective commercialization strategy is their capacity to educate and train new scientists and technologists for work in remote sensing applications. Future advances in the use of remote sensing data and growth of a viable commercial market will depend not only on the availability of data but also on the availability of trained professionals who can employ the data in applied settings. These people are prepared for employment in universities. One of the ironies of the U.S. policy to encourage the private sector to assume what had previously been governmental responsibilities in remote sensing is that the private sector has not done well in creating a commercial market outside the government for its products. Even the so-called science market for commercial imagery has been subsidized by the federal government through the Science Data Buy. The emphasis of commercial image providers has been on developing, launching, and operating the satellites rather than on nurturing commercial markets for the data. Providing a separate stream of free and open remote sensing data for scientists in nonprofit institutions could begin to rectify a part of this problem by expanding the pipeline of trained technical experts for commercial remote sensing applications.

Making commercially produced data freely available to scientists in universities for purposes of research and education will not resolve all the issues raised by the transfer of what had originally been a function of federal science agencies to the private sector. Archiving and providing access to heritage or legacy data and the ongoing bias in data acquisition practices that responds to actual data orders (the nonscientific market) rather than the scientific need for continuous monitoring are two issues that still need to be addressed.

These issues, and the cost of licensing data, have meant that the privatization of remote sensing has limited and will continue to limit scientific access to the new high-resolution data even as it has provided a new type of data for research. The worst-case result of the federal government's policy of commercialization in the field of satellite remote sensing is that the private sector remote sensing firms do not survive. The industry has relied on the federal government to guarantee short-term returns from scientific markets for data, continuing in a traditional model of public-private collaboration in which private sector firms work under government contract rather than building new and independent commercially robust markets for their data. True commercialization requires that the private sector cultivate its strengths, that is, expand into new markets, build new capacity, and introduce profitable economies of scale. These have been difficult to accomplish in the remote sensing industry, but by enlisting university scientists as participants in the process rather than merely as customers for the data, the private sector may be able to succeed.

Notes

1. Spatial resolution is the term used to describe the size of objects that a satellite sensor can detect on the ground. Spectral bands refer to the bands in the electromagnetic spectrum that are differentiated by a satellite sensor. Panchromatic sensors provide data from one broad band; multispectral sensors can differenti-

ate between three and seven color bands; and hyperspectral sensors use many spectral bands.

2. Sunsat 1, a land-based observation satellite, was launched for Stellenbosch University by the U.S. Air Force in February 1999. The satellite is no longer in operation, but a successor, Sunsat 2, is currently under construction.

3. As part of its attempt to increase the user base for Landsat, NASA had commissioned a study of technology transfer of remote sensing to the private sector. One of the presumptions of this study was that private sector adoption of the technology had been held back because of the fear that there would not be continuity in data availability over time. See OAO (1981).

4. NASA is also engaged in space observation, both by satellite (such as the Hubble Space Telescope) and in other types of missions.

5. There is an inverse relationship between resolution and swath width. Low-resolution data have a wider swath width than high-resolution data.

References

Braunschvig, David, Richard I. Garwin, and Jeremy C. Maxwell. 2003. "Space Diplomacy." *Foreign Affairs* 82(4): 156–64.

Colwell, Robert N. 1984. "From Photographic Interpretation to Remote Sensing." *Photogrammetric Engineering and Remote Sensing* 30(9): 1305–7.

Dehqanzada, Yahya A., and Ann M. Florini. 2000. *Secrets for Sale: How Commercial Satellite Imagery Will Change the World.* Washington, D.C.: Carnegie Endowment for International Peace.

Entwistle, Barbara, Stephan J. Walsh, Ronald J. Rindfuss, and Aphichat Chamratrithirong. 1998. "Land-Use/Land-Cover and Population Dynamics, Nang Rong, Thailand." In *People and Pixels: Linking Remote Sensing and Social Science,* edited by Diana Liverman, Emilio F. Moran, Ronald R. Rindfuss, and Paul C. Stern. Washington: National Academy Press.

Fritz, Lawrence W. 1996. "The Era of Commercial Earth Observation Satellites." *Photogrammetric Engineering and Remote Sensing* (January): 39–45.

International Council of Scientific Unions (ICSU). 1996. Panel on World Data Centers. *World Data Center System Guide.* Paris: ICSU.

Jensen, John R. 2000. *Remote Sensing of the Environment: An Earth Resource Perspective.* Upper Saddle River, N.J.: Prentice Hall.

Krepon, Michael. 2001. "Lost in Space: The Misguided Drive Toward Antisatellite Weapons." *Foreign Affairs* 80(May–June): 3.

Land Remote-Sensing Commercialization Act of 1984. 1984. Public Law 98-365, 98 Stat. 451 (July 17).

Land Remote-Sensing Policy Act of 1992. 1992. Public Law 102-555, 106 Stat. 4163 (October 28).

Logsdon, John M., ed. 1998. *Exploring the Unknown: Selected Documents in the History of the U.S. Civilian Space Program.* Vol. 3, *Using Space.* Washington: National Aeronautics and Space Administration.

Mack, Pamela E. 1990. *Viewing the Earth: The Social Construction of the Landsat Satellite System.* Cambridge, Mass.: MIT Press.

———. 1998. "LANDSAT and the Rise of Earth Resources Monitoring." In *From Engineering Science to Big Science: The NACA and NASA Collier Trophy Research Project Winners,* edited by Pamela E. Mack. NASA History Series. Available at: www.history.nasa.gov/SP-4219/contents.html (accessed July 15, 2002).

Mack, Pamela E., and Ray A. Williamson. 1998. "Observing the Earth from Space." In *Exploring the Unknown: Selected Documents in the History of the U.S. Civilian Space Program.* Vol. 3, *Using Space,* edited by John M. Logsdon. Washington: National Aeronautics and Space Administration.

McDougall, Walter A. 1985. . . . *The Heavens and the Earth: A Political History of the Space Age.* New York: Basic Books.

McLucas, John L. 1991. *Space Commerce.* Cambridge, Mass.: Harvard University Press.

Miller, Roberta Balstad, and Harold K. Jacobson. 1991. "International Collaboration in Science: Building on the Past." Paper presented at the American Association for the Advancement of Science. Washington, D.C.

Morain, Stanley. 1998. "A Brief History of Remote Sensing Applications, with Emphasis on Landsat." In *People and Pixels: Linking Remote Sensing and Social Science,* edited by Diana Liverman, Emilio F. Moran, Ronald R. Rindfuss, and Paul C. Stern. Washington: National Academy Press.

National Research Council (NRC). 1982. Committee on Basic Research in the Behavioral and Social Sciences. *Behavioral and Social Science Research: A National Resource.* Washington: National Academy Press.

———. 1985. Space Applications Board. *Remote Sensing of the Earth from Space: A Program in Crisis.* Washington: National Academy Press.

———. 1995. Space Studies Board. *Earth Observations from Space: History, Promise, and Reality.* Washington: National Academy Press.

———. 1999. Committee on Global Change Research. *Global Environmental Change: Research Pathways for the Next Decade.* Washington: National Academy Press.

———. 2001. Steering Committee on Space Applications and Commercialization. *Transforming Remote Sensing Data into Information and Applications.* Washington: National Academy Press.

———. 2002. Steering Committee on Space Applications and Commercialization. *Toward New Partnerships: Government, The Private Sector and Earth Science Research.* Washington: National Academies Press.

Nelson, Richard R. 2001. "On the Complexities and Limits of Market Organization." Unpublished paper.

OAO Corporation. 1981. *Analysis of the Private Market for Landsat Products and Applications: Final Report, prepared for the Office of Space and Terrestrial Applications, NASA.* Beltsville, Md.: OAO Corporation.

Pozzi, Francesca, Christopher Small, and Gregory Yetman. 2003. "Modeling the Distribution of Human Population with Nighttime Satellite Imagery and Gridded Population of the World." *Earth Observation Magazine* 12(4): 24–30.

Reining, Priscilla. 1980. *Challenging Desertification in West Africa: Insights from Landsat into Carrying Capacity, Cultivation and Settlement Sites in Upper Volta and Niger.* Papers in International Studies, Africa Series 39. Athens: Ohio University Center for International Studies, Africa Program.

Sheffner, Ed. 1999. *Landsat Program Management/EOSAT Agreement.* April 6, 1999. Available at: landsat.gsfc.nasa.gov/project/apr11.htm (accessed April 14, 2002).

Skole, David, and Compton Tucker. 1993. "Tropical Deforestation and Habitat Fragmentation in the Amazon: Satellite Data from 1978 to 1988." *Science* 247: 1431–38.

SpaceNews Business Report. 2002. *Space News Top 50:2001.* Accessed July 14, 2002, at: www.space.com/spacenews/top50_2001.html.

Specht, Jeff. 2002. "Remembering Where It All Began." *Imaging Notes* 17(2): 4.

U.S. Congress. 1994. Office of Technology Assessment. *Civilian Satellite Remote Sensing: A Strategic Approach.* OTA-ISS-607. Washington: U.S. Government Printing Office (September 1994).

U.S. House of Representatives. 1983. Committee on Science and Technology. *The Commercialization of Meteorological and Land Remote-Sensing Satellites: Hearing before the Subcommittee on Natural Resources, Agricultural Research, and Environment, and the Subcommittee on Space Science and Applications of the Committee on Science and Technology.* Committee report on April 14, June 21, June 28, November 8, and November 9, 1983.

Williamson, Ray A. 1997. "The Landsat Legacy: Remote Sensing Policy and the Development of Commercial Remote Sensing." *Photogrammetric Engineering and Remote Sensing* 63(7): 877–85.

Wood, Charles, and David Skole. 1998. "Linking Satellite, Census, and Survey Data to Study Deforestation in the Brazilian Amazon." In *People and Pixels: Linking Remote Sensing and Social Science,* edited by Diana Liverman, Emilio F. Moran, Ronald R. Rindfuss, and Paul C. Stern. Washington: National Academy Press.

Zygielbaum, Arthur, ed. 1993. *Earth and Space Sciences Information Systems.* Proceedings of the American Institute of Physics Conference. New York: American Institute of Physics.

Part IV

PROTECTING THE PUBLIC
AND THE STATE

P ART IV is concerned with two functions that are widely agreed to be the
responsibility of government: protecting the public health and running
elections and the legislative process. In contrast with the activities and sectors considered up to now, for which a case can be made (and, of course, argued
against) that some form of market governance is appropriate, no one really disputes that these activities fall under the province of government. The issue in
these two areas is how much marketlike activity to allow around the edges.

An earlier chapter treats the current disputes about how to organize and
govern private medical care. The stakes here clearly are high. Yet it almost certainly is the case that the improvements in health and longevity experienced in
relatively affluent countries over the past century have had much more to do
with effective public health measures than with advances in private medicine.

Chapter 12 addresses the system of public health care. Public health measures include activities like eradicating and keeping under control insect populations that spread disease and diagnosing and organizing treatments to contain
potential epidemics, which directly involve the use of public funds. The work
may or may not be contracted out to private firms, but the demand is for a public good. Public health activity also includes regulatory activities, like ensuring the safety of water supplies and the cleanliness of restaurants. Some public
health measures, like ensuring an adequate level of vaccination for contagious
diseases, yield private benefits as well as public but would not proceed far
enough absent regulatory enforcement.

The issue of how to govern and organize public health activities is interesting in its own right. The discussion of that issue in this volume also is interesting because many of the issues relating to public health are typical of
activities providing public goods more generally.

Chapter 13, which addresses the impact of financing on public elections
and legislation, concerns activities that are innately considered governmental
and in which there are good reasons to fence out markets. Actually, in a wide
range of human activities, keeping markets away is the problem. Thus, as the
metaphor suggests, many people believe that love should not be for sale; but

of course it is, at least in some circumstances and to some degree. Parents are not expected to use their children for their personal gain if doing so works against the children's best interests, and there are laws to guard against it; however, the issues that arise here are often difficult to sort out. When religious organizations or their leaders are viewed as going hard after personal financial gain, that is widely viewed as a problem; but it is also widely recognized that churches and church activities need financial support. As noted in the introduction to this volume, a long-standing intellectual tradition sees the market as a greater threat to cooperative civil society than the state. But the activities of civil society often make significant use of market mechanisms.

Perhaps the most important arena in which the purpose of the activities would seem to call for fencing out the market, or severely constraining its influence, is the domain of democratic politics and governance, where the basic ideology is of equal rights and equal voice for all citizens. It is basic to democratic principles that police should not be bribed, or juries or judges bought, or elections or the votes of elected officials swayed by money. But of course money, and markets, have influence in all of these areas.

12

PUBLIC HEALTH

Kristine M. Gebbie

W HAT IS "public health"? Concern for the public's health is long-standing in organized societies, but the term "public health" has multiple meanings, some of which contribute to a confusing debate on the application or impact of market forces. Public health has most recently been described by the Institute of Medicine as those organized activities undertaken by a community or society to create the conditions within which people can be healthy (Committee on Assuring the Health of the Public in the 21st Century 2003). Stated another way, public health consists of the steps taken to protect, preserve, and promote the physical and mental health of people in a community (town, county, state, or country). In another approach, organizations representing public health in the United States have articulated their ultimate vision for the impact of public health as "healthy people in healthy communities," with the specific mission of agencies and organizations being to "promote physical and mental health and prevent disease, injury and disability" (U.S. DHHS 1994, 1). In all these discussions, public health measures are understood to be concerned with the conditions of health of a community, as contrasted with the health of particular individuals, although individuals, of course, benefit from public health measures, and a healthy community includes many healthy individuals.

In some cases, public health measures can be clearly described as distinct from individual ones: clearing a mosquito breeding pond or requiring (and enforcing) sanitary practices in restaurants by law are actions taken to ensure or improve the health of all. In other cases, there is a strong overlap, such as the mutual community and individual benefit derived from the vaccination of children or the treatment of tuberculosis. The vaccinated child or treated tubercular patient benefits individually, while the community-wide risk of epidemic is reduced. Finally, there is the blurred distinction between public and private health that occurs in the course of providing strictly individual, personal care, during which the physician, nurse, or other caregiver is on the alert for and expected to report potentially contagious diseases.

For a variety of reasons, all of medical care is often referred to as health care, and, indeed, medical care does share many of the concerns of public health. However, the activities of diagnosis, prescription, treatment, and patient education as done in offices and hospitals by physicians, nurses, and others have as their focus improving the well-being of each individual patient, not the collective whole. That some of these personal care services are delivered in public facilities (for example, public hospitals or clinics) at public expense (for example, Medicaid or special grant support) does not make them public health. A true public health focus is always on some group or community, one that is usually defined by a geopolitical boundary. This population focus remains true even when public health workers have contact with individuals and may engage in specific activities that are also part of the delivery of personal care.

Identifying Public Health

As already noted, many of the observable actions of public health workers look just like activities undertaken for other purposes. In fact, there are many times when one action fulfills both interests, as in the case of vaccines. Immunization against infectious diseases (measles, polio, hepatitis B, to name a few) is a personal health measure that can be taken at individual discretion based upon a personal level of risk aversion or family fiscal resources. Limitation of epidemic spread of these conditions, any one of which can cause significant discomfort, disability, and death, is dependent upon achieving "herd immunity." This public health term refers to a sufficiently high proportion of the population being immunized such that, while there may be an occasional individual case, there are not sufficient susceptible individuals to sustain an epidemic (Turnock 2003). At the peak of an epidemic, widespread fear of infection may stimulate many to request or even demand access to vaccine. However, once epidemic levels of the disease have been eliminated, individuals might perceive the risks of the vaccine (for there always are some) as being greater than the risk of the disease, preferring to rely for protection on the herd immunity created by immunization choices made by others. The only way we have been able to achieve the necessary high level of immunization and sustain the dramatic reduction in disease experienced in the developed world by the late twentieth century has been by using the police power of public health to enforce immunizations.

Many more tasks done by public health agencies resemble tasks done in the private sector. For example, public health laboratories operated by every state health department and many large local ones perform (among other examinations) a wide range of tests on samples of blood or other human tissue. Many of the tests are directly associated with epidemiologic investigation, such as the diagnosis of tuberculosis or sexually transmitted disease. Some are specialized confirmatory tests that back up diagnostic tests done by hospital or other laboratories in the state, for example, in order to ensure that correct antibiotics are used. Some of these tests are universal to a specific population within the jurisdiction, as when a state makes the decision to test newborn infants for inborn errors of metabolism that, undiagnosed and untreated, will lead to serious mental retardation. Other tests are for conditions that occur only sporadically, such as rabies, for which it is extremely inefficient to maintain widespread laboratory capacity.

The laboratory services provide a vivid illustration of the role public health agencies play in emergency conditions. An emergency might be a large outbreak of rash diseases in a school, requiring quick determination of rubella antibody titer, or a sudden surge in reports of exposure to powdery substances that might contain anthrax spores. The public health laboratory system must be ready to absorb suddenly up to several thousand specimens over a matter of hours or days. The test result information is critical to public health decisions such as the closure of schools or hospitals, or the administration of medication to a large segment of the population. In some of these cases, the initial samples may have to be tested for a range of possible organisms to determine the cause; in other instances, human samples may also be accompanied by a wide range of environmental samples. The laboratories have to be able to maintain clear records (which may have to stand up to court scrutiny on "chain of evidence") and may be working with specimens requiring a high level of personal protective equipment and environmental containment. Commercial laboratories and hospital clinical laboratories are not equipped for such surges of demand and, in fact, rely on public health laboratory expertise for backup in many areas.

It is also the case that some public health laboratories do routine individual laboratory testing in support of whatever personal care services an individual health department may be providing, such as prenatal care or primary care for the uninsured. In these cases, it is primarily the result of one of two business decisions by the local governing body. It may be cheaper because of volume or salary for staff to perform the tests directly rather than purchase them from an outside laboratory. Alternatively, the conduct of routine tests may be a part of maintaining the critical mass of laboratory capacity on which the needed public health expertise and surge capacity can be built.

Longer Life from Good Public Health

The successes of public health in the United States in the twentieth century have included the reduction of vaccine-preventable diseases, increased motor vehicle safety, safer workplaces, control of many infectious diseases, reduced deaths from coronary heart disease and stroke, safer and healthier foods, healthier mothers and babies, planned pregnancies, fluoridation of drinking water, and the recognition of tobacco use as a health hazard (Centers for Disease Control and Prevention 1999). By far most of the thirty-year increase in longevity over the past century has come through activities taken at the community level—safe drinking water, safe food, sanitary waste disposal, the provision of safer housing, and improved overall nutrition—rather than those related to specific individuals. At the beginning of the twentieth century, responsibility for the full range of governmental public health activities, though small by today's standards, often rested in a single agency, with the local health officer (sometimes doubling as the local police chief) being given general authority to isolate and quarantine those suspected of spreading disease, inspect lodging houses, close borders, stop stagecoaches, or other dramatic interventions.

This list of historic public health actions illustrates the intersection of public health action with other public policy activities. A full listing of the public policy arenas having an impact on public health would have to include, at a minimum, housing, education, employment, transportation, and communications. Agriculture, labor, recreation, and energy are also appropriate to include. A number of programs in these spheres had their origin in public health actions before evolving into full-fledged, separate agencies. In many of these instances, the public health agency's role has continued to be the conduct of epidemiologic studies that identify the specific relationship of environmental and human factors contributing to the existence of the problem and making information on potential areas of intervention available to partner agencies and policy makers.

Records of boards of health from the first quarter of the twentieth century include major struggles, for example, to ensure that milk sold came from cows that were free of tuberculosis and was pasteurized to limit the spread of disease, moves that were often vigorously opposed by dairy owners fearing the loss of business or the expense of compliance. This debate continues today in the form of arguments about whether consumers should have access to milk that has not been pasteurized. There is a market for such milk, demonstrated by the continued presence of dairies in the business. There is also a continuing record of outbreaks of infectious disease associated with unpasteurized milk, outbreaks not limited to the supposedly informed adult purchaser of the risky product but involving children and other household contacts who had no choice in the matter.

In addition to the public health activities, one facet of longer life is access to medical care by those individuals needing it. Public health has not been entirely left out of this aspect of policy, though it is not a central issue. Public health agencies are seen and used by many policy makers as the provider of care of last resort. Because full achievement of the vision of a healthy public includes access to needed personal medical care, many practitioners of public health advocate for universal access to care. But there are many conditions for which individuals seek personal medical attention that have only minimal or very delayed impact on the rest of the community. Many skin conditions, heart disease, and joint disease are examples. Cosmetic plastic surgery's positive impact may be an economic one primarily in the employment it offers one group of practitioners rather than any measurable health change. This is in contrast to the impact on the community of undiagnosed or untreated tuberculosis, gonorrhea or other sexually transmitted disease, or lack of access to reproductive health services and contraceptives. Every state makes at least some provision for public health resources to treat these latter conditions, and many also see the public health agency as having a special responsibility for identification of new and special problems. Public health agencies were charged, for example, with assessing the health of the Southeast Asian refugees entering the United States at the end of the Vietnam War and developing the expertise needed to diagnose and treat the rare (to us) parasitic diseases from which some of them suffered.

Public Health as a Public Good

The nature of public health as a public good is clearly illustrated by the case of providing potable drinking water and safe food for the public. It is possible for individuals (or a family) to ensure that drinking water is probably safe to drink by boiling all water for human consumption for at least ten minutes before using. But this is extremely inefficient in time and energy use; every home would need storage space for the cooling, boiled water, and the fluctuating daily requirements mean that shortcuts would often be taken. "Clean" water generally does not look different from water that might cause disease, so that no simple "look first" warning is sufficient. Large-scale treatment of water before delivery by pipeline to every building becomes the community method of choice and has been for decades. While this may be an economic decision in terms of cost (both time and money), it is also a good public health decision because it ensures protection for all. The individual who, for whatever reason, contracts a water-borne disease from insufficiently treated water is not only at individual risk but also presents a risk to all in the community. A large outbreak of cryptosporidium infection in Milwaukee, Wisconsin, resulting in thousands ill and many deaths, provided an all too vivid lesson in the need for water supply protection.

The same line of reasoning applies to the oversight of food supplies. While it is sometimes possible to identify, before serving it, whether a food substance has been grossly contaminated by sewage, many forms of food adulteration or contamination cannot easily be identified and are not simply countered in ordinary food preparation processes. The creation of today's federal Food and Drug Administration is the direct result of the realization that public intervention and oversight were needed if the public at large was to be able to purchase and consume meals safely. Current debate about testing beef for infectious agents (E. coli and BSE [bovine spongiform encephalitis]) further illustrates the concerns about public health regulation as the Department of Agriculture struggles to balance the mission of supporting meat producers with the need to protect the public from harm.

With a public concern for governmental efficiency and interest in the use of the private sector to perform as many services as possible, the nature of public health as a public good has been overshadowed by other debates. Public health agencies have been pushed to charge fees for services, make use of private contractors for services, or quit offering some services that are seen as competitive with private providers. This process threatens the core capacity of public health agencies and decreases access to important services in some communities. In the matter of fees, for example, it is certainly possible to establish a cost-based fee for a visit to a clinic treating sexually transmitted diseases. However, there is no public benefit, and some harm, from discouraging sexually active teens or those with no health insurance from seeking needed care and thus unintentionally spreading disease. Nor is it realistic to include in the clinic visit fee the complete cost of the subsequent public health investigation of a new case of tuberculosis or syphilis conducted to locate both the source of the treated infection and any subsequent infections it may have been caused.

It may be realistic to see a restaurant or day care center license as a rightful business expense, even a fee that escalates if the practices are such that repeat inspections are required. But there is no realistic way to match license fees to a full-scale investigation of a food-borne outbreak that may have spread from a day care center to the community through an infected but nonsymptomatic parent working at a restaurant. Making the connections, breaking the chain of infection, and ensuring that treatment is available is a public good for which some form of general revenue support is more realistic.

The increasing numbers of uninsured Americans over the last part of the twentieth century led to another area in which the public-private debate has flourished. The growing number of uninsured has meant an increasing number of persons turn to their local health departments for help when they need health care or consultation but are not so ill as to require emergency room care. Health departments have been sensitive to the number of women giving birth who have received inadequate prenatal care (an indicator of higher probability of child health problems in the future) and the potential for more unimmunized children. Community concern and compassion has meant that in many communities, what were originally classic public health education or consultation services have been expanded to include clinical services. In some cases, this expansion has been supported by funds from the state Medicaid program. The Medicaid-reimbursable services may have provided the critical mass that allowed for a full-time rather than a part-time nurse or for some routine physician hours in the health department. However, the general provision of care is not strictly a public health function; it is use of public health to fulfill another of society's interests. As Medicaid policies have changed (higher reimbursement rates, the use of managed plans of care), previously unattractive patients have become of greater interest to other providers in the community. Some health departments have been able to leave the clinical care business and return to the core mission of protecting the health of the whole community, though with severely tightened resources (Gebbie 1995).

The Limits of Motivation

One question asked about public health and the need for a communal effort to support it is whether enlightened self-interest on the part of individuals would be sufficient to ensure a healthy public. Unfortunately, evidence strongly suggests that this is not the case. For example, parents generally are motivated to protect their children from harm, including the potential harm of epidemics of diseases such as diphtheria, rubella, measles, or polio. Just telling parents about the wonders of vaccine, however, even those who are positively inclined, has not proved sufficient. Protection of children (and their parents, caretakers, and neighbors) is achieved only when the desired herd immunity level, usually at least 90 percent, is achieved. At that point, with less than 10 percent of the population vulnerable to infection, an epidemic could not be sustained even if the infectious organism were introduced into the community. From a public health viewpoint, there is little concern about which specific children are in the 90 percent receiving the vaccine. The pediatrician, however, is concerned about each individual child who comes in for care and will make decisions about offering, or pushing for, immunization based on the needs and preferences of the specific child and his or her parents. These two interests do coincide in many ways, and practitioners from the two fields are often working in partnership, but the analytic skills and the actions taken will differ greatly.

A community that has decided to achieve high immunization levels to reduce premature death, long-term disability, and school and work absenteeism rates, and knows that simply providing information will not accomplish the goal, has a number of policy options. In the case of introduction of a new vaccine with potential for dramatic impact, such as the introduction of the two polio vaccines in the 1950s, there was little debate about decisions to offer the vaccine through public clinics and community vaccine days. The images of children in iron lungs provided an incentive that we no longer have, after half a century of successful immunization. Furthermore, with insured populations regularly taking children for growth and development supervision to a pediatric office, the dominant current expectation is that vaccines are a part of routine personal medical care.

The flaw in this approach is that there are families who lack a regular source of well-child care or fail to understand the need for routine visits. Today's immunization levels have been achieved only by combining provider and public education and advertising about immunization with the supply of low-cost and free vaccine to all children who are not reached through the private sector and the additional use of police power through "no shots, no school" laws. These laws do, it should be pointed out, allow for children who are medically unable to tolerate the vaccine or whose parents claim a religious or philosophical objection to vaccination, to be exempted. (The numbers fitting these exemptions are small.) As with the full public health response to communicable diseases, some general revenue source is needed to support the tracking of immunization levels and outreach to underserved populations.

The supply of childhood vaccines illustrates another aspect of public health as a public good. Vaccines are produced by pharmaceutical companies, participants in one of the regularly successful sectors of the private economy. As is the case with any pharmaceutical product, vaccines are not risk free. Over the last quarter of the twentieth century, public aversion to risk, or public interest in receiving compensation for a bad outcome, led to increasing use of lawsuits against vaccine manufacturers for the small number of problems occurring in well children receiving recommended childhood vaccines. Furthermore, some states increased the use of their purchasing power to provide lower-cost vaccines not only through public clinics but also through private providers. In the face of reduced profits and increasing liability, a number of companies ceased the manufacture of vaccines. To ensure that at least one company continued to manufacture each desired vaccine, a publicly administered no-fault compensation program was initiated under the guidance of the Centers for Disease Control and Prevention, and strict guidance on the use of publicly purchased vaccines was provided.

Police Powers

The ultimate legal basis for public health practice is the application of the police power of the state to protect the vulnerable. Effective public health has been built throughout history on government action that allows control of the behavior of those individuals who are putting others at risk of disease or death. Public health begins with the long-standing requirement to report births, deaths, and infectious diseases or other untoward events. This provides the factual basis for all other public health actions and can be sustained only with the combination of the legal mandate to report coupled with legal assurance that information received will be handled in such a way that individuals are protected from discrimination or unwarranted disclosure of personal information.

This highlights one of the major balancing points of public health as a public good: it exists at the point at which the actions or health of any one individual may have an impact on the health of others. While many people are willing and able voluntarily to adjust their actions so as not to harm others, there are those who need strong encouragement and even threatened or actual negative sanction before they curb personal choice when they do not see a direct, personal benefit. Some individuals with active, contagious tuberculosis disease decline to take needed medication, either because it is inconvenient or because some side effect of the medication is seen as a greater concern than untreated disease, and take the prescribed drugs only when made aware that if they fail to do so a court will order isolation and continuous supervision. This need for occasional application of the police power of public health extends not only to individuals but to corporations: many business operators will voluntarily take action to ensure that the health of employees, customers, and neighbors is not threatened; others act only when under both regulation and regular inspection.

The delicate balancing point in both writing and enforcing public health laws is to focus on those behaviors that put others at risk without becoming "moral police" on matters that are strictly individual choice. The efforts to dramatically restrict smoking in all workplaces is based on good science about the impact of secondhand or sidestream smoke. If smoking is allowed in a workplace such as a restaurant, it is not only the individual smoker who is exposed to all the chemicals in the smoke but every patron and the entire staff, as well. Making certain that the public's health is protected may require elimination of indoor smoking, but it should be done in such a way that the adult who continues to smoke, whether by addiction or by choice, is not labeled morally unfit in some way.

The Power of Market Forces to Diminish Public Health

Restaurant food safety provides an example of a setting in which customer satisfaction is often associated with the aesthetics of the setting or the taste and appearance of the food. None of these is related to whether the raw ingredients came from safe sources, were prepared under safe conditions, have been stored at appropriate temperatures, and are served by staff with hands free of infectious organisms. The cost to a restaurant owner of discarding a large quantity of food because it has spent a short time at the wrong storage temperature may loom sufficiently large to lead to a decision to use the food anyway. That restaurateur is gambling that the contamination is too slight to cause illness or that those who become ill will be far down the road, will have eaten at several places within a short time, or will be otherwise unable to associate a subsequent disease with a specific source. Environmental health staff inspecting food establishments report regular debates about the level of cleanliness to be demanded. Many of those who regularly eat out are aware of the addition of gloves to the standard wardrobe of food preparers.

Removal of lead paint as part of the demand for safe housing is another area in which there has been a long-running struggle to sort out what level of expense to place on property owners to minimize the risk of exposure to lead-based paint. Although the product has been off the market for many years, older housing stock contains many layers of old paint, some of which is constantly exposed through chips, cracks, and leaks. The economics of low-cost housing have provided no incentives for removal of the hazardous paint. While a complete removal of this risk involves policy outside of the usual public health authority, public health agencies have been funded to ensure that children at risk are tested for lead exposure and treated, if affected, and that the homes of lead-injured children are tested, identified hazards removed, and parents taught about how to minimize exposure in the future. This public service is supported because failure to invest in monitoring child health and abating risk results in the unacceptable human cost of lead-poisoned children whose minds fail to develop appropriately.

Community Support for the Public Good

Isolation of infected individuals to limit the further spread of disease is possibly the public health action most clearly supported by communities as a public good, sometimes even when such isolation has little or no impact on the actual spread of disease. Every state health authority has some ability to order individuals to remain away from others, in home isolation, off the job, or detained in a hospital, when interaction with others would lead to an increase in disease spread. Even in the face of increasing concern about inappropriate detention, and with an interest in ensuring that current understanding of due process is respected, new public health laws continue to include such authority (Gostin 2000). There is even a Model Emergency Public Health Powers Act (Gostin 2001a) being used as a guideline by some legislative bodies to ensure that the public health authority can act decisively and forcefully in the face of a threat to the community.

Why keep public health out of the market? Some of those who advocate universal access to personal health services have talked as if such an achievement would obviate the need for public health. It is certainly possible to imagine a world in which every single member of the community has direct, easy, and affordable access to a clinician able to diagnose and treat a problem such as salmonella infection, a common food-borne disease. Such access is the norm in other economically developed countries. It is not likely, however, that the diagnosing and treating physician will also be in a position to interview the patient and family about where they have eaten, and what, for the past several days, identify the likely source of the contaminated food, inspect the reported restaurant or grocery to identify the specific source of the infection, identify others who may need treatment, and ensure that the problem is corrected before more members of the community become ill.

The rapid collaboration between emergency rooms, pediatricians, and public health in the fast food–associated epidemic of E. coli 0157 in Seattle in 1993 provides a vivid example of the needed collaboration (Centers for Disease Control and Prevention 1993). Without skilled physicians and an alert emergency room, the illness suddenly striking a number of preschool children might have been misdiagnosed, treatment might have been delayed or less than aggressive, and multiple deaths might have occurred as a consequence. Failure to report the problem to the health department would have meant the continued serving of undercooked hamburger in kiddy meals. As an added measure, aggressive retraining of all day care centers in hand washing and sanitation precluded secondary transmission of the disease across the most susceptible population. These latter activities transcended the individual interests of the directly affected parties and could have been effectively carried out only by a publicly authorized body financed out of a common resource.

Data gathering to monitor the public's health is the cornerstone of public health policy making. Someone must be put in a position to review the causes of death, the state of health at birth, the rate of occurrence of preventable conditions, levels of threats to health in the environment, the range and quality of care available, and risk-taking behavior and to assemble the disparate bits of information into meaningful data that can serve as the basis for policy making (Lumpkin and Richards 2002). Assembling the data, however, requires exception to the growing body of regulation regarding confidentiality of data about individual health and illness and businesses' proprietary information. The most far-reaching recent national legislation in this area, the Health Insurance Portability and Protection Act (Gostin 2001b), includes specific language exempting public health data from some provisions of the law to ensure that federal, state, and local public health authorities have appropriate access to information.

The individual interests in health have not been sufficient to build an adequate picture of a community's health such as that reflected in the government's 2000 report, *Healthy People 2010* (U.S. DHHS 2000). The hundreds of individuals and associations coming together to construct this set of health goals for the nation also strongly supported the continuation of publicly financed health data systems, such as the system of vital statistics and the national health surveys conducted under the auspices of the National Center for Health Statistics.

Yet another example of public support for a nonmarket approach to protecting the public health is in the control of vectors of disease such as mosquitoes. In many mosquito-prone areas of the country, special mosquito control districts have been created to collect taxes and use them for draining standing water, supplying larvae-eating fish for ponds, and spraying insecticides. Locales that had not invested in such efforts quickly added mosquito control to public health budgets after the mosquito-borne West Nile virus was identified as newly arrived in the United States, causing illness and death (Centers for Disease Control and Prevention 2003). The diffuse nature of the risk and the economies of scale in general applications has led to public support for the actions. Some regulation of businesses and property owners could be used to accomplish the programs in lieu of publicly employed field staff, but even in that case, oversight and enforcement would be needed.

As people now live longer and experience fewer communicable diseases, chronic diseases such as heart disease, lung disease, and cancer have attracted public health attention. The role of tobacco, for example, was the subject of a surgeon general's report (U.S. Surgeon General's Advisory Committee on Smoking and Health 1964) in the mid-1960s, and by the 1990s almost every state health department had at least some cancer prevention activities. At mid-century, some predicted the end of the era of concern for infectious diseases, a prediction demolished by the emergence of human immunodeficiency virus (HIV) and the global movement of a variety of old and emerging conditions (Turnock 2003). While the shift toward chronic diseases has been applauded by many, it has also moved public health more directly into areas in which individual human behavior is seen as responsible for disease and thus in which public activity is suspect.

Bringing a public health analysis to traffic safety is credited with the huge savings in life and property that accumulated over the latter part of the twentieth century. Use of this model led to understanding that traffic deaths and injuries were the result of interaction among the environment (roads, streets, bridges), the vector of injury (the automobile, truck, bicycle), and the host (the driver or passenger) (Baker 1989). From this perspective, communities (and national agencies) were stimulated to take a wide range of actions. Breakaway road signs (part of transportation policy), bumpers of consistent heights and car hoods that "accordion pleat" (to absorb crash energy rather than transmit energy through the steering column into the driver's liver), and graduated permit programs for newly licensed teen drivers (presenting driving as a publicly granted privilege, not an automatic right) all have played a part in the health improvement.

It has been extremely difficult, however, to clarify the overlapping roles that advertising, community norms, and peer influence have on the beginning of cigarette use. There are many who would like to consider smoking a purely personal choice, of no more public interest than the decision to wear a certain style of clothing, rather than an epidemic subject to public health intervention. The market for tobacco, as for other addicting substances, does not seem to be controllable through strictly market forces, nor are nonsmoking individuals protected from the smoke of others. Despite the controversy, the authority of the state (or the city or county government) is now being used, for example, to ensure that the air inside any publicly accessible building is free of tobacco smoke. Data show that the more difficult it is to smoke, the less likely people are to smoke, so the protection of the nonsmoker also contributes to the health of the smoker. Similarly, we are only beginning to focus on the epidemic of obesity in the United States, with associated increases in diabetes and heart disease. We have yet to complete the research to understand fully the complex mix of overproduction of calories (nearly double what is needed by the population each day), advertising ("Just super-size it"), reduced exercise (whole communities with no sidewalks), and self-image (too thin may be glamorous, but it is bad) that appear to be contributors and could be addressed on a community-wide basis.

Over the course of the twentieth century, average length of life in the United States was extended by approximately thirty years. Only five of those added years are attributable to increased sophistication and effectiveness of medical intervention; the other twenty-five derive from improved public health (McKinlay, McKinlay, and Beaglehole 1989). There may be a few individuals living in isolated circumstances who are not recipients of public health services from one year to the next, but in our increasingly urbanized society they are rare indeed. Developing effective public policy that creates and sustains the conditions under which people can be healthy is an increasingly complex challenge. Public health's "patient" is the body politic and its chosen leaders. It takes great skill to plan the best course of medical care for a complex illness, explain it to a patient, and then help that patient to follow it for an extended period of time. Similarly, the exact blend of services needed to support the public good of public health in any one jurisdiction must be carefully negotiated. The precise mix will vary from one location to another, but given the mobile nature of our population and the failure of health threats to understand boundaries, there is a need to work toward consistency. Furthermore, the actions that can be done in the explicitly public health sector will be enhanced or impeded by the degree to which related public policies in housing, transportation, and education are developed. There is every reason to believe that the average length of life will be extended further as we move into the twenty-first century. Assuring that the longer life is a healthier life is public health's opportunity and a public challenge.

References

Baker, S. P. 1989. "Injury science comes of age." *JAMA* 262(16): 2284–85.

Centers for Disease Control and Prevention. 1993. "Update: Multistate Outbreak of escherichi coli 0157:H7 Infections from Hamburgers—Western United States, 1992–1993." *MMWR* 42(14): 257–63.

———. 1999. "Ten great public health achievements." *MMWR* 48(12): 241–43.

———. 2003. "Epidemic/Epizootic West Nile Virus in the United States: Guidelines for Surveillance, Prevention, and Control." *MMWR* 51 (April 2001, updated August 8, 2003): 1129–33.

Committee on Assuring the Health of the Public in the 21st Century. 2003. *The Future of the Public's Health in the 21st Century.* Washington: National Academies Press.

Gebbie, Kristine M. 1995. "Follow the Money: A Commentary on Funding Streams and Public Health Nursing." *Journal of Public Health Management and Practice* 1(3): 23–28.

Gostin, Lawrence O. 2000. "Public Health Law in a New Century." Pt. 1, "Law as a Tool to Advance the Community's Health." *JAMA* 283: 2837–2841.

———. 2001a. "Model state emergency health powers act, draft as of Dec, 2001." Baltimore: Johns Hopkins Bloomberg School of Public Health Center for Law and the Public's Health. Available at: www.publichealthlaw.net/MSEHPA/MSEHPA2.pdf (accessed October 17, 2003).

———. 2001b. "National health information privacy: regulations under the Health Insurance Portability and Accountability Act." *JAMA* 285(23): 3015–21.

Lumpkin, John R., and Margaret S. Richards. 2002. "Transforming the public health information infrastructure." *Health Affairs* 21(6): 45–56.

McKinlay, J. B., S. M. McKinlay, and R. Beaglehole. 1989. "A review of the evidence concerning the impact of medical measures on recent mortality and morbidity in the United States." *International Journal of Health Services* 19(2): 181–208.

Turnock, Bernard J. 2003. *Public Health: what it is and how it works.* 2nd ed. Sudbury, Mass.: Jones and Bartlett.

U.S. Department of Health and Human Services (DHHS). 1994. Public Health Functions Steering Committee. *Public Health in America.* Washington: U.S. Department of Health and Human Services, Office of Disease Prevention and Health Promotion.

———. 2000. *Healthy People 2010.* Washington: U.S. Government Printing Office.

U.S. Surgeon General's Advisory Committee on Smoking and Health. 1964. *Smoking and health: report of the advisory committee to the Surgeon General of the Public Health Service.* Washington: U.S. Government Printing Office.

13

CAMPAIGN FINANCE

Richard Briffault

O UR DEMOCRATIC political process is predicated on two norms that reject fundamental characteristics of markets. First, whereas markets rely on the private use of economic resources, so that actors are entitled to deploy their economic endowments—which may vary wildly—in pursuit of their goals, democratic politics is based on the equal status of the members of the political community. All adult resident citizens are presumptively entitled to vote; each person casts an equally weighted vote; and wealth, income, or property ownership criteria may not be used to determine eligibility to vote or hold office.

Second, markets involve the voluntary exchange of economic resources, including the trading of goods and services for money. In politics, however, the market mechanism is usually prohibited. Politicians may not buy—and voters may not sell—votes; nor may interested individuals buy government offices or government decisions. To be sure, politicians and voters may exchange favors, and politicians may make deals that involve the trading of one legislative vote for another. But neither politicians nor voters can sell their political decisions for money.

Although private wealth and market transactions are excluded from the political process, that process is surrounded, indeed, interpenetrated, by both economic resources and market transactions. Politicians may not be able to buy votes, but they have to compete for those votes in contested elections, and they need economic resources to fund their election efforts. So, too, although individuals and interest groups may not buy government decisions, they can deploy their economic resources to support the election of candidates sympathetic to their concerns, to influence the decisions of officeholders, and to affect public opinion generally. Economics and markets affect politics even if they are kept out of its core.

Campaign finance law mediates the relationship between our egalitarian and market-free elections and the economically unequal and market-filled world that surrounds them. Today, federal law provides for the disclosure of most contributions, limits the size of large contributions, restricts the campaign activities of certain interest groups, and provides for public grants to presidential candidates. However, few observers think federal campaign finance law has been effective at keeping markets and economic inequality entirely out of elections for federal office. Belying the norm of one person, one vote, a relatively small number of individuals and organizations provide a large portion of campaign funding. Although wealth tests for voting and holding office have been eliminated, personal wealth can provide a great boost to a candidate's political fortunes—as the recent ascents of enormously wealthy political newcomers to a U.S. Senate seat in New Jersey and to the mayoralty of New York City demonstrate. Although evidence that political contributions directly influence the actions of elected officials is slim, both the public and many elected officials believe that the role of campaign money in the political process is enormous.

To some extent, our failure to create a fully egalitarian, market-free campaign finance system is inevitable. Our Constitution guarantees the ability of the people to influence their government, but the process of influencing government will often involve the use of private wealth. Drawing a line between improper wealth-based influence on elections and government, on the one hand, and constitutionally protected speech, press, assembly, and associational activities aimed at affecting government decision making, on the other, is no easy matter. More important, competitive elections require the expenditure of money so that the voters may be informed and campaign participants can bring their messages to the electorate. To the extent that money comes from private sources—and nearly all of it does—wealth inequality and market forces will reenter the electoral process.

Two Norms of Democratic Politics

Two central features of market organization are the assumption that people will express their preferences through the deployment of their economic resources, and that they will do so through the process of exchange, that is, the market itself. Democratic politics, however, challenges both of those features and is, instead, based on two very different fundamental principles—that people will voice their preferences through votes, not dollars, and that they may not exchange their votes for something else, such as money. These two features, in turn, have broader implications and raise broader questions. The reliance on votes has given rise to a norm of electoral equality sharply at odds with the economic inequality characteristic of market organization. The rejection of vote-trading has raised questions about other marketlike features of the political process, such as the private donation of campaign contributions to candidates for elected office.

Electoral Equity

Equality, regardless of wealth, is the hallmark of our electoral system. As a matter of constitutional doctrine, the right to vote cannot be limited based on wealth, income, or the failure to pay a tax, such as a poll tax or a property tax (for example, Harper v. Virginia Board of Elections, 383 U.S. 663 [1966]; City of Phoenix v. Kolodziejski, 399 U.S. 204 [1970]). Nor can the right to run for public office be conditioned on the payment of a fee (for example, Bullock v. Carter, 405 U.S. 134 [1972]; Lubin v. Panish, 415 U.S. 709 [1974]).

The elimination of the wealth test from elections came relatively late in our constitutional development. In the eighteenth century, voting was considered not a natural right but a state-granted privilege—as the term "franchise" suggests—and the privilege was extended only to those believed capable of providing the polity with sound governance (Keyssar 2000, 9). For the most part, that meant property-owning adult white males. Property ownership was believed to supply the independence necessary to make judgments about questions of community governance. Those without property were presumed to be economically dependent on and subservient to others and, as a result, subject to political manipulation and control by their economic patrons and social betters (Keyssar 2000, 3–21; Steinfeld 1989). To be sure, the propertied often expressed the contrary fear that the propertyless were not just pawns of elites but might instead use political power to advance their own distinct economic interests, which might be in conflict with those of the propertied (Keyssar 2000, 11). But the dominant argument for a property test was the sense that property provided the capacity for independent judgment essential for a healthy polity.

Over the first half of the nineteenth century, property requirements were progressively relaxed, and most were ultimately abolished. Initially, property ownership tests were replaced by tax-payment requirements. By the Civil War, most states had eliminated both property and tax-payment tests. These changes reflected the growing sense that all members of the political community—still largely limited to white men—were affected by government decisions and, therefore, ought to have a right to participate in the process of producing a government (Keyssar 2000, 26–52).

Nonetheless, some forms of property or wealth criteria persisted for another century. Some states used property or tax-payment requirements for certain local elections, such as votes on school taxes or bond issues (Keyssar 2000, 130–34). In these states, ownership of property or the payment of taxes indicated that an individual had a sufficient economic stake in the election that he or she ought to be entitled to vote. Many states continued to exclude paupers—that is, persons living in poorhouses run by state or local governments or receiving "out-door" poor relief—from voting (Keyssar 2000, 61–62, 134–36). At the end of the nineteenth century, many Southern states responded to the Fifteenth Amendment's enfranchisement of blacks by adopting poll-tax requirements, which, along with other voting qualifications, excluded many blacks (and poor whites) from voting (Keyssar 2000, 111–12).

Only in the late 1960s did the Supreme Court hold that voting is a fundamental right for purposes of the Equal Protection Clause of the Fourteenth Amendment, so that restrictions on the vote would be subject to strict judicial scrutiny (Kramer v. Union Free School District, 395 U.S. 621 [1969]). The Court proceeded to invalidate all requirements based on tax payment, property ownership, or possession of wealth. At the same time, the Court and Congress also banned two other long-standing restrictions on voting—durational residency requirements (Dunn v. Blumstein, 405 U.S. 330 [1972]) and literacy tests (Oregon v. Mitchell, 400 U.S. 112 [1970]). Combined with the Court's articulation and implementation of the one person, one vote rule for legislative apportionment, equality emerged as a constitutionally mandated hallmark of the electoral process. All adult resident citizens are presumptively entitled to vote—and to cast equally weighted votes—regardless of their wealth or the lack of it.

Since the early 1970s, the principal legal questions concerning the equal right to vote have involved whether a particular arrangement involves a political election—or an election at all. For example, one person, one vote does not apply to shareholder voting in corporate elections or to homeowner voting in homeowner association elections. In those nongovernmental contexts, one share, one vote, or arrangements otherwise linking voting power to the size of one's financial commitment to the enterprise, are entirely permissible. In a sense, the connection between economic stake and votes in the business context only underscores the contrasting commitment to equality in the context of democratic politics. The Supreme Court has also held that voting rights in certain special limited-purpose districts—such as water supply or flood control districts—can be based on property ownership (for example, Ball v. James, 451 U.S. 355 [1981]) and one federal court of appeals extended that holding to business improvement districts (Kessler v. Grand Central District Management Association, Inc., 158 F.2d 92 [2d Cir. 1998]). Although these entities are clearly governmental, the courts have emphasized that the districts are operationally quasi-private, functioning more like firms in providing a market-type service to customers than like governments that regulate and tax citizens. Once again, in a businesslike context, votes may be tied to economic stake. But for truly "political" bodies, universal suffrage and equally weighted votes regardless of wealth, property ownership, or tax-payment are the constitutional ground rules.

The right to an equally weighted vote is limited to elections. Thus one person, one vote does not apply to appointive bodies. Regional bodies composed of representatives of cities and suburbs throughout a metropolitan area can allocate governing board seats on the basis of one town, one vote, regardless of size, if the board is appointed rather than elected (see, generally,

Briffault 1993). More generally, political activities not involving the election of public officials, such as legislative lobbying, grassroots organizing, and campaigns aimed at influencing public opinion generally, are not subject to the equality norm. Under the First Amendment, government cannot impose a wealth or property ownership test as a condition for engaging in lobbying or media campaigns, but neither can government limit the ability of the well-heeled to spend more on efforts to influence public opinion or government action. As a result, different groups can spend different amounts of money, reflecting differences in their economic resources, in efforts to influence political views and decisions outside of elections.

In short, the domain of political equality—of one person, one vote—is limited to political elections and does not apply to corporate elections; and within the political context, equality without regard to wealth is further limited to elections; it does not apply to other political activity. The first limitation has not been the source of much difficulty in the campaign finance context. But drawing the line between elections, where equal voting rights is the norm, and other political activity, where wealth differences may constitutionally be translated into differences in the scope and intensity of political appeals, has been a central difficulty for campaign finance law.

Prohibition of the Purchase of Political Decisions

A second political norm fundamentally at odds with market principles is the prohibition of the purchase of political decisions. This prohibition takes two forms. First, both federal and state laws have long prohibited the buying of voters' votes, that is, the payment of money to anyone in exchange for that person's vote for a candidate, as well as the receipt or acceptance of such an expenditure by anyone who has a vote to sell (see, generally, Hasen 2000). Second, our laws have also long prohibited bribery, that is, the offer or promise of something of value to a public official to influence or induce an official act or a public official's demand for or acceptance of something of value in return for being influenced or induced with respect to an official act (see, generally, Lowenstein and Hasen 2001).

One justification for barring the purchase of political decisions is equality. The poor, who have few other assets, will be more likely to sell their votes, and will sell for a smaller sum, than those who are wealthy. Conversely, the wealthy are in a better position to buy votes. If vote buying were allowed, then, the rich would be able to purchase the votes of the poor and would be able to use them to advance their own interests. (In a sense, this restates the concern of eighteenth-century thinkers who feared that propertyless voters would be manipulated by the wealthy.) As a result, vote buying is inconsistent with political equality (Hasen 2000, 1329–31). Equality concerns also support the prohibition of bribery, since the rich would benefit particularly if government decisions were up for sale.

The egalitarian argument against vote selling is ultimately paternalistic, since it denies voters the opportunity to profit from their political rights or to determine for themselves whether they are better off casting their votes their own way or selling them to the highest bidder. As the poor have equal voting rights with the rich, even though they lack equal material resources, the ban on vote selling arguably burdens the poor more heavily.

A second and perhaps more fundamental reason for the ban on vote buying is that the sale of votes corrupts the political decision-making process (Hasen 2000, 1335–37). This goes to the heart of the distinction between markets and politics. Market decisions are supposed to be based on self-interest. But political decisions—both by the general public, when acting as voters, and by public officials, when attending to official business—are supposed to be based on public concerns and the public interest rather than the decision maker's narrow self-interest in receiving a payment. It is in the best interests of the polity as a whole—including the poor—for political decisions to be based on the public interest and thus free of the self-interest advanced by monetary exchange.

The commitment to a public-regarding basis for political decisions sometimes results in a ban broader than the prohibition on monetary transactions. Some states bar legislative logrolling, that is, an agreement by one legislator to cast his or her vote one way on a particular measure in exchange for the commitment of another legislator to cast his or her vote in a certain way on another measure (Hasen 2000, 1338–48). The ban on logrolling is logically connected to the prohibition of vote buying. Both reflect the view that public officials ought to make their decisions based on the merits of the matter at hand rather than on their interest in advancing another concern. To be sure, antilogrolling rules are rarely enforced (Hasen 2000, 1340), but they illustrate the power of the principle that political decisions should be based on the decision makers' perception of the merits rather than on self-interest.

On the other hand, that legislative logrolling is generally not subject to restriction—and some states expressly exempt legislative deal making from the general ban on vote buying—should tip us off to some of the difficulties with the goal of public-regarding decision making. It is difficult for public decision makers to disregard private interests entirely when making decisions. Indeed, it is difficult even to define the public interest without taking into account the sum of the private interests of the individuals who collectively compose the public. Notwithstanding the ban on vote buying, it is considered appropriate for both voters and elected officials to take some aspects of self-interest into account when they vote.

So, too, it is legitimate for candidates and interest groups to appeal to voters' self-interest when they attempt to sway voting decisions. When Ronald Reagan famously asked voters to consider whether they were "better off now than four years ago," he was asking them to cast their ballots based on economic self-interest, that is, on their evaluation of which presidential candidate would improve their own circumstances. No one condemned this as illegal. So, too, Bill Clinton's "It's the economy, stupid" mantra was intended to get voters to focus on which candidate would benefit them economically. This was considered shrewd campaigning, not corruption. Indeed, although vote buying is everywhere prohibited, the Supreme Court has expressly held that the First Amendment protects candidate appeals to voter self-interest: "The fact that some voters may find self-interest reflected in a candidate's commitment does not place that commitment beyond the reach of the First Amendment. We have never insisted that the franchise be exercised without taint of individual benefit" (Brown v. Hartlage, 456 U.S. 45, 56 [1982]).

Similarly, we assume that officeholders can consider some aspects of self-interest in their official decision making; indeed, at times we prefer it. Thus an official can agree to follow the dictates of his or her party's leader rather than make an independent judgment. This is not considered corrupt even if the official's motive is to gain personal power by advancing within the party hierarchy; instead, some observers would applaud a legislator's voting the party line and thereby vindicating the values of party governance. So, too, elected officials may base their votes on the preferences of their constituencies, as indicated by polling data, even if what motivates their actions is the desire for reelection rather than a belief in the wisdom of the local electorate.

Nor is legislative vote trading always considered to be an abdication of the lawmaker's duty to make a decision on the merits. Logrolling may provide a means of registering differences in intensities of preference, which may be an appropriate means of taking the interests of minorities and dissenters into account. More generally, in our pluralist political system in which many different interests struggle for legislative attention and legislative votes, logrolling may be a necessary means of achieving compromises and building the broad support necessary for legislative action.

In short, although buying votes with, or selling votes for, money is always illegal, casting a vote based on personal self-interest is often legal, and appeals to self-interest are both widespread and constitutionally protected. The legitimacy of voting based on self-interest—and of appeals to the officeholder's or voter's self-interest—also complicates efforts to regulate campaign finance.

The Two Political "Markets"

Our laws prohibit the purchase and sale of both voters' votes and officeholders' official actions. Yet the electorate and elected officials participate in two critically important, albeit metaphoric, political markets. There is, first, the competition by candidates, political parties, and interest groups to persuade voters to cast their ballots for one candidate or another. Second, there is the competition among individuals and groups—including corporate, labor, trade, and ideological organizations—to influence government action.

In the first market—the competition for voters' ballots—voters choose among candidates based on what they know about the candidates. Voters typically know relatively little about the candidates at the start of a campaign and know even less about challengers and newcomers than about incumbents and officeholders. The media may provide some information, but this is usually quite limited in amount and, typically, is focused on only the most prominent contests. In some jurisdictions, a government agency may publish and distribute a voter information pamphlet that provides brief biographies of and statements from the candidates. Most states and localities do not do this, and even when they do, the information so provided is likely to be rather scant and more useful to the voters already attentive to politics than to the larger portion of the electorate who are less interested.

As a result, for most voters the most usable information is provided by the campaign participants, that is, the candidates themselves, the political parties, and politically active interest groups. Through television, radio, and newspaper ads, mailings, telephone calls, Internet websites, and other means of communications, candidates, parties, and interest groups compete to provide the voters with vital facts and arguments concerning the records, programs, issue positions, and personalities of the candidates; to link up the candidates to particular parties, interest groups, political actions, or celebrities; and to challenge the arguments and assertions of other political advertisers. The claims in these ads may be at times inflammatory, tendentious, inaccurate, unfair, simplistic, delivered in brief sound bites, and repeated over and over again without nuance or variation. But for most voters, most of the information that enables them to make decisions about the election and choose among the candidates comes from the election campaign.

Beyond communications, candidate, party, and interest group expenditures also register and mobilize voters. Organizational endorsements, election day operations, and get-out-the-vote drives are critical in persuading and helping favorably inclined voters actually to cast their ballots. Together, electoral communications and voter mobilization activities shape the competition for voters' votes.

The election of candidates, of course, is only a step in the ongoing struggle over political power, the resolution of public policy questions, and the determination of public actions. This broader and virtually endless competition among groups, organizations, and individuals seeks to influence government decisions both before and after elections. The competition for political influence intersects with election campaigns in two important ways.

First, interest groups may promote the election of candidates favorable to their interests. They may do so by providing those candidates with financial support directly, thereby enabling those candidates to conduct more vigorous campaigns. They may also communicate with the voters directly, providing reasons for voters to support the candidates the interest groups favor or to oppose the candidates the groups oppose. Together, these efforts constitute what is known as an "electoral" strategy.

Second, interest groups can focus less on the election of candidates favorable to their interests and more on making sure that whoever is elected is responsive to their concerns. Interest group contributions and expenditures taking this approach would be aimed not at affecting the election but at securing the gratitude of, or at least access to and the favorable attention of, the winner. This kind of campaign spending resembles lobbying and is known as a "legislative" or "access" strategy. Ideological groups are more likely to pursue an electoral strategy; conversely, groups that pursue a legislative strategy are less likely to be interested in ideology and more likely to give to both parties and even to both candidates in the same race. A group may also pursue both electoral and legislative strategies simultaneously—although there may be some risk that an electoral strategy in support of the candidate who turns out to be the loser may get in the way of a legislative strategy aimed at having access to the winner.

The Structure and Development of Federal Campaign Finance Law

Federal campaign finance law today relies on four regulatory techniques:

- Reporting and disclosure rules obligate candidates and other organizations, such as political parties and political action committees, that raise and spend money in connection with election campaigns to disclose the sources of funds and amounts provided for contributions over a threshold amount and to report expenditures of campaign funds over a threshold level.

- Contribution restrictions take two forms: there are limits on the amount of money a donor can give to a candidate or to a political organization for electoral purposes. There are also laws that bar some groups, such as corporations or unions, from making any contributions at all.

- Expenditure restrictions are similar to contribution restrictions. There may be limits on the amounts a candidate or political organization can spend on campaigns aimed at the voters, and there may be laws that prohibit expenditures by certain individuals or groups outright.

- Public subsidies can be provided to qualifying candidates or parties to defray some of the costs of campaigning. Many public subsidy programs require the candidate who receives the funds to agree to accept a limit on his or her total campaign expenditures.

Each of these techniques has an effect on one or the other of the political markets. Indeed, given the interconnections between the two markets, a technique that operates primarily in one market will also have an effect on the other.

Reporting and disclosure requirements operate directly in the market for voters' votes. By providing voters with information concerning a candidate's donors, the voters may be better able to assess the candidate and to cast an informed vote. Disclosure, however, may have effects that are broader than voter information. Disclosure rules may discourage contributions by donors who prefer not to have their political choices publicized and may discourage donations to unpopular candidates. Disclosure might also discourage donations that are so large that they draw public comment. As a result, disclosure could reduce the funds available for campaigning for all or some candidates and thus interfere with the competition for voters' votes. By potentially discouraging very large donations or discouraging candidates from accepting donations from unpopular donors, disclosure can also indirectly affect the market for influence over officeholders.

Contribution restrictions operate directly on the market for influence over government. Their purpose is to reduce the ability of large donors, or certain categories of donors, to make candidates dependent on, and grateful for, their donations. But they also indirectly affect the competition for voters' votes since they can make it more difficult for candidates to obtain the funds they need to campaign. Indeed, by exacerbating the burdens of fundraising, contribution restrictions can raise barriers to entry into the electoral market.

Expenditure restrictions operate directly on the market for voters' votes by limiting the ability of candidates or their supporters to bring their case to the voters. This could have the benefit of equalizing the competition for votes by checking the ability of the better-funded candidate to outspend his opponent. On the other hand, if the limits are set too low, then expenditure restrictions could benefit the candidate who is better known before the election, such as the incumbent or a celebrity. Expenditure restrictions also affect the market for political influence. Large expenditures by interest groups in support of or opposition to a particular candidate may win the gratitude of the candidate who benefits from the spending; capping expenditures would reduce the opportunity to win such gratitude. Moreover, if the total amount of money candidates are permitted to spend is limited, they will need to raise less money than otherwise. Thus they may be less dependent on, and less grateful to, large donors than if there were no limits on spending.

Public funding operates directly in the market for voters' votes by providing candidates with resources for campaigns. This should improve the ability of candidates to communicate and the ability of voters to make informed choices. Since public funding is particularly beneficial to candidates who have difficulty raising private contributions, public funding may also level the playing field among the candidates. Public funding can also have an important impact on the market for political influence. By providing candidates with funds not tied to any donor or interest group, public funding reduces the influence of private donors on government decision making.

The Evolution of Federal Campaign Finance Law

Disclosure, contribution restrictions, and expenditure restrictions have been part of federal campaign finance law for nearly a century, although until the 1970s the relevant federal laws had little effect. There were no public subsidies before the 1970s, and even now federal public subsidies are limited to presidential elections.

Historically, the first federal campaign finance law focused on contributions from business corporations. Responding to public reports of lavish corporate campaign contributions in the elections of the Gilded Age, Congress in 1907 passed the Tillman Act, which barred federally chartered corporations from making campaign contributions and barred all corporations from making contributions in connection with an election for federal office (see, generally, Mutch 1988).

Congressional attention then shifted from corporate donations to the disclosure of campaign receipts and expenditures. In 1910 Congress passed the Federal Corrupt Practices Act, generally known as the Publicity Act, which required party committees operating in two or more states to file postelection reports on contributions and expenditures made in connection with general elections for the House of Representatives. The 1911 amendments to the Publicity Act extended the reporting requirement to Senate campaigns and to primary elections and required preelection as well as postelection reports. In addition, the 1911 amendments provided the first expenditure limitations. The law limited House campaign expenditures to a total of $5,000 and Senate campaign expenditures to $10,000 or any lesser amount set by state law (Mutch 1988, 8–16). In 1921, however, the Supreme Court curbed the effect of the 1911 amendments when it invalidated the limits on spending in Senate primary elections, holding that Congress lacked authority to regulate primaries since these were not "elections" in the constitutional sense (Newberry v. United States, 256 U.S. 232 [1921]).[1]

Congress revisited campaign finance regulation in the 1920s, in the aftermath of the Teapot Dome scandal. Teapot Dome illustrated some of the shortcomings of the 1911 disclosure law. The $1.5 million contribution by oil magnate Harry F. Sinclair to the Republican Party had not been reported because he made the contribution in a nonelection year and the disclosure law applied only to election year contributions. The Federal Corrupt Practices Act of 1925 strengthened disclosure by requiring all political committees active in two or more states to file quarterly financial reports listing contributions of

$100 or more with the clerk of the House (for House races) or the secretary of the Senate (for Senate races), even in nonelection years. In addition, the act revised the spending limits for congressional general elections to $5,000 for House races and up to $25,000 for Senate elections.

The 1925 law's disclosure requirement, however, had little impact: "It did not mandate publication of the reports or public access to them; it did not ensure that the reports would be accurate, or even that they would be filed at all. The increasingly strong wording of the law distracted attention from the fact that it contained no provisions for enforcement" (Mutch 1988, 25). The relevant House and Senate officers had no authority to require campaign committees to submit the reports required by law; to examine submitted reports for errors or omissions; or to publicize the reports. They were not even required to keep the reports as a permanent record; instead, after two years, the reports could be destroyed (Mutch 1988, 25–26).

The 1925 act's expenditure limitations were no more effective than its disclosure requirements:

> Because the limits were applicable to party committees, they were easily skirted by creating multiple committees for the same candidate or race. Each of these committees could then technically comply with the spending limit established for a particular race, while the total monies funneled into that race greatly exceeded the amount intended by law. These multiple committees also facilitated evasion of disclosure. Donors could provide gifts of less than $100 to each committee without any reporting obligation, or give larger amounts to a variety of committees, thus obscuring the total given to any candidate. (Corrado 2002, 6)

Indeed, "in the history of the 1925 act, no one was prosecuted for failing to comply with the law" (Corrado 2002, 6).

Campaign finance law was modified again in 1939 and 1940, in reaction in part to the expansion of the federal government during the New Deal, the growing cost of campaigns, and the increased political power of labor unions. The Hatch Act of 1939 expanded the prohibition of the 1883 Pendleton Act on political activity by federal civil service employees to so-called unclassified employees and expressly barred the solicitation of contributions from relief workers (Mutch 1988, 33–34). In effect, these measures prohibited the one-sided "government subsidy" that would result if public employees and public dependents were required to provide financial support to the party in power; at the same time, they also protected such employees and aid recipients from the potential for extortion resulting from their dependence on the federal government for income.

The 1940 amendments to the Hatch Act imposed a $5,000 annual limitation on individual contributions to federal candidates or national party committees and a $3 million annual limit on the total amount that a party committee operating in two or more states could receive or spend; applied the contribution limits to federal candidates participating in primary elections; and prohibited federal contractors from making contributions to candidates or party committees. "Like earlier regulations, these restrictions had little effect on political giving. Donors could still contribute large sums by giving to multiple committees or by making contributions through state and local party organizations, which were not subject to the $5,000 limit" (Corrado 2002, 7). Moreover, the limits on the national party committees did not apply to unofficial "nonparty organizations" operating independently of party committees. Owing to the independent committee loophole and the state and local party committee exemption, "the contribution and expenditure ceilings failed completely" (Mutch 1988, 35).

The final campaign finance measure coming out of the post–New Deal period was the restriction on union political activity. Paralleling the earlier prohibition on corporations, Congress in 1943 prohibited labor unions from using their treasury funds to make contributions to federal candidates or other expenditures in connection with a federal election. The ban on union activity was adopted as a war measure, with provision for a sunset six months after the end of the war. The ban, however, was made permanent by the Taft-Hartley Act of 1947. This limit, however, was to a considerable degree circumvented by the unions' invention of the political action committee (PAC). The PAC collected contributions from union members and then used the funds to make contributions to candidates and to finance political education programs and voter mobilization activity. The contributions had to be voluntary, not the commitment of obligatory dues. Although PACs could not use union treasury funds for campaign purposes, they provided labor with an opportunity for a significant campaign finance role (Mutch 1988, 152–65).

Federal campaign finance law took its current form with a series of measures adopted in the 1970s: the Federal Election Campaign Act (FECA) of 1971, the significant amendments to FECA adopted in 1974, and further amendments adopted in 1976 and 1979. Although FECA is sometimes described as a reaction to Watergate, Congress had actually devoted considerable attention to the question of campaign finance before Watergate; indeed, the 1971 act predates the scandal. Campaign expenditures had risen sharply in the 1950s and 1960s as television and other media spending became increasingly integral to campaigns. In addition, although political parties were still important, campaigns had become increasingly candidate centered. "Candidates for federal office established their own committees and raised funds independent of party efforts" (Corrado 2002, 8). This, too, drove up costs and thereby increased the need for large contributions.

The FECA of 1971 (which took effect in 1972) established contribution limits on the amount candidates could give to their own campaigns; set ceilings on the amount candidates could spend on media; and strictly tightened disclosure, including new provisions for public inspections. The 1971 act's restrictions, however, had little impact on overall spending. Dissatisfaction with the act and evidence of significant financial improprieties in connection with the Nixon reelection campaign led Congress to overhaul the law dramatically in 1974. (More minor changes were made in 1976 and 1979.) Following the 1974 act, the basic elements of federal campaign finance law are as follows:

- Candidates, political parties, political action committees, and other organizations engaged in electoral campaigning are required to disclose the sources and amounts of contributions and their expenditures. A newly created agency, the Federal Election Commission, is empowered to receive all campaign reports and enforce the disclosure requirement.

- There are dollar limitations on the amount of money individuals may contribute to candidates, political parties, and political committees generally, as well as on the amounts that parties and political committees may contribute to candidates. The Federal Election Campaign Act also carries forward the older laws barring corporations and unions from using their treasury funds to make any contributions to candidates, parties, or political committees. Corporations and unions may, however, set up and control "separate, segregated funds"—that is, political action committees—that are authorized to raise voluntary contributions from corporate officers, directors, and shareholders and from union members and coworkers and may then use the contributions so raised to make donations to candidates and parties, subject to dollar limits on the amount of such contributions. The law also imposed dollar limitations on the amounts candidates could spend on their own campaigns and on the amounts that individuals, organizations, and parties may spend on "independent expenditures" that expressly support or oppose candidates but are not coordinated with candidates. The Supreme Court, in the landmark Buckley v. Valeo (424 U.S. 1 [1976]) decision in 1976, found these expenditure restrictions were unconstitutional, although the Court upheld the accompanying statutory disclosure requirements for such expenditures and the contribution limits on donations to candidates.

- The 1974 law provided federal subsidies for candidates in the presidential primaries and the presidential general election. Qualifying primary participants—qualification involves raising a certain threshold amount of money from donors in a number of states—receive public matching funds based on the amount of private contributions the candidate has raised, with public funds matching up to $250 per donor, subject to a statutory cap on the total amount any candidate may receive. In the general election, the major party nominees receive a large flat grant; nominees of minor parties that received above a threshold percentage of the popular vote in the prior presidential election receive a fraction of the major party grant; other candidates who receive above a threshold percentage of the popular vote (5 percent) are eligible for a fractional grant after the election. To receive public funds, a candidate must agree to accept a spending limit (and a limit on the use of personal funds). In the general election, the major party candidate's spending limit (which was set in 1974 and then indexed for inflation) is equal to the public grant. The spending limit in the primary election is one-half the major party limit in the general election. The Supreme Court has held that the spending limit condition for presidential public funding is constitutional since candidates are subject to the limit only if they agree to it; the limit is not imposed on candidates who decline public funds (Buckley v. Valeo, 57 n. 65). A number of states and cities have also adopted partial public funding programs for some state and local elections.

Campaign Finance Regulation and the Supreme Court

In Buckley v. Valeo, the Supreme Court for the first time comprehensively reviewed federal campaign finance law. The Court ruled that the regulation and restriction of campaign contributions and expenditures directly implicated the First Amendment (Buckley v. Valeo, 14–23), but the Court sharply distinguished between laws affecting the market for voters' votes and laws regulating the market for political influence.

The Court held that the primary acceptable justification for regulating campaign finance activity is the prevention of corruption and the appearance of corruption: "To the extent that large contributions are given to secure a political *quid pro quo* from current and potential office holders, the integrity of our system of representative democracy is undermined. . . . Of almost equal concern as the danger of actual corruption is the impact of the appearance of corruption stemming from public awareness of the opportunities for abuse inherent in a regime of large individual financial contributions" (Buckley v. Valeo, 26–27). The Court also minimized the speech element of campaign contributions. A contribution does not entail an expression of political views; rather, "it serves as a general expression of support for the candidate and his views but does not communicate the underlying basis for the support" (Buckley v. Valeo, 21). The real speech is undertaken by the candidate or political organization that spends the contribution, not the contributor. Consequently, the Court upheld FECA's contribution restrictions and has, since Buckley, consistently sustained limitations on the amount of money donors can give to candidates. In a recent case, the Court indicated that its principal concern with contribution limits is that they not be set so low as to make it too difficult for candidates to obtain the funds necessary to wage competitive campaigns (Nixon v. Shrink Missouri Government PAC, 528 U.S. 377, 397 [2000]).

The concern about the potential impact of campaign donations on the market for political influence also played a role in the Supreme Court's validation of the optional public funding program for presidential candidates. As the Court noted in Buckley, one of the benefits of public funding—in addition to reducing the burdens of fundraising—is that it can "reduce the deleterious influence of large contributions on our political process" (Buckley v. Valeo, 91).

With respect to the regulation of the competition for voters' votes, the Court has sharply distinguished between rules that would limit that competition and rules that would supplement it. Buckley v. Valeo flatly rejected limitations on candidate expenditures and expenditures by independent individuals or committees intended to influence the voters. Direct communications to the voters—and other expenditures incurred in support of or in connection with such communications—were held to be the highest form of campaign finance activity and thus entitled to the greatest constitutional protection. The Court dismissed the argument that expenditures could be limited to promote equality among candidates or among the interests seeking to influence voter opinion: "The concept that government may restrict the speech of some elements of our society in order to enhance the relative voice of others" was pronounced "wholly foreign to the First Amendment" (Buckley v. Valeo, 48–49). The Court specifically rejected the relevance to campaign finance law of the one person, one vote doctrine and the constitutional case law invalidating wealth restrictions on the right to vote or run for office: "The principles that underlie invalidation of governmentally imposed restrictions on the franchise do not justify governmentally imposed restrictions on political expression. Democracy depends on a well-informed electorate, not a citizenry legislatively limited in its ability to discuss and debate candidates and issues" (Buckley v. Valeo, 49 n. 55).

Buckley, however, upheld those regulations of the market for voters' votes that increase the amount of information available to voters or increase the ability of candidates to communicate with the electorate. Thus the Court sustained FECA's disclosure requirements, finding that disclosure provides the electorate with useful information concerning the sources of campaign money and thus aids the voters in evaluating candidates: "It allows voters to place each candidate in the political spectrum more precisely than is often possible solely on the basis of party labels and campaign speeches. The sources of a candidate's financial support must also alert the voter to the interests to which a candidate is most likely to be responsive and thus facilitate predictions of future performance in office" (Buckley v. Valeo, 67).[2] In the Court's view, the validity of disclosure and the invalidity of expenditure limitations go hand in hand in fostering a competitive market for voters' votes. The Court similarly upheld the provision of public funds to presidential candidates, finding that public funding is justified by Congress's purposes "to facilitate communication by candidates with the electorate, and to free candidates from the rigors of fundraising" (Buckley v. Valeo, 91). The reduction in fundraising would enhance the electoral marketplace by allowing candidates to spend more time on campaigning and by ameliorating one of the great disincentives to candidacy.

Complicating the Court's preference for subsidies over limitations in the market for voters' votes is the later decision in Austin v. Michigan Chamber of Commerce (494 U.S. 652 [1990]) in which the Court sustained the constitutionality of the long-standing ban on campaign expenditures by corporations. The Court's reasoning relied on the "unique state-conferred" advantages that corporations enjoy, such as limited liability and unlimited life, as well as the fact that corporate resources reflect success in the economic marketplace but "have little or no correlation to the public's support for the corporation's political ideas" (Austin v. Michigan Chamber of Commerce, 659–60). Austin's implication that political expenditures ought to reflect underlying political support does not easily square with Buckley's flat rejection of one person, one vote as a theory of limiting campaign spending. Nor is it clear that the benefits afforded to corporations by state law are distinctly different from those provided to other economic actors who participate in politics (including corporate officers, directors, and shareholders). Austin suggests the continuing power of the political equality model of election competition, Buckley notwithstanding.

The political equality concern, however, remains limited to corporations (and presumably unions) and, specifically, to the use of corporate and union treasury funds.[3] Indeed, corporate and union political action committees, whose funds presumably reflect the support of their donors rather than success in the marketplace, are free to spend unlimited amounts in support of or opposition to candidates. With the exception of the corporate and union treasury fund restrictions (and a handful of other contribution and expenditure prohibitions involving special cases, such as government contractors and nonresident foreign nationals), there are no limits on the ability of candidates, parties, or interest groups to spend money in campaigning to the voters.

Stresses in the Campaign Finance System

The federal campaign finance system inaugurated by Congress in 1971 and 1974, and modified and sustained by the Supreme Court in 1976, has been subject to severe strains over the past three decades. These strains can be grouped into three broad categories. First, there are the difficulties of distinguishing the more heavily regulated market for political influence from the less regulated market for voters' votes. The Court's protection of free competition for votes has handicapped legislative efforts to curtail the market for political influence. Second, there is the difficulty of distinguishing campaign finance from other political activities. Many of the rules, such as contribution limits and disclosure requirements, that the Court upheld in the electoral context would be unconstitutional if applied to nonelectoral political activity. The line between elections and nonelectoral politics has become increasingly blurred as election participants have developed new means to portray their activities as political rather than electoral in order to escape the restraints on electoral activities.

Finally, there is the growing tension between our increasingly wealth-driven campaign finance system and our nominal commitment to egalitarian electoral participation. In the absence of spending limits and public funding, campaign expenditures have grown sharply. Some campaigns have been marked by lopsided funding imbalances between the candidates. Most campaigns have witnessed either a dramatic rise in large private contributions or a growing role for multimillionaire self-funded candidates (or both). These developments do not sit easily in a system that bars the buying of votes, offices, and political decisions.

Distinction Between Contributions and Expenditures

At the heart of contemporary campaign finance law is the combination of contribution restrictions and unlimited expenditures. This requires maintaining a sharp distinction between contributions and expenditures—a distinction that may be more easily sustained in theory than in practice.

Independent expenditures blur the distinction. Independent expenditures are, in form, expenditures and involve the communication of ideas, information, and arguments to the voters. But by supporting or opposing candidates, such expenditures can both advance the political causes of those groups—by electing sympathetic candidates and defeating opponents—and, especially, win the spender useful influence with the candidates who are benefited thereby. Independent expenditures thus provide political committees the opportunity to pursue both electoral and legislative strategies for political influence.

The Supreme Court has consistently held that independent expenditures—so long as they are undertaken without prearrangement or coordination with a candidate—are entitled to the same constitutional protection as candidate expenditures (for example, Colorado Republican Federal Campaign Committee v. FEC, 518 U.S. 604 [1996]). The Court's suggestion that, owing to the lack of coordination, independent expenditures are less beneficial to candidates and do not pose a real danger of a quid pro quo seems naive. Observers have noted that candidates and independent committees can exchange information concerning campaign themes and the placement of ads so that independent expenditures can be beneficial to candidates even in the absence of formal coordination.

Beyond the difficulty of maintaining the contribution-expenditure distinction, the combination of contribution caps with unlimited expenditures fuels the campaign finance arms race that is a defining feature of our system. Without expenditure limitations, campaign costs have soared. Between 1976 and 1996, congressional campaign expenditures rose 667 percent—between three and four times the rate of inflation. This reflects the sharply rising costs of broadcast media and mailings, the growing role of information technologies and computers in polling and other campaign activities, and the replacement of unpaid volunteers by paid campaign specialists. Campaigns are far costlier than they used to be, but contribution limitations were frozen between 1974 and 2002. Candidates have had to raise more and more money in—in inflation-adjusted terms—smaller and smaller amounts (Association of the Bar of the City of New York 2000, 58–59). This has had several consequences, including the following:

- the rise of intermediaries, such as political action committees and so-called "bundlers" like EMILY's List, that play a key role in collecting political money from large numbers of individuals and passing it on to candidates. (Political parties also function as campaign intermediaries and have done well under the system.) In effect, the contribution restriction rules, in limiting the role of wealthy individuals, stimulated the formal organization of political interests into PACs.

- the strengthening of incumbents, who are better known to begin with and thus have a better chance of raising money. Incumbents particularly benefit from the many political action committees that pursue the "legislative" strategy of maintaining friendly ties with elected officials. The greater public awareness of incumbents, and their higher reelection rate to begin with, bolsters incumbents' standing with the PACs, who presume they are likely to be reelected. That helps enable the incumbents to amass significantly larger campaign treasuries than their challengers, reinforcing their electoral advantages and making their reelection all the more likely.

- the rise of wealthy self-funded candidates, who can raise money in unlimited amounts from their own accounts and thus are not burdened by contribution restrictions (Association of the Bar of the City of New York 2000, 73–74).

- the ever-growing burden of fundraising, which, according to anecdotal evidence, has discouraged some people from becoming candidates, has led many officeholders to devote a disproportionate time to raising campaign money, and has led the media, senior political figures, prospective donors, and opinion leaders to look to the ability of a candidate to amass a campaign war chest as a key test of the candidate's seriousness (Association of the Bar of the City of New York 2000, 60).

The Line Between Elections and Politics

Central to campaign finance law is the distinction between election finance, which may be regulated, and political finance generally, which is constitutionally protected from regulation. In making that distinction and sustaining FECA's requirements and restrictions, the Supreme Court read federal campaign law narrowly, holding that it applies only to "communications that in express terms advocate the election or defeat of a clearly identified candidate for federal office" (Buckley v. Valeo, 44). Such activities are now known as "express advocacy." All other political communications are now called "issue advocacy," even though they may not involve the discussion of issues at all.

Buckley's express advocacy test reflects two concerns. First, despite—or perhaps because of—the close connection between elections and politics, the Supreme Court sought a standard that clearly distinguished election-related spending from other political spending. To avoid vagueness and the chilling effect on political speech that can result from vague regulation, Buckley requires the definition of election-related speech to be sharply drawn. Second, the Court seemed worried about unwelcome administrative or judicial probing of the intentions of speakers. Express advocacy appeared to constitute a clear, objective test that fully protected political speech while permitting regulation of activities that were plainly election related.

Over the course of the 1990s, it became clear that the express advocacy test was easily and regularly evaded by both political parties and independent committees. It proved to be child's play for political advertisers and campaign professionals to develop ads that effectively advocated or opposed the cause of a candidate but stopped short of the formal express advocacy that the courts made a prerequisite for regulation. The most common tactic for political advertisers was to include in an ad some language calling for the reader, viewer, or listener to respond by doing something other than voting, such as calling the sponsor or the candidate criticized to obtain more information or vent their views. Hundreds of millions of dollars were spent on issue advocacy during federal election campaigns (Briffault 1999a).

The issue advocacy exemption had three effects. First, because reporting and disclosure requirements apply only to express advocacy, not issue advocacy, various "stealth" organizations with anodyne names like Americans for Good Government emerged during campaigns and made significant expenditures praising or criticizing candidates without having to disclose the identities of their donors. Second, the restrictions on corporate and union treasury funds did not apply, so that corporations and unions could spend unlimited amounts on issue advocacy. Third, the restrictions on contributions to political parties, political party contributions to candidates, and party expenditures coordinated with a candidate—such coordinated expenditures are normally treated as contributions, not expenditures—did not apply, either. The parties could receive unlimited donations from corporations, unions, and wealthy individuals and spend those sums without limit on issue advocacy in support of their candidates or in opposition to the candidate of the opposing party. This enabled the parties to avoid both the general limits on party support for candidates and the spending limits on publicly funded presidential candidates. As a result, the nominally publicly funded presidential general election became increasingly privately funded.

Party issue advocacy was a key component of party "soft money," that is, party expenditures funded by contributions not subject to federal restrictions. Soft money originally emerged out of the complications of federalism. The Federal Election Campaign Act regulates only federal elections, but federal and state elections typically occur concurrently, with candidates for federal and state elections appearing on the same ballot. Political party committees may undertake campaign efforts that assist federal and state candidates simultaneously. Spending with respect to federal candidates must satisfy FECA, but assistance to state candidates is subject only to state law. Many state campaign finance laws are less restrictive than FECA. Some permit corporations or unions to support candidates; some do not limit individual or PAC contributions. The Federal Election Commission held that money not subject to FECA—in other words, corporate and union treasury funds and large individual and PAC contributions—could be used to pay for party activities that do not directly benefit federal candidates, such as staff salaries and overhead, and for the "nonfederal share" of joint federal-state activities, such as voter registration and get-out-the-vote drives. Starting around 1995, the national parties also began to use such soft money for issue advocacy, on the theory that such advocacy is not about the election of federal candidates. In the 2000 election, soft money accounted for 40 percent of major party expenditures. Contributions to party soft money accounts became a major mechanism for channeling special interest moneys into election campaigns and thus into the market for political influence (see, generally, Briffault 2000).

Inequality in the Competition for Votes

Inequality—both the inequality of candidates and the inequality of influence of donors—is a central theme in our campaign finance system, particularly in congressional campaigns. With respect to candidate competition, in most campaigns one candidate, usually the incumbent, significantly outspends his or her opponent. In 1998 the average House incumbent spent $657,000, and the average House challenger spent $265,000; on average, then, incumbents outspent challengers by 2.4 to 1. Similarly, in 1996 the average House incumbent spent $750,000, and the average House challenger spent $279,000, an imbalance of 2.7 to 1. More important, in 1998 half of all House challengers raised less than $100,000, and only one-third raised as much as $200,000. Sixty percent of House incumbents either had no significant financial opposition or outspent their opponents by a margin of ten to one or more (Association of the Bar of the City of New York 2000, 65–66).

Although funding parity is not essential for competitive elections, if only one candidate is able to obtain adequate financing, the election is likely to be politically noncompetitive. In 1998 House challengers who spent less than $200,000 on average received less than 40 percent of the two-party vote. Overall, across the 1994, 1996, and 1998 elections, the average winner outspent the average loser by between 2.5 and 3 to 1, and the biggest spender won in 95 percent of House races. Financial competition was less one-sided in the Senate, but there too in 1996 and 1998 incumbents outspent challengers by 1.5 to 1, and winners outspent major party losers by 1.7 and 1.8 to 1 (Association of the Bar of the City of New York 2000, 67–68).

Our frequently financially noncompetitive elections are also elections in which a relatively small number of donors dominate the process. Large individual donations (in excess of $200) and PAC contributions provide the bulk of campaign contributions. Moreover, a relatively small number of large PACs dominate PAC giving. In 1998, 55 percent of all PACs made contributions of less than $5,000, and another 27 percent made contributions of between $5,000 and $50,000. At the other end of the spectrum, there were 34 PACs that contributed $1 million or more, for a total of $52.6 million, or one-quarter of all PAC spending. An additional 51 PACs made contributions ranging from $500,000 to $1 million, for a total of $35.7 million. Altogether, the top 179 PACs (3.8 percent of all PACs) made $118.5 million in contributions (56.1 percent of all PAC contributions). The inequalities are even greater among individual donors. In 1995 and 1996, just 235,000 people—one-tenth of 1 percent of the total population and one-fifth of 1 percent of those who cast ballots in the presidential election—provided one-third of all individual donations. The vast majority of voting-age residents make no campaign contributions at all (Association of the Bar of the City of New York 2000, 61–65).

Large donors are not a politically or demographically representative sample of the general population. A study of donors who gave $200 or more to one or more congressional candidates found that affluent men, whites, and people engaged in high-status occupations make up a far higher proportion of the large donor group than of society as a whole (Briffault 1999b, 563, 575 n. 42).

The central role of large individual and PAC donations poses a sharp challenge to the principle of voter equality. Although elections are not always won by the biggest spender, the big spender does win in the vast majority of cases. To be sure, scholars have been unable to determine whether the big spender wins by virtue of being the big spender or whether the winner is the big spender because he or she is also usually the biggest recipient of campaign contributions, and the same factors that lead voters to vote for a candidate independently lead donors to give to that candidate. Yet campaign spending surely has some effect on campaigns. Indeed, the theory underlying the Supreme Court's protection of campaign expenditures is that those expenditures do affect how voters vote.

Thus our campaign finance system gives a small and unrepresentative number of individuals and organizations the opportunity to use their contributions to candidates, as well as their expenditures on direct communications with the voters, to affect electoral outcomes. Their votes are not tabulated in the ballot result, but they play a role in influencing how the ballots are cast. In a sense, both candidates and the public at large are indebted to these donors, for, under current law, without their contributions campaigns would have to consist entirely of the self-financed efforts of candidates and their families and the meager coverage provided by the media. A greater percentage of candidates would be multimillionaires, voter ignorance even higher, and voter turnout still further reduced. Yet campaign funding predicated on extremely unequal levels of contributions, reflective in part of underlying differences in the distribution of wealth as well as of engagement with politics, is in sharp tension with the norm of voter equality.

Reforming Campaign Finance Reform

On March 27, 2002, President George W. Bush signed into law the most significant and comprehensive changes in United States campaign finance regulation in more than a generation. Enacted after almost six years of contentious debate, the Bipartisan Campaign Reform Act (BCRA) of 2002—known as Shays-Meehan in the House of Representatives and McCain-Feingold in the Senate—addresses a broad range of campaign finance issues, including fundraising on federal property, contributions by foreign nationals, donations to presidential inauguration committees, electronic filing of and Internet access to federal campaign finance reports, and penalties for the violation of federal campaign finance law. But at the heart of BCRA is the effort to strengthen FECA's regulation of the market for political influence through the imposition of new restrictions on "soft money" and "issue advocacy."

The act bans soft money contributions to the national political parties and prohibits the use of soft money to fund the federal election activities of state and local parties, with a limited exception permitting large individual donations for party-led voter registration and get-out-the-vote drives. The act also addresses issue advocacy, albeit in three different ways.

- With respect to political parties, BCRA treats all public communications that refer to a clearly identified candidate for federal office and promote or oppose a candidate for that office as express advocacy, subject to federal regulation.

- The act prohibits business corporations and unions from spending money on "electioneering communications," which it defines as "any broadcast, cable or satellite communication" that refers to a clearly identified candidate for federal office and that is aired within sixty days of a general election or thirty days of a primary election (*Bipartisan Campaign Reform Act of 2002*, 116 Stat. 81, §201). Not-for-profit corporations that finance their election-related activities solely from individual donations, and do not accept corporate or union support, are exempt from the ban.

- Other organizations and individuals can spend without limit on election-eering communications, but any person or entity that spends in excess of $10,000 on electioneering communications during a calendar year must file reports that disclose the identities of the principal contributors financing those expenditures.

In addition, BCRA requires the Federal Election Commission to adopt a new definition of coordinated expenditure that will permit the limitation of such expenditures even in the absence of a formal agreement or collaboration be-tween the individual or organization making the expenditure and the candi-date who benefits from it.

A broad coalition of interest groups brought suit to challenge BCRA's constitutionality the day it was signed. Many politicians and party committees entered the suit against the statute as well. In a highly unusual September 2003 sitting devoted solely to the suits against BCRA, the Supreme Court met to hear four hours of argument challenging and defending the statute. In De-cember 2003, in McConnell v. FEC (124 S. Ct. 619 [2003]), a divided Supreme Court issued a sweeping judgment that upheld all of the key provi-sions of the act, including the restrictions on political party soft money, the regulation of "electioneering communications," and the requirement of a new definition of coordination.

In so doing, the Court made several important contributions to the evolv-ing jurisprudence of campaign finance regulation. First, the Court appeared to broaden its definition of corruption used to justify regulation of campaign con-tributions. In the past, the Court had focused on the concept of the quid pro quo, that is, a campaign contribution would be considered corrupt if the donor re-ceived some benefit in exchange for the donation. In McConnell v. FEC (664), the Court broadened the concept of corrupt benefit to include not just a partic-ular vote cast or favor granted but also the "special access" to officeholders that donors obtain from their contributions. The Court repeatedly focused on the use of campaign donations to "buy preferential access to federal officeholders" and thereby "open the doors of the offices of individual and important Members of Congress and the Administration" (McConnell v. FEC, 668, 663 n. 46). By fo-cusing on special access, McConnell reframed the corruption analysis from the consideration of the impact of contributions on formal decisions to their effect on the opportunity to influence government actions. By treating preferential ac-cess as a problem in itself, the Court has made it easier for Congress and the states to justify and prove the need for restrictions.

Second, the Court expanded the theoretical basis for regulating the financing of political parties. The Court had previously sustained restrictions on party support for candidates on the theory that the parties could be used as conduits for potentially corrupting contributions from private donors to candidates (FEC v. Colorado Republican Federal Campaign Committee, 533 U.S. 431 [2001]). But many of BCRA's soft money restrictions went beyond money given to parties to be funneled to specific candidates. The act restricted *all* donations to national parties—including donations for expenditures that do not support any candidates as well as state and local party spending on voter registration, get-out-the-vote, and generic party spending—that might benefit party candidates generally but did not closely link a particular donor with a particular candidate. Nevertheless, looking to the "special relationship and unity of interest" (McConnell v. FEC, 661) that links a party to its officeholders and candidates, as well as to the unique role parties play in mobilizing voters and organizing Congress, the Court found that donations to party committees raise the same dangers of corruption as donations to candidates and therefore may be regulated.

Third, the Court gave surprisingly little weight to the First Amendment arguments raised against the more expansive definition of "electioneering communication." The Court was persuaded that the old "express advocacy" test had failed to distinguish effectively between speech that was election related and speech that was not and that BCRA's test suffered from neither vagueness nor overbreadth.

Finally, and most important, McConnell to a considerable degree reframed the way the Court addressed the constitutionality of campaign finance regulation. Instead of treating campaign finance restrictions as a threat to freedoms of speech and association and therefore a challenge to constitutional values, the Court gave great weight to the interests in fair, informed democratic decision making it found to be advanced by contribution limitations, disclosure requirements, and restrictions on corporate and union spending. The Court found that campaign finance law involves not a single set of constitutional principles but the reconciliation of "competing constitutional values" (Nixon v. Shrink Missouri Government PAC, 403 [Breyer, J., concurring])—not just freedom of speech but free speech and government integrity. Indeed, McConnell appears to have placed the democracy-promoting features of campaign finance regulation at the heart of the Court's analysis. The McConnell majority clearly viewed many of BCRA's restrictions and requirements not as burdens on speech but as desirable efforts to promote democracy.

To be sure, the Court was sharply divided. Of the three principal components of campaign finance doctrine at issue in McConnell—disclosure, contribution limits, and the special restrictions on corporate and union funds—only the disclosure principle appears to enjoy broad support within the Court. Four justices vehemently dissented from the portions of the decision upholding the soft money restrictions and the ban on corporate and union electioneering communications. Thus McConnell was a precarious victory for reform as well as a sweeping one. Both the specific holdings and the Court's basic approach could be dramatically transformed if and when the membership of the Court changes.

Although BCRA is now law, it is not clear what its effects will be. The 2004 elections will be the first to be run under the new rules, and at this early stage it is impossible to tell whether BCRA will reduce the political influence of interest groups over officeholders or instead simply restructure that influence in arguably undesirable ways.

The Bipartisan Campaign Reform Act's toughest limitations are on money given to and spent by the political parties. Consequently, the act could enhance the role of nonparty groups and shift political campaigns further from candidates and parties and into the hands of ideological organizations—such as the National Rifle Association or the Sierra Club—and wealthy individuals willing to spend money independently to promote their ideas and the candidates they favor. Arguably, the ability of the political parties to hold together candidates, party organizations, and ideological and economic interest groups will be curtailed, and the role of independent spending will rise.

These concerns have considerable force, but they may be misplaced. Inducing interest groups to shift money away from the parties to independent spending follows from BCRA's concern with curtailing the legislative strategy for pursuing political influence. Right now, wealthy individuals, corporations, unions, and interest groups seek to influence officeholders by giving to party committees often controlled by the party's elected officials, deploy their funds in support of party candidates, work with candidates, and rely on candidates and officeholders for party fundraising. Soft money contributions to the parties are comparable to direct contributions to candidates in terms of the capacity for creating quid pro quos and the appearance of quid pro quos. Independent spending by individuals and interest groups may still benefit candidates, but it may be less beneficial, and less directly the source of political influence with candidates, than large soft money contributions to the parties. Independent spending is more likely to be part of an election strategy of electing sympathetic officeholders than a legislative strategy of obtaining access to whoever wins, and the Supreme Court has made it extremely difficult to curtail election strategy expenditures. To be sure, some of the integrative function of the parties—in holding diverse officeholders and interests together—may be jeopardized. But soft money restriction is consistent with our campaign finance system's long-term focus on reducing the ability of individuals and interests to use their campaign donations to obtain influence with officeholders.

A more troubling criticism of BCRA is that it does little to reform the market for votes; indeed, it probably aggravates the inequalities that beset that market. The act could reduce the campaign finance role of political parties. Although that may be a useful means of controlling donor efforts to obtain political influence, the parties, more than any other campaign participants (for example, wealthy individuals and PACs), are likely to support challengers and incumbents at risk of losing rather than incumbents generally. Parties play an exclusively electoral strategy, not a legislative strategy, and they do that by sending money to competitive races. Parties thus promote competition in the market for voters' votes. Reducing their role could reduce the opportunity for competitive elections.

By eliminating most soft money donations and preelection issue advocacy expenditures by business corporations and unions, the act may also reduce the amount of money spent on election campaigns and thus the amount of campaign information available to voters generally. This, however, is not certain. To offset the contribution losses resulting from the restriction of soft money, BCRA doubled FECA's limits on individuals' hard money donations to candidates and parties and party donations to candidates. These were the first increases in the contribution limits since 1974. Moreover, BCRA provided that, for the first time, these limits will be indexed for inflation. The amount of hard money should thus increase substantially.

The soft money restrictions, even offset by the increase in hard money limits, may make it harder for candidates to compete against personally wealthy opponents. One unusual feature of the act provides that if candidates use personal wealth to spend over a threshold amount on their campaigns, then the limitations on contributions to their opponents are progressively relaxed, so that the more big spenders commit to their campaigns the more their opponents can accept from individual donors. This may make races involving wealthy candidates more financially competitive—provided their opponents can actually persuade donors to contribute larger sums. On the other hand, it also authorizes extremely large donations to certain candidates, so that greater competition among candidates in the market for voters' votes increases the ability of large donors to dominate the market for political influence. The implications of this so-called millionaires' provision nicely illustrate the difficulty of reconciling all of the values—prevention of corruption as well as promotion of equality—affected by a campaign finance system, as well as the impact that regulation in the market for voters' ballots can have on the market for political influence.

Although the millionaires' provision may mitigate one aspect of candidate inequality, BCRA does nothing to promote voter equality. The combination of soft money and issue advocacy restrictions, hard money increases, and the rolling relaxation on donations to candidates running against wealthy self-financing opponents does nothing to increase the equal voice of voters in the campaign finance process. At best, the very large influence of million-dollar soft money gifts will be marginally democratized by a shift to smaller hard money gifts—although with the hard money ceiling at $2,000 for individual donations to candidates and $25,000 on gifts to party committees, BCRA hardly limits large donations. Rather, the very small number of donors ready to give the statutory maximum will most likely continue to dominate campaign financing. With many large donors pursuing the legislative strategy of using contributions to secure access to officeholders, the candidates likely to benefit most from larger hard money contributions are incumbents, political insiders, preelection favorites, and the candidates of the stronger party in the district or state. Most congressional elections are likely to be no more financially competitive under BCRA than before its passage.

Public Subsidies and the Market for Voters' Votes

At an early stage in the legislative process that produced the 2002 law, Congress considered a proposal to provide free broadcast time to candidates who voluntarily agreed to abide by spending limits. That provision dropped out of BCRA, so that the new law contains no public subsidies to enhance competition in the market for votes—with the arguable exception of the informational subsidy provided by the enhanced disclosure requirements for electioneering communications. Congress has shown little interest in providing public funding for congressional candidates.

This should come as no surprise. By making it easier for newcomers and challengers to compete, public funding may be a threat to the incumbents who decide what campaign finance laws are adopted. Moreover, the presidential public funding system has been less than a complete success. Despite the fact that the major party nominees have consistently accepted public funds, with the attendant limits on private contributions, private money has come flooding back into the system. The rigidities of the funding formula have also had peculiar results. Ross Perot's respectable 8.4 percent showing in the 1996 election meant that millions of dollars in public funds were available to his Reform Party, even though the Reform Party candidate in 2000, Pat Buchanan, had meager public support and only limited ties to the prior Reform Party agenda. Conversely, Perot, when he ran in 1992 and had enormous public backing, and Ralph Nader, who had significantly more public support than Buchanan in 2000, were both ineligible for preelection public funds, as both were the candidates of new parties. Presidential public funding has also suffered from a loss of public support as reflected by the declining percentage of taxpayers who have been willing to check off a contribution to the public funding program on their tax returns.

Of course, some of the problems with presidential public funding are the result of particular features of that system rather than the concept of public funding generally. When Congress adopted public funding in 1974, it set the basic general election grant in an amount significantly below that spent by the loser, George McGovern, in 1972. The public grant did not reach the nominal dollar amount spent by the 1972 winner, Richard Nixon, until 1996. As a result, presidential election campaigns have been significantly underfunded. Indeed, owing to the low levels of public funding, in recent years a growing number of major party candidates have declined to participate in the primary election phase of the public funding program. In 2000 George W. Bush opted out of the public funding program during the prenomination phase of his campaign, relying instead on a record amount of privately raised contributions and the resulting ability to spend far in excess of the prenomination spending limit. In 2004 not only did President Bush again decline to take primary public funds and to accept a prenomination spending limit but so also did two of the leading Democratic contenders, including the ultimate winner of the Democratic nomination, John Kerry.

The low level of public funding in the presidential election system was an important factor fueling the rise of soft money (Briffault 1999b, 586). Soft money's growth, in turn, fueled public discontent with campaign finance generally, perhaps contributing to taxpayers' unwillingness to donate to the public funding program. To be effective, public funding requires adequate financing. So, too, different criteria could be used for determining which candidates are eligible for public funding and what level of funding candidates receive.

Although Congress has demonstrated no interest in public funding for congressional elections or in strengthening the presidential public funding system, many states and localities have implemented public funding programs. In some places, like New Jersey, the focus has been on the gubernatorial election. But elsewhere, including Arizona, Maine, Minnesota, and New York City, public funding initiatives have included legislative elections. The most dramatic of these measures—the "clean money" laws of Arizona, Maine, Massachusetts, and Vermont—would largely replace private funding with public grants for participating candidates. These laws were adopted only in the late 1990s, and the Massachusetts program has yet to be funded, so it is too early to tell how well they work. Older laws, such as those in Minnesota and New York City, are more comparable to the presidential primary public funding system in that they aim to supplement private funding with public dollars, not to completely replace private funds. Because of its most recent amendments, New York City now offers a generous 4-to-1 public match for private donations up to $250, subject to a cap on the total public grant to each candidate. These laws have been considered successful in helping challengers, independents, and newcomers.

Public funding would make our campaign finance system more congruent with our egalitarian electoral norms, curtail the ability of donors to factor campaign financing into the market for political influence, and improve competition in the market for voters' votes. With publicly financed campaigns, all voters have an equal role in campaign finance and thus an equal say in the campaign to influence voters' votes. Money from the public fisc comes from everyone and thus from no one in particular. No one gains influence over the election through public funding. The more the funds for election campaigns come from the public treasury, the more evenly is financial influence over election outcomes spread across the populace.

Public funding breaks the tie between campaign finance and interest group influence over the political process. Public funding also reduces the leverage of large donors over government. The more campaign funds come from the public fisc, the less sensitive elected officials need to be to the views of large private donors, and the more they can act on their own view of what the public interest requires.

Public funding can also promote competition among candidates in the market for voters' votes. In general, incumbents, politically favored candidates, and major party candidates benefit from the current system in which private contributions are frequently given to advance strategies for obtaining influence within the legislature or the executive branch. Donors who want to be with the winner give to incumbents, the candidate of the locally dominant party, or the preelection favorite, and, in consequence, campaign donations often become self-fulfilling prophecies. The challengers most financially capable of taking on incumbents or the dominant party's candidate are the self-financing multimillionaires. Public funding would level this playing field by making it easier for less affluent challengers to raise funds.

To be sure, the effectiveness of a publicly funded system in promoting electoral competition would turn crucially on the precise details of how candidates qualify for funds, how much funding a candidate qualifies for, and what percentage of funding will consist of public dollars. A small public grant would do little; a high threshold might exclude many potential challengers; a low spending limit would make it more difficult for challengers to take on incumbents. Still, given the bias toward incumbents of the current system and the general lack of financially competitive races, it is difficult to believe that public funding would worsen electoral competition, and there is every reason to believe that public funds would make elections more competitive.

Of course, public funding is not a panacea. As Michael Bloomberg demonstrated when he spent more than $70 million of his own funds in his successful quest to become mayor of New York City, so long as mandatory campaign spending limits are unconstitutional, even a well-funded public funding system cannot eliminate the role of private wealth. Still, public funding provided Bloomberg's opponent, Mark Green, with millions of dollars that significantly supplemented his privately raised funds and enabled him to spend more than any prior New York City mayoral candidate, even if it was significantly less than Bloomberg. The Bloomberg-Green race was certainly competitive, even if the enormous role played by Bloomberg's personal wealth was at odds with the norm of political equality.

A Comparative Perspective on Campaign Finance

The difficulties of regulating the markets for votes and for political influence without unduly impinging on electoral competition or political freedom are not limited to the United States. Most democratic countries regulate important aspects of their campaign finance systems, utilizing the same basic regulatory techniques that have long been part of the American campaign finance tool kit. A recent survey of political finance laws in 111 countries found widespread use of disclosure requirements, contribution prohibitions and limitations, expenditure limitations, and public subsidies of candidates or parties (Tjernström 2003). The mix of techniques, however, differs from the United States.

A majority—53 percent—of the countries surveyed required some form of disclosure of contributions to parties or candidates. But outside the United States such disclosure typically involves a postelection report rather than American-style preelection disclosure. Postelection disclosure may have some mild effect in discouraging potentially corrupting contributions, but it is useless for informing the voters and influencing the competition for votes. Moreover, in many countries the scope of disclosure is more limited than in the United States. Although the effectiveness of the federal disclosure requirements have been criticized, the United States appears to do comparatively well with disclosure.

With respect to contributions, although 55 percent of the countries surveyed banned some form of contributions, the restrictions tended to be targeted on foreign contributions and government contractors. These contributions are also banned in the United States, but the primary targets of the American contribution prohibitions have been corporations and unions, while relatively few other countries ban political donations by these groups. For example, corporate and union contributions were permissible in Australia, Canada, New Zealand, and the United Kingdom.[4] Similarly, although monetary contribution limits are a fundamental component of American campaign finance law and have been strongly validated by the Supreme Court, only 27 percent of the countries surveyed imposed any monetary limits on the size of contributions. Again, there were no monetary contribution limits in national elections in Australia, Canada, New Zealand, or the United Kingdom.

On the other hand, although the U.S. Supreme Court has largely prohibited expenditure limitations (other than limitations on corporate and union treasury funds), 24 percent of the countries surveyed have spending limits. The United Kingdom has imposed spending limits on candidates at the constituency level since 1883, and the Political Parties, Elections, and Reform Act of 2000 added national spending limits for the national political parties. Canada imposed spending limits on parties and candidates in 1974, and New Zealand did so in the 1990s (Geddis 2002).

Public funding also seems to be a more popular option outside the United States, with the money provided primarily to parties rather than, as is the usual practice in the United States, to candidates. Often, however, in other systems the money is provided after the election, as a reimbursement to parties that obtained a specified level of voter support, rather than beforehand for actual financing of the campaign. Such postelection support is the practice in Australia and in the province of Quebec. Federal election law in Canada provides a more limited form of public support: donors to parties and candidates and parties that enjoy a specified level of electoral support can claim a tax credit up to a statutory ceiling.

One big difference between the United States and most other countries involves the regulation of broadcast media. The majority (64 percent) of the 111 countries surveyed provide their parties with free political broadcasts. Free media is effectively a public subsidy.

Although it is difficult to generalize, the principal focus of campaign finance regulation in the United States, compared with other countries, is the campaign contribution. This derives partly from the actions of Congress, which first restricted contributions in 1907 and made limits on contributions a centerpiece of campaign finance law in 1974. Equally important has been the role of the Supreme Court, which has invalidated most expenditure limitations. As a result, it appears that the United States places greater weight on regulating the market for political influence than do the other countries; by contrast, the other countries have focused on regulating the market for voters' votes.

Moreover, focusing specifically on the market for voters' votes, the United States—again due in part to the Supreme Court—has aimed primarily at increasing voter information through disclosure and at preventing the limits on voter information that might result from spending caps. By the same token, the United States has given little weight to the role of political equality in campaigning for voters' votes. The Supreme Court has made the spending caps that might level the playing field among candidates unconstitutional, while Congress has made only limited provision for public funding. In contrast, other countries, through their expenditure caps, limits on paid advertising, and provision of some free air time, appear to take political equality in the competition for votes more seriously as a campaign finance value.

Although their laws are different, many foreign countries are encountering problems similar to the those of the American campaign finance system. In recent years both Canada and the United Kingdom have grappled with their equivalents of the issue advocacy dilemma. Those countries limit the campaign expenditures of candidates and then tightly limit the election-related spending of independent interest groups. As a result, courts in both countries have had to determine both what constitutes an election-related expenditure as well as the propriety of favoring parties and candidates over nonparty actors (see, generally, Geddis 2001).

The Limits and Possibilities of Campaign Finance Reform

The impetus for campaign finance reform over the past several decades has been the concern that our election campaigns increasingly depart from our norms of equality of electoral participation and exclusion of market transactions from political decision making. Our current system of relying heavily—and, in congressional elections, exclusively—on private funds is marked by considerable inequality, with a tiny fraction of the community supplying the bulk of campaign funds and thus enjoying disproportionate influence in the electoral process. Private funding constrains competition in the market for votes, producing many financially noncompetitive elections. Private funding also offers wealthy individuals and interest groups the opportunity to use their control over the supply of campaign funds to influence the decisions of elected officials.

Ultimately, the only way to ensure equality of participation and eliminate the concern that campaign contributions can "buy" official decisions would be to require all candidates to rely on public funds for their campaigns and to bar, or tightly limit, the use of private funds for independent expenditure. Private funding of campaigns inevitably gives different individuals and groups different levels of influence over the election and over the actions of elected officials.

Mandatory and exclusive public funding of elections is constitutionally forbidden, however, according to the Supreme Court's interpretation of the First Amendment. Candidates and interest groups have a constitutional right to present their views concerning an election to the voters and to spend as much money as they want in presenting those views.

Moreover, a purely publicly funded electoral process would give the government an enormous say in shaping our elections. Government determination of who gets public funding and how much particular candidates receive would determine the nature and scope of electoral competition. Public funding rules tied to past electoral success—as in presidential public funding—could favor the major parties and hurt new parties and independents. Even public funding criteria linked to current levels of support would tend to favor incumbents, major parties, and, in general, candidates popular at the outset of the campaign and would make it difficult for newcomers and those initially less popular to get their views to the voters.

Moreover, a ban on private funding would also exclude interest groups interested in raising particular issues—issues that the candidates and major parties want to keep off the electoral agenda but other groups think ought to be a part of the electoral debate. Election campaigns would become the exclusive domain of the candidates and parties. Neither Eugene McCarthy's 1968 antiwar presidential campaign, which was financed by a handful of financial angels, nor Ross Perot's 1992 antideficit presidential campaign, nor the independent electoral activities of a range of term-limits, right-to-life, environmental, and pro- and anti-abortion-rights groups would have been possible without a considerable role for private funds. Yet surely these candidates and organizations broadened the electoral debate and brought a wider range of issues into the electoral decision.

As a result, even if a purely publicly funded election were constitutionally possible, it is not clear it would be desirable. Completely excluding private funding would make the electoral system more rigid and more subject to control by government and the major parties. Some private funding can enable a wider range of voices to participate in the electoral process, even if it also injects economic inequality into election campaigns.

Nor would public funding of elections completely eliminate the ability of wealthy individuals and special interests to have an undue impact on the political process. Economic and organizational resources not committed to election campaigns could still be used for lobbying, for shaping public opinion, and for mobilizing group members for political action. Wealth and organization have central roles to play in politics, even if they are kept out of elections.

Nonetheless, even if the price of our relatively open electoral system is some inequality in campaign financing and some spillover from campaign financing into government decision making, our campaign finance system can be made more congruent with the egalitarian, market-free norms of democratic politics. By barring very large individual, corporate, and union donations to the political parties and subjecting all electioneering communications—not just so-called express advocacy—to the contribution, expenditure, and disclosure rules that apply to election campaigns, the newly enacted Bipartisan Campaign Reform Act pushes special interest money further away from candidates and reduces the potential for campaign finance to "buy" government decisions.

The act by itself, however, does little to address the problems of unequal financing of election campaigns or the undue influence big spenders and donors can have in influencing voter decision making. Some significant, albeit partial and voluntary, public funding will be necessary if we wish to really curtail the impact of campaign financing on government decision making and respect the norm of political equality in the financing of election campaigns. Perfect equality of voter influence in campaign financing is probably not possible; indeed, it may not even be desirable if we also want to keep our system open to new entrants and noncandidate participants. So long as private money is involved, campaign contributions will have some impact on the political process. But significant public funding would increase the equal influence of voters, reduce the role of private wealth, and promote financially competitive elections.

Notes

1. The Supreme Court ultimately reversed its position on the nature of primaries, holding that primaries to select nominees for federal office are elections subject to federal regulation, in United States v. Classic (313 U.S. 299 [1941]).
2. The Court acknowledged that the disclosure of contributions could chill certain donations, particularly those to politically unpopular groups. It held, however, that disclosure requirements are generally valid and placed the burden of proof on individuals or groups seeking exemption from the general rule of disclosure to demonstrate that disclosure constitutes a "serious" threat to their First Amendment rights. See Buckley v. Valeo (424 U.S. 1, 71 [1976]). Subsequently, in a case involving the Socialist Workers Party, the Court found that a minor party had made out a sufficient case that disclosure would chill legitimate contributions that the Court exempted the party from a state disclosure law. See Brown v. Socialist Workers '74 Campaign Committee (459 U.S. 87 [1982]).
3. Not only may corporate expenditures be prohibited, but the Court has also upheld the federal law barring corporate contributions directly to candidates for federal office. See FEC v. Beaumont (123 S. Ct. 2200 [2003]).
4. In Canada, the province of Quebec bars contributions by corporations, unions, and associations in provincial elections. See Massicotte (2002).

References

Association of the Bar of the City of New York, Commission on Campaign Finance. 2000. *Dollars and Democracy: A Blueprint for Campaign Finance Reform.* New York: Fordham University Press.

Bipartisan Campaign Reform Act of 2002. 116 Stat. 81–116. Pub.L. 107–55. 107th Congress, 2nd Session (March 27, 2002).

Briffault, Richard. 1993. "Who Rules at Home? One Person/One Vote and Local Government." *University of Chicago Law Review* 60(2): 339–424.

———. 1999a. "Issue Advocacy: Redrawing the Elections/Politics Line." *Texas Law Review* 77(7): 1751–1802.

———. 1999b. "Public Funding and Democratic Elections." *University of Pennsylvania Law Review* 148(2): 563–90.

———. 2000. "The Political Parties and Campaign Finance Reform." *Columbia Law Review* 100(3): 620–66.

Corrado, Anthony. 2002. "A History of Federal Campaign Finance Law." In *The New Campaign Finance Sourcebook,* edited by Anthony Corrado, Thomas E. Mann, Daniel Ortiz, and Trevor Potter. Washington, D.C.: Brookings Institution Press.

Geddis, Andrew C. 2001. "Democratic Visions and Third-Party Independent Expenditures: A Comparative View." *Tulane Journal of International and Comparative Law* 9(spring): 5–107.

———. 2002. "Regulating Campaign Funding in New Zealand's Changing Election Process." Paper presented at the Institute of Advanced Legal Studies Research Seminar on Funding of Political Parties. Columbia University (July 5–6).

Hasen, Richard L. 2000. "Vote Buying." *California Law Review* 88(5): 1323–71.

Keyssar, Alexander. 2000. *The Right to Vote: The Contested History of Democracy in the United States.* New York: Basic Books.

Lowenstein, Daniel Hays, and Richard L. Hasen. 2001. *Election Law: Cases and Materials.* 2d ed. Durham, N.C.: Carolina Academic Press.

Massicotte, Louis. 2002. "Financing Parties at the Grass Roots Level." Paper presented at the Institute of Advanced Legal Studies Research Seminar on Funding of Political Parties. Columbia University (July 5–6).

Mutch, Robert E. 1988. *Campaigns, Congress and Courts: The Making of Federal Campaign Finance Law.* New York: Praeger.

Tjernström, Maja. 2003. "Matrix on Political Finance Laws and Regulations." In International IDEA, *Handbook on Funding of Political Parties and Election Campaigns.* Stockholm: International Institute for Democracy and Electoral Assistance.

Steinfeld, Robert J. 1989. "Property and Suffrage in the Early American Republic." *Stanford Law Review* 41(2): 335–76.

14

CONCLUSION

Richard R. Nelson

MARKET ORGANIZATION has shown itself to be a valuable and flexible component of the way we govern a wide range of human activities. Given broad agreement on this premise, this book develops three arguments. First, U.S. society is able to use market organization effectively in such a wide range of areas in large part because we have learned how to supplement basic market organization with a diverse structure of nonmarket forms of governance tailored to the specific characteristics of different fields of activity. Second, there are certain activities and sectors where market organization is problematic as a basic governing mode, and by and large society has stayed clear of heavy reliance on market organization in these areas. Third, in recent years, at least, the American polity has tended to forget what it once understood about the complexities and limits of market organization and to push simple market organization as a general-purpose governing mode. The results in many cases have not been happy ones.

The position we espouse here most emphatically is not an antimarket position. It is no more antimarket than the position that families need extrafamily assistance in carrying out various parts of their charge to raise their children well, or that for certain things, like the question of whether or not their children should be inoculated for certain infectious diseases or should attend school, the decision should not rest solely with family, is an antifamily position. It does not help the case for market organization to be blind to supplements that often are needed if market organization is to work well or to the activities for which market organization is not well suited as a central form of governance.

Economists have long recognized this. They have developed a collection of theoretical concepts that identify conditions under which markets need supplementary apparatus to work well or are inappropriate. These concepts include public goods—goods or services that should be made public on grounds of equity or other normative reasons—externalities, asymmetric information or knowledge between provider and user, and natural monopolies. Certainly, these concepts are extremely useful in analyzing what is needed for effective governance of an activity. However, they provide no easy, transparent formula for determining just how much use of market organization is appropriate in an area of activity and how much and what kind of nonmarket organization.

They do not, first of all, because what economists call "market failures" are almost always a matter of degree, not kind. Furthermore, a number of the categories of market failure depend on people's values, and there may be limited agreement about what values should count, and with what strength, in an area of human activity. Second, while simple market organization is not a perfect solution for all (or perhaps any) activity, the supplements and alternatives to market organization have their limitations and problematic elements, too. The question of how to organize and govern an activity inevitably requires careful analysis of a variety of mixed and complex alternatives, none of which will score as perfect in all dimensions.

Third, and this is a matter that even many sophisticated economists tend to overlook, because it has market organization as the default solution, the language of market failure for analyzing this class of issues is implicitly biased toward market organization and represses the fact that different modes of governance have particular desirable attributes that make them suitable for certain kinds of activities. In many cases, nonmarket modes of governance are employed not so much because of market failure but because they are more appropriate for those activities. The court system, for example, is operated through government rather than through the market because legal justice is an innately governmental function, not because of market failure, although it is obvious that given what we want out of a court system, market organization is simply not appropriate. Similarly, as a rule, young children are cared for by their parents because this arrangement is broadly deemed appropriate and desirable, not because of market failure.

Some readers of this book may have been looking for simple, sharp answers to two questions. First, where does market organization work well, and where does it not work well? Second, which of the recent efforts toward using more market and less nonmarket have been successful, and which ones not, and why? The message of this book is that there are no sharp, simple answers to either question.

Market organization is not a single thing, as a careful look at the panoply of governing mechanisms that are operative in sectors generally assumed to be market governed makes clear. The way airline service is governed is very different from the way pharmaceuticals are governed, even though in both there is customer choice and considerable reliance on for-profit firms. Because customer choice is present, both sectors are broadly thought of as market governed. However, both involve complex regulatory structures, and in both sectors government provides important parts of the infrastructure. On the other hand, the regulatory structures in the two industries are different in terms of what they are trying to do and in the way they are organized. Public support of infrastructure also differs in the two industries in the way support is oriented and organized.

I do not want to argue that there are no activities or industries for which the simple market organization of the economic textbooks provides a reasonably satisfactory governing structure. However, if society were stuck with that simple form of market organization, we would use it much less widely than we do. The range of sectors and activities where society can make good use of market elements is dependent on the range of supplementary mechanisms we have learned to use in different contexts. Provision of medical services through for-profit organizations and private physicians is acceptable these days only because we have learned to put in place public programs that ensure that most people have access to medical care, regardless of their ability to pay directly. Over the long run, the viability of using for-profit health insurance companies to administer publicly financed programs will depend on our ability to set up a regulatory structure that prevents such companies from ripping off their customers and the public fisc. The point that needs to be understood is that the sectors that are thought of as market organized tend, in fact, to have a variety of nonmarket mechanisms involved in their operations and their governance and that the structures differ widely from sector to sector.

The sectors and activities that are generally regarded as outside of the market also tend to be complex in their structures, often employing market mechanisms to a considerable degree, and varied. Thus while national security is generally regarded as a government responsibility, virtually all of the equipment for the armed forces is procured from private enterprise, using market mechanisms. While the decisions of government organizations are generally assumed to be made either by political process or through the determinations of appointed public officials, such science funding agencies as the National Science Foundation and the National Institutes of Health rely heavily on peer review to determine what applications for support are accepted and rejected. Just as stylized models of how markets work get in the way of seeing what actually is happening, so too do stylized models of government or other nonmarket operation.

How about the successes and failures of the policies that have tried to bring in more market, reducing the role of nonmarket elements, in the governance of various economic sectors? This question, like the one about where market organization works well, implicitly presumes that these policies are all of a piece. In fact, they have been quite varied.

The chapters of part I of this book provide a window into the debate about increasing the role of market governance, and decreasing regulation and other nonmarket elements, in sectors that used to be considered public utilities. A principal element of the public utility concept is that the activity is a natural monopoly and thus competition would be unstable and, in any case, wasteful.

Another characteristic of public utilities is that the services they provide are generally regarded as essential in a wide range of human activities and therefore should be available to all potential users. Policies of deregulation, or denationalization, clearly have yielded positive results, at least for customers of the services involved, when there was no good reason to treat the sector as a regulated public utility in the first place or where circumstances had changed to eliminate or greatly reduce the natural monopoly elements involved in the key activities and make competition potentially both possible and fruitful. Trucking is a good example of the first case; airlines, telephone service, and possibly bank clearing services, of the second. But where there remain significant aspects of natural monopoly, the results of deregulation have been problematic. Electric power is a good example.

As the cases in part I clearly show, it matters whether the "public utility" in question is a growing sector or a declining one. The case of passenger rail in the United States now is not so much about public or private provision (this has been pretty much settled) or regulation or deregulation but rather about whether there should be government subsidy to prevent the sector from further decline.

As shown in the chapters of part II, the argument about the appropriate roles of market mechanisms in the provision of basic human services has had a very different orientation. Here, there is no issue of natural monopoly. However, as in the public utility cases, the policy debate is strongly influenced by beliefs that these services—the ones considered in this volume are primary and secondary education, extra-family care for preschool-age children, and medical care—should be available to all, with good quality, regardless of ability to pay. In these areas, there is no strong pressure to reduce government financial support; rather, if anything, the pressure is the other way. The issue of whether the providers should be for-profit firms or nonprofit or governmental organizations is mostly secondary, although questions of appropriate regulation are involved in the argument about what kind of role for-profit providers should play.

Primary and secondary education differs from the other two sectors in that at the present time the providers are largely public organizations. There is advocacy of privatizing the supply of education, as well as enlarging the range of choice available to families, but thus far the advocates of privatization have not had a major impact on policy.

The wide range of activities involved in the advance of science and technology, the subject matter of the chapters in part III, have long operated with a mix of public and private funding and public and private organizations doing the work. The cases of fundamental research and satellite data are ones in which recent polices have expanded the role of market governance and diminished the role of the public sector. The authors of both of these chapters argue that significant values have been lost in that shift.

The Internet case is really two cases wrapped in one package. The development of the Internet is an example of a technological project that started in the public sector and was successfully taken on by the private sector as the commercial potentials of the technology became clear. Hence, it is a healthy antidote to general arguments that the government can never lead technological development down paths that have economic payoff, although it is interesting that in this case this was not the purpose of the early government programs. The debate about the present operation of the Internet, and about what kind of regulation may be needed for it best to serve its users, is a fine example of the kind of policy debate that arises when a new industry emerges. The debate is about the range of nonmarket elements that are needed to enable this "market" sector to work decently.

The interesting thing about the cases in part IV is that they show areas of activity in which there is no argument against a central role of government. No one is arguing against a governmental responsibility for public health, although there is argument about the range of measures that are appropriate. No one is arguing that it is not a governmental responsibility to run, and to run well, the essential activities of democratic government. Rather, the issue is about the role that private money should play in influencing those processes.

Modern economies, political economies, social economies, are complex and variegated. They defy simple characterization. Long ago Friedrich Hayek (in *The Fatal Conceit: The Errors of Socialism* [1988]) observed the tendency of humans to view the economy, and especially to develop views of what the economy should look like, through simplifying glasses and to plunge ahead with what they thought were reforms based on a highly oversimplified view. Hayek was, of course, referring to the communist planned economies of the Soviet Union and Eastern Europe. If I may end this book on a provocative note, it would appear that the promarket zealots of the 1980s and 1990s were guilty of the same tendency to believe a highly oversimplified model was, in fact, an accurate picture of the economy and at least provided a good guide to what it should look like. The central purpose of this book has been to get into clearer view the complexities and limits of market organization.

Reference

Hayek, Friedrich. 1988. *The Fatal Conceit: The Errors of Socialism.* Chicago: University of Chicago Press.

Index

Boldface numbers refer to figures and tables.

ACT. *See* automated clearinghouse

African Americans, educational inequity for, 165–66

agency, expertise asymmetry and the problem of consumer, 15–16, 214, 227

Agrawal, Ajay, 240

American Bankers Association, 130

American Economic Association, 5

American Telegraph and Telephone (AT&T): the future of telecommunications and, 71–72; in the history of telecommunications development and regulation, 49–58, 61, 67; interconnection policies, 73*n*3–4; the Internet and, 261, 275, 281, 288–89*n*9; Internet telephony and, 69–70; long-distance revenues, share of, **57**; market share of interstate minutes, **56**; switched services and access charges, average revenue per minute from, **58**

American Telegraph & Telephone, United States v., 54

America Online (AOL), 68, 268

America Online (AOL)/Time Warner, 68

Amtrak: creation of, 93–97; efficiency of, 90–91; long-distance trains, cost of eliminating, 89–90; policy debate regarding, 97–101; proposed reorganization of, 78, 100; ridership on, 82; services and revenues, 87–88; subsidization of, 87–88

Amtrak Reform and Accountability Act of 1997, 97–98

Amtrak Reform Council (ARC), 97–100

Andreesen, Marc, 268–69, 289*n*16

Andrew, A. Piatt, 147*n*56

AOL. *See* America Online

ARC. *See* Amtrak Reform Council

Armitt, John, 105–6

Arora, Ashish, 247

ARPANET, 264, 266–67, 271

ARMS. *See* automated teller machines

AT&T. *See* American Telegraph and Telephone

Austin v. Michigan Chamber of Commerce, 351

Australia, 44*n*2, 365–66

automated clearinghouse (ACH): the Federal Reserve and, 114, 126–28, 130–32, 137–38; network, consolidation and influence of, 122–23; transactions, processing of, 119

automated teller machines (ATMs), 119–20, 122–23

Bacon, Francis, 241

banks, payments system and. *See* payments system

Baran, Paul, 264

Barnard, Henry, 162

Bar-Shalom, Avital, 248, 255

basic science. *See* research, basic scientific

Bauer, Paul W., 147*n*61

Bayh-Dole Act of 1980, 244, 246, 252–56

BORA. *See* Bipartisan Campaign Reform Act of 2002

Beatty, Barbara, 188

Bell, Alexander Graham, 53

Bell South, 67–68

Bergmann, Barbara, 199

Bernal, J. D., 241–42
Berners-Lee, Tim, 268, 279, 290*n*21, 290*n*29
Bettinger, Eric, 174
Biehl, Andrew, 144*n*35
Bipartisan Campaign Reform Act of 2002 (BCRA), 357–62, 368
Bismarck, Otto von, 213
Bloomberg, Michael, 364–65
Blyth, Mark, 6–7
Bok, Derek, 252, 254
Borenstein, Severin, 36, 43
Bowker, Richard, 109
Britain. *See* United Kingdom
British Rail, privatization of, 101–9
Brown v. Socialist Workers '74 Campaign Committee, 369*n*2
Buchanan, Pat, 362
Buckley v. Valeo, 348–51, 354, 369*n*2
Bush, George W., 307, 363
Bush, Vannevar, 234, 241–43
Bushnell, James, 43

Cailliau, Robert, 268
California: charter schools in, 173–74; electric power industry in, 36–37, 40–43; telecommunications market in, 55
campaign finance, 319–20, 335–36; a comparative perspective on, 365–67; contributions and expenditures, distinguishing between, 352–53; elections and politics, distinguishing between, 339, 353–55; electoral and access strategies, 342–43; inequality in the competition for votes, 355–57; public funding, 362–65; regulation of, evolution of federal, 345–49; regulation of, reforming federal, 357–62, 367–69; regulation of, structure and development of federal, 343–45; regulation of and the Supreme Court, 338, 345, 348–54, 358–60; soft money, 355, 357, 361; stresses in the system of, 351–57. *See also* elections
Campbell, Donald, 239
Canada, 221, 365–67
Cannon, James, 129
capitalism: historical development of, 4–7; progress and innovation associated with, 9–10. *See also* market organization

Capitalism, Socialism, and Democracy (Schumpeter), 5, 9, 237
Carnoy, Martin, 176
Carter, Jimmy, 221, 301–2
Cerf, Vinton, 264–66, 271
Chandley, John, 40
charter schools, 172–74
child care. *See* early childhood education and care
Child Care and Development Fund, 194–96, 202
Chile, 33, 176–77
CHIPS. *See* Clearing House Interbank Payment System
Classic, United States v., 369*n*1
Clearing House Interbank Payment System (CHIPS), 117, 119, 125, 139, 142*n*15, 144*n*35
Cleveland voucher program, 171–72
Clinton, Bill, 61, 224, 306, 341
CLS. *See* Continuous Linked Settlement bank
Coase, Ronald, 13
Cohen, Wesley, 247
Coleman, James, 169
Colyvas, Jeanette, 254
Comcast, 67
Commercial Space Act of 1998, 294
Committee for Economic Development, 198
Committee on the Federal Reserve in the Payments Mechanisms (Rivlin Committee), 117, 123, 126–27, 137
CompuServe, 268
Connolly, Paul, 128
Conrail, 93, 100
Continental Illinois, 132
Continuous Linked Settlement (CLS) bank, 125, 139, 144*n*35
Cook-Deegan, Robert, 248, 255
Coons, Jack, 179–80
Council of Economic Advisors, 1962 report, 6
credit cards, 119–20, 122
Crocker, Steve, 265
CYCLADES, 288*n*6

DARPA. *See* Defense, United States Department of, Defense Advanced Research Projects Agency

David, Paul, 287

Davies, Donald, 264, 288*n*6

debit cards, 119–20

Defense, United States Department of, Defense Advanced Research Projects Agency (DARPA), 264, 266–67, 270–73. *See also* ARPANET

Demaine, Linda, 249

demand externalities, 120–21

deregulation: bias toward market organization and, 2; of the electric power industry (*see* electric power industry); of infrastructure systems, experience with, 26; of public utilities, 14–15; restructuring, requirements for effective, 27–28; of the telecommunications industry (*see* telecommunications industry). *See also* market organization; privatization

DigitalGlobe, 300

Dowd, Kevin, 133

Downes, Tom, 144*n*32

Dreyfuss, Rochelle, 251

early childhood education and care (ECEC), 185–87, 207–8; family, role of, 205–7; government funding of, 195–99; historical perspectives on, 187–95; historical roots of, 188–92; historical variation by the children's age, 192–93; market organization of, 157–58; private sector role, arguments for and against, 199–205; private sector role, history of, 193–95; quality of care, regulations, and standards, 202–5

earth observation. *See* satellite remote sensing

Earth Observation Satellite Company (EOSAT), 303–5

Eberts, Randall, 174

ECC. *See* early childhood education and care

economic governance: alternatives, need for evaluation of, 8; continuing challenges of, 20–21; economy and community life, 18–19; economy and the state, 17–18; planning, experience and arguments regarding, 8–9; as political issue, 3–4. *See also* market organization; state, the

economics: Austrian school of, 9; classical, 5; network, 51; public science and, 243; of transportation, 84–90

education, early childhood. *See* early childhood education and care

education, primary and secondary: annual earnings, educational attainment and, **165**; charter schools, 172–74; choice programs, large-scale in other countries, 174–77; concerns regarding, 163–67; history of, 161–63; market organization of, 157–58, 161, 167–74; market solutions for educational inequity, 180–81; math and science test scores, by country, **164**; voucher experiments: design issues, 177–80; vouchers, 170–72

Education for All Handicapped Children Act of 1975, 167

Eisenberg, Rebecca, 247, 255

Eisenmenger, Robert, 128

elections: equality as a norm for political, 337–39; political markets and electoral strategies, 341–43; vote-buying, ban on, 339–41. *See also* campaign finance

electric power industry: assessing the results of restructuring, 42–44; "avoided cost" defined, 44*n*4; basic model of restructuring, 34–35; in California, 39–42; federal wholesale trading policies, 32–33; groundwork for restructuring, 31–33; history of regulation in, 29–31; independent power producers, emergence of, 31–32; industry overview, 28–29; institutional requirements of restructuring, 35–39; regulation and restructuring of, 27–28; restructuring of, 33–34

Ellwood, Paul, 220, 223

email, 264

Energy Policy Act of 1992, 33, 45*n*6

Enron Corporation, 37

Enthoven, Alain, 223

Entwistle, Barbara, 300

environmental and global change, remote sensing data regarding, 299

ACED. *See* Earth Observation Satellite Company

Ethernet, 289–90*n*20

Europe, health care and insurance in, 225–27

European Union, telecommunications regulation by, 53, 66, 74*n*19–20

Eurostar, 83–84
Expedited Funds Availability Act of 1987, 140*n*2
expertise, asymmetric, problem of, 15–16, 214
externalities: demand, 120–21; liquidity, 120–21; as market failure, 13–14

families, role of in early childhood education and care, 205–7
FCC. *See* Federal Communications Commission
FECA. *See* Federal Election Campaign Act
Federal Communications Commission (FCC): competitiveness in the long-distance market, 56; creation of, 54; the Internet and, 49, 275, 277, 287, 290*n*24; local-exchange carriers, entry into the long-distance market, 62–64; MCI application to provide long-distance service, rejection of, 53; technical standards, failure regarding definition of, 75*n*24; Telecommunications Act of 1996, litigation regarding, 71, 74–75*n*22
Federal Corrupt Practices Act of 1925, 345–46
Federal Election Campaign Act (FECA), 347–50, 353–55, 357
Federal Election Commission, 348, 358
Federal Energy Regulatory Commission (FERC), 32–33, 41
Federal Highway Administration, 96
Federal Power Act of 1935, 32
Federal Rail Administration, 96, 100
Federal Reserve Act, 129
Federal Reserve Bank: automated clearinghouse, 114, 119, 122–23, 126–28, 130–32, 137–38; in the check-clearing market, **118**; clearing and settlement markets, share of, **124**; dual roles of and the payments system, 114–15; funds transfers, share of, **128**; interbank payments system, role in, 117–19; in the market for payments services, 123–28; privatization in the payments system and, 137–40; as standards coordinator and clearinghouse of last resort, 128–33
Federal Trade Commission, 283–84

Federal Transit Administration, 96
Fedwire, 117, 122–23, 126, 140
Fellmeth, Aaron, 249
FERC. *See* Federal Energy Regulatory Commission
Ferrier, Gary D., 147*n*61
financial clearing systems. *See* Federal Reserve Bank; payments system
Florida, 45*n*9
Food and Drug Administration, 326
France: early childhood education and care in, 190–91, 194, 206, 208*n*2; electric power industry in, 44*n*2; remote sensing capabilities of, 300, 303
Francis, Stewart, 109
Friedman, Milton, 169–70
Froebel, Friederich, 188, 190
Fukuyama, Francis, 6
Fuqua, Don, 302

General Electric, 300–301, 305
Georgia, 204
Germany: early childhood education and care in, 206, 208*n*2; health care and insurance in, 225–26
Gilbert, R. Alton, 123, 125–26, 131, 139–40, 142*n*20, 143*n*27, 145*n*38
Global Crossing, 55
global positioning data, 295–96
Goodman, John, 219
Gorton, Gary, 135–36
governance. *See* economic governance
government. *See* state, the
Great Transformation, The (Polanyi), 5
Green, Edward J., 140*n*1
Green, Mark, 364
Greenstein, Shane, 144*n*32
GTE, 61
Gunn, David L., 89
Guston, David, 241

Hamilton, Alexander, 5
Hanushek, Eric, 168
Hart, David, 241
Harvey, Scott, 40
Hatch Act, 346–47
Hayek, Friedrich, 9, 375

Head Start, 186, 189, 198–99

health care and insurance: European interest in market forces, 225–27; government, role of, 213–16; managed care and HMOs, 220–23; managed competition, 223–25; market organization of, 157–59; markets, retreat and return of, 216–23; markets and government, interdependence of, 213, 227–28; not-for-profit and for-profit institutions, roles of, 228*n*1. *See also* public health

Health Insurance Portability and Protection Act, 331

health maintenance organizations (HMOs), 220–23

Hegel, Georg Wilhelm Friedrich, 16

Helburn, Suzanne, 199

Heller, Michael, 247

Henderson, Rebecca, 240

Hertz, Heinrich, 238

Hess, Frederick, 172

High Speed Ground Transportation Act of 1965, 84

Hispanics, educational inequity for, 165–66

HMOS. *See* health maintenance organizations

Hobbes, Thomas, 17

Hoffer, Thomas, 169

Hogan, William, 40

Hollenbeck, Kevin, 174

home schooling, 163

Hope Schools, 172

Hoxby, Caroline M., 168, 172, 174, 178, 181*n*6

Hsieh, Chang-Tai, 176

human services: child care and early education (*see* early childhood education and care); education (*see* education, primary and secondary); health care and insurance (*see* health care and insurance); market organization and, 157–59, 374

Hunt, Sally, 28, 36–37, 41, 43–44

ICANN. *See* Internet Corporation for Assigned Names and Numbers

Idaho, 45*n*9

IETF. *See* Internet Engineering Task Force

independent system operator (ISO), 37–38

information, asymmetric, problem of, 15–16, 214, 227

infrastructure: electric power (*see* electric power industry); financial clearing systems (*see* payments system); natural monopolies in, 14, 25, 29, 108–9; the state and, 17–18; systems activities, market organization of, 25–26; telecommunications (*see* telecommunications industry); transportation (*see* passenger rail)

intellectual property rights. *See* patents and intellectual property rights

International Geophysical Year, 309

International Polar Commission, 308–9

Internet, the, 232, 259–63, 375; access charges and Internet penetration in OECD countries, **276**; commercialization of, 269–70, 272–73; early computer networks, 264–66; governance of, 261–62; governing applications: regulation and markets, 282–86; history of the development of, 263–70; infrastructure development and growth, 266–69; innovation related to, sources of, 270–74; privacy on, 283–86; private investment in R&D and deployment, 273–74; privatization of the IETF, 280; public R&D investment in, 271–73; regulation and technical coordination of, 49, 274–82; standard setting for, 277–82; telecommunications and, 68–69, 275–77; venture capital investment in information technology and health care, **270**; voice-over Internet protocol (VOIP), 50, 69–72

Internet Architecture Board, 278–79

Internet Assigned Numbers Authority, 278, 281

Internet Configuration Control Board, 278

Internet Corporation for Assigned Names and Numbers (ICANN), 261, 281–82

Internet Engineering Task Force (IETF), 262, 266, 278–82

Internet service providers (ISPs), 261, 277

Internet Society, 266, 278

Internet telephony, 50, 69–72

Interstate Commerce Commission, 79–80, 93–94

Interstate Highway Act of 1956, 94

Iowa, 45*n*9

ISO. *See* independent system operator
IMPS. *See* Internet service providers
Israel, 226
Italy: early childhood education and care in, 191, 194, 206, 208*n*2; electric power industry in, 44*n*2

J. P. Morgan, 135
Jefferson, Thomas, 161–62
Jencks, Christopher, 170, 179
Jessup, Paul, 145*n*44
Joskow, Paul, 29, 35, 39–40, 43, 45*n*12
Judson, Horace, 245
Justice Department, United States: telecommunications antitrust suits, 54–55; telecommunications mergers, blocking of, 66

Kaestle, Carl, 162–63
Kahn, Robert, 264–65
Kaiser-Permanente Health Plan, 220
Kerry, John, 363
Kilgore, Harley, 242
Kilgore, Sally, 169
Kitcher, Philip, 239
Kleinrock, Leonard, 264
Koch, Robert, 238

Land Remote-Sensing Commercialization Act of 1984, 303, 306
Land Remote-Sensing Policy Act of 1992, 304–5
Landsat data, 297–305, 312
Langlois, Richard N., 148*n*62, 271
Large Area Crop Inventory Experiment, 298–99
Lau v. Nichols, 167
Lessig, Lawrence, 282
Level 3, 55, 69
Lincoln, Abraham, 92
Lincoln Trust, 135
liquidity externalities, 120–21
Locke, John, 17

Madey v. Duke, 250
magnetic levitation technology, 82–83
Major, John, 101
Mann, Horace, 162

Marconi, Guglielmo, 238
market failure theory, 10, 372; bias of, 16; expertise/information asymmetry and consumer agency, 15–16; externalities, 13–14; infrastructure for markets and, 18; monopoly and the costs of competition, 14–15; public goods, 11–13
market organization: the case for, 7–10; competition, costs and benefits of, 14–15; folk theory of, 1–2; as governing structure, 3–4 (*see also* economic governance); historical development of, 4–7; problems with (*see* market failure theory); sectors/areas of economic activity and the limits of, 2–3, 371–75. *See also* deregulation; privatization
Marx, Karl, 9
Massachusetts, 46*n*14
Maxwell, James Clerk, 238
MCA. *See* Monetary Control Act of 1980
McAndrews, James, 122, 132, 141*n*9, 142*n*19, 144*n*30, 144*n*35, 146*n*50
McCarthy, Eugene, 368
McConnell v. FEC, 358–60
McEwan, Patrick, 176
McGovern, George, 363
MCI, 53, 55, 66–67
MCI-WorldCom, 61, 66, 74*n*19–20, 261
MediaOne, 67
Medicaid, 218, 326–27
medical savings accounts, 219
Medicare, 218–22
Merton, Robert, 234, 245
Metcalfe, Robert, 289*n*20
Michigan, 173–74
Microsoft, 75*n*23, 278–79
Mill, John Stuart, 5
Milwaukee Parental Choice Program, 170–72, 174–75
mixed economy, 6
Model Emergency Public Health Powers Act, 330
Moen, Jon, 135
Monetary Control Act of 1980 (MCA), 114, 123, 125, 131, 137, 139–40
monopoly: natural, 14, 25, 29, 108–9; problem of private, 14–15
moral hazard, health insurance and, 215, 218–19, 223–24, 227

Mowery, David, 271
Mueller, Milton, 144*n*32
Musgrave, Gerald, 219

Nader, Ralph, 362
Napster, 68
NASA. *See* National Aeronautics and Space Administration
National Aeronautics and Space Administration (NASA), 297–98, 300–307, 309, 313
National Assessment of Educational Progress, 165–66
National Automated Clearinghouse Association, 130–31
National Center for Supercomputing Applications, 289*n*16
National Institutes of Health (NIH), 242, 255–56, 373
National Oceanographic and Atmospheric Administration (NOAA), 297–98, 302–6, 309
National Rail Passenger Corporation (NRPC), 95–98, 100. *See also* Amtrak
National Science Foundation (NSF), 242, 263, 266–67, 271–74, 308, 373. *See also* NFSNET
"Nation at Risk, A," 161, 164–65
Nelson, Richard, 196, 199, 295
Netherlands, the: health care and insurance in, 226; school choice in, 175
Netscape, 263, 269, 278–79
Network Rail, 102–6, 109
networks: chicken and egg problem, 130; network economics, 51; payments system as, 119–23
New York: electric power industry restructuring in, 39, 42; prekindergarten programs in, 204
New York Clearing House (NYCH), 119, 129, 134–36
New Zealand: campaign finance laws in, 365–66; electric power industry in, 34, 43, 44*n*2; school choice in, 175–77
NFSNET, 263, 266–68, 271–72, 289*n*12
NIH. *See* National Institutes of Health
Nixon, Richard, 189, 298, 363
NOAA. *See* National Oceanographic and Atmospheric Administration

Norway, 43
NRPC. *See* National Rail Passenger Corporation
NSF. *See* National Science Foundation
NYCH. *See* New York Clearing House

Oklahoma, 204
Orbital Sciences Corporation, 300

Pacific Gas and Electric, 41
Pacific Railway Act, 92
PACs. *See* political action committees
Parke-Davis & Co. v. H. K. Mulford & Co., 248
passenger rail, 77–78, 108–10; the Amtrak policy debate, 97–101; consumer preference and government subsidy, 81–82; economics of, 84–90; history: creation of Amtrak, 93–97; history: origins of rail service, 92–93; history: separation from freight service, 93–95; privatization in Britain, 100–109; public intervention, case for, 90–91; selective history in contemporary policy debates, 78–81; technological possibilities for, 82–84
Pasteur, Louis, 238
Pasteur's Quadrant (Stokes), 235–36
patents and intellectual property rights: as barriers to research, 247; protecting the scientific commons through, 248–51; as threat to the scientific commons, 233, 244–46; universities and, 253–56
payments system: description of, 115–19; the Federal Reserve in the markets for, 123–28; the Federal Reserve *vs.* privatization in, 114–15, 137–40; lender of last resort, private clearinghouses as, 133–37; national bank panics, 1873–1914, **134**; network perspectives on, 119–23; standards coordinator and clearinghouse of last resort, the Fed as, 128–33
Pennsylvania, electric power industry in, 39, 42, 46*n*14
Perot, Ross, 362, 368
Personal Responsibility and Work Opportunities Reconciliation Act of 1996, 196
Plato, 16

Polanyi, Karl, 5, 19
Polanyi, Michael, 234, 241–42
political action committees (PACs), 347, 351, 353, 355–56
politics: campaign finance (*see* campaign finance); economic governance and, 3–4, 20–21; norms of democratic, 336–41
Popper, Karl, 239
Porter, Roy, 245
Postel, Jon, 265
power: private, concerns regarding, 14–15; state (*see* state, the)
Pozzi, Francesca, 299
preschool. *See* early childhood education and care
Price, Don, 241
privatization: bias toward market organization and, 2; of child care services, 200–201; of the Internet, 266, 280; passenger rail and, 78, 80, 98–109; of the payments system, 137–40 (*see also* payments system); of remote sensing, 302–4, 309–14 (*see also* satellite remote sensing); of scientific research, 233, 235–36 (*see also* research, basic scientific). *See also* deregulation
Prodigy, 268
property rights, patents and intellectual. *See* patents and intellectual property rights
public choice theory, 79–80
public goods: domain of public science and, 243–44; economic governance and, 3–4; market failure and, 11–13; passenger rail as, 78 (*see also* passenger rail); public health as, 325–27, 329
public health, 319; definition of, 321–22; identifying, 322–23; limits of individual motivation and the need for a communal effort, 327–28; police powers and, 328–29; power of market forces to diminish, 329–30; as public good, 325–27, 329; public support for a nonmarket approach to, 330–32; successes and longer life from good, 323–25, 332–33. *See also* health care and insurance
public utilities: concept of, 373–74; private power and regulation of, 14–15. *See also* infrastructure

Public Utility Holding Company Act of 1935, 30–31
Public Utility Regulatory Policy Act of 1978, 31–32, 34–35

Qwest, 55, 68–69

Rai, Arti, 255
railroads. *See* passenger rail
Railtrack, 102–5
Rajan, Samira, 122, 144*n*30
RBOC. *See* regional Bell operating companies
Reagan, Ronald, 6, 202, 340–41
Redenius, Scott A., 143*n*27
regional Bell operating companies (RBOCs), 55–58, 60–62, 66–67, 71–72
regulation: drawbacks and costs of, 52–53; reasons for, 48–50; of telecommunications, reasons for, 50–52. *See also* deregulation
religion, education and, 163
research, basic scientific, 231–32; patent law, protecting the scientific commons through, 248–51; public science, governance of, 241–46; scientific commons, importance of protecting, 246–47; scientific commons and the danger of privatization, 233–36; technology, coevolution with, 236–40; universities and defending the scientific commons, 251–56
Reseaux IP Européen, 266, 290*n*25
restructuring. *See* deregulation
Rhode Island, 39
Ritchie, Dennis, 288*n*9
Rivkin, Steven, 168
Revlon Committee. *See* Committee on the Federal Reserve in the Payments Mechanisms
Roberds, William, 136, 141*n*9, 147*n*58
Robertson, Paul L., 148*n*62
Rosenberg, Nathan, 238

Saloner, Garth, 143*n*23
satellite industry, commercial sectors of, 295–96
satellite remote sensing, 232; commercialization of, 294–95, 305–6; development of, 297–98; national policy for civilian,

300–305; new capabilities, 300; public and private sector involvement in, 296–97; scientific and other uses of, 298–300; scientific research, data for, 307–9; scientific research, impacts of commercialization for, 309–14

Schmidt, Harrison, 301

school choice, 14

Schumpeter, Joseph, 5, 9–10, 237, 270

science and technology: Internet, the (*see* Internet, the); research, basic scientific (*see* research, basic scientific); satellite remote sensing (*see* satellite remote sensing); state and market in the governance of, 231–32, 374–75

Science Data Purchase Program, 307

Shepard, Andrea, 143*n*23

Shockley, William, 238

Sinclair, Harry F., 345

Small, Christopher, 299

Smith, Adam, 5, 7, 17–18

Socialist Workers Party, 369*n*2

Southwestern Bell, 67–68

Space Imaging, 300

Spahr, Walter E., 145*n*44

Sprague, O. M. W., 135, 137, 146*n*52, 147*n*57

Sprint, 55, 66

Stanislaw, Joseph, 6

state, the: campaign finance (*see* campaign finance); the community and, 18–20; early childhood education and care, support for, 195–99 (*see also* early childhood education and care); education, role in (*see* education, primary and secondary); the Federal Reserve (*see* Federal Reserve Bank); health care and insurance, role in, 213–16 (*see also* health care and insurance); infrastructure for markets provided by, 17–18 (*see also* infrastructure); the Internet, public investment in, 271–73; police powers to promote public health, 328–29; rights and the role of government, 19; subsidy of transportation systems (*see* passenger rail); theories of, 16–18

Stefanadis, Chris, 144*n*35

Stevens, Ed, 146*n*45

Stokes, Donald, 235

Stone, Bernell K., 131, 147*n*61

Strahan, Philip, 132

Strategic Rail Authority, 102–3, 109

Sugarman, Stephen, 180

Summers, Bruce J., 123, 125–26, 131, 139–40, 142*n*20, 145*n*38

Supreme Court, United States, federal campaign finance regulation and, 338, 345, 348–54, 358–60

Sweden: early childhood education and care in, 191, 194, 206, 208*n*2; health care and insurance in, 219, 226

Tallman, Ellis, 135

TCI, 67

TCP/IP. *See* Transmission Control Protocol/Internet Protocol

technology. *See* science and technology

Telecommunications Act of 1934, 54

Telecommunications Act of 1996, 48, 50, 58–66, 69–71, 277

telecommunications industry, 48–50; the AT&T near monopoly, 54–55; breakup of AT&T, years following, 55–59; deregulation and the Internet, 275–77; the future of, 70–72; Internet telephony, 50, 69–72 (*see also* Internet, the); local-exchange carriers entering the long-distance market, FCC approval of, **63–64**; meltdown of 2000–2003, 68–69; mergers, current wave of, 66–68; regulation, reasons for, 50–53; regulation in the U.S., 53–59; satellite communications, 295 (*see also* satellite remote sensing); Telecommunications Act of 1996, 48, 50, 58–66; universal service, goal of, 62–66

Temporary Assistance for Needy Families, 194, 196, 201, 202

Thatcher, Margaret, 6

Thompson, Kenneth, 288*n*9

Thompson, Tommy, 189

Timberlake, Richard, 147*n*60

Time Warner, 67–68

Todd, Richard M., 140*n*1

Transmission Control Protocol/Internet Protocol (TCP/IP), 259–60, 264–66, 272–75, 279

transportation, economics of, 84–90. *See also* passenger rail
Transportation Act of 1958, 94
Transportation Security Administration, 96
Trust Company of America, 135

United Kingdom: campaign finance laws in, 365–67; early childhood education and care in, 189–90, 194, 208*n*2; health care and insurance in, 220, 226; privatization of passenger rail, 100–109; public science, debate over the governance of, 241–42; restructuring of the electric power industry in, 34, 43
United States Telecom Association v. FCC, 71
United States v. AT&T, 54
United States v. Western Electric, 54
universities, patents and the scientific commons, 251–56. *See also* research, basic scientific
Urban Mass Transit Act of 1964, 96
Urban Mass Transit Administration, 96
Urquiola, Miguel, 176
U.S. West, 68

vaccines, 327–28
venture capital, the Internet and, 269–70
Verizon, 67

Victor, David, 34
Vincenti, Walter, 239, 249
voice-over Internet protocol (VOIP), 50, 69–72
VOIP. *See* voice-over Internet protocol
vouchers, 170–72

Walsh, John, 247
W3C. *See* World Wide Web Consortium
Wealth of Nations, The (Smith), 5, 17–18
West, E. G., 169
Western Electric, United States v., 54
Williams, 55
Williamson, Oliver, 29
Wilson, Woodrow, 79
Wisconsin, University of, 255
WorldCom, 66–67
World Wide Web, 260, 268
World Wide Web Consortium (W3C), 262, 279–80, 290*n*29

Yao, Dennis, 282
Yergen, Daniel, 6
Yetman, Gregory, 299

Zelman v. Simmons-Harris, 163, 169, 171
Ziman, John, 239
Zimmerman, Phil, 283